# Business Law for Financial Services Professionals

*Second Edition*

LOMA (Life Office Management Association, Inc.) is an international association founded in 1924. LOMA is committed to a business partnership with the worldwide members in the insurance and financial services industry to improve their management and operations through quality employee development, research, information sharing, and related products and services. Among LOMA's activities is the sponsorship of several self-study education programs leading to professional designations, including the prestigious Fellow, Life Management Institute (FLMI) program. For more information on the FLMI program and all of LOMA's education programs, please visit www.loma.org.

*Statement of Purpose: LOMA Educational Programs Testing and Designations.*

Examinations described in the LOMA Education and Training Catalog are designed solely to measure whether students have successfully completed the relevant assigned curriculum, and the attainment of the FLMI and other LOMA designations indicates only that all examinations in the given curriculum have been successfully completed. In no way shall a student's completion of a given LOMA course or attainment of the FLMI or other LOMA designation be construed to mean that LOMA in any way certifies that student's competence, training, or ability to perform any given task. LOMA's examinations are to be used solely for general educational purposes, and no other use of the examinations or programs is authorized or intended by LOMA. Furthermore, it is in no way the intention of the LOMA Curriculum and Examinations staff to describe the standard of appropriate conduct in any field of the insurance and financial services industry, and LOMA expressly repudiates any attempt to so use the curriculum and examinations. Any such assessment of student competence or industry standards of conduct should instead be based on independent professional inquiry and the advice of competent professional counsel.

# Business Law for Financial Services Professionals *Second Edition*

**LOMA Education and Training**
**Atlanta, Georgia**
**www.loma.org**

**Information in this text may have changed or been updated since its publication date.**
**For current updates visit www.loma.org.**

**PROJECT TEAM:**

| | |
|---|---|
| Content Authors: | Harriett E. Jones, J.D., FLMI, ACS, AIRC |
| | Monica R. Maxwell, J.D., FLMI, AIRC |
| Manuscript Editor: | Barbara Foxenberger Brown, FLMI, ACS, AIAA, AIRC |
| Examinations Editor: | Martha Parker, FLMI, ACS, ALHC, AIAA |
| Permissions Coordinator: | Steven R. Silver, J.D., FLMI, AFSI, ACS, AIRC, AIAA |
| Workflow Coordinator: | Kelly Neeley, FLMI, ALHC, ACS, AIAA, PAHM |
| Copy Editor: | Robert D. Land, FLMI, ACS |
| Indexer: | Robert D. Land, FLMI, ACS |

## Text Production:

| | |
|---|---|
| AVP, Marketing: | Paul Wilson |
| Figure Designers: | Susan Austin |
| | Sean Schaeffer Gilley, FLMI, ACS, HIA, CEBS, AIAA, MHP, AIRC, ARA, FLHC |
| | Amy Stailey, ACS, ALMI |
| Typesetter: | Amy Stailey, ACS, ALMI |
| Production Coordinator: | Amy Stailey, ACS, ALMI |
| Production Proofreader: | Natalie K. Cape Sanders |
| Production Gatekeeper: | Kelly Neeley, FLMI, ALHC, ACS, AIAA, PAHM |
| Graphic Designers: | Marlene McAuley |
| | Amy Stailey, ACS, ALMI |
| Cover Designer: | Amy Stailey, ACS, ALMI |

## Product Marketing:

| | |
|---|---|
| Product Marketing: | Kathryn Brown |
| Graphic Designers: | Marlene McAuley |
| | Amy Stailey, ACS, ALMI |

## Portal Production:

| | |
|---|---|
| Project Management: | Gene Stone, FLMI, ACS, CLU |
| Portal Design: | Stephen Hill |
| | Marlene McAuley |
| | Amy Stailey, ACS, ALMI |
| Portal Text Editor: | Stephen Hill |
| | Gene Stone, FLMI, ACS, CLU |
| Videos: | William P. Maura, AVP Marketing Operations |
| | John Rocchetti, Multi-Media Tech Specialist |
| | James Aldridge, AV Assistant |
| | Frank Robinson Jr., Multi-Media Specialist |
| Learning Aids: | ProEdit, Inc. |

Top Ten Tough Topics:    Vivian Heeden, FLMI, FFSI, CLU, FLHC, AIRC, AAPA, AIAA, PCS, ARA

Elizabeth A. Mulligan, FLMI, FLHC, PCS, PAHM, AAPA, AIRC, ARA, AIAA

Sean Schaeffer Gilley, FLMI, ACS, AIAA, AIRC, FLHC, AAPA, ARA, CEBS, HIA, MHP, PAHM

Brian Laframboise

**TPG Production:**

TPG Online Conversions:    David A. Lewis, FLMI, ACS

TPG Authors:    Vivian Heeden, FLMI, FFSI, CLU, FLHC, AIRC, AAPA, AIAA, PCS, ARA

Elizabeth A. Mulligan, FLMI, FLHC, PCS, PAHM, AAPA, AIRC, ARA, AIAA

David A. Lewis, FLMI, ACS

Martha Parker, FLMI, ACS, ALHC, AIAA

ISA    David A. Lewis, FLMI, ACS

Manager, Product Sourcing:    Carol Wiessner, ACS

Product Sourcing Coordinator:    Natalie K. Cape Sanders

Administrative Support:    Mamunah Carter

Portal Build    Stephen Hill
Brian Laframboise

ISBN 978-1-57974-396-3

# *Contents*

## Module 2: Organization and Regulation of Business (Chapters 3–5)

## Module 4: Sale and Performance of Financial Services Products (Chapters 10–15)

# *Preface*

*Business Law for Financial Services Professionals* provides an overview of the types of legal issues that financial services professionals may face as they perform their jobs. Although the text primarily focuses on U.S. laws, the concepts and legal principles presented here are similar in most countries. The text is divided into four modules:

■ Module 1: Introduction to Business Law (Chapters 1–2)

■ Module 2: Organization and Regulation of Business  (Chapters 3–5)

■ Module 3: Areas of Business Law (Chapters 6–9)

■ Module 4: Sale and Performance of Financial Services Products (Chapters 10–15)

## Acknowledgments

LOMA texts are the result of a joint effort between industry experts and LOMA's own staff. Both groups make invaluable contributions to the success of LOMA's texts, and *Business Law for Financial Services Professionals* is no exception.

### LOMA 311 Textbook Development Panel

*Business Law for Financial Services Professionals* benefited from a panel of industry experts who reviewed the text and made many substantive comments on the chapters, provided suggestions for content, and answered numerous questions. The reviewers cared enough about the educational needs of current and future industry employees to volunteer their time and expertise to this project. The following individuals devoted countless hours to this text review, for which we are most grateful:

Maria Sandra J. Bustos, RFC, FLMI, LUTCF, ACS, ARA, AIAA, AIRC
Assistant Vice President and Head, SMG Training and Education Department
The Insular Life Assurance Co., Ltd.

Nicolle Galipeau, J.D., FLMI, LTCP, HCAFA, ARA
Senior Attorney
Transamerica Long Term Care

Shirley Grossman, FLMI, FLHC, AIRC, ACS, ARA, CCP
Vice President, Compliance Officer
Lincoln Heritage Life Insurance Company

Stephen Horton, J.D., FLMI, CLU, ChFC, CPCU, CRCP
Associate General Counsel
State Farm Life Insurance Company

Luke McClaren, J.D., MBA, CLU, RHU, FLMI, FFSI, AAPA, ACS, AIAA, AIRC, ARA
FASG Counsel
USAA

James R. Ruegg, FLMI/M, CLU, AIRC, CCP, PCS, ARA, AIAA
Senior Assistant Vice President
Amica Life Insurance Company

Cesar Y. Salera, FLHC, ALHC, AIRC, ACS
Senior Assistant Vice President, Legal Unit
The Insular Life Assurance Co., Ltd.

Tan Eng Bee, SRN, ANZIIF (Senior Associate), ACS, FLMI, FLHC,
FAHM, MBA (UK), CFP$^{CERT\ TM}$
Technical Advisor
Asia Assistance Network (M) Sdn. Bhd.

We also want to thank the following individuals, who reviewed portions of the text
and advised us on the course content:

Marc E. Cavadel, J.D., FLMI, AIRC, ACS
AVP—Product Development and Regulatory Compliance
Protective Life Insurance Company

Chow Yiu Ming Andrew, MBA, FLMI, ANZIIF (Fellow), CPCU, FCII
General Manager & Chief Underwriting Officer
Hang Seng General Insurance (Hong Kong) Company Limited

## LOMA 311 Course Project Team

The author wishes to thank the LOMA 311 project team members for all of their
hard work. The LOMA 311 course is the result of the collaborative efforts of a
dedicated project team of LOMA staff members and consultants.

Thanks also go to Stephen Quina, ALMI, PCS, Director, International Industry
Solutions, International Operations, LL Global, Inc., who advised us about international content and helped recruit industry experts for the textbook development
panel.

Finally, a very special thank you to Julia K. Wooley, FLMI, ACS, ALHC, HIA,
MHP, Assistant Vice President, Learning Content, who served as Project Manager and provided guidance and support throughout the project and Katherine C.
Milligan, FLMI, ACS, ALHC, Vice President, Education & Training Division,
who provided leadership, guidance, resources, support, and encouragement for
this project.

Harriett E. Jones, J.D., FLMI, ACS, AIRC
Atlanta, Georgia
2012

# *Introduction*

The purpose of *Business Law for Financial Services Professionals* is to provide an overview of the types of legal issues that financial services professionals may face as they perform their jobs. To enhance your learning experience, LOMA has developed a Course Portal for this course that is accessible upon course enrollment in LOMANET. A LOMA Course Portal is an online resource from which learners access everything they need to study and prepare for the course examination. The Course Portal organizes the assigned text material into convenient Modules—chapter clusters that help to focus the learning process by breaking up the course content into meaningful sections. In addition to the assigned study materials, the Course Portal provides access to an array of blended learning resources, including some multimedia features designed to enhance the learning experience. The LOMA 311 Course Portal provides access to

■ An introductory course video

■ Protected PDFs of the assigned text and Test Preparation Guide, which can be printed or read online

■ The interactive version of the Test Preparation Guide's Practice Questions and Sample Exam

■ Review tools, including Learning Aids—animations of important concepts—and a "Top Ten Tough Topics" tutorial

■ Recommended study plans to help you set goals and manage your learning experience

■ Related links which help you apply the course instruction to the real world

LOMA 311—*Business Law for Financial Services Professionals*—is part of the Fellow, Life Management Institute (FLMI) program. Students preparing to take the examination for LOMA 311 will find that the assigned study materials—the protected PDFs of the text and Test Preparation Guide—include many features designed to help learners more easily understand the course content, organize their study, and prepare for the examination. These features include lists of Learning Aid topics available on the Course Portal, chapter outlines, chapter learning objectives, key terms, figures containing real-world examples of course content, and a comprehensive glossary. As we describe each of these features, we give you suggestions for studying the material.

■ **Learning Aids and Top Ten Tough Topics.** A list of Learning Aids is provided in the protected PDF for the entire text as well as for each Module. Review this list to become familiar with topics for which an animated learning aid is available on the Course Portal. Viewing these Learning Aids allows you to see topics in action or to view topics from a different perspective than from simply reading about them in the text. Also included is a Top Ten Tough Topics tutorial. This tutorial contains animations and study tips for topics that learners often find difficult when answering questions on the examination. Both the Learning Aids and the Top Ten Tough Topics tutorial enhance the learning experience, appeal to a variety of learning styles, and offer a great way for learners to advance their understanding and retention of course content.

- **Learning Objectives.** The first page of each chapter contains a list of learning objectives to help you focus your studies. Before reading each chapter, review these learning objectives. Then, as you read the chapter, look for material that will help you meet the learning objectives. The interactive version of the Test Preparation Guide's Practice Questions and Sample Exam questions (accessible from the Course Portal) are linked to the learning objectives to give you an idea of how the learning objective might be measured on an examination, as well as to help you assess your mastery of the learning objectives.

- **Chapter Outline.** Each chapter contains an outline of the chapter. Review this outline to gain an overview of the major topics that will be covered; then scan through the chapter to become familiar with how the information is presented. By looking at the headings, you can gain a preview of how various subjects in each chapter relate to each other.

- **Key Terms.** This text explains key terms that apply to the text material and, where appropriate, reviews key terms previously presented in LOMA courses. Each key term is highlighted with *bold italic type* when the term is defined and is included in a list of key terms at the end of each chapter. All key terms also appear in a comprehensive glossary at the end of the protected PDF of the text. As you read each chapter, pay special attention to the key terms.

- **Figures.** We include figures throughout the text to illustrate and bring a real world perspective to the text's discussion of selected topics. Information contained in figures may be tested on the examination for the course.

- **Glossary.** A comprehensive glossary that contains definitions of all key terms appears at the end of the protected PDF of the text. Following each glossary entry is a number in brackets that indicates the chapter in which the key term is defined. The glossary also references important equivalent terms, acronyms, and contrasting terms.

**LOMA may periodically revise the assigned study materials for this course. To ensure that you are studying from the correct materials, check the current LOMA *Education and Training Catalog* available at www.loma.org or on the Course Portal. Also be sure to visit the Announcements page on the Course Portal to learn about important updates or corrections to the assigned study materials.**

## Using the Test Preparation Guide

LOMA's *Test Preparation Guide for LOMA 311 (TPG)* is assigned reading for students preparing for the LOMA 311 examination. It contains Practice Questions organized by chapter and a full-scale Sample Exam. The TPG is available in two versions, both accessible from the Course Portal: (1) a printable, protected PDF that includes answer keys for all questions, and (2) an interactive version that can be used online or downloaded for offline use. The interactive version has the added advantage of answer-choice explanations for all Practice Questions and Sample Exam questions. The TPG is designed to help you learn the course content and prepare for the examination. Used along with the assigned text, the TPG will help you master the course material. **Studies indicate that students who use LOMA TPGs consistently perform significantly better on LOMA examinations than students who do not use TPGs.**

# *Learning Aids*

The LOMA 311 Course Portal, available online at www.LOMANET.org, includes several Learning Aids designed to reinforce concepts covered in the assigned text. If you are not already using the online Course Portal but would like access to the Learning Aids for this course, please follow the log-in instructions provided in your enrollment confirmation email, or call 1-800-ASK-LOMA or email education@loma.org for assistance.

**PLEASE NOTE:** Examination questions will be based only on content presented in the assigned text.

## Module 1: Introduction to Business Law
### (Chapters 1–2)

- ✓ U.S. Federal and State Court Systems

- ✓ Specific Intentional Torts

- ✓ Legal vs. Equitable Remedies

## Module 2: Organization and Regulation of Business
### (Chapters 3–5)

- ✓ Types of Business Organizations

- ✓ Directors and Officers

- ✓ Economic Concepts

- ✓ Employee vs. Independent Contractor

- ✓ Regulation of Financial Services Companies

- ✓ Insurance Holding Companies vs. Financial Holding Companies

## Module 3: Areas of Business Law
### (Chapters 6–9)

- ✓ Types of Contracts
- ✓ Contractual Capacity of Individuals
- ✓ Agency Agreement
- ✓ Principal's Liabilities to Third Parties
- ✓ Forms of Property Ownership
- ✓ Testamentary Transfers
- ✓ Negotiable Instruments
- ✓ Bankruptcy Proceedings

## Module 4: Sale and Performance of Financial Services Products
### (Chapters 10–15)

- ✓ Contractual Capacity for Insurance Policies
- ✓ Insurable Interest
- ✓ Class Designations—Per Capita, Per Stirpes
- ✓ Revocable and Irrevocable Beneficiaries
- ✓ Trust Agreements
- ✓ Policy Settlement Options
- ✓ Incontestability Provision
- ✓ Equitable Remedies
- ✓ Standard Claim Procedures
- ✓ Special Claim Situations
- ✓ Group Life Insurance Contract Provisions
- ✓ Who's Who in Retirement Plans?
- ✓ Regulation of Retirement Plans

*Chapter 1*

# The Legal Environment of Business

## Objectives

### *After studying this chapter, you should be able to*

- Identify the primary sources of law and explain how they are created
- Explain how the three primary governmental functions are divided among the branches of government
- Distinguish among the various types of legal systems
- Define ethics and explain the value of a corporate culture that encourages ethical conduct
- Describe the organization of the federal and state court systems in the United States and describe the decision-making procedures that courts follow
- Describe the purpose of the U.S. Federal Sentencing Guidelines and explain their significance to a company's compliance and ethics program

# Outline

**Sources of Law**
- Constitutions
- Statutes
- Administrative Regulations
- Treaties and International Agreements
- Case Law

**Legal Systems**
- Common Law Systems
- Civil Law Systems
- Mixed Legal Systems

**Court Systems**
- State Court Systems
- Federal Court System

**Business Ethics**

Within any given country, everyone is constantly affected by the country's legal system, which includes the specific laws that regulate conduct and the legal process by which those laws are enforced. The laws provide guidelines and rules designed to help individuals, organizations, and governments interact in an orderly fashion. The legal process is used to punish those who break laws, provide remedies for victims of certain wrongs, and resolve specific types of disputes. The legal system enables people and organizations to anticipate the outcomes of their actions with some degree of certainty, conduct their affairs with a minimum of conflict, and when conflicts do arise, resolve them in an equitable manner.

This text is designed to help people working in the financial services industry to identify and understand some of the legal issues that they may face as they do their jobs. Financial services companies and their employees have a range of legal duties and legal rights. The more you understand those duties and rights, the better prepared you will be to handle various types of transactions and conduct business to protect your rights and the company's rights. You also will be better able to protect yourself and your company against legal liability for harming others or violating their legal rights.

Although the text focuses on the United States, the same types of legal issues arise in most countries. For students who work outside the United States, familiarity with the information in this text should help prepare you to conduct business within your own legal system. Although specific laws vary from country to country, the types of legal issues that businesses face are similar around the world. In addition, the globalization of the financial services industry means that businesses now operate in more and more parts of the world. Financial services companies and their employees must be familiar with the laws in every country in which they do business.

I'm new to the insurance industry and I'm working in claims. I guess I'm wondering what the laws in other countries have to do with *my* job. Isn't this why we have a legal department?

You'd be surprised! Having worked in a financial services legal department for 17 years, I've seen many cases where big problems could have been avoided if employees had known more about the legal environment surrounding our products and services. Keep reading, and you'll see what I mean!

## Sources of Law

Determining what the law is concerning any given matter may require consulting one or more sources of the law. In most countries, the primary sources of the law are (1) constitutions, (2) statutes, (3) administrative regulations, and (4) treaties and international agreements. In many countries, including the United States, case law created by the courts is also a primary source of the law. Figure 1.1 presents an overview of the typical sources of the law.

### Figure 1.1 Sources of the Law

**Constitution:**

A relatively permanent document or group of documents which set out the fundamental principles that determine the powers and duties of a jurisdiction's government and the rights of the people of the jurisdiction

**Statutes:**

Laws enacted by the legislative branch of a government

**Administrative regulations:**

Rules or orders adopted by agencies within the executive branch of a government

**Treaties and international agreements:**

Formal agreements between two or more countries

**Case law:**

Law created by a jurisdiction's courts and found in the courts' written decisions

## Constitutions

Almost every country has adopted a **constitution**, which is a document or group of documents that sets out the fundamental principles that determine the powers and duties of the government and the rights of the people. It is one of the most basic aspects of a country's legal system and is intended to be a relatively permanent and primary source of law. A constitution typically is considered the supreme law of the land, and any laws that are found to violate a country's constitution generally are invalid.

A constitution usually establishes the organizational structure of a nation's government. In the United States and most other countries, governmental powers are divided among the following three branches of government:

- The **legislative branch**, which consists of one or more legislative bodies that are responsible for enacting laws to govern the applicable jurisdiction

- The **executive branch**, which consists of a number of agencies or ministries that are responsible for administering, enforcing, or carrying out the jurisdiction's laws

- The **judicial branch**, which consists of a system of courts that are responsible for applying and interpreting the jurisdiction's laws

Figure 1.2 illustrates the three primary governmental functions of (1) creating laws, (2) administering those laws, and (3) resolving disputes.

Like many constitutions, the U.S. Constitution establishes a system of checks and balances that places restraints on each branch of government and, thus, seeks to prevent the concentration of power in any branch. By contrast, other countries are **parliamentary democracies** in which the legislative branch of government, usually known as the *Parliament*, has ultimate authority for making all laws. A general description of the operation of parliamentary democracies is set forth in Insight 1.1.

---

### Figure 1.2 Governmental Organization

**Governments typically are configured to carry out at least three functions:**

✔ **Creating the laws** → Nations establish some type of legislative body, often referred to as a *legislature* or *parliament*

✔ **Administering and enforcing the laws** → Nations establish a system of administrative agencies, often referred to as departments or ministries

✔ **Settling disputes that arise within the jurisdiction** → Nations typically establish a court system, and many nations promote alternative dispute resolution methods

---

## Insight 1.1 Parliamentary Democracies

Many countries—including countries within the British Commonwealth, most European countries, India, and Singapore—are organized as parliamentary democracies in which the legislative branch of government, known as the Parliament, has ultimate authority for making all laws. Although specific details of how a parliamentary system operates vary from country to country, the executive branch of government typically is headed by a *prime minister*. The prime minister is the individual who heads the political party—or coalition of parties—that holds a majority of elected seats in the Parliament. Upon taking office, the prime minister names a *Cabinet* of individuals who serve as advisers to the prime minister.

The individuals who make up the executive branch hold office as long as the Parliament has confidence in how the executive branch is leading the government. If the Parliament votes that it no longer has confidence in the executive branch's ability to lead the government, then the prime minister and the Cabinet resign, Parliament is dissolved, and elections are held to create a new Parliament from which the next prime minister will be elected.

A number of countries, including the United States, have established a ***federal system*** in which a federal government and a number of lower level governments share governmental powers. In other words, a group of sovereign states have agreed to unify as a nation. For example, the United States is a federation of 50 states, the District of Columbia, and a number of territories. Figure 1.3 identifies some other countries that have a federal system of government.

## Figure 1.3 Examples of Federal Systems of Government

- Argentina is a union of 23 provinces and a federal district

- Brazil is a union of 26 states and a federal district

- Canada is a federation of 10 provinces and 3 territories

- Germany is a union of 16 states

- India is a union of 28 states and 7 territories

- Indonesia is a union of 30 provinces, 2 special regions, and a federal district

- Malaysia is a federation of 13 states and 3 territories

- Mexico is a federation of 31 states and a federal district

- South Africa is a union of 9 provinces

In a federal system, the federal constitution is the nation's supreme law, and all other laws must be consistent with the constitution. Typically, each state also has adopted a state constitution that serves as the state's fundamental law. All state laws must be consistent with the federal constitution and the applicable state constitution. The federal constitution typically provides a method of dividing governmental powers between the federal and state governments. As an example, the U.S. Constitution enumerates the specific powers that are delegated to the federal government; all governmental powers not specifically given to the federal government are left to the state governments. The U.S. states are responsible for a range of functions, including regulating businesses and professions within their borders, providing for public schools, and protecting the health and safety of people. States delegate some of their governmental authority to local governmental units such as counties and municipalities. Local governments, for example, typically provide police and fire protection.

## Statutes

The legislative branch of government is composed of one or more legislative bodies that are authorized to enact laws to govern the applicable jurisdiction. (For the sake of consistency, we use the term *legislature* to refer to such a legislative body.) As noted in Figure 1.1, the laws enacted by a legislature are referred to as **statutes**, which typically declare, command, or prohibit something. These legislative enactments create the body of law known as **statutory law**. The authority of a legislature to enact laws is limited by the applicable constitution. When a legislature exceeds its constitutional powers in enacting a law, that law is unconstitutional and therefore illegal and void.

The U.S. federal and state constitutions authorize the creation of legislatures, which typically consist of two houses known as the Senate and the House of Representatives. The legislative branch of the federal government is referred to as the **Congress**. The legislative branch of a state government typically is referred to as the **state legislature**.

All of the laws enacted by each legislative body are compiled and organized into a collection of laws that typically is referred to as a *code*. The names given to such codes vary from jurisdiction to jurisdiction. In the United States, all of the federal statutes have been compiled as the **U.S. Code**. The laws enacted by a given state typically are known as the **state code**. The U.S. and state codes are further subdivided into discrete sections that each regulate a specific area. For example, the federal tax laws are found in a portion of the U.S. Code that is generally referred to as the *Internal Revenue Code (I.R.C.)*. Similarly, a portion of each state code is devoted to regulating the insurance industry within the applicable state; that portion of the state code is often known as the **state insurance code**.

## Administrative Regulations

The executive branch of government is authorized to administer or carry out a jurisdiction's laws. In the United States, the federal executive branch, headed by the President, is responsible for carrying out federal laws. The executive branch of a state government, headed by the state's governor, is responsible for carrying out the laws of that state. Each executive branch of government consists of a variety of departments, sometimes referred to as *administrative agencies*, that are responsible for administering specific aspects of the law. Figure 1.4 identifies just a few of the many U.S. federal and state administrative agencies.

## Figure 1.4 Examples of U.S. Administrative Agencies

### Federal Administrative Agencies:

**Department of the Treasury.** The federal agency that has primary responsibility for administering federal banking and tax laws.

**Department of Justice (DOJ).** The federal agency that is responsible for enforcing federal criminal laws, representing the United States in federal cases, and providing legal advice to other federal officials and departments.

**Securities and Exchange Commission (SEC).** The federal agency that administers federal laws governing securities and the investment industry.

### State Administrative Agencies:

**Office of the Secretary of State.** A state agency that is responsible for licensing corporations and businesses.

**Office of the Attorney General.** A state agency that is authorized to enforce the state's criminal laws, represent the state in all legal matters, and provide legal advice to the governor and other state administrative officials.

In the United States and many other jurisdictions, the legislatures enact statutes in relatively general terms and delegate authority to the executive branch to adopt regulations to fill in the details of the law. *Regulations* are rules or orders that are issued by administrative agencies and that have the same force and effect as statutes; such regulations make up the type of law known as *administrative law*. The regulations of each governmental unit are compiled into that jurisdiction's *administrative code*. For example, the regulations of a given state are compiled into that state's administrative code.

In the United States, the administrative agency responsible for administering a specific aspect of the law also is responsible for adopting regulations to fill in the details of that aspect of the law. For example, each state has created an administrative agency, typically known as the ***state insurance department***, that is responsible for enforcing the state insurance code and ensuring that insurance companies conducting business within the state comply with all state insurance laws. The state insurance department is responsible for adopting regulations that fill in the details of the state insurance code and for enforcing those regulations.

I think I've got it. *Statutes* are the laws enacted by the federal or state legislatures, and *administrative regulations* are the rules that explain how to follow the laws. So a jurisdiction's department of insurance is an administrative agency that creates regulations which insurance companies must follow to comply with the laws enacted in that jurisdiction.

## Treaties and International Agreements

A ***treaty*** is a legally binding agreement entered into by two or more nations, which agree to abide by the terms of the treaty. Treaties may be referred to by various terms, including *conventions* and *pacts*. When a nation agrees to a treaty, it generally agrees to enforce the terms of the treaty within its borders and to cooperate with other nations in enforcing the treaty. In the United States, a treaty may be entered into by the President, with the advice and consent of the Senate.

Countries enter into many types of treaties. Political treaties are used to establish military alliances, end wars, and settle boundary issues, among other things. Commercial treaties deal with trade and tariff issues. Countries also enter into legal treaties under which they agree to abide by common patent and copyright protections. These are just a few examples of various types of treaties.

## Case Law

In common law jurisdictions, the written decisions of the courts form a body of law known as ***case law***. All governments have established some type of judicial system—or court system—that is responsible for applying the laws to specific cases. The types of laws that the courts apply to specific cases are known as ***substantive laws***, which are laws that create, define, and regulate legal rights and duties. In addition, each jurisdiction has adopted laws, known as ***procedural laws***, which define the methods that exist to enforce substantive laws. Procedural laws specify the types of cases that each court has jurisdiction to hear. In this sense, ***jurisdiction*** refers to the authority of a court to hear specific cases.

The organization of the court system varies from jurisdiction to jurisdiction. Nevertheless, court systems typically have a variety of ***trial courts***, which often are referred to as *courts of original jurisdiction* because they are the courts that first hear disputes. In addition, most court systems have ***appellate courts*** that are authorized to review the decisions of lower courts. Thus, a party that loses a case heard by a trial court may have the right to appeal—or contest—that decision by asking an appellate court to review the trial court's decision. State and federal appellate courts issue a written opinion for most noncriminal cases they decide. These appellate court decisions are published in a series of volumes known as *reports* or *reporters*.

Most courts also engage in the important function of interpreting statutes and regulations. For example, statutes usually are expressed in relatively general terms that are designed to cover a wide range of situations. As a result, a law's intent may be clear, but its application to a specific situation may be unclear. In such cases, the courts generally have authority to interpret the meaning of statutes. Thus, the courts serve as a source of law.

# Legal Systems

Even though each country has established its own distinct legal system, we can identify several basic types of legal systems: common law systems, civil law systems, and mixed legal systems. Figure 1.5 identifies some of the countries that have adopted each type of legal system.

## Common Law Systems

A *common law system* is a legal system that is based on the common law of England. A *jurisdiction*—a geographic area of legal authority—that bases its legal system on the common law of England is referred to as a *common law jurisdiction*. Most English-speaking countries that were colonized by England—including the United States—have adopted common law systems. Many non-English-speaking jurisdictions also have adopted elements of the common law system, which was created in feudal England. During that time, the English created courts that were authorized to resolve disputes in accordance with the customs of the local area; these local customs often were referred to as *common laws*. Over the years, the courts developed an unwritten body of general principles of law based both on local customs and on public policy. In its broadest sense, the **common law** is an unwritten body of general principles and rules of law developed and followed by the courts. Today, this body of common law principles, known as *case law*, is found in the courts' written decisions. These general common law principles supplement the laws enacted by the legislature and thus form a large component of the law of a common law jurisdiction.

An important feature of the common law system is that, in making decisions, the courts follow a general rule known as the *doctrine of stare decisis*.[1] According to the doctrine of stare decisis, when a court finds that a specific principle of law applies to a certain set of facts, the court will apply that principle to all future cases in which the facts are substantially the same. The decision in such a prior case is known as a *precedent*. A court in a common law jurisdiction is bound to adhere to its own precedents and to the precedents established by higher courts in the same jurisdiction. By relying on precedent, the courts are able to enforce the laws in a uniform, predictable, and impartial manner.

Although the common law courts are bound to follow precedent, the doctrine of stare decisis is not totally inflexible. The courts have authority to depart from precedent when the facts of a case warrant it or when strong public policy reasons favor such a departure. For example, a court can depart from a precedent by distinguishing the case under consideration from the precedent. In other words, the court can find ways in which the two cases differ so that it can arrive at a different decision. A court also may depart from a precedent when following the precedent would cause an unjust result.

## Figure 1.5 Examples of Countries with Various Types of Legal Systems

**Common Law Systems:**

- Antigua and Barbuda
- Australia
- Bahamas
- Barbados
- Bermuda
- Canada
  (except the province of Quebec)
- Fiji Islands
- Ireland
- Jamaica
- New Zealand
- Trinidad and Tobago
- United Kingdom
- United States
  (except the state of Louisiana)

**Civil Law Systems:**

- Argentina
- Austria
- Belgium
- Brazil
- Chile
- Colombia
- France
- Germany
- Italy
- Mexico
- Poland
- Portugal
- Spain
- Turkey
- Venezuela
- Vietnam

**Mixed Legal Systems:**

- Hong Kong–mixture of common law and customary law
- India–mixture of common law, civil law, and Islamic law
- Japan–mixture of civil law and customary law
- Philippines–mixture of common law and civil law
- Malaysia–mixture of common law, civil law, and Islamic law
- People's Republic of China–mixture of civil law and customary law
- Singapore–mixture of common law and Islamic law
- Taiwan–mixture of civil law and customary law

**Source:** University of Ottawa, Faculty of Law, Civil Law Section, http://www.juriglobe.ca/eng/sys-juri/index-syst.php (17 August 2010).

A precedent remains in force until (1) a court overturns the precedent or (2) a statute is enacted that changes the legal principle that underlies the precedent. Over time, therefore, the courts and the legislatures are able to modify and change the law so that the law keeps pace with changing times and circumstances.

Sometimes, no statute or precedents apply to an issue before a court. In such cases, the courts apply the general principles of common law.

## Civil Law Systems

A *civil law system* is a legal system based on the Roman legal system in which the laws are codified into written codes enacted by the legislature. A *code* is a comprehensive written statement of rules that embody the general principles of law that apply in a given civil law jurisdiction. Each jurisdiction has enacted a *civil code* that contains the general principles of law that apply to relationships between people that arise through birth, adoption, marriage, death, contracts, and personal liability. The civil code usually also regulates property rights. Each jurisdiction also has enacted other codes that govern other areas of the law. For example, a *commercial code* regulates commercial transactions and business organizations. Other codes contain laws that apply specifically to insurance companies, banks, financial instruments, and so on.

Many countries in Europe and in Central and South America have adopted civil law systems. The French brought civil law systems to the United States. Only a few states, primarily Louisiana, have based any part of their legal systems on the civil law. Instead, the U.S. federal government and most state governments have adopted the common law system.

Civil law courts follow a different decision-making procedure than that followed by common law courts, as illustrated in Figure 1.6; even so, the courts in both types of jurisdictions often arrive at similar decisions on similar issues. A court in a civil law jurisdiction looks first to the jurisdiction's codes for the applicable rules of law. If the codes do not specifically cover the subject at issue, the court decides the issue in accordance with the general principles of law that are set out in the applicable code. Although civil law courts are not bound to follow precedents as common law courts are, courts in civil law jurisdictions are influenced by their own prior decisions and the decisions of the jurisdiction's higher courts on similar issues.

## Mixed Legal Systems

The legal systems in many countries are *mixed legal systems* that contain elements of more than one basic type of legal system. In some countries, for example, the legal system includes elements of both the common law system and the civil law system. In addition, the legal systems in many countries have been greatly influenced by the religion of Islam. Under an *Islamic legal system*, the law is set out in the book of scripture known as the *Koran* (or *Qur'an*), and the law of the Koran is unchanging. The legal systems in these countries often have elements of common law systems and/or civil law systems *and* elements of Islamic law.

Many other countries have mixed legal systems that include a common law system and/or a civil law system *and* a *customary law system* in which members of a community have accepted local customs as binding on the community's members. The matters in which customary law may be applied vary considerably from jurisdiction to jurisdiction. For example, customs may govern the personal affairs of individuals within a community by establishing rules for marriage, separation, divorce, and adoption. In some areas of the world, customary laws help communities maintain their physical well-being by establishing rules for how houses must be constructed and how the community provides itself with food. Customary laws often set out the punishments that the community imposes on individuals who violate the customary laws. In a number of countries, the government has formally recognized customary laws as being binding and enforceable by the government.

## Figure 1.6 Overview of Courts' Decision-Making Procedures

**Common Law System**

A court first looks to the applicable written law—statutes and regulations.

If no statutes or regulations apply, then the court applies the doctrine of stare decisis by following precedents, unless strong reasons justify a departure from precedent.

If no precedents apply, then the court applies general principles of the common law.

**Civil Law System**

A court first looks to the applicable code.

If no code applies, then the court applies the general principles of law set out in the applicable code.

Although not bound to follow precedents, the court will be influenced by its own prior decisions and decisions of higher courts on similar issues.

# Court Systems

In the United States, the federal government and each of the state governments have established a court system, and each court system operates as a separate and independent unit. In this section, we describe the organization of the state and federal court systems in the United States. Insight 1.2 provides two other examples of how judicial systems are organized.

## State Court Systems

As noted earlier, each state court system includes a variety of trial courts. In the United States, each trial court is presided over by a judicial officer, who is generally called a *judge*. Most states have two levels of appellate courts. The higher level appellate court—usually known as the state *supreme court*—has authority to review the decisions of the lower appellate court—often known as the state *court of appeal*.

---

## Insight 1.2 Examples of Judicial Systems

**Argentina:** Like the United States, Argentina has a federal system of government and a federal court system. Argentina also has created a provincial court system. Federal courts have jurisdiction over matters involving the federal government, conflicts between provinces, and certain matters specified by federal law. Provincial courts have jurisdiction over all other matters, and federal and provincial courts have overlapping jurisdiction in many matters.

The federal Supreme Court of Justice is the highest court in the nation. Specialized federal courts, known as *forums,* each have jurisdiction over specific matters; such courts include a civil forum, a criminal forum, a labor forum, an administrative forum, a family forum, and a commercial forum. The provincial court systems are similarly organized, with a Supreme Court and specialized courts. Provincial court systems usually include at least three forums: a civil forum, a criminal forum, and a labor forum.

**Hong Kong:** Although Hong Kong is a region of China, it has an independent court system composed of a number of courts. Lower courts include the District Court, which is a court of original jurisdiction that hears both civil and criminal cases; a number of Magistrates' Courts that hear criminal cases; the Labour Tribunal that handles disputes between employers and employees; and the Small Claims Tribunal that hears civil cases involving less than a stated sum of money. The highest appellate court is the Court of Final Appeal; it hears both civil and criminal appeals from the High Court. The High Court consists of two separate courts:

- The Court of First Instance is a court of original jurisdiction and hears a variety of civil and criminal matters. It also hears appeals from lower courts.

- The Court of Appeal hears appeals from the Court of First Instance and the lower courts.

**Source:** "Ernesto Nicolás Kozameh et al., "Guide to the Argentine Executive, Legislative and Judicial System," LLRX, 14 July 2001, http://www.llrx.com/features/argentina.htm (6 December 2010); Gisela Monge Roffarello, et al., "Update: A Research Guide to the Argentine Legal System," *GlobaLex*, January 2006, http://www.nyulawglobal.org/globalex/argentina1.htm#_Judicial_Power (6 December 2010); "About Us: Introduction," Judiciary of the Hong Kong Special Administrative Region of the People's Republic of China, http://www.judiciary.gov.hk/en/crt_services/pphlt/html/guide.htm (6 December 2010).

## Federal Court System

The U.S. federal court system consists of three levels of courts, as follows:

- *District courts* sit in every state and territory and act as trial courts with jurisdiction to hear only specific types of cases as set out in the Constitution and various federal laws. Figure 1.7 identifies the cases over which the Constitution gives jurisdiction to the federal courts.

- Thirteen *circuit courts of appeal* have jurisdiction to hear cases in which the decision of a district court is appealed by one of the parties involved in a trial.

■ The *Supreme Court* is the country's highest court; it hears only certain appeals from lower courts and cases involving any of the states or a foreign official, such as an ambassador. The Court primarily reviews cases that involve a matter of national importance, such as cases that involve the U.S. Constitution or cases in which two or more lower courts have reached different results.

## Figure 1.7 Jurisdiction of the U.S. Federal Courts

**The U.S. Constitution identifies the following types of cases over which the federal courts have jurisdiction:**

- All cases arising under the U.S. Constitution and under federal laws and treaties

- All cases affecting ambassadors, other public ministers, and consuls

- All cases of admiralty and maritime jurisdiction

- Controversies to which the United States is a party

- Controversies between two or more states

- Controversies between a state and citizens of another state

- Controversies between citizens of different states

- Controversies between citizens of the same state claiming lands under grants of different states

- Controversies between a state—or citizens of a state—and foreign states, citizens, or subjects

**Source:** U.S. Constitution, Article III, Section 2.

The federal court system also includes a variety of special courts that have only limited jurisdiction over a narrow range of cases. For example, the *U.S. Tax Court* has jurisdiction to hear controversies between taxpayers and the federal Internal Revenue Service (IRS) involving the payment of federal taxes.

## Business Ethics

Throughout this text, we discuss many of the legal and regulatory issues that financial services companies face. But simply doing what is legal and required by law does not always mean that a business operates ethically. Sometimes employees must make decisions that cannot be based solely on legally established rules. In these situations, they must look to moral and ethical standards on which to base their decisions.

By *ethics* we mean a system of accepted standards of conduct and moral judgment that combines the elements of honesty, integrity, and fair treatment. Making ethical business decisions involves behaving in accordance with accepted legal and moral principles of right and wrong. Acting ethically means, among other things, upholding promises to customers, operating in a responsible manner, treating customers and employees equitably, and keeping confidential information private.

Even before the creation of organized legal systems, cultures around the world created ethical codes designed to maintain order and resolve conflicts within communities. Although ethical codes vary somewhat from culture to culture, most codes include prohibitions against lying, cheating, stealing, and physically harming others. Businesspeople, however, often are faced with situations for which there are no clearly defined rules of right and wrong. In such situations, the decision a person makes is likely influenced by his own personal values and standards, as well as by the likelihood of receiving support for his decision within the organization. Thus, the organization's corporate culture affects the person's decision. By *corporate culture* we mean the values, beliefs, goals, and patterns of behavior that employees of an organization share. Businesses that value ethical conduct typically try to create a corporate culture that encourages such conduct. Today, many businesses—especially large corporations—have adopted written standards of ethical conduct.

Financial services companies can benefit in many ways from operating ethically. For example, ethical companies enhance their good reputations, which enables them to gain the trust of their customers and others, including regulators and stockholders. By operating ethically, companies are better able to hire and retain top-quality employees; avoid costly lawsuits, antitrust actions, and even criminal prosecutions; and satisfy and retain customers. As a result, maintaining a high standard of ethics is a valuable asset in a company's efforts to earn a profit.

An effective compliance and ethics program also can help companies detect and prevent fraud and other crimes. Like many countries, the United States has enacted criminal laws that apply to businesses as well as to individuals. Businesses, for example, can be found guilty of crimes such as fraud, tax evasion, and antitrust violations. If convicted, a business can be subject to paying fines, being placed on probation, and being ordered to make repayments to injured parties.

The *Federal Sentencing Guidelines* are U.S. federal rules that set out uniform policies for sentencing individuals and organizations that have been convicted of serious federal crimes.[2] Federal judges are required to consider the guidelines when setting a punishment, but they may consider other factors in addition to the guidelines. Although the guidelines are federal rules, they have influenced many state regulators. For example, state insurance departments voluntarily follow some of the practices contained in the guidelines, especially the practice of assessing the degree of blame to place on a company for allowing illegal activities to occur.

The guidelines provide incentives—in the form of reduced penalties—for organizations to take steps to prevent illegal conduct by individuals within the organizations. According to the sentencing guidelines, if criminal conduct occurs within an organization that has an effective compliance and ethics program, the court can reduce the penalties it otherwise would have imposed on the organization. Penalties are reduced further if the organization reported the offense to appropriate governmental authorities, fully cooperated in the government's investigation, and clearly accepted responsibility for its criminal conduct. To establish an effective compliance and ethics program, an organization must exercise due diligence to prevent and detect criminal conduct and must promote an organizational culture that encourages ethical conduct and a commitment to compliance with the law. To establish an effective compliance and ethics program that meets the standards set by the sentencing guidelines, an organization must

- Establish compliance standards and procedures to prevent and detect criminal conduct by the organization's personnel.

- Place responsibility for overseeing the organization's compliance with its established standards and procedures on high-level executives in the organization. Many companies have created a new staff position—the *ethics officer* or *compliance officer*—who is a high-level company employee responsible for overseeing the company's ethics program.

- Ensure that individuals who have substantial discretionary authority to act on behalf of the company are of high character.

- Effectively communicate the organization's standards and procedures to all personnel. The organization can, for example, require participation in training programs or provide employees with written materials that explain in a practical manner what the organization's standards and procedures require.

- Take reasonable steps to achieve compliance with the organization's standards. Such steps include the use of monitoring and auditing systems that are reasonably designed to detect criminal conduct by personnel and the establishment of a reporting system whereby personnel can report criminal conduct by others within the organization without fear of retribution.

- Consistently enforce the organization's standards through appropriate disciplinary mechanisms, including disciplining individuals who are responsible for the organization's failure to detect an offense.

- Take reasonable steps after an offense has been detected to respond appropriately to the offense and to prevent further similar offenses. If necessary, the organization must modify its standards and procedures to more effectively prevent and detect future violations of law.

By establishing such a program, a company can provide a solid foundation for ethical company operations.

Wow, I didn't realize that all that compliance and ethics training we participated in could have this big an impact on our organization if something goes wrong internally. I guess maybe it really is worth the time.

See? I told you that learning about the legal environment not only helps you understand how laws and legal systems work, but also how you can play a part in keeping our company in compliance with regulatory requirements.

## Key Terms

| | |
|---|---|
| constitution | substantive laws |
| legislative branch | procedural laws |
| executive branch | jurisdiction |
| judicial branch | trial courts |
| parliamentary democracy | appellate courts |
| federal system | common law system |
| statute | common law |
| statutory law | doctrine of stare decisis |
| Congress | precedent |
| state legislature | civil law system |
| U.S. Code | code |
| state code | civil code |
| state insurance code | mixed legal system |
| administrative agencies | Islamic legal system |
| regulations | customary law system |
| administrative law | judge |
| administrative code | ethics |
| state insurance department | corporate culture |
| treaty | Federal Sentencing Guidelines |
| case law | |

## Endnotes

1. *Stare decisis* (star-ē di-sī-sis) is a Latin term that means "to stand by that which is decided."

2. United States Sentencing Commission *2010 Federal Sentencing Guidelines Manual*, http://www.ussc.gov/Guidelines/2010_guidelines/ToC_HTML.cfm (18 May 2011).

10/22      Exam Score : 56%    5/9
Not that difficult of a test

*Chapter 2*

# Civil Disputes

## Objectives

_____

*After studying this chapter, you should be able to*

- Identify the three stages of a civil action and describe the rules and procedures that are followed in the civil litigation process in the United States

- Describe the general principles of tort law and explain how liability for tortious conduct can be based on intentional torts, negligence, and strict liability

- Distinguish between legal remedies and equitable remedies and describe the types of damages that may be awarded in civil actions

- Describe the equitable principles that equity courts apply to determine whether to grant an equitable remedy to a plaintiff

- Identify and describe two alternative dispute resolution methods

# Outline

**Civil Litigation Process**
- The Parties
- Procedural Stages

**Tort Law**
- Intentional Torts
- Negligence
- Strict Liability

**Civil Remedies**
- Legal Remedies
- Equitable Remedies
- Restitution

**Alternative Dispute Resolution**

Although we describe some aspects of criminal law, this text's primary focus is on issues of civil law. In common law jurisdictions, *criminal laws* are laws that define certain acts as crimes and provide specific punishments for each crime. In a criminal court case, the government is the party that prosecutes its case against the individual charged with the crime. By contrast, *civil laws* are laws that are concerned with private—that is, nongovernmental—rights and remedies.

So a dispute about who has a right to receive life insurance policy proceeds is a civil dispute?

That's right. And civil laws govern the dispute.

Civil law jurisdictions typically categorize these areas of the law as public law and private law. *Public law* refers to those areas of the law that affect the public interest and that govern relationships between the government and nongovernmental parties. *Private law* refers to those areas of the law that primarily involve disputes between nongovernmental parties.

Although most private (civil) disputes are settled by the parties involved, some disputes cannot be resolved between the parties. Governments typically establish a system for resolving such disputes within their jurisdictions. In many jurisdictions including the United States, the parties generally turn to the courts to resolve civil disputes. *Civil litigation* is a judicial process by which private parties go to court to enforce a legal right or to obtain a remedy for a civil wrong.

To file a successful civil lawsuit, a person or business that is a party to a dispute must have a valid cause of action. A *cause of action* is a set of facts that gives a person the right to judicial relief. A cause of action arises when (1) one person has a legal right, (2) another person has a legal duty to observe that right, (3) the second person breaches her legal duty, and (4) the first person suffers a loss or injury as a result of that breach. All four elements must be present to create a cause of action. The civil litigation process is designed to help the courts determine whether the elements of the cause of action are present and, if so, what judicial relief is appropriate.

Common law jurisdictions provide for two general types of civil causes of action: breach of contract actions and tort actions. A *contract* is a legally enforceable agreement between two or more parties; the agreement consists of a promise or a set of promises. A *breach of contract* is the failure of a party to perform a contractual obligation. A *tort* is a private wrong—other than a breach of contract—for which the law provides a remedy to the wronged party.

# Civil Litigation Process

Each court system has established rules which specify the procedures that must be followed in civil court proceedings. Although specific rules and procedures vary slightly from jurisdiction to jurisdiction, the general procedures and principles we describe are fairly uniform across the United States.

## The Parties

Judicial proceedings begin when an injured party, known as the *plaintiff*, files papers with the court setting out her cause of action against the other party, who is known as the *defendant*. The plaintiff and defendant are known as the *parties* to the action. Any legal person can be a party to a civil action. In this context, a *person* is a natural person or an entity, such as a corporation, that the law recognizes as having legal rights and duties.

## Procedural Stages

A civil action consists of three distinct stages: (1) the pleading stage, (2) the discovery stage, and (3) the trial stage. Note, however, that the parties have the right to settle their dispute at any time. As a result, a civil action may terminate by agreement of the parties at any time before the court reaches a verdict. Figure 2.1 outlines the stages of the civil litigation process.

### The Pleading Stage

The *pleadings* are the formal, written statements that set out the claims and defenses of each of the parties to a lawsuit. Pleadings serve to

- Define the issues that are in dispute

- Set out the material facts that are involved in the dispute

- Define the judicial relief that the parties seek from the court

The two basic types of pleadings are the complaint and the answer. Civil proceedings begin when the plaintiff files a complaint with the appropriate court official, such as the clerk of the court. A *complaint* is a written document that sets out the cause of action on which the plaintiff bases her claim against the defendant. The procedural rules of each jurisdiction specify the proper form of a complaint, which usually must be personally served on—that is, presented to—the defendant in accordance with specific procedural rules. *Service of process*, the act of delivering—or serving—the complaint to the defendant, provides the defendant with official notification of the proceeding so as to afford him the opportunity to appear and be heard.

## Figure 2.1 Overview of the Civil Litigation Process

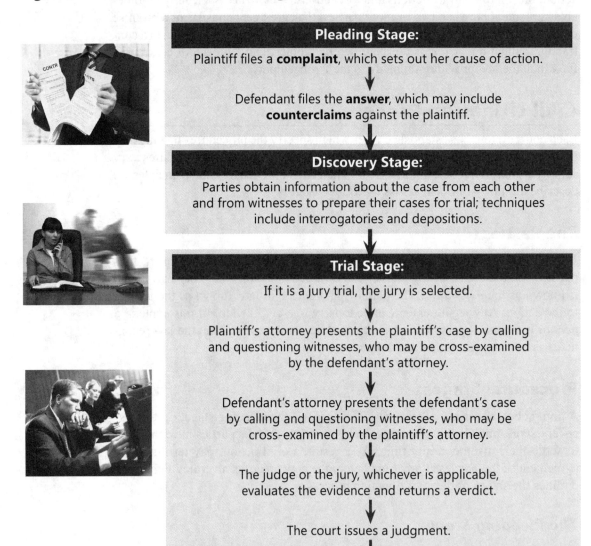

**Pleading Stage:**

Plaintiff files a **complaint**, which sets out her cause of action.

↓

Defendant files the **answer**, which may include **counterclaims** against the plaintiff.

↓

**Discovery Stage:**

Parties obtain information about the case from each other and from witnesses to prepare their cases for trial; techniques include interrogatories and depositions.

↓

**Trial Stage:**

If it is a jury trial, the jury is selected.

↓

Plaintiff's attorney presents the plaintiff's case by calling and questioning witnesses, who may be cross-examined by the defendant's attorney.

↓

Defendant's attorney presents the defendant's case by calling and questioning witnesses, who may be cross-examined by the plaintiff's attorney.

↓

The judge or the jury, whichever is applicable, evaluates the evidence and returns a verdict.

↓

The court issues a judgment.

↓

The losing party may have the right to appeal the judgment.

When a defendant is served with a complaint, the defendant has a specified number of days in which to respond to the plaintiff's complaint by filing with the court a written document known as an *answer*. In his answer, a defendant can (1) admit or deny each of the facts that the plaintiff alleged in her complaint or (2) answer that he has no knowledge of a fact that the plaintiff alleged. The defendant also may include affirmative defenses and counterclaims in the answer.

■ An *affirmative defense* is an allegation of facts that constitute a defense to the plaintiff's claim. For example, the voluntary assumption of a known risk, which we describe later in the chapter, is an affirmative defense that totally bars a plaintiff's claim.

Business Law for Financial Services Professionals

Chapter 2: Civil Disputes | **2.5**

- A *counterclaim* is a claim by the defendant against the plaintiff that arises out of the same facts on which the plaintiff's claim is based. In contract disputes, for example, both parties often have claims against each other. Counterclaims allow all of the disputes between the parties to be joined together for resolution in one civil proceeding.

If a party fails to file a required pleading or files defective pleadings, the action may be ended fairly quickly with either a default judgment or a dismissal of the action. A *default judgment* is a judgment entered against a defendant who fails to plead—that is, to file an answer within the required time—or who otherwise fails to defend the lawsuit. A *dismissal* is a court order or judgment that concludes a lawsuit without a trial of the issues involved in the lawsuit. Typically, a lawsuit is dismissed because the plaintiff either failed to prosecute her case or failed to state a valid claim and therefore is not entitled to judicial relief.

## The Discovery Stage

*Discovery* is a process in which the parties to a civil lawsuit gather information that is relevant to the lawsuit so that they can prepare to present their respective cases at trial. Discovery serves the following functions:

- Permits the parties and witnesses to be questioned early on in the litigation process while their memories are fresher and to preserve their testimony

- Allows facts to be revealed so that the parties can narrow the issues and can identify those that are actually in dispute and thus reduce the time needed to try the action

- Facilitates settlements because the parties are able to determine the relative strengths of their own case and the other party's case

- Seeks to prevent a party from hiding information in order to surprise the other party at trial and thus gain an unfair advantage

Ultimately, the discovery process is designed to aid the court in discovering the truth of the matter under consideration.

A number of discovery techniques are available to the parties. The following are some important discovery techniques:

- *Interrogatories* are written questions that one party prepares and that the other party must answer in writing within a specified time. The answers to interrogatories are submitted in the form of an *affidavit*, which is a written statement made under oath. When an individual knowingly makes false statements under oath, the individual has committed *perjury*, which is a crime in all jurisdictions.

- Parties and other witnesses may be questioned by attorneys for each party in a procedure known as a *deposition*, in which the person orally testifies under oath. The testimony is recorded by a court reporter, who provides each of the parties with a written transcript of the deposition.

- A *request to produce documents and things* is a request by one party that the other party produce defined documents and items related to the lawsuit.

That sounds like discovery can be a lot of trouble.

You're right. The scope of what can be discovered is very broad. It can take a lot of time, especially if you have to locate and produce many documents. That's one reason we want to avoid lawsuits if at all possible.

The court has the authority to compel plaintiffs, defendants, and third parties to comply with the rules of discovery. When a plaintiff does not cooperate with the defendant's discovery attempts, the court can dismiss the plaintiff's action. Alternatively, when the defendant does not comply, the court can enter a default judgment. In addition, the court can find parties or persons who are not parties to the action in contempt of court for failure to comply with proper discovery requests. *Contempt of court* is any act that hinders the court in administering justice or that lessens the authority and dignity of the court. A person found in contempt of court is subject to a variety of penalties, including the seizure of property, imprisonment, or a monetary fine.

## The Trial Stage

A *trial* is a formal proceeding at which the parties appear in court along with their respective attorneys and present their cases to the court. An action may be tried by a judge alone or by a judge and a jury. In most U.S. trial courts, the parties have the right to request a trial by jury.

A civil proceeding may involve issues of law as well as issues of fact. An *issue of law* is an issue in which the parties disagree on how the law should be applied to a given set of facts. An *issue of fact* is an issue in which the parties disagree as to the facts involved in the action. In all cases, the judge is responsible for deciding issues of law. In a jury trial, the judge instructs the jury as to the laws that apply to the case. Issues of fact are decided by the *trier of fact*, which is the judge in a nonjury trial and the jury in a jury trial. Thus, when a case is tried by a judge alone, the judge decides both issues of law and issues of fact. When a case is tried by a judge and a jury, the judge instructs the jury as to the applicable laws; then the jury decides which facts to believe and applies the law to those facts to reach a verdict.

|  | Nonjury Trial | Jury Trial |
|---|---|---|
| **Who decides issues of law?** | Judge | Judge |
| **Who decides issues of fact?** | Judge | Jury |

If a case is to be tried by a judge and a jury, the jury must first be selected and sworn in. The trial proceeds with the presentation of the plaintiff's case. The plaintiff's attorney calls and examines each plaintiff's witness, who testifies under oath. The defendant's attorney has the right to cross-examine each witness. At the conclusion of the plaintiff's case, the defendant's attorney presents the defendant's case by calling and examining the defendant's witnesses, who testify under oath; the plaintiff's attorney has the right to cross-examine these witnesses.

## The Rules of Evidence

*Evidence* is the means by which the disputed facts in an action are proved or disproved. To be admissible at trial, evidence must be relevant and material to the facts at issue—that is, evidence must tend to prove or disprove a relevant fact. Evidence is presented through the testimony of witnesses and through the production of documents and other items.

The ***rules of evidence*** are procedural rules that govern the admissibility of evidence at trials and determine whether the evidence presented is sufficient to prove the issues involved in an action. The goal of the rules of evidence is to aid the court in ascertaining the truth by winnowing out unreliable evidence.

The rules of evidence determine which party bears the burden of proving a given fact. The term *burden of proof* has two meanings. First, ***burden of proof*** means the duty to present evidence to prove a given fact or set of facts. Second, *burden of proof* means the duty to persuade the trier of fact that an alleged fact is true.

The burden of presenting evidence often shifts between the plaintiff and defendant throughout a trial. Initially, the plaintiff has the burden of presenting evidence because the plaintiff must first prove all of the elements of his cause of action. The plaintiff's initial burden of proof is the burden to present a prima facie case. A ***prima facie case*** is evidence that is sufficient to prove the elements of a party's case and that entitles the party to judicial relief unless the opposing party presents evidence to the contrary.[1] A plaintiff who fails to present a prima facie case has failed to meet his initial burden of proof, and the court probably will dismiss such a plaintiff's lawsuit. If the plaintiff presents a prima facie case, then the burden of producing evidence shifts to the defendant, who will probably lose the case unless she is able to present evidence sufficient to disprove the plaintiff's prima facie case.

In general, the burden of persuading the court that a particular fact is true rests with the party who alleges that fact as being true. As noted, the plaintiff has the burden of persuading the court of the truth of all of the facts necessary to constitute the plaintiff's prima facie case. Likewise, if the defendant filed a counterclaim against the plaintiff, then the defendant bears the burden of proving all of the elements of that counterclaim. Unlike the burden of presenting evidence, which shifts from party to party throughout a trial, the burden of persuasion regarding a specific element of the case remains throughout the proceedings with the party who alleged that element.

The rules of evidence also specify the degree of proof required for a party to meet his burden of persuasion. The degree of proof generally required in a civil action is a preponderance of the evidence. A ***preponderance of the evidence*** means that the decision as to an issue of fact must be supported by the greater weight of the evidence. In other words, the trier of fact must evaluate the evidence and decide the issue in favor of the party that presented the more convincing evidence concerning the disputed fact. By contrast, the degree of proof required of the prosecution in a criminal action is *proof beyond a reasonable doubt*. The trier of fact may not find a defendant guilty of a crime if the trier of fact has any reasonable doubt about the defendant's guilt. Proving a fact beyond a reasonable doubt is a much higher standard of proof than proving a fact by a preponderance of the evidence.

So, in a civil action, the degree of proof needed is a preponderance of the evidence. The trier of fact decides which party presented the more convincing evidence. How is that different than the proof needed in a criminal case?

You've probably heard that the prosecution in a criminal case has to prove a defendant's guilt beyond a shadow of a doubt. That's a much higher standard of proof than the standard in a civil case.

The rules of evidence also include a legal device known as a presumption. A ***presumption*** is a rule of law under which a fact is assumed to be true because another fact or set of facts was proven. Presumptions stand in the place of facts that have not been proven. For example, if the facts surrounding a death indicate that the death could have resulted from either suicide or accident, the law in most jurisdictions presumes that the death was accidental. The law includes a variety of presumptions, many of which we discuss throughout this text.

A presumption can be either conclusive or rebuttable. A ***conclusive presumption*** is a presumption that cannot be refuted. The law contains very few conclusive presumptions. An example of a conclusive presumption in most U.S. jurisdictions is that a child under a specified age is conclusively presumed to be incapable of committing certain crimes. In such jurisdictions, the conclusive presumption means that a child who is younger than the specified age cannot be charged with the specified crimes.

A ***rebuttable presumption*** is a presumption that can be disproven but that stands until adequate evidence is presented to the contrary. A rebuttable presumption shifts the burden of producing evidence from one party to another. In other words, once a party produces evidence sufficient to create a rebuttable presumption, the presumption stands unless the other party produces evidence to rebut or disprove it.

> **Example:**
> An insurer denied a claim for life insurance policy proceeds on the ground that the insured died as a result of suicide during the suicide exclusion period. The beneficiary filed an action to recover the policy proceeds and presented a prima facie case that the insured died while the policy was in force and that the death was accidental. The beneficiary's evidence raised the rebuttable presumption that the insured's death was accidental. As a result, the burden of producing evidence shifted to the insurer, which had to produce evidence sufficient to rebut the presumption that the death was accidental. Unless the insurer can produce evidence sufficient to convince the trier of fact that the insured's death was not accidental, the beneficiary will prevail in the action.

## The Applicable Law

As we have noted, laws vary from jurisdiction to jurisdiction, and many legal issues arise from actions or transactions that involve more than one jurisdiction. In cases that involve the laws of more than one jurisdiction, the courts must first determine which jurisdiction's substantive laws apply to the case. *Conflict of laws* is the area of the law that determines which substantive laws apply to each issue in a case when the laws of more than one jurisdiction are involved in the action. Procedural rules in each jurisdiction around the world guide the courts in making conflict-of-laws determinations.

## The Judgment

A civil action is completed when the court issues a judgment. A *judgment* is an official decision of a court that resolves a dispute and determines the rights and obligations of the parties to the action. Typically, the judgment incorporates the verdict of the trier of fact. However, if the judge in a jury trial finds that the jury's verdict is not reasonably supported by the facts or is contrary to the law, then the judge may set aside the jury's verdict and refuse to incorporate it into the judgment. If the parties agree to settle their dispute before the case is presented to the trier of fact, then their settlement agreement is incorporated into the court's judgment. In any case, once a judgment is issued, it is filed with the court and usually becomes part of the public record.

A losing party may have the right to appeal the judgment of the trial court. The right to appeal exists only when it is granted by statute, and, in some cases, an appellate court must first grant a party permission to appeal. Appeals must be filed within the time limit prescribed by the applicable rules of procedure and can be based on issues of fact and/or on issues of law. Appellate courts have the power to affirm the judgment of a trial court, order a new trial, or change a trial court judgment in whole or in part.

If there is no appeal in a civil action, the judgment becomes final and binding on the parties, and the cause of action may not be the subject matter of a subsequent action. The finality of judgments is based on the judicial doctrine of res judicata. *Res judicata* means that a matter has been decided.[2] The purpose of this doctrine is to ensure that parties will not relitigate matters that the courts have already decided. The doctrine thus promotes judicial efficiency and enables the parties to rely on the finality of judgments.

### The Legal Process in Civil Law Jurisdictions

The United States and Canada are unique in providing parties in criminal and civil cases the right to a jury trial. Although jury trials are available in some public (criminal) cases in civil law jurisdictions, private disputes typically are heard by a judge or panel of judges. A case involving a private dispute begins when the parties file pleadings, which state the issues in general terms. Rather than culminating in a trial as in common law jurisdictions, a case in a civil law jurisdiction usually proceeds with a series of meetings, hearings, and written documents through which evidence is presented. The judge guides the evidence-gathering process, questions all witnesses, and evaluates the admissibility and weight of all evidence presented. The judge renders the verdict at the final hearing on the matter.

## Tort Law

In the United States, each state has developed a body of tort law that creates rights and imposes corresponding duties on individuals and apportions responsibility when a breach of a legal duty results in loss to another person. Although laws vary somewhat from state to state, we describe some of the general principles of tort law found in the laws of most states. As described in Insight 2.1, similar laws are included in the civil codes of civil law jurisdictions around the world. Further, virtually all countries provide remedies to those who are injured by another person's wrongful (tortious) actions as described in this section.

---

### Insight 2.1 The Law of Obligations in Civil Law Jurisdictions

The civil code of many civil law jurisdictions includes a section that sets out the jurisdiction's **law of obligations**, which includes laws that govern a range of civil duties and liabilities. An **obligation** is a duty that one person owes to another, and it may arise from a number of sources. Obligations may arise as a result of a contract or when one person damages another through negligence or fault. In the Canadian province of Quebec, for example, the two sources of noncontractual civil liability are

- Delicts, which are intentional faults that damage another person
- Quasi-delicts, which are unintentional faults that damage another person

In most jurisdictions, the law of obligations also typically includes rules that govern special types of agreements such as leases, partnerships, and insurance contracts.

---

The law of torts focuses on compensating the victims of torts rather than on punishing the wrongdoers. An individual who breaches a legal duty that she owes to another person and thereby harms the other person is financially liable for the loss to the injured person. Whether an individual has met her legal duty depends on whether her conduct met the standard of care required by the law.

The common law recognizes three general theories on which liability for tortious conduct can be based: intentional torts, negligence, and strict liability.

## Intentional Torts

An ***intentional tort*** is a private wrong committed by a person who intended to do something that the law declares a wrong. The common law imposes liability for a variety of specific intentional torts, which are either wrongs against another person or wrongs against another person's property. Intentional torts against another person include assault, battery, defamation, fraudulent misrepresentation, and inducing a breach of contract. Intentional torts against another person's property include trespass to land and conversion.

### *Specific Intentional Torts*

***Assault*** is the intentional creation of a reasonable fear in the mind of the victim of imminent bodily harm. ***Battery*** is an intentional harmful or offensive physical contact with another person. Note that an assault consists of a threat to harm another, whereas a battery occurs when a person touches, strikes, or otherwise physically harms another person. A battery is often preceded by an assault, and thus, these two torts typically are linked together. Assault and battery also are criminal acts, and a person who commits an assault and battery is subject to criminal prosecution in addition to being sued in a civil action.

I thought that assault and battery were criminal issues.

They are, and criminal laws are in place to punish wrongdoing. But an injured person also can sue the wrongdoer for civil damages.

The tort of ***defamation*** occurs when a person makes false statements that injure the good name or reputation of another person. Defamation takes two forms: (1) *slander*, when the defamatory statements are made orally, and (2) *libel*, when the statements are made in writing. To succeed in a civil action for defamation, a plaintiff typically must prove that (1) the defendant made a false statement about the plaintiff, (2) the defendant communicated the statement to a third party, and (3) the statement injured the plaintiff's reputation.

*Fraudulent misrepresentation* occurs when a person knowingly or willfully makes a false statement with the intent that another person will rely on the statement and will be harmed as a result of that reliance. To prove that a defendant knowingly or willfully made such a false statement, the plaintiff must prove that the defendant made a misrepresentation either (1) with knowledge of its falsity, (2) without belief in its truth, or (3) with reckless or careless disregard for whether it is true.

> **Example:**
>
> An officer of a corporation intentionally overstated the corporation's profits to several major shareholders in order to induce them to purchase more of the corporation's stock. In reliance on the misrepresentation, the shareholders purchased more stock and as a result lost most of their investments. The shareholders have a cause of action against the corporate officer for fraudulent misrepresentation.

*Inducing a breach of contract* is an intentional tort that occurs when a person who is not a party to a contract persuades a contracting party to breach a contractual obligation.

> **Example:**
>
> Sally Badger persuaded three of Carlos Romero's employees to breach their employment contracts and to come to work for her. Mr. Romero has a cause of action against each of the employees for breach of contract, and he has a cause of action in tort against Ms. Badger for inducing the breaches of contract.

*Trespass to land* is the unauthorized physical invasion of another's land. For example, a person who walks onto another person's land without the right to do so has trespassed and may be liable in tort. *Conversion* is the unauthorized exercise of dominion and control over another person's property. Acts of conversion include theft, embezzlement, and damaging or destroying another's property.

## Elements of a Cause of Action

The elements of a cause of action based on an intentional tort vary depending on the specific tort involved. To prevail in any cause of action based on an intentional tort, however, the plaintiff usually must prove that the defendant acted with intent. A defendant acts with intent when she desires to produce the results that follow from her wrongful act.

> **Example:**
>
> Ms. Gregg aimed and fired a rifle in an effort to shoot Mr. Barker. If she succeeded in shooting Mr. Barker, then she brought about the result she intended, and her actions constitute the tort of battery. By contrast, assume that Ms. Gregg aimed and fired a rifle at a target but accidentally shot Mr. Barker. Ms. Gregg's conduct produced an undesired result, and therefore she did not commit an intentional tort by shooting Mr. Barker. Her conduct, however, may have been negligent.

# Negligence

In most cases, liability in tort is the result of conduct that is considered negligent rather than conduct that is intentionally harmful. *Negligence* is a private wrong committed by a person who failed to exercise the legally required degree of care in (1) doing something that is otherwise legally permissible or (2) omitting to do something that is otherwise legally required.

## Elements of a Cause of Action

To prevail in a civil action based on negligence, a plaintiff generally has the burden of proving the following four elements of a cause of action:

1. **The defendant had a legal duty to the plaintiff to act in accordance with a prescribed standard of care.** Whether a defendant owed a duty to the plaintiff is a question of law for the court. The law imposes a general duty of care on all activities: a person typically has a legal duty to act as a reasonably prudent person would in the situation. Insight 2.2 describes this standard of care.

2. **The defendant breached his legal duty.** Whether a defendant breached a legal duty is a question of fact for the trier of fact to answer.

3. **The plaintiff suffered a loss.** The loss may result from physical injuries that lead to medical expenses, lost income, and pain and suffering. The plaintiff also may have financial losses resulting from damage to, or loss of, property. Whether a loss occurred and the extent of the loss are questions of fact.

4. **The defendant's conduct was the cause of the plaintiff's loss.** Whether a defendant's conduct was the cause of the plaintiff's loss is a question of fact.

## Insight 2.2 The Standard of Care

In most tort actions, the trier of fact must decide whether the defendant acted as a reasonably prudent person would have acted in the same situation. To make that decision, the trier of fact must evaluate all of the circumstances surrounding the defendant's conduct and sometimes must take into account some facts about the defendant.

- Children generally are held to a lower standard than are adults. A child generally is required to act like a reasonable person of the child's age, experience, and intelligence. Thus, actions taken by a child may not be negligent, whereas the same actions taken by an adult might be negligent.

- Professionals, such as physicians, attorneys, and accountants, generally are held to a higher standard of care than are non-professionals. A professional is required to act as a reasonably prudent person of like knowledge and skill would have acted in the same situation. Thus, professionals are required to have the special knowledge and skills needed to carry out their professions and to use reasonable care as they use their special knowledge and skills.

## *Defenses*

A defendant who is sued for negligence often defends the lawsuit by trying to prove that he was not negligent. For example, the defendant may try to show that she did not owe the plaintiff a duty of care or that her actions were not the cause of the plaintiff's loss. Even if a plaintiff's injuries were the result of the defendant's negligence, the defendant may be able to defeat the plaintiff's claim in whole or in part with an affirmative defense such as contributory negligence or assumption of the risk.

*Contributory negligence* is a plaintiff's own negligence that contributes to his loss. According to the original common law rule of contributory negligence, a plaintiff who was responsible to any extent for his loss was denied any recovery from the defendant. To reduce the harshness of this rule, most states have modified their laws by adopting a system of *comparative negligence* that allows a plaintiff who was contributorily negligent to recover from the defendant, but the amount of that recovery is reduced in proportion to the plaintiff's fault. Each party must bear the cost of that portion of the plaintiff's losses that the party caused. For example, assume that the trier of fact determines that a plaintiff was 25 percent at fault for her losses and the defendant was 75 percent at fault. The defendant will be held liable to the plaintiff for 75 percent of her losses. Insight 2.3 describes comparative negligence in more detail.

---

### Insight 2.3 Comparative Negligence

Most states have adopted a system of comparative negligence under which the amount a plaintiff can recover for losses caused by the defendant's negligence is reduced when the plaintiff also was negligent. The states, however, have adopted two different versions of comparative negligence:

- In some states, the plaintiff and defendant each bear their proportionate share of the losses regardless of which party was most at fault.

- In other states, a plaintiff can recover from the defendant only if the defendant was 50 percent or more at fault. In some of these states, a plaintiff can recover only if the defendant was more than 50 percent at fault.

---

*Assumption of the risk* is an affirmative defense that totally bars a plaintiff's claim when the plaintiff understood the nature of the risk presented by the defendant's conduct and voluntarily incurred that risk. Whether a plaintiff voluntarily assumed the risk is a question of fact.

> **Example:**
> Your friend offered to give you a ride in his truck but warned you that something was wrong with the truck's brakes. While riding in your friend's truck, the brakes failed, the truck hit a tree, and you were injured. It is likely that the trier of fact would find that you had voluntarily assumed the risk of being injured because you knew about the defective brakes and chose to ride in the truck.

Many states have abolished the common law defense of assumption of the risk by merging the rule into a system of comparative negligence. Some states have adopted laws of comparative fault that are similar to comparative negligence laws but are broader and include tortious conduct other than negligence, such as intentional torts.

## Strict Liability

*Strict liability*—that is, liability without regard for whether the defendant was at fault—is applied only in very restricted situations, such as when a defendant engages in extremely hazardous activities. For example, blasting with dynamite is a hazardous activity that may cause harm to others. A defendant is liable for losses caused by such activities even if the defendant was not negligent or otherwise at fault for the losses.

# Civil Remedies

A plaintiff files a civil action to obtain redress from the defendant for a wrong the defendant committed. Thus, the plaintiff seeks a remedy for the wrong she suffered as a result of the defendant's conduct. The remedies available to a plaintiff vary depending on the nature of the plaintiff's cause of action.

In common law jurisdictions, remedies generally are categorized as either *legal* or *equitable*. This categorization results from the way that remedies were developed by England's common law courts. Originally, English courts followed rigid, formalized procedures that provided only limited and specific remedies, which came to be known as *legal remedies*. These remedies primarily involved the payment of money damages to injured parties. Over time, legal remedies were inadequate to remedy some wrongs, and separate courts, known as *courts of equity*, were created to provide new remedies. The courts of equity were not bound by rigid procedures and were given discretionary power to base their decisions on moral rights and concepts of justice. The remedies developed by the equity courts were known as *equitable remedies*. Today, the courts in common law jurisdictions are empowered to grant both legal and equitable remedies.

Let's see if I understand this. The basic legal remedy for civil wrongs is damages, and common law courts grant both legal and equitable remedies, right?

 Correct. But there is more than one type of damages.

 Why does that not surprise me?

## Legal Remedies

The basic legal remedy for most civil wrongs is *damages*, which consists of monetary compensation that may be recovered by a plaintiff who suffered a loss or injury as a result of a defendant's wrongful conduct.

### *Compensatory Damages*

Civil damages awards generally provide a plaintiff with *compensatory damages*, which are damages intended to compensate an injured party for the amount of the monetary losses that resulted from the defendant's wrongful conduct. Compensatory damages are sometimes referred to as *actual damages*.

The amount of compensatory damages to be awarded a plaintiff is a question of fact. Once a defendant's liability has been established, the trier of fact must determine the amount of damages to be awarded the plaintiff. The measure used to determine the amount of damages varies depending on the specific facts of the case. In all cases, the plaintiff has the burden of proving with reasonable certainty the amount of her losses. In addition, a defendant generally is liable only for those losses that were the foreseeable result of his actions. A loss is foreseeable if it would ordinarily be expected to result from the wrongful actions or the defendant knew of specific facts that would make the loss likely.

In an action for breach of contract, compensatory damages generally are measured as the *benefit of the bargain*. The damage award is that amount that will put the plaintiff in the financial position he would have been in if the contract had been performed.

> **Example:**
>
> The defendant agreed to pay the plaintiff $5,500 for certain goods. The defendant breached the contract and refused to complete the purchase, and the plaintiff sold the goods to another buyer for $4,500. Had the contract been performed, the plaintiff would have realized an additional $1,000 on the sale of the goods. Thus, the plaintiff is entitled to receive $1,000 in compensatory damages from the defendant.

In an action based on tort, compensatory damages generally include losses for personal injuries and/or property damage. Personal injury losses include physical, mental, and emotional injuries and typically consist of the amount of the plaintiff's medical expenses and loss of earnings, including the loss of future earnings. Damage awards also include amounts to compensate the plaintiff for the pain and suffering that resulted from the defendant's wrongful conduct.

## Other Types of Damages

*Punitive damages*, or *exemplary damages*, are awarded in addition to compensatory damages when a defendant's wrongful conduct was malicious or willful. The purpose of a punitive damage award is to punish the defendant and to deter others from similar conduct. For example, punitive damages may be awarded in intentional tort cases and occasionally in cases based on negligence. Punitive damages generally are *not* available in actions based on breach of contract unless the breach was wanton, willful, and deliberate.

Sometimes, a plaintiff is awarded *nominal damages* when he was wronged but he did not suffer a loss as a result of the wrong, cannot prove the amount of the loss with reasonable certainty, or the loss was trivial. In such cases, the plaintiff is not entitled to compensatory damages, because he failed to prove the amount of his damages with reasonable certainty. If the defendant's conduct was wrongful, however, the trier of fact may award the plaintiff a small sum. For example, assume that the defendant trespassed on the plaintiff's land but did not damage the plaintiff in any measurable way. The trier of fact might award the plaintiff nominal damages of one dollar. Nominal damages may be awarded in both tort and contract actions.

The rules we have described are the most common rules concerning damages. The facts of each case determine the specific measure used to calculate the amount of damages that are awarded. Figure 2.2 describes some other types of damages that may be awarded in a civil action.

## Duty to Mitigate Damages

The plaintiff in a civil action always has a duty to make a reasonable effort to *mitigate*—that is, to minimize—the amount of damages that result from the defendant's wrong. The plaintiff cannot recover damages for a loss that she could have avoided or lessened by reasonable efforts. Thus, the plaintiff's failure to mitigate damages is an affirmative defense to a civil action. The defendant may use the affirmative defense to reduce the amount of damages that he is required to pay.

> **Example:**
> The plaintiff entered into an employment contract to create a computer software program for the defendant, who agreed to pay the plaintiff $10,000. Before the plaintiff began the project, the defendant breached the contract by firing the plaintiff and refusing to pay him. The plaintiff found other employment on a similar project, but was paid only $9,000. Had the plaintiff been unable to find other employment, the amount of his loss would have been $10,000. Because he was able to mitigate his damages by earning $9,000, the amount of loss he actually suffered was $1,000.

## Figure 2.2 Civil Damages

**The following types of damages are sometimes awarded in civil lawsuits:**

- **Liquidated damages:** A sum of money that the parties to a contract have specified in their agreement as the amount of damages to be recovered by a party if the other party breaches the contract. The courts generally enforce a liquidated damages provision if it appears that the contracting parties set the amount of damages fairly.

- **Prospective damages:** Damages that have not occurred at the time of the trial of a case but that are reasonably likely to occur as a result of the defendant's conduct.

- **Statutory damages:** Damages that are awarded under the provisions of a statute rather than under the common law rules governing damages for civil wrongs. Some statutes, for example, increase the damages to be awarded in certain cases above what would be available under the common law rules.

**The following types of damages generally are *not* awarded in civil actions in the United States:**

- **Remote damages:** Damages for losses that the defendant could not reasonably have anticipated resulting from a given set of facts. Generally, civil damages are awarded only for those losses that a reasonable person in the defendant's position could have foreseen would result from the defendant's actions.

- **Speculative damages:** Damages that may occur in the future as a result of the defendant's actions but that also depend on the occurrence of other uncertain contingencies.

Whether a party made reasonable efforts to mitigate his damages is a question of fact. Returning to our example, assume that the defendant breached the employment contract, and the plaintiff did not find other employment and thus lost $10,000. The defendant argued that the plaintiff failed to mitigate his damages by not looking for other work. The trier of fact must decide whether the plaintiff made reasonable efforts to mitigate his damages. If the plaintiff failed to make such reasonable efforts, then the trier of fact will reduce the amount of damages awarded to the plaintiff by the amount the plaintiff could have earned from other sources.

## Equitable Remedies

The English equity courts developed principles to aid them in determining when an equitable remedy should be granted. According to these principles, to be granted equitable relief, a plaintiff in a civil action

- **Must have no adequate remedy at law.** In most cases, the legal remedy of damages is adequate to compensate a plaintiff's losses. Equity will intervene only when damages do not adequately compensate a plaintiff. Insight 2.4 gives some examples illustrating how the courts apply principles of equity.

- **Must come into court with clean hands.** The purpose of equity is to do justice, and equity will not aid a party who has acted unfairly or dishonestly. As a result, equity will deny relief to any party who has unclean hands in the matter before the court. Unclean hands can consist of any conduct that equity considers to be unfair or unethical.

- **Must not be guilty of laches.** A plaintiff is guilty of *laches* when he unreasonably delayed in pursuing a claim for relief and the defendant was harmed in some way as a result of the undue delay.

The courts have created additional equitable principles, and they have a great deal of discretion to fashion remedies and make decisions based on what is fair to the parties. The following equitable remedies may be available in a breach-of-contract action:

- *Reformation* is an equitable remedy in which a written contract is rewritten to express the original agreement of the contracting parties. Reformation is available when the parties entered into a written contract, but the document does not accurately reflect their agreement. If the parties cannot mutually agree to correct such a mistake, then one party may ask a court to correct the mistake and rewrite the contract. Whether the written contract accurately reflects the parties' agreement is a question of fact.

- *Rescission* is an equitable remedy in which a contract is cancelled—or *rescinded*—and the parties are returned to the positions they would have been in had no contract ever been created. The remedy of rescission is of special importance to insurers. We describe in Chapter 13 situations in which a life insurance contract may be rescinded.

- *Specific performance* is an equitable remedy that requires a party who has breached a contract to carry out the contract according to its terms. Courts, for example, sometimes order specific performance of contracts for the sale of land, as illustrated in the first example in Insight 2.4. Because of the uniqueness of land, when a contract is breached, the buyer often suffers a loss that cannot be compensated with money damages. Courts, however, will not order the specific performance of certain kinds of contracts, such as employment contracts.

Figure 2.3 describes some other equitable remedies that parties sometimes seek.

## Insight 2.4 Putting Equitable Principles into Practice

**No adequate remedy at law:** Ike Stern was planning to develop a shopping mall and purchased all of the land needed for the project except one parcel, which belonged to the defendant. Although the defendant had entered into a contract to sell his land to Mr. Stern, the defendant changed his mind and refused to sell the land. Because of the defendant's breach of contract, Mr. Stern was unable to develop the mall and was left with the land he had already purchased and could no longer use as planned. Money damages will not adequately compensate Mr. Stern for his injury. The only remedy that will make him whole is to require the defendant to perform the contract and sell the land to Mr. Stern at the price agreed on in the contract.

**Clean hands:** In a 1948 case, the Campbell Soup Company had a contract with a farmer to purchase a specialized type of carrot. The farmer breached the contract by selling his carrots to another buyer at a much higher price than what he would have received from Campbell Soup. Campbell Soup sued the farmer and asked the court to force the farmer to perform the contract. The court found that the contract, which was written by Campbell Soup, contained provisions that were so unfair to the farmer that it would not be fair to require the farmer to perform the contract.[3]

**Laches:** The defendant built an elaborate stone fence between his land and the plaintiff's land. The design was quite intricate, and it was an expensive project. Soon after construction began, the plaintiff discovered that the fence was inadvertently being built on her land. Construction took several months, and several months after the fence was completed, the plaintiff filed a civil lawsuit asking the court to force the defendant to remove the fence from her land. The doctrine of laches probably will bar the plaintiff's claim. The plaintiff stood by and watched as the fence was built on her land. Had she spoken to the defendant when she discovered the fence being built on her land, the defendant could have taken action to make changes in the fence to ensure it was not on the plaintiff's land. Instead the plaintiff allowed the defendant to complete the fence before letting him know the fence encroached on her land, and it would be unfair to make the defendant remove the fence.

I've heard of an injunction. What exactly is that?

An injunction is an order from a court that someone not do something. Let's say that your neighbor makes it a practice to drive his truck across your property. You could go to court and ask for an injunction to legally prevent your neighbor from driving across your property.

## Figure 2.3 Additional Equitable Remedies

**Declaratory judgment:**

A judicial statement that declares or denies the parties' legal rights but does not include specific relief or any means to enforce those rights. Declaratory judgments are available in a variety of situations, including to determine personal rights such as marital rights, to interpret statutes, and to interpret contracts.

**Injunction:**

A court order that prohibits a party from committing a specific act. Typically, injunctions are issued in cases in which a defendant is committing or is threatening to commit an act that would harm the plaintiff.

## Restitution

**Restitution** is sometimes a legal remedy and other times an equitable remedy under which a party is ordered to return property to its owner or to the person entitled to it. The basic purpose of restitution is to prevent unjust enrichment; a person should not be allowed to profit or be enriched as a result of a wrong committed at the expense of another person. Restitution is available in civil actions in which it is more appropriate to restore to the plaintiff what the defendant received than to award damages in the amount of the plaintiff's losses. For example, assume that a person overpays an amount owed to another. The party who receives such an overpayment would be unjustly enriched if she keeps the amount overpaid and, thus, may be ordered to repay that amount. Similarly, a person who wrongfully takes the property of another may be ordered to return the property to its owner.

## Alternative Dispute Resolution

Anyone who has been involved in a civil lawsuit in the United States knows that years can pass between the time a complaint is filed and the time the dispute is resolved by a court judgment. As we noted, the parties are free to settle their dispute at any time, and they sometimes try to settle the matter by means of alternative dispute resolution methods. By **alternative dispute resolution (ADR) methods** we mean any nonjudicial method of resolving civil disputes. For example, parties usually first try to settle their disputes themselves by means of formal or informal negotiations. Mediation and arbitration are two other common forms of dispute resolution in the United States.

- **Mediation** is a process in which an impartial third party, known as a **mediator**, facilitates negotiations between the parties in an effort to create a mutually agreeable resolution of the dispute. If the parties are not able to resolve their dispute through mediation, they typically have the right to arbitration or civil litigation.

- **Arbitration** is a process in which impartial third parties, known as **arbitrators**, evaluate the facts in dispute and render a decision that usually is binding on the parties. Appeals of arbitrators' decisions are generally possible only if the arbitration was conducted improperly. Contracts often require that any disputes that arise between the contracting parties be resolved through arbitration rather than through civil litigation.

Alternative dispute resolution methods are available in most countries, although the terminology varies and the specific operation of the procedures also varies. In many countries, for example, **conciliation** is a dispute resolution method that is similar to mediation in that the parties are encouraged to come to a mutually acceptable agreement; a third party facilitates the parties' negotiations and helps them resolve the dispute themselves. If the parties are not able to resolve their dispute through conciliation, they typically have the right to resort to the courts. Another variation in some countries is that the mediator's role is to present a nonbinding solution that the parties are encouraged to accept. As described in Insight 2.5, ADR methods are preferred to civil litigation in some countries.

## Insight 2.5 Dispute Resolution in China

Mediation and arbitration are the preferred methods for resolving civil disputes in China. In fact, many laws require parties to first try to resolve their disputes through mediation, and the courts are required to promote the process of mediation for resolving civil disputes brought to the courts. When parties reach a mediation agreement, that agreement usually becomes enforceable by the courts. If the parties do not agree to mediation or are unable to resolve their dispute through mediation, they typically may ask the court to resolve the matter.

In some cases—especially disputes involving contracts—the parties are encouraged to arbitrate disputes that cannot be resolved through mediation. Because of this emphasis on arbitration of contract disputes, contracts typically include provisions that require the parties to resolve any disputes through arbitration and that specify the location where such arbitration will be conducted. When a dispute is resolved through arbitration, the arbitrators issue a written arbitration decision, which becomes legally binding on the parties.

**Sources:** Gabrielle Kaufmann-Kohler and Fan Kun, "Integrating Mediation into Arbitration: Why It Works in China," *Journal of International Arbitration* 25, no. 4 (2008): 479–492, http://www.arbitration-icca.org/media/0/12319139722760/ 00951635.pdf (14 February 2011); "Legal System of China: Mediation System," Chinalawedu.com, 21 February 2010, http://www.chinalawedu.com/new/23223_23225/2010_2_21_ji84013635431122010215408.shtml (14 February 2011).

## Key Terms

| | |
|---|---|
| criminal laws | conclusive presumption |
| civil laws | rebuttable presumption |
| public law | conflict of laws |
| private law | judgment |
| civil litigation | res judicata |
| cause of action | intentional tort |
| contract | assault |
| breach of contract | battery |
| tort | defamation |
| plaintiff | fraudulent misrepresentation |
| defendant | inducing a breach of contract |
| parties | trespass to land |
| person | conversion |
| pleadings | negligence |
| complaint | contributory negligence |
| service of process | comparative negligence |
| answer | assumption of the risk |
| affirmative defense | strict liability |
| counterclaim | legal remedies |
| default judgment | equitable remedies |
| dismissal | damages |
| discovery | compensatory damages |
| interrogatories | punitive damages |
| affidavit | nominal damages |
| perjury | mitigate |
| deposition | laches |
| request to produce documents and things | reformation |
| | rescission |
| contempt of court | specific performance |
| trial | declaratory judgment |
| issue of law | injunction |
| issue of fact | restitution |
| trier of fact | alternative dispute resolution (ADR) methods |
| evidence | |
| rules of evidence | mediation |
| burden of proof | mediator |
| prima facie case | arbitration |
| preponderance of the evidence | arbitrators |
| presumption | conciliation |

## Endnotes

1. *Prima facie* (prī-ma fā-sha) is a Latin term that means "at first view."

2. *Res judicata* (rās jūd-i-kät-a) is a Latin term that means "the thing has been decided."

3. Campbell Soup Company v. Wentz, 172 F.2d 80 (3d Cir.1948).

10/22 Exam Score 7/11 64% 2, 8, 9, 11
More Difficult

*Chapter 3*

# Business Organizations

## Objectives

### *After studying this chapter, you should be able to*

- Identify and distinguish among the three primary types of business organizations
- Identify the three primary groups of people who are involved in the management of a corporation and explain each group's legal rights and duties
- Distinguish between common and preferred stock
- Describe methods by which corporations can change their corporate structures
- Explain the situations in which the dissolution of a corporation may occur
- List some similarities and differences between corporations in the United States and other countries
- Define a multinational corporation and identify ways in which companies can operate in a foreign country

# Outline

B usiness organizations take various forms, and every business must be organized and operated in accordance with applicable laws. In this chapter, we describe the basic forms of business organizations in the United States, focusing on corporations. We also describe the legal environment of international business.

# Types of Business Organizations

People who want to start a business first must decide how the business will be organized. They must decide which jurisdiction will serve as the organization's home jurisdiction, and they must comply with that jurisdiction's laws regarding the formation of the business. Laws in all countries provide for a number of forms of business organizations. In the United States, the primary forms of business organizations are sole proprietorships, partnerships, and corporations.

## Sole Proprietorships

A **sole proprietorship** is a business that is owned and operated by one individual, who is known as the *sole proprietor*. A sole proprietorship is the simplest form of business organization, and the sole proprietor generally can conduct business without taking any specific steps to formally establish the business as a sole proprietorship. In other words, no government action is necessary to create a sole proprietorship. Like any business, however, the proprietor may be required to obtain a local business license or local permit to operate the business, but such requirements typically are imposed on all businesses in the locale without regard to the legal form of the business.

A sole proprietorship and the individual who owns the business are one and the same legal person. The business continues only as long as the sole proprietor wants the business to continue, and the sole proprietorship ceases to exist when the proprietor dies. The sole proprietor reaps all profits and is personally responsible for paying all the debts of the business. Thus, if the proprietor fails to pay a business debt, the proprietor's creditors can sue the proprietor personally and can obtain a court judgment against the individual; such a judgment enables the creditor to recover the debt by taking the sole proprietor's personal property. For U.S. federal income tax purposes, the proprietor files an individual tax return and reports all profits from the business as income, which is taxed at individual tax rates. The sole proprietorship is not taxed as a legal entity.

## Partnerships

A *partnership* is an association between two or more individuals, known as the *partners*, who enter into an agreement to own and operate a business for profit. The partnership agreement, which may be oral or written, governs the operation of the partnership. Applicable state laws also govern many aspects of the operation of partnerships.

A partnership has the following similarities to a sole proprietorship:

- No specific government action is necessary to create a partnership. The only legal requirement the partners must meet before conducting business is that they must obtain any required local business license or local permit to operate a business.

- The partners share the profits of the business, and they have unlimited personal liability for the debts of the business.

- A partnership does not have an unlimited life; rather it continues as long as the partners choose to continue it or until the occurrence of certain events. For example, a partnership dissolves by operation of law upon the death or bankruptcy of any of the partners. After such an event, the remaining partners may agree to re-form the partnership under a new partnership agreement.

- For U.S. federal income tax purposes, a partnership is not taxed as a legal entity. Instead, each partner reports her share of profits from the partnership on her individual tax return, and those profits are taxed at individual tax rates.

The partnerships that we have described, in which all of the partners have unlimited personal liability for partnership debts, are referred to as *general partnerships*, and the partners are known as *general partners*. All states now permit other forms of business organizations that enable individuals to participate in a business without accepting the unlimited liability associated with a general partnership. These and other forms of business organizations are described in Insight 3.1.

## Corporations

A *corporation* is a legal entity that is created by the authority of a governmental unit, such as a state or nation, and that is separate and distinct from the people who own it. Unlike sole proprietorships and partnerships, corporations are created by governmental action. Corporations have two characteristics that set them apart from sole proprietorships and general partnerships.

- As a legal entity that is separate from its owners, a corporation can sue or be sued, enter into contracts, and own property. The corporation's debts and liabilities belong to the corporation itself. The owners are not personally responsible for the corporation's debts. Instead, the personal liability of an owner for the corporation's debts generally is limited to the amount of the owner's investment in the corporation. Thus, the owner may lose no more than the amount of her investment in the corporation.

■ A corporation continues beyond the death of any or all of its owners. This characteristic of corporations provides a business an element of stability and permanence that a sole proprietorship and partnership cannot guarantee. Such stability makes the corporation the ideal form of business organization for financial services companies. For example, to protect the rights of the individuals and businesses that own its insurance policies, an insurance company must be a permanent and stable organization that can continue indefinitely. To ensure such protection of policyholders, laws in all states and in many other countries require insurance companies to operate as corporations.

## Insight 3.1 Alternate Forms of Business Organizations

A **limited partnership (LP)** is a partnership consisting of one or more general partners, who are responsible for running the business and have unlimited personal liability for partnership debts, and one or more **limited partners**, who invest in the business (contribute capital) but are not involved in running the business. A limited partner who does not become involved in running the partnership is not personally liable for partnership debts beyond the amounts he contributed to the partnership.

Most states also permit certain types of professionals, such as accountants, health care providers, attorneys, and architects, to create another type of partnership. Such a partnership, known as a **limited liability partnership (LLP)**, protects a partner from personal liability for the negligent acts committed by other partners or by employees who are not under the partner's direct control.

Many small businesses now are choosing to organize as a **limited liability company (LLC)**, which is a legal entity that has some characteristics of sole proprietorships and partnerships and some characteristics of a corporation. LLC owners can choose to be taxed like a sole proprietorship or partnership, with each owner reporting and paying federal income taxes on LLC profits as individuals. Alternatively, they can choose for the LLC to be taxed as a corporation, which means that the company files a corporate tax return and the company's profits are taxed at corporate rates, which generally are lower than individual rates. Then, each owner files an individual tax return and pays taxes at individual rates on the income he earned from the LLC. An LLC is like a corporation in that (1) certain documents must be filed with the applicable state in order to create an LLC and (2) the owners have limited personal liability for the debts of the business.

Typically, corporations are not allowed to provide services that require a license, such as legal, medical, and accounting services that may be provided only by a licensed professional. Most states, however, allow for the creation of a **professional corporation (PC)**, which is a corporation composed of individuals who provide services that require a professional license. A licensed professional who is a member of a PC is personally liable for his own acts of malpractice, but he generally is not liable for acts of malpractice by other professionals in the firm.

Corporations can be classified in various ways. From the point of view of a given jurisdiction, a ***domestic corporation*** is a corporation that was incorporated within that jurisdiction. The jurisdiction in which a business incorporates is known as its ***domicile*** or *domiciliary state*. In the United States, a ***foreign corporation*** is a corporation incorporated under the laws of another U.S. state, and an ***alien corporation*** is a corporation incorporated under the laws of another country. By contrast, most other countries classify corporations as either *domestic corporations* incorporated within the country or *foreign corporations* incorporated under the laws of another country.

So the term "foreign corporation" means different things in different countries?

Right. In the United States, it refers to a company formed in a different *state*; in most other countries it means a company formed in another *country*.

Corporations also can be classified according to how their stock is sold. Large corporations, including financial services companies, tend to be publicly traded corporations. A ***publicly traded corporation*** is a corporation whose stock is available for sale to the general public. By contrast, a ***close corporation*** or *closely held corporation* is a corporation that has issued stock which is owned by a relatively small group of people—often members of the same family—and which is not available for sale to the general public. Throughout this text, we are concerned with financial services corporations whose stock is traded to the general public.

# Formation of a Corporation

Laws in each state specify the steps that must be followed to incorporate a business in the state, and those requirements vary from state to state. Throughout this chapter, we base our discussion on the *Model Business Corporation Act*, which is a model law drafted by the American Bar Association; most states have based their laws on this model law.[1] A ***model law***, which is sometimes referred to as a *model act*, is a sample law that has been created and adopted by a national or international organization of regulators, lawmakers, lawyers, and/or academics; the sponsoring organization then encourages legislatures to enact laws based on the model. A model law is only a proposed law; no model law is effective until a state or national legislature enacts a law based on the model. Insight 3.2 describes model laws in more detail.

To incorporate a business in a given state, a stated number of adults, referred to as the *incorporators*, usually must file specified documents with a specific state administrative agency. In most states, the documents must be filed with the secretary of state's office or with the state's corporation commission. The primary document that generally must be filed is the corporation's ***articles of incorporation***, which is a document that describes some of the essential features of the corporation.

The following information usually must be included in a corporation's articles of incorporation:

- **The names and addresses of the incorporators.**

- **The name of the proposed corporation.** Each corporation must have a unique name that is not the same as or deceptively similar to the name of any other domestic corporation's name. A corporation's name also must include one of the following words or an abbreviation of one of them: *corporation, incorporated, company,* or *limited.* The inclusion of one of these words puts the public on notice that the business is incorporated.

- **The street address of the corporation's registered office and the name of the corporation's registered agent at that address.** The *registered agent* is the individual whom the corporation has appointed as its agent within the state for purposes of service of process.

- **The number of shares of stock that the corporation is authorized to issue.** The individuals and businesses that buy the stock the corporation issues become the owners of the corporation. The owners of a corporation's stock are known as its *stockholders,* or *shareholders.*

## Insight 3.2 Model Laws

Variations in state laws are commonplace, and laws also vary across national borders. Many businesses engage in interstate and/or international commerce, and they must comply with the laws in each jurisdiction in which they operate. Complying with different laws and regulatory requirements across jurisdictions can greatly increase the costs and administrative burdens of doing business. One method of making laws more uniform is the enactment of model laws. The following are just a few of the many U.S. and international organizations that draft model laws and encourage legislatures to adopt the models as laws:

- The **Uniform Law Commission (ULC),** also known as the National Conference of Commissioners on Uniform State Laws, is a nonprofit association of more than 300 U.S. lawyers, judges, and law professors appointed by the states. The organization studies and reviews the laws of the states to determine which areas of law should be uniform across the United States, and then they draft model laws in those areas and encourage their enactment by the state legislatures.

- The *National Association of Insurance Commissioners (NAIC)* is a nonprofit association of the insurance commissioners of all U.S. states and territories. One of its primary functions is to promote uniformity of state regulation by developing model insurance laws and regulations.

- The **United Nations Commission on International Trade Law (UNCITRAL)** is a body within the United Nations authorized to prepare and promote the adoption of new international treaties and model laws concerning international trade. UNCITRAL has fostered uniform laws in matters such as electronic commerce, commercial arbitration, and international sales of goods.

Articles of incorporation are permitted to include other types of information, such as the names and addresses of the corporation's directors.

Unless the articles of incorporation state otherwise, the corporation's existence begins when the articles of incorporation are filed with the appropriate administrative agency.

# Operating and Managing a Corporation

Many aspects of a corporation's organization and operation are spelled out in the corporation's articles of incorporation and its *bylaws*, which are the basic rules under which the corporation operates. The bylaws state information such as the duties of the corporation's officers, the meetings that will be held by the directors and the stockholders, and the rules under which the corporation's stock will be issued. In addition, state laws impose a range of requirements that govern the operation of domestic corporations.

In a broad sense, three groups of people are involved in the management of a corporation: the board of directors, the officers of the corporation, and the stockholders.

## Board of Directors

*Directors* are individuals who are appointed or elected by the stockholders to manage and direct the affairs of a corporation. Collectively, the directors are known as the corporation's *board of directors*. Directors who are otherwise employed by the corporation or are major stockholders of the corporation are known as *inside directors*; those who are not otherwise employed by or have no significant direct interest in the corporation are referred to as *outside directors*. Inside directors typically are officers of the corporation.

The incorporators usually appoint the corporation's initial board of directors. Thereafter, the directors usually are elected at annual meetings of the corporation's stockholders. A corporation's articles of incorporation or bylaws must specify the number of individuals who are to be included on the board of directors; laws in some states specify a minimum number of directors that domestic corporations must have. Articles of incorporation or bylaws also specify the length of each director's term in office. Typically, directors' terms are staggered so that only a portion of a corporation's board is elected each year. Articles of incorporation or bylaws may include specific qualifications that the corporation's directors must have.

Actions of a board are legally binding on the corporation if they are the result of a legal vote by at least a quorum of the board members. A *quorum* is a specified percentage of an entire body, in this case, a board of directors. State laws and corporate articles of incorporation or bylaws may establish the number or percentage of directors who must be present in order to constitute a quorum. In the absence of such controlling authority, a simple majority of directors constitutes a quorum.

Boards of directors typically meet at scheduled times and must meet at least once a year. All directors must be given adequate notice of the time and place where such meetings will be held. If such notice has not been provided, then actions taken by the board at such a meeting are not valid and binding on the corporation. A board of directors typically also may act without an in-person meeting if all directors consent to the action in writing.

## Duties of Directors

A corporation's directors have ultimate responsibility for managing and overseeing the corporation's affairs. The directors exercise that responsibility by delegating their authority. For example, directors are responsible for appointing the corporation's officers. The directors then have a duty to ensure that the officers manage the corporation in a lawful manner and carry out their responsibilities competently. The larger the corporation, the less direct involvement the corporation's directors are able to have in the corporation's ongoing operations. In all cases, however, directors must have at least a basic understanding of the business that the corporation conducts, and they have a duty to keep informed about the corporation's affairs.

Directors are fiduciaries who are obligated to act in the best interests of the corporation's stockholders. A *fiduciary* is an entity or individual who holds a special position of trust or confidence when handling the affairs of another and who must put that other's interests above the fiduciary's own. As fiduciaries, directors have the following duties:

- **Duty of loyalty and good faith.** To carry out this duty, directors must act in good faith and in the best interests of the corporation and the stockholders. Directors must not misuse corporate assets or take a corporate opportunity for their own personal benefit. In addition, directors must fully disclose any conflicts of interest they may have. If a director has a personal interest in an issue that the board is voting on, then the director must disclose his conflict of interest to the board and must not try to influence the board to act for the director's own benefit. A director also should abstain from voting on matters that could involve a conflict of interest.

- **Duty to exercise due care in carrying out responsibilities.** To meet this duty of care, a director must use that degree of care that an ordinarily prudent person would use in carrying out her own affairs. Whether a director has exercised due care in a given situation is a question of fact.

Because the financial health of financial services companies is of such importance to so many people, financial services companies occupy a special position of public trust. As a result, financial services companies are regulated more heavily than are most other types of businesses. Consequently, directors of corporations that hold a position of public trust typically are held to a higher standard of care than are directors of other types of businesses.

Although directors have a duty to use due care, they also have a right to rely on information they receive from corporate officers and employees whom the directors reasonably believe are reliable and competent to provide the information. Directors also may rely on statements and information provided by qualified attorneys and accountants who are competent to provide such information. Before relying on such people, however, directors have a duty to ensure that the individuals are, in fact, qualified and competent to provide the information.

In all cases, if a director's review of the corporation's affairs would raise questions in the mind of a reasonably prudent person, then the director has a duty to inquire further. For example, directors may not ignore misconduct or evidence of potential illegal activities.

### Liability of Directors

Directors may be held legally liable if they violate—or breach—their fiduciary duties. However, U.S. courts generally protect directors against such personal liability for breach of fiduciary duties by applying the business judgment rule. The **business judgment rule** states that directors will not be held personally liable for making business decisions if there is a reasonable basis to believe that the directors acted in good faith and with due care. By contrast, corporate directors generally will be personally liable if they

- **Act in bad faith.** *Bad faith* is essentially the opposite of good faith and occurs when an individual knowingly commits a wrong or fails to fulfill a legal duty with a dishonest motive.

- **Abuse their discretion.** Directors abuse their discretion when their actions are not reasonably justified or are clearly not reasonable, given the circumstances.

- **Are guilty of gross negligence.** *Gross negligence* occurs when an individual knowingly fails to perform a legal duty in reckless disregard of the consequences of that failure.

- **Commit fraud.** *Fraud* is an act by which someone intentionally deceives another party and induces that other party to part with something of value or to give up a legal right.

## Officers

*Officers* of a corporation are the individuals, such as the president and treasurer, who are responsible for carrying out important management functions for the day-to-day operation of the corporation. A corporation's board of directors usually appoints the top-level officers in accordance with applicable state laws and the corporation's articles of incorporation and bylaws. Such appointed officers often are authorized to appoint additional officers.

Corporate officers, like directors, are fiduciaries who are obligated to act in the best interests of the corporation and its stockholders. Officers have a duty of loyalty and a duty to exercise due care in carrying out their responsibilities. In addition, laws in some states specifically require officers to disclose all relevant information to the board of directors so that the board is fully informed before making decisions on behalf of the corporation.

Officers are employees of the corporation, and they often enter into contractual agreements with the corporation, including employment contracts and related types of agreements. Such a contract often imposes additional duties on the employees, who may be held legally liable to the corporation for violating those duties. For example, an officer may have a contractual duty not to disclose certain information about the corporation and the corporation's operations.

Like directors, officers may be personally liable if they breach their duties and obligations to the corporation. Unlike directors, however, officers generally are not afforded protection under the business judgment rule, and they may be personally liable for acts that are negligent. Recall that directors may be liable for gross negligence, which involves an element of willful misconduct. By contrast, negligent conduct involves only an element of inattention or thoughtlessness in acting or failing to act.

## Stockholders

The stockholders exercise ultimate control over a corporation's management because they have the right to elect the corporation's board of directors. They also have a number of other ownership rights in the corporation that issued their stock, including the right to

- **Inspect the corporation's financial records, books, and papers.** This right, however, is limited to inspections that are carried out in good faith and with a proper and honest purpose.

- **Attend annual stockholder meetings and vote on certain important corporate matters.** In addition to the right to elect the corporation's directors, stockholders have the right to vote on matters such as whether the corporation should be dissolved or merged with another corporation. Insight 3.3 describes annual stockholder meetings. Stockholders also have the right to change the corporation's bylaws, which typically are adopted by the corporation's board of directors and may later be changed by the directors or the stockholders.

- **Share in the corporation's profits when dividends are declared.** A *dividend* is a payment of a portion of the corporation's profits to the corporation's owners. A corporation's board of directors must authorize the payment of dividends, which are paid from the corporation's surplus. Insight 3.4 describes the declaration and payment of dividends.

### Insight 3.3 Annual Stockholder Meetings

State corporation laws require corporations that issue stock to hold regular meetings of their stockholders, and they must hold at least one meeting each year. A corporation's board of directors sets the time and place of such meetings and is responsible for notifying stockholders in advance so that they may attend if they choose.

Stockholder meetings provide a forum for stockholders to get information from and ask questions of corporate directors and officers and to vote on important corporate matters that require stockholder approval. Large publicly traded corporations are owned by stockholders who are geographically scattered and generally are unable to attend such meetings. Stockholders who are not able to attend, however, may vote on corporate matters by means of proxies. A *proxy* is a written authorization given by one person, such as a stockholder, to another person who is thereby enabled to act on behalf of the first person. Thus, a valid proxy enables someone else to vote on behalf of a stockholder at a stockholder meeting.

Most stockholders vote by proxies they receive from the corporation's board of directors. Before each annual stockholder meeting, the board sends out a proxy statement to each stockholder. The proxy statement identifies the proposals that stockholders will vote on at the meeting and states the board's recommendation for each proposal.

## Insight 3.4 Dividends Paid to Stockholders

A corporation's board of directors is responsible for deciding when the corporation will pay dividends to stockholders and the amount of any dividends. Many publicly traded corporations pay dividends on a quarterly basis as profits warrant. When a board declares a dividend, it specifies the amount of the dividend and the date—known as the **record date**—on which a person must be a registered stockholder of the company to be entitled to receive the dividend. Stockholders who are listed on the corporation's records on that date are entitled to receive a dividend. The dividend announcement also specifies the date on which the dividend will be paid, known as the **distribution date** or *payment date*. For example, an announcement might state that the corporation will pay a dividend of $1 per share to stockholders of record on September 1, 2012, and that the dividend will be paid on September 8, 2012. On the distribution date of September 8, stockholders who were listed on the corporation's records as owning stock on the record date of September 1 will receive a dividend.

The articles of incorporation spell out the various classes of stock that the corporation will issue and identify the specific rights that owners of each class of stock will have. Stock can be common stock or preferred stock, and a corporation may issue various classes of each type of stock. **Common stock** is an equity security that entitles its owner to share in the issuing corporation's dividends and provides its owner with the right to vote on certain corporate matters. As a general rule, only owners of a corporation's common stock have the right to elect the corporation's board of directors. **Preferred stock** is an equity security that entitles its owner to certain preferences—or first rights—that common stockholders do not have. Typically, preferred stockholders have first right to receiving dividends; thus, any profits available for payment to stockholders must be paid to preferred stockholders before they may be paid to common stockholders. Preferred stockholders generally do not have the right to vote for the corporation's board of directors; however, they may have the right to vote on certain matters such as the sale of substantially all of the corporation's assets. Figure 3.1 describes some special types of preferred stock that corporations may issue.

If the corporation is liquidated (dissolved), then any funds or assets that remain after creditors' claims are paid belong to the corporation's owners. Preferred stockholders are given priority over common stockholders to the assets of the corporation that remain after creditors' claims are paid.

## Figure 3.1 Types of Preferred Stock

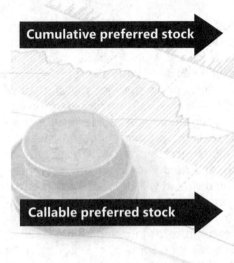

**Cumulative preferred stock**

Preferred stock that requires the issuing corporation to pay all declared but unpaid dividends that have accrued over time before any dividends may be paid to the owners of the issuing corporation's common stock. In other words, declared dividends that are not paid accumulate over time. Preferred stock also may be **noncumulative**, which means that the issuing corporation must pay only currently declared dividends before it is permitted to pay any common stock dividends.

**Callable preferred stock**

Preferred stock that includes a **call feature**, which enables the issuing corporation to redeem—or repurchase—the stock at a stated price, known as the **call price**.

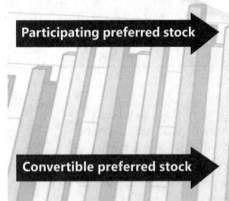

**Participating preferred stock**

Preferred stock that entitles the stockholder to receive, in addition to regular preferred dividends, an additional dividend when common stock dividends are greater than a specified amount. Preferred stock also may be **nonparticipating**, which entitles the stockholder to receive only those dividends the issuing corporation declares on the preferred stock.

**Convertible preferred stock**

Preferred stock that gives the stockholder the right to convert the stock into a stated amount of common stock.

Let's see if I've got this right: People who buy a company's stock actually own the company. These stockholders elect or appoint directors, who ultimately are responsible for overseeing the company. And the directors appoint officers to actually run the company.

You've got it! And remember, it's the stockholders who have ultimate control over the company's management, because they choose the directors.

# Changing the Corporate Structure

To grow and prosper, corporations sometimes change their organizational structure. Such changes can enable corporations to attract new sources of capital or can create new, profitable uses for existing capital. Two types of transactions, known as *mergers* and *acquisitions*, result in a change in the ownership of an asset—the controlling interest in a corporation.

■ A *merger* is a transaction in which one corporation is absorbed into another corporation by combining its assets and liabilities with those of the surviving corporation. The merged corporation ceases to exist after it is liquidated. Thus, only one corporation survives the merger transaction.

■ An *acquisition* is a transaction wherein one corporation purchases a controlling interest in another corporation, resulting in a linkage between formerly independent corporations. After the transaction, both corporations survive as separate legal entities.

Successful mergers and acquisitions require the input and advice of a range of professionals, including attorneys, accountants, and investment advisers because various federal and state laws regulate such transactions. The following are some of the regulatory issues that companies considering a merger or acquisition must address:

■ U.S. antitrust laws prohibit mergers and acquisitions that tend to lessen competition. *Antitrust laws* are designed to protect commerce against the monopolization of market power and unlawful restraints of trade, such as price discrimination and price fixing. In Chapter 4, we describe antitrust laws, which are known as *competition laws* in most countries outside the United States. Depending on the circumstances, companies considering a merger or acquisition must file documents with specified government agencies, which review the filings to ensure that antitrust laws will not be violated by the transaction.

■ When stock will be issued as part of the transaction, the issuing corporation must comply with federal and state securities laws.

■ When financial services companies participate in such transactions, additional regulatory approvals must be obtained before the transactions are completed. For example, a transaction in which one entity will either acquire control of an insurer or merge with an insurer usually requires the approval of the insurance department of the insurer's domiciliary state.

# Dissolution of a Corporation

In the United States, the creation and dissolution of a corporation are both governed by state corporation laws. By *dissolution*, we mean the termination of a corporation's legal existence. Although a corporation generally has a perpetual existence, the articles of incorporation may state that the corporation will exist only for a specified, definite time. In such a case, the corporation ceases to exist at the end of that specified time. In other cases, a corporation ceases to exist upon its voluntary or involuntary dissolution.

A voluntary dissolution of a corporation occurs as a result of a vote of the corporation's stockholders, who agree to the dissolution. For example, a voluntary dissolution occurs when a corporation agrees to be merged into another corporation. After the stockholders agree to a dissolution, the corporation must deliver articles of dissolution to the appropriate state agency; the dissolution is effective when the articles of dissolution are filed with the state.

An involuntary dissolution can occur as the result of the following types of proceedings:

- A corporation's domiciliary state has the right to dissolve the corporation in certain circumstances, such as when the corporation has failed to file required annual reports, pay applicable taxes and fees, or appoint and maintain a registered agent in the state.

- A court may order the dissolution of a corporation in a proceeding begun by the corporation's stockholders. Such a legal proceeding may be brought if the corporation's directors are hopelessly deadlocked in how to manage the corporation or the stockholders are deadlocked and unable to agree on a board of directors. Other reasons for such a proceeding include cases in which those managing the corporation are acting illegally or fraudulently or when corporate assets are being wasted or looted.

- A court may order the dissolution of a corporation in a proceeding begun by a creditor of the corporation. Such a proceeding can occur when a creditor has obtained a court judgment against a corporation and has been unable to satisfy its judgment because the corporation is insolvent.

After a corporation's dissolution, it may no longer carry on business and must conclude its affairs and liquidate the business. *Liquidation* is a process in which a corporation that is being dissolved pays its debts or makes arrangements to pay those debts. If any assets remain after the debts are paid, then those assets are distributed on a pro rata basis to the corporation's stockholders in the order of their priorities—that is, preferred stockholders have priority over common stockholders.

This section has described the general rules that apply to most U.S. corporations. Special laws govern the liquidation and dissolution of insurance and financial services companies, which are more closely regulated than are most corporations. We defer that discussion to Chapter 5.

# Legal Environment of International Business

Jurisdictions around the world allow for the creation and operation of business organizations that have many of the features of U.S. corporations. Such organizations generally are known as *corporations* or *companies* depending on the jurisdiction, and they typically have the following characteristics that are similar to U.S. corporations:

- The business exists as a legal entity that is separate from its owners, and it has the legal rights and liabilities of a natural person, including the right to sue and be sued and the right to own property.

- The owners of the business have limited liability for the debts of the business.

- The business continues to exist beyond the death of its owners. In some jurisdictions, however, the business is given a life of only a specific number of years. For example, a corporation in the Philippines has a 50-year lifetime, after which time it is renewable for another 50 years.

- A board of directors is responsible for managing the affairs of the business.

- The owners (typically stockholders) have the right to make certain important decisions for the business.

Company or corporation laws around the world also contain some features that differ from U.S. laws. The following are some examples of such differences:

- Some jurisdictions impose minimum capital requirements for every corporation. In the United States, insurance and other financial services companies must meet such minimum capital requirements, but most other types of U.S. businesses are not subject to such requirements.

- Some jurisdictions, such as India, recognize two forms of companies that provide their owners with limited liability. In these countries, an owner's liability may be either *limited by shares* or *limited by guarantee*. A ***company limited by shares*** is a company whose owners' liability is limited to the investment they made when they purchased the company's shares. A ***company limited by guarantee*** is a company whose owners agree to pay up to a stated amount if the company is liquidated.

- Some jurisdictions—such as China, Malaysia, and Mexico—have created state-owned businesses, which are operated by the government for the benefit of the people.

Foreign companies are permitted to operate in most jurisdictions by either (1) incorporating a business in the host country that operates as a subsidiary of the foreign company, (2) opening a branch in the host country that is properly registered with the host government, or (3) entering into a joint venture with a local company. A ***joint venture*** is an arrangement between two otherwise independent businesses that agree to undertake a specific project together for a specified time period. In some countries, the amount that may be invested in a local business is subject to regulatory requirements.

A ***multinational corporation*** is a corporation that operates in more than one country and makes major operational decisions within a global context. Because they operate across jurisdictional borders, multinationals are faced with unique legal and regulatory compliance issues, including the following:

- They must comply with laws and regulations of their own home country.

- They must comply with laws and regulations in each country in which they conduct business.

- In some cases, multinationals are affected by international laws, such as treaties. Figure 3.2 describes just a few of the many treaties that have affected international business operations.

## Figure 3.2 International Treaties

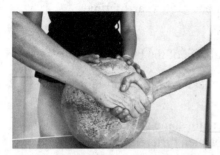

**Convention on Contracts for the International Sale of Goods (CISG):**

Adopted by the United Nations Commission on International Trade Law, the Convention is the law for international sales of goods between parties from member nations. The Convention governs the formation of sales contracts and the rights and duties of the buyer and seller arising from such contracts. Almost 50 nations have adopted the CISG.

**International Convention for the Suppression of the Financing of Terrorism:**

This United Nations convention prohibits any person from providing funds that are intended to be used to carry out acts of terrorism. The 132 signing countries agreed to enact laws to criminalize such financing and to impose appropriate penalties. Such laws, often referred to as **anti-money laundering acts**, require financial institutions to monitor customer activity and report suspicious or unusually large transactions to appropriate authorities.

**OECD Convention on Combating Bribery of Foreign Public Officials in International Business Transactions**

Adopted by the Organization for Economic Cooperation and Development (OECD) and signed by 35 nations, the Convention represents an agreement for countries to adopt rules to punish companies and individuals who engage in bribery.

**General Agreement on Trade in Services (GATS)**

Entered into by members of the World Trade Organization (WTO) in 1995, this agreement covers almost all types of services, including insurance, banking, and other financial services. Its goal is to promote the international flow of services, and the agreement addresses four ways of trading services: (1) services supplied across borders, (2) consumption of services in another country, (3) establishing a commercial presence in another country, and (4) individuals travelling from one country to provide services in another. The World Trade Organization (WTO) is an international organization created to ensure that trade flows smoothly and predictably and as freely as possible. With more than 140 member countries, which make up most of the world's trading nations, the WTO helps member nations negotiate agreements that are designed to help producers of goods and services, exporters, and importers conduct their business. The WTO also provides a forum for resolving disputes that arise between trading partners.

## Key Terms

sole proprietorship
partnership
partners
general partnership
general partner
corporation
domestic corporation
domicile
foreign corporation
alien corporation
publicly traded corporation
close corporation
model law
National Association of Insurance
    Commissioners (NAIC)
articles of incorporation
stockholders
bylaws
directors
board of directors
inside directors
outside directors

quorum
fiduciary
business judgment rule
bad faith
gross negligence
fraud
officers
dividend
proxy
record date
distribution date
common stock
preferred stock
merger
acquisition
antitrust laws
dissolution
liquidation
company limited by shares
company limited by guarantee
joint venture
multinational corporation

## Endnote

1. American Bar Association Committee on Corporate Laws of the Section of Business Law, *Model Business Corporation Act* (2005), http://apps.americanbar.org/buslaw/committees/CL270000pub/nosearch/mbca/assembled/20051201000001.pdf (10 February 2011).

*10/23 Exam Score: 7/11 64%    5, 7, 10, 11*

*Not terribly difficult chapter*

## Chapter 4

# Regulation of Business

## Objectives

### After studying this chapter, you should be able to

- Define the basic economic concepts underlying the goals of antitrust laws

- Identify federal antitrust laws and the types of activities that antitrust laws typically prohibit

- Describe federal consumer protection laws that protect consumers who enter into credit transactions and that regulate trade practices

- Describe electronic commerce laws that are designed to facilitate electronic signatures and contracts and to ensure the privacy and security of customers' personal information

- Explain the types of workplace standards, nondiscrimination requirements, and required benefits that U.S. federal and state laws typically impose on employers

# Outline

**Antitrust Regulation**
- Basic Economic Concepts
- U.S. Antitrust Laws
- International Antitrust Regulation

**Consumer Protection Regulation**
- Consumer Credit Protection
- Unfair Trade Practices

**Electronic Commerce Regulation**
- Electronic Signatures, Contracts, and Records
- Privacy
- Conflict of Laws

**Employment Regulation**
- Employment Relationship
- Workplace Standards
- Nondiscrimination Requirements
- Required Benefits

All governments have enacted laws that regulate how businesses operate within their jurisdictions. In this chapter, we describe some of the primary areas of business regulation worldwide: antitrust, consumer protection, electronic commerce, and employment. The laws we describe apply to almost all businesses that operate within a given jurisdiction, including financial services companies. We describe the specifics of regulation of the financial services industry in Chapter 5.

# Antitrust Regulation

Virtually all countries have enacted antitrust laws—referred to in many countries as *competition laws*—designed to prevent marketplace practices that are viewed as anticompetitive. Governments seek to promote marketplace competition because competition encourages the efficient use of economic resources and tends to keep down the costs of producing goods and providing services. By keeping down costs, competition also keeps down the prices of goods and services.

To fully understand how antitrust laws operate to ensure competitive markets, you must be familiar with economic theory. A complete discussion of economic theory is beyond the scope of this text, but the next section provides a very broad overview of economic concepts so that you can have some understanding of the basic goals of antitrust laws. Then we describe antitrust laws in the United States and other countries.

## Basic Economic Concepts

*Economics* is the study of how societies allocate their resources. Like many economies around the world, the U.S. economy is a **market economy** because it relies primarily on the market forces known as *supply* and *demand* to allocate resources. In this context, a **market** is an environment in which buyers and sellers of a product or service meet. *Supply* represents the amount of goods and services that producers are willing and able to provide the marketplace. According to economic theory, the supply of any given product tends to vary in relation to the price of the product—as a product's price *increases*, the supply of the product also tends to *increase* as producers seek to increase their profits by selling more goods at higher prices. This relationship between price and supply is illustrated graphically as the *supply curve* in Figure 4.1.

## Figure 4.1 Demand and Supply Curves

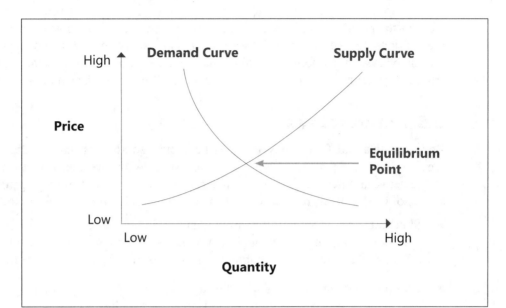

Demand represents the willingness and ability of consumers to purchase goods and services at a given price. Like supply, the demand for a product tends to vary in relation to variations in price. In this case, however, as the price of a product increases, the demand for the product tends to *decrease* as consumers seek to obtain the most value for their spending dollars. The relationship between price and demand is illustrated graphically as the *demand curve* in Figure 4.1.

In theory, the market forces of supply and demand operate to help producers establish a product's price and production levels at the point that maximizes their own profits and at the same time satisfies consumer demand. This point, known as the *equilibrium point*, which is illustrated in Figure 4.1, is the point at which the supply curve and demand curve intersect.

So far, we have described a scenario in which the market for a product operates in a state of ***pure competition***—that is, there are many producers and consumers of the product, and prices are established by market forces with no interference from outside economic forces. In theory, pure competition results in the production of the greatest output of a product at the lowest price. In reality, no market operates in a state of pure competition. Rather, each market operates somewhere on a continuum that ranges from pure competition to pure monopoly. A ***monopoly*** is a situation in which one firm, or a group of firms acting together, controls the production and distribution of a product. In other words, under a monopoly, there is no competition. Without competition, prices tend to increase and producers are less responsive to consumer demand.

U.S. antitrust laws are designed to promote free and open competition in the marketplace by preventing monopolies and specified business practices that are deemed to unfairly restrain trade. In other words, antitrust laws seek to enable markets to operate as closely to a state of pure competition as possible by ensuring that markets are free and open. A *free and open market* is a market in which prices are established by the forces of supply and demand with little or no intervention from the government or other powerful economic entities, such as monopolies.

## U.S. Antitrust Laws

Both the state and federal governments have enacted antitrust laws. State laws regulate activities that occur within a given state. Activities that involve commerce between states are governed by federal antitrust laws, which are the primary source of U.S. antitrust regulation. The principal federal antitrust laws are the

- **Sherman Act**, which prohibits individuals and companies from (1) monopolizing or attempting to monopolize any part of interstate or foreign trade or (2) engaging in contracts, combinations, or conspiracies in restraint of trade.[1]

- **Clayton Act**, which makes it unlawful to engage in certain actions that are believed to lessen competition and to lead to monopolies.[2]

- **Federal Trade Commission Act**, which established the *Federal Trade Commission (FTC)* and gave it the power to enforce federal antitrust laws.[3] The FTC is an independent administrative agency of the federal government responsible for enforcing both federal antitrust laws and federal consumer protection laws.

The federal antitrust laws are written in very broad terms, and they leave it to the courts to decide what specific activities are illegal based on the facts and circumstances of each case. The courts have identified certain activities that are so harmful to consumers that they are conclusively presumed to violate the antitrust laws. Such prohibited activities, which are referred to as *per se violations*, include agreements among competitors to fix prices or output, rig bids, or divide markets by allocating customers, suppliers, or territories. The courts evaluate all other cases under a *rule of reason analysis*, in which they evaluate the overall competitive effect of the parties' conduct and weigh the competitive harm against the competitive benefits. The specific analysis used varies depending on the facts of each case.

### Specific Prohibitions

An illegal monopoly exists when a business controls the market for a product or service, and the business obtained that power through anticompetitive conduct. Anticompetitive tactics include those that unreasonably exclude businesses from the market or that significantly impair others' ability to compete in a market. A monopoly, however, is not always illegal. A business that gained monopoly power through fair competition and legitimate tactics has not violated the antitrust laws. For example, a company can gain a monopoly by being the only business that is able or willing to produce a specific good.

Certain activities are prohibited by federal antitrust laws when the activities are part of an agreement between competing businesses. The following are some examples of such prohibited agreements between competitors:

- Competitors may not enter into an agreement to divide up a market by geographical territory or by customers. Such agreements are per se violations because they essentially are agreements not to compete in a given market.

- Competitors may not agree to restrict the output or production of goods, which tends to drive up the price of those goods.

- Price-fixing agreements are per se antitrust violations because of their anti-competitive effects. *Price fixing* occurs when competitors act together to affect the price of a product or service. For example, competing businesses may not enter into agreements to (1) set minimum or maximum prices for goods or services, (2) limit the production of goods or services so as to affect the price, or (3) eliminate competitive bidding.

Antitrust laws also prohibit some agreements between parties in a buyer-seller relationship, such as a retailer who buys from a manufacturer. For example, it is a violation for a manufacturer and a retailer to agree on the fixed minimum resale price of a product. Figure 4.2 describes some other activities that are prohibited by U.S. antitrust laws.

Antitrust laws don't prohibit all monopolies then?

No, their goal is to prevent *illegal* monopolies—those created through unfair competition or dishonest practices.

## *Enforcement Procedures*

Both the Department of Justice (DOJ) and the FTC are authorized to enforce the federal antitrust laws. To avoid duplication of efforts, the two agencies generally consult before they begin an antitrust investigation and decide which agency will take primary responsibility for handling the case. Each agency has developed expertise in overseeing certain industries and businesses. The FTC, for example, typically is responsible for overseeing markets for consumer products, including health care, pharmaceuticals, food, and energy. The DOJ is responsible for overseeing certain industries, including telecommunications, railroads, and airlines. Insight 4.1 describes one of the many responsibilities shared by the DOJ and the FTC to enforce federal antitrust laws: the review of mergers and acquisitions.

Various legal sanctions may be imposed against individuals and businesses that violate federal antitrust laws. Some violations are crimes that are handled by the DOJ and punishable by fines and/or imprisonment. Civil penalties, including substantial fines, also may be imposed.

## Figure 4.2 Practices Prohibited by U.S. Antitrust Laws

### Unfair price discrimination:

Price discrimination occurs when a seller agrees to sell goods to a buyer at a price that is lower than the price charged other buyers under the same circumstances. Price discrimination is prohibited only when it is used unfairly against competitors. For example, a seller has the right to give a purchaser a volume discount and, thus, may sell the same goods at different prices to different buyers. As long as a seller enters into price agreements that are administered fairly and in an otherwise nondiscriminatory fashion, the seller is not violating federal antitrust laws.

### Tying arrangements:

A tying arrangement is an illegal arrangement under which a business will sell one product to a purchaser only if the purchaser also buys a second different product from the firm.

### Boycotts:

A boycott is a concerted effort by competitors in which they agree not to do business with another business. Often, companies engaging in a boycott use coercion and intimidation to force others to join in the boycott.

## Insight 4.1 Regulatory Review of Mergers and Acquisitions

Although mergers and acquisitions may benefit competition, they sometimes lessen competition because they create monopoly power. Federal law requires that parties to certain mergers or acquisitions notify the Federal Trade Commission (FTC) and the Department of Justice (DOJ) before completing the proposed transaction. Whether a particular transaction must be reported depends on the value of the acquisition and the size of the parties, as measured by their sales and assets. Large acquisitions, acquisitions involving large parties, and other acquisitions that are likely to raise antitrust concerns must be reported and are subjected to agency scrutiny.

When the FTC and DOJ are notified of a proposed merger or acquisition, they have a stated time in which to evaluate the proposed transaction. The agencies' evaluation is aimed at determining whether the transaction would substantially concentrate market power and make it difficult for new firms to enter the market. If the FTC or DOJ believes that a proposed transaction violates the antitrust laws, they may seek an injunction in federal district court to prohibit the parties from completing the transaction. A party who violates an injunction is subject to fines and/or imprisonment.

A person who has been harmed by a violation of federal antitrust laws has the right to file a lawsuit in federal court against the business or individual who committed the violation. A plaintiff who is successful in such a lawsuit is entitled to recover from the defendant *treble damages*—an amount equal to three times the actual damages—and reasonable attorneys' fees. The cost of defending such a lawsuit plus the amount of any potential treble damage award is perhaps the most effective enforcement tool provided by federal antitrust laws.

## International Antitrust Regulation

Specific laws relating to competition vary from jurisdiction to jurisdiction. Although not all countries have enacted antitrust laws, most countries have done so. The same types of activities prohibited in the United States as described in the previous section generally are prohibited in other nations, and specific governmental agencies are charged with enforcing applicable laws. U.S. antitrust laws, however, are unique in the following respects:

- As a general rule, no other country has antitrust laws that are as strict as those in the United States, and the United States more vigorously enforces its antitrust laws than do most other countries.

- Anticompetitive conduct that affects U.S. domestic or foreign commerce may violate the U.S. antitrust laws regardless of where such conduct occurs or the nationality of the parties involved. Other countries generally do not try to regulate such conduct when it occurs beyond their own geographic borders.

- Violation of most countries' antitrust laws may result in the imposition of fines, but such violations typically are not considered crimes punishable by imprisonment as is true in the United States.

Insight 4.2 gives some brief descriptions of competition laws in selected countries.

# Consumer Protection Regulation

Governments around the world have enacted laws designed to protect the welfare of consumers. For most regulatory purposes, a ***consumer*** is a natural person who purchases or tries to purchase goods or services that are to be used primarily for personal, family, or household purposes. Businesses and business organizations generally are not considered consumers, and thus, are not protected by consumer protection laws.

But businesses also buy goods and services. It doesn't seem fair that they aren't protected by these laws.

It's true that businesses aren't protected as consumers, but other laws govern transactions between businesses. You'll learn about those laws in later chapters.

## Insight 4.2 Examples of Competition Laws

**China:** As part of its process of changing from a planned economy system into a socialist market economy system, China has enacted laws designed to promote competition and is establishing a regulatory system to carry out its competition policies. The *Anti-Monopoly Law*, which became effective in 2008, and the *Law for Countering Unfair Competition (LCUC)*, are the primary laws designed to protect competition. Prohibited practices include tying arrangements, damaging a competitor's reputation by making false statements, price-fixing agreements, and squeezing competitors out by selling goods at below-cost prices.[4]

**Mexico:** Mexico's Constitution prohibits monopolies and monopolistic practices. In addition, the *Federal Law of Economic Competition* protects competition by prohibiting monopolies and practices that impair or prevent competition. The Federal Competition Commission is the administrative agency responsible for enforcing the law.[5]

**Taiwan:** The *Fair Trade Law* is the principal law governing competition, and the Fair Trade Commission is the primary authority in charge of Taiwan's competition policy. The Fair Trade Commission is charged with drafting fair trade policy, laws, and regulations and with investigating and handling various acts that impede competition, such as monopolies, mergers, concerted actions, and other restraints on competition or unfair competitive practices by businesses.[6]

The following types of consumer protection laws are common in many jurisdictions around the world:

- **Consumer product safety laws**, which require consumer products designed for personal, family, and household use to meet minimum standards. These laws are intended to protect the health and safety of consumers.

- **Consumer credit laws**, which require providers of consumer credit—such as banks, finance companies, and credit card companies—to disclose all the terms of a consumer credit transaction and to use properly any personal information obtained about consumers. These laws are intended to promote the informed use of credit and to protect consumers' privacy.

- **Laws that prohibit deceptive and unfair sales practices**, which are designed to provide consumers with fair and accurate information about consumer goods and services.

- **Laws that prohibit false, deceptive, and misleading advertising**, which are intended to protect consumers by ensuring that advertisements are truthful and are reasonably clear to the average person.

Most jurisdictions, including the United States, have enacted general consumer protection laws that apply to all types of businesses as well as specific laws that apply only to certain types of businesses. For example, some laws regulate only businesses that produce specific types of goods or services. Many such general and specific laws apply to financial services institutions. In this section, we describe just a few of the many consumer protection laws that apply to financial services organizations operating in the United States.

## Consumer Credit Protection

Both federal and state laws have been enacted to protect consumers who enter into credit transactions in which they purchase goods or services and finance those purchases over time. One of the broadest federal laws is the ***Consumer Credit Protection Act***, which regulates many aspects of how businesses provide credit to consumers in the United States.[7] The Act requires that creditors

- Provide consumers with certain written disclosures concerning all finance charges and related aspects of credit transactions.

- Adhere to restrictions on the garnishment of a debtor's wages. ***Garnishment*** is a legal process by which a creditor can obtain a debtor's property that is in the possession of a third party. For example, certain creditors are able to garnish the wages of a debtor, which means that the debtor's employer is required to pay a specific portion of the debtor's wages to the creditor in payment of the debt.

- Refrain from discriminating on the basis of race, color, religion, national origin, sex, marital status, or age when they extend credit.

The ***Fair Credit Reporting Act (FCRA)*** regulates the reporting and use of consumer credit information and seeks to ensure that consumer credit reports contain only accurate, relevant, and recent information.[8] For purposes of the FCRA, a ***consumer credit report*** is any communication of information by a consumer reporting agency that (1) bears on a consumer's creditworthiness, credit standing, credit capacity, character, general reputation, personal characteristics, or mode of living and (2) is used or collected as a factor in establishing a consumer's eligibility for insurance or credit. FCRA requirements govern the types of information that can be included in consumer credit reports and the permissible uses of information in consumer credit reports.

The FCRA regulates (1) ***consumer reporting agencies***, which are private businesses that assemble or evaluate information on consumers and furnish consumer credit reports to third parties in exchange for a fee, and (2) third parties, such as banks and insurance companies, that obtain consumer credit reports. Before obtaining such a report, a third party must disclose in writing to the consumer that it will obtain the report. In addition, when a third party takes an adverse action based on information contained in such a report, the third party has certain duties to the affected consumer. An ***adverse action*** means a denial or revocation of credit or insurance coverage, a change in the terms of an existing credit arrangement or insurance coverage, or a refusal to grant credit or insurance in substantially the amount or on substantially the terms requested. When it takes an adverse action based on a consumer credit report, a third party must

- Provide the consumer with information about the consumer reporting agency that provided the report

- Notify the consumer of her right to dispute with the reporting agency the accuracy or completeness of any information contained in the report

- Notify the consumer that she has the right to obtain a free copy of the credit report from the reporting agency

 We sometimes want an applicant's credit report to use in underwriting. And we always notify the applicant that we're doing that.

 Good! That's what the law requires us to do before getting someone's credit report.

 And, if we reject an application because of information in a credit report, we give the applicant the required information about the credit report.

## Unfair Trade Practices

Federal and state laws also regulate trade practices and advertising. The FTC Act, which we mentioned earlier, prohibits unfair or deceptive acts or practices that affect commerce and false or deceptive advertising. In addition to investigating unfair or deceptive conduct, the FTC is responsible for enforcing various consumer protection statutes that prohibit specifically defined trade practices. Examples of such federal consumer protection laws are the Equal Credit Opportunity Act, the Truth-in-Lending Act, the FCRA, the Cigarette Labeling Act, and the Fair and Accurate Credit Transactions Act of 2003.

Most states have enacted unfair trade practices laws that place broad restrictions on deceptive or unfair trade practices. Most states also prohibit specific practices that are considered unfair or deceptive, including

- Passing off goods or services as those of another party

- Causing the likelihood of confusion as to the source, sponsorship, or certification of goods or services

- Representing that goods or services have characteristics, ingredients, uses, or qualities that they do not have

- Disparaging the goods or services of another party by misrepresenting facts

Usually, the state attorney general's office is responsible for enforcing a state's unfair trade practices laws. Enforcement authorities can get cease-and-desist orders to stop businesses from engaging in deceptive trade practices. In addition, consumers may file civil lawsuits against businesses that engage in deceptive practices and may be awarded monetary damages.

# Electronic Commerce Regulation

Most businesses today use the Internet to help them market goods and services, meet customers' demands, and compete effectively in the marketplace. Governments around the world have enacted laws to regulate such electronic commerce, also known as *e-commerce*. These laws seek to facilitate electronic transactions while protecting the rights and interests of customers and businesses.

## Electronic Signatures, Contracts, and Records

To be legally binding, some contracts traditionally require one or both parties to sign a specified paper document. With the rise of e-commerce transactions, governments around the world have enacted laws that enable parties to effectively contract electronically, using electronic signatures and document records. An *electronic signature* is a generic term that means a signature on an electronic document. Essentially, an electronic signature is whatever the parties to a transaction agree that it is. In other words, if the parties intend to be bound by the "signature," then they can agree on the action that will create the signature.

On the Internet, I've been asked to click an "I Accept" button to show that I agree to something.

Yes, that's a common way to give an electronic signature. Another example is that you may be asked to type your name or initials into a box. If you agree to that and enter your name in that box, then you've given an electronic signature.

In the United States, the federal *Electronic Signatures in Global and National Commerce Act (E-SIGN)* eliminates legal barriers to the use of electronic technology to form and sign contracts, collect and store documents, and send and receive notices and disclosures.[9] E-SIGN applies to commercial, consumer, and business transactions that affect interstate or foreign commerce and to transactions that are regulated by both the federal and state governments. E-SIGN has the following legal effects when all of the parties to a transaction agree to use an electronic medium:

- An electronic signature is the legal equivalent of a pen-and-ink signature.

- A contract in electronic form is the legal equivalent of a contract written on paper.

- Electronic documents are the legal equivalent of legally required written documents—known as *records*.

In addition to the federal E-SIGN, almost all states have enacted laws based on the *Uniform Electronic Transactions Act (UETA)*, which is a model law adopted by the National Conference of Commissioners on Uniform State Laws (NCCUSL) to provide for the effectiveness of electronic signatures.[10] However, specific provisions of individual state laws vary greatly.

If a provision of a state law based on the UETA is inconsistent with E-SIGN, then E-SIGN preempts that state law provision. To the extent a state law is not inconsistent with E-SIGN, then the state law is effective and is not preempted by E-SIGN. As a result, businesses still need to consider state laws when planning their electronic signature strategy.

Under E-SIGN and the UETA, consumers cannot be required to use electronic records, signatures, or contracts. Instead, a consumer must affirmatively consent to the use of electronic notices and records, and the consumer must receive a clear and conspicuous statement of (1) her right to receive paper records, (2) the consequences of later withdrawing consent to receive electronic records, and (3) the hardware and software requirements for access to and retention of electronic records.

Under the provisions of E-SIGN and the UETA, certain legal documents and transactions cannot be completed with electronic signatures. Legal documents and transactions that still require hand-written signatures include

- Wills and testamentary trusts

- Notices of the cancellation of health insurance or of life or health insurance benefits

- Court orders

- Mortgage foreclosures

Laws in the United States are designed to make it clear that an electronic signature is valid, but they do not directly address the reliability of such signatures. Reliability relates to how parties can authenticate that a person is who he purports to be. Some countries have enacted laws that address the reliability and adequacy of electronic signatures. For example, the *UNCITRAL Model Law on Electronic Signatures* establishes criteria for the technical reliability of electronic signatures.[11] Countries that have adopted laws based on the UNCITRAL Model Law include China, India, Jamaica, Mexico, Nicaragua, Paraguay, Thailand, and Vietnam. The European Union (EU) has adopted the *Electronic Signatures Directive*, which sets up a system by which certification service providers that are regulated by the EU member states must verify electronic signatures.

## Privacy

When conducting business electronically, firms and their customers exchange a great deal of information. Ensuring the privacy and security of customers' personal information increases consumers' willingness to engage in electronic transactions.

Governments have enacted laws designed to ensure the privacy of information that is transmitted electronically, but those laws vary from place to place. The European Union has led the way with its *Directive on Privacy and Electronic Communications*, which seeks to ensure the free flow of information while protecting the privacy of personal information. The EU Directive requires providers of publicly available electronic communications services to take specific steps to safeguard the security of their services and ensure the privacy of electronically transmitted information. The EU's comprehensive laws require, among other things, the creation of independent government data protection agencies, registration of databases with those agencies, and in some instances prior approval before personal data processing may begin. By contrast, U.S. privacy laws have been enacted on a sector-by-sector basis and, thus, privacy protections vary depending on the type of transaction.

The EU Directive prohibits the transfer of personal information from the EU to a non-EU country unless the non-EU country provides adequate protection for the information. EU member states are authorized to enforce this provision by levying fines on EU organizations and ordering the discontinuation of data flows to foreign countries and organizations that do not comply with requirements of the Directive. Insight 4.3 describes how the United States has responded to the EU Directive. We defer our discussion of U.S. privacy laws to Chapter 5.

## Conflict of Laws

By bringing together businesses and customers from around the world, e-commerce results in transactions that may be affected by laws in many jurisdictions. When e-commerce transactions cross jurisdictional boundaries, questions arise as to which jurisdiction's laws govern such transactions. Questions also may arise as to how a party in one country can pursue its legal remedies against a business located in another country. As a general rule, electronic commerce laws in the United States and other countries have not changed the underlying conflict of laws rules that apply to various types of transactions. Thus, a contract for the sale of goods would be treated the same regardless of whether the contract is completed in a face-to-face setting or by means of an electronic transaction. Some e-commerce laws do, however, clarify the conflict of laws rules that will be applied to electronic transactions.

# Employment Regulation

Most countries have enacted laws that govern the relationship between employers and employees. In the United States, federal, state, and local laws regulate many aspects of the employment relationship. Most such laws govern the employer-employee relationship only; independent contractors generally are not covered by such laws. An *employee* is a person in the service of another, the *employer*, who has the power or right to control and direct how the employee performs the work. An *independent contractor* is a person who contracts to do a specific task according to his own methods and who generally is not subject to the employer's control except as to the end product or final result of the work. Thus, the main distinction between an employee and an independent contractor concerns the employer's power or right to control how the work is performed.

Parties often characterize their relationship as either employer-employee or employer-independent contractor. Regardless of what the parties call themselves, whether a person is acting as an employee or an independent contractor is a question of fact. Figure 4.3 identifies some of the factors that U.S. courts typically consider in determining whether a specific individual is an employee or an independent contractor.

## Insight 4.3 U.S. Safe Harbor for EU Privacy Directive

 The European Union approach to regulating e-commerce has been much more comprehensive and restrictive than has the U.S. regulatory approach. With the enactment of the EU Directive on Privacy and Electronic Communications, the U.S. government recognized that U.S. businesses needed a way to ensure continued access to personal information from Europe. The U.S. Department of Commerce in consultation with the European Commission developed a "safe harbor" framework that enables U.S. companies to provide evidence that they are in compliance with the EU Directive. EU member countries permit the transfer of personal information to those U.S. companies that comply with the safe harbor principles, which require the following:

**Notice:** An organization must notify individuals about the purposes for which the organization collects and uses information about them. The organization also must provide information about how individuals can contact the organization with any inquiries or complaints, the types of third parties to which it discloses the information, and the means the organization offers for limiting its use and disclosure of information.

**Choice:** Organizations must give individuals the opportunity to choose (opt out) whether their personal information will be disclosed to a third party or used for a purpose incompatible with the purpose for which it was originally collected or subsequently authorized by the individual.

**Onward Transfer (Transfers to Third Parties):** Before disclosing personal information to a third party, organizations must apply the notice and choice principles.

**Access:** Individuals must have access to personal information about them that an organization holds and, with some exceptions, must be able to correct, amend, or delete that information where it is inaccurate.

**Security:** Organizations must take reasonable precautions to protect personal information from loss, misuse, unauthorized access, disclosure, alteration, and destruction.

**Data integrity:** Personal information must be relevant for the purposes for which it is to be used.

**Enforcement:** To ensure compliance with the safe harbor principles, there must be (a) readily available and affordable independent recourse mechanisms so that each individual's complaints and disputes can be investigated and resolved and damages awarded where the applicable law or private sector initiatives so provide, (b) procedures for verifying that the commitments companies make to adhere to the safe harbor principles have been implemented, and (c) obligations to remedy problems arising out of a failure to comply with the principles.

**Source:** "Safe Harbor," U.S. Department of Commerce, www.export.gov/safeharbor (29 June 2011).

### Figure 4.3 Employee or Independent Contractor?

The following factors help the courts determine whether a given individual was an employee or an independent contractor:

**Who controlled how the work was performed?**

Control by the employer is evidence that the individual was an employee. Control by the individual is evidence that he was an independent contractor. Control includes the ability to supervise and direct the work and to set the time and place where the work is performed.

**Who supplied the tools used to perform the work?**

The employer's provision of the tools or equipment is evidence that the individual acted as an employee. An individual who provides her own tools or equipment likely acted as an independent contractor.

**How was the individual paid?**

Payment of regular wages or a salary is evidence that the individual was an employee. If the individual was paid a commission or a lump sum upon completion of the task, then it is likely that he was hired as an independent contractor.

I get a monthly salary and work a standard 40-hour week here in the company's home office. I guess I'm considered an employee and not an independent contractor.

That's right. We're both employees, which means that all those employment laws govern the terms of our employment.

## Employment Relationship

State laws govern the employment relationship, and in most states employees are considered to be *employees at will*, which means that either the employer or the employee can terminate the employment relationship at any time for any lawful reason. Although most employment relationships are at-will relationships, the parties can change the nature of that employment relationship by entering into a contract. The contract may spell out the terms of the employment relationship, including the length of the employment period. When the parties enter into such an employment contract, the employer and employee must honor its terms and are liable for breach of contract if they violate the contract terms.

Whereas U.S. state laws generally are based on the concept that the employment relationship is an at-will relationship, laws in many countries do not provide for an employment-at-will relationship. Instead, laws in these countries are based on the idea that every employment relationship is a contractual relationship and the terms of that relationship are governed by the employment contract. Although, as a general rule, the parties are free to enter into any contract that they choose, laws in most countries provide some minimum statutory protections for employees, and employment contracts may not limit these protected areas.

## Workplace Standards

Like laws in most other countries, U.S. federal and state laws impose a variety of standards on the employment relationship. Wage and hour standards and health and safety standards are probably the most common types of regulatory requirements imposed by governments around the world. As with other areas of the law, the specific standards imposed vary greatly from jurisdiction to jurisdiction.

In the United States, the federal *Fair Labor Standards Act* imposes minimum requirements on the wages that employers must pay workers.[12] Most states also have established minimum wage requirements that are the same as the federal minimum wage amount. In states that have set a minimum wage requirement that is higher than the federal minimum requirement, employers must pay the higher amount.

State and federal laws do not set maximum limits on the number of hours that workers may be required to work each week. With certain exceptions, however, employees who work more than 40 hours a week must be paid at an overtime rate of at least 1½ times their normal hourly wage rate.

The federal *Occupational Safety and Health Act (OSHA)* governs almost all employers and their employees and sets a wide range of safety and health standards for workplaces. The Act requires employers to eliminate dangerous conditions and take action to achieve safe and healthy working conditions.[13] Both civil and criminal penalties may be imposed on employers that violate the Act.

## Nondiscrimination Requirements

A number of state and federal laws seek to ensure that employees are treated equally in the workplace by prohibiting employment discrimination. Employers in any given state must comply with that state's employment laws, as well as with all applicable federal laws. Federal laws prohibit discrimination in employment on the basis of various factors, which we describe in this section. State and local laws also prohibit such discrimination and often provide broader protections and remedies than are provided by the federal laws. These federal and state laws modify the employment-at-will relationship by prohibiting employers from discriminating in hiring and firing on the basis of certain factors.

The federal *Civil Rights Act of 1964* is one of the broadest federal antidiscrimination laws. It applies to employers that are engaged in interstate commerce and that have 15 or more employees.[14] Title VII of the Civil Rights Act prohibits employment discrimination on the basis of race, color, sex, religion, or national origin.[15] The term "on the basis of sex" includes on the basis of pregnancy, childbirth, and related medical conditions. Employers are required to treat pregnancy, childbirth, and related medical conditions the same as any other medical condition.

The federal ***Americans with Disabilities Act (ADA)*** protects people with disabilities against all types of discrimination, including employment discrimination.[16] The ADA applies to all employers with 15 or more employees. Discrimination is prohibited in regard to job application procedures; the hiring, advancement, or discharge of employees; employee compensation; job training; and other terms and conditions of employment. Unless an employer would be subjected to an undue hardship, the employer is required to make reasonable accommodations to the physical and mental impairments of otherwise qualified individuals. What is a reasonable accommodation varies depending on a specific situation, but it may include job restructuring and making physical facilities reasonably accessible to the disabled person.

The federal ***Age Discrimination in Employment Act (ADEA)*** protects workers who are age 40 and older from being discriminated against because of their age.[17] The ADEA applies to employers with 20 or more employees. It prohibits those employers from refusing to hire and from firing individuals 40 and older because of their age. Employers also cannot discriminate regarding compensation and other terms and conditions of employment because of an individual's age.

The federal ***Equal Pay Act*** applies to employers with two or more employees and prohibits sex-based wage discrimination between men and women in the same establishment who are performing the same job under similar working conditions.[18] Thus, women who are performing the same job as men and are working under similar conditions must be paid at the same rate as the men. Different wage rates are permitted only when such wages are paid under (1) a seniority system, (2) a merit system, (3) a system that measures earnings by quantity or quality of production, or (4) a system that differentiates wages based on any factor other than sex.

The federal ***Equal Employment Opportunity Commission (EEOC)*** is the U.S. federal agency responsible for administering the federal antidiscrimination laws described in this section. In general, individuals who wish to pursue discrimination complaints in federal court must first file an administrative charge of discrimination with the EEOC. If the EEOC determines there is "reasonable cause" to believe discrimination has occurred, it tries to conciliate the charge by reaching a voluntary resolution between the parties to the complaint. If conciliation is not successful, the EEOC may file a lawsuit in federal court. The EEOC also may issue a right-to-sue-notice to the party who alleges the discrimination, allowing the charging party to file an individual action in court without the EEOC's involvement. Thus, before an individual is permitted to file a civil lawsuit, he must pursue his claim with the EEOC.

Like the United States, most countries have enacted laws that prohibit certain types of employment discrimination. The specific classes of employees that are protected by such laws vary from place to place. Figure 4.4 lists some specific protections in selected countries.

## Figure 4.4 Examples of Nondiscrimination Laws

**European Union:**

Workers are protected against employment discrimination based on their sex, racial or ethnic origin, sexual orientation, age, disability, or religion.

**Hong Kong:**

Employers may not discriminate on the grounds of sex, race, pregnancy, marital status, responsibility for caring for an immediate family member, or disability.

**Japan:**

Workers are protected against employment discrimination based on race, creed, sex, social status, or family origin.

## Required Benefits

The U.S. federal *Family and Medical Leave Act (FMLA)* requires employers with 50 or more employees within a 75-mile radius of each other to allow eligible employees in specific circumstances to take up to 12 weeks of unpaid leave within any 12-month period.[19] The Act defines *eligible employee* as an employee who has been employed by a covered employer for at least 12 months and who has worked for the employer at least 1,250 hours in the previous 12 months. The Act provides 12 weeks of unpaid leave in a 12-month period in any of the following circumstances:

- The employee becomes a parent or foster parent

- The employee has a serious health condition

- The employee has a spouse, parent, or child with a serious health condition

An employee who returns from such leave must be reinstated to the position she held immediately prior to taking the leave or to an equivalent position. In addition, the employer must continue to provide medical insurance coverage for employees while they are on leave. Employees may be required to continue contributing their portions of the premiums for medical coverage during such leave.

Most countries have enacted laws that require employers to provide certain minimum benefits to employees. In many countries, laws entitle employees to a wider range of employee benefits than do U.S. laws. For example, many countries specify the minimum number of vacation days and paid holidays that employers must provide employees. Women workers in most countries are entitled to paid maternity leave, and some countries also provide at least some period of paid paternity leave. Figure 4.5 gives examples of parental leave benefits provided around the world. Multinational businesses must ensure that they comply with the employment laws in each country in which they hire workers.

## Figure 4.5 Examples of Parental Leave Laws

**Argentina:**

- After the birth of a child, women workers are required to take 90 days paid leave. Fathers are entitled to 2 days paid paternity leave. Benefits are paid by a centralized fund that is financed by government and employer contributions.

**Brazil:**

- Women are entitled to 120 days of paid maternity leave. Fathers are entitled to 5 days paid paternity leave. Benefits are provided by a government insurance program.

**China:**

- After giving birth, women workers are entitled to at least 90 days leave with full pay.

**Japan:**

- Women workers are entitled to a maximum of 14 weeks paid maternity leave. They are entitled to 6 weeks paid leave before giving birth and are required to take 8 weeks after the birth.

- All workers (other than day laborers) are entitled to unpaid parental leave until the child reaches age one.

- Specified workers are entitled to up to 3 months leave to care for a family member (spouse, child, parent, or parent of a spouse) due to injury, sickness, or disability.

**Source:** ILO Database on Conditions of Work and Employment Laws. ILO, Geneva. Available at: http://www.ilo.org/dyn/travail (30 June 2011).

## Key Terms

economics

market economy

market

pure competition

monopoly

free and open market

Federal Trade Commission (FTC)

price fixing

consumer

Consumer Credit Protection Act

garnishment

Fair Credit Reporting Act (FCRA)

consumer credit report

consumer reporting agency

adverse action

electronic signature

Electronic Signatures in Global and National Commerce Act (E-SIGN)

Uniform Electronic Transactions Act (UETA)

employee

independent contractor

Fair Labor Standards Act

Occupational Safety and Health Act (OSHA)

Civil Rights Act of 1964

Americans with Disabilities Act (ADA)

Age Discrimination in Employment Act (ADEA)

Equal Pay Act

Equal Employment Opportunity Commission (EEOC)

Family and Medical Leave Act (FMLA)

## Endnotes

1. 15 U.S.C. §§ 1–2 (2011).

2. 15 U.S.C. §§ 12 et seq. (2011).

3. 15 U.S.C. §§ 41 et seq. (2011).

4. "China Unveils New Rules against Anticompetitive, Monopolistic-type Behavior," Xinhua Net, 5 January 2011, <http://english.mofcom.gov.cn/aarticle/newsrelease/commonnews/201101/20110107348396.html (28> June 2011); "Competition Policy: People's Republic of China," APEC Competition Policy & Law Database, <http://www.apeccp.org.tw/doc/China/Competition/cncom1.html (28> June 2011).

5. "Legal Framework," Federal Competition Commission of Mexico, http://www.cfc.gob.mx/index.php/en/nocitias-cfc/programas-de-la-cfc (28 June 2011).

6. "Organization and Duties," Taiwan Fair Trade Commission, http://www.ftc.gov.tw/internet/english/doc/docDetail.aspx?uid=198&docid=12193 (28 June 2011).

7. 15 U.S.C. §§ 1601 et seq. (2011).

8. 15 U.S.C. § 1681 (2011).

9. 15 U.S.C. §§ 1701 et seq. (2011).

10. "Electronic Transactions Act Summary," National Conference of Commissioners on Uniform State Laws, http://uniformlaws.org/ActSummary.aspx?title=Electronic%20Transactions%20Act (29 June 2011).

11. United Nations General Assembly, Resolution 56/80, "Model Law on Electronic Signatures," 12 December 2001, http://www.uncitral.org/pdf/english/texts/electcom/ml-elecsig-e.pdf (29 June 2011).

12. 29 U.S.C. §§ 201 et seq. (2011).

13. 29 U.S.C. §§ 651 et seq. (2011)

14. 42 U.S.C. §§ 1981 et seq. (2011).

15. 42 U.S.C. §§ 2000(e) et seq. (2011).

16. 42 U.S.C. §§ 12101 et seq. (2011).

17. 42 U.S.C. §§ 621 et seq. (2011).

18. 29 U.S.C. § 206(d) (2011).

19. 29 U.S.C. §§ 2601 et seq. (2011).

*[handwritten note]* 10/23 Exam Score 6/11 55% 2,6,7,8,11
Little more difficult but was falling asleep reading it

## Chapter 5

# Regulation of Financial Services Companies

## Objectives

### After studying this chapter, you should be able to

- ■ Explain how the federal government regulates the financial services industry in the United States

- ■ Define the components of a holding company system and describe how insurance holding companies are regulated in the United States

- ■ Identify the two primary types of state insurance laws and describe the four primary features of state insurance regulatory systems

- ■ Explain the role of the federal government in regulating insurance

- ■ Identify types of depository institutions and explain how banks in the United States are governed by federal and state banking laws and international banking standards

- ■ Identify financial products that qualify as securities and describe the types of regulatory requirements that federal securities laws impose on securities and the individuals and companies that issue and sell securities

- ■ Describe the types of regulatory requirements that state, federal, and international privacy laws impose on financial institutions to protect personal consumer information

# Outline

**Regulation of Holding Companies**
- Insurance Holding Companies
- Financial Holding Companies

**Regulation of Insurance**
- State Regulation
- Federal Regulation of Insurance
- International Insurance Regulation

**Regulation of Banking**
- Federal Banking Laws
- State Banking Laws
- International Banking Standards

**Regulation of Securities**
- Registration Requirements
- Regulation of the Sale of Securities

**Privacy Protection Laws**
- U.S. Privacy Laws
- International Privacy Laws

The financial services industry is an integral part of the economy of all developed nations, and it can be an important factor in helping a developing nation create a well-balanced economy. Because the financial health of financial services companies is of such importance to so many people, these companies occupy a special position of public trust. That special position has led most governments to enact laws to regulate financial services companies in an effort to safeguard the public interest. This chapter describes how the U.S. state and federal governments regulate the financial services industry.

Historically, the various segments of the U.S. financial services industry were separated by regulatory barriers designed to protect the country's overall economic system. Because of these legislative restrictions, each type of financial institution was governed by a separate regulatory system. The various segments of the financial services industry are identified in Figure 5.1.

Congress removed many of the regulatory barriers to affiliations between institutions in the various segments of the U.S. financial services industry in 1999.[1] With the removal of regulatory barriers, financial institutions began to move into each others' traditional businesses. Many institutions expanded their operations

## Figure 5.1 Segments of the Financial Services Industry

**Depository Institutions**
- Commercial banks
- Thrift institutions
- Credit unions

**Insurance Companies**
- Life and health insurers
- Property/casualty insurers

**Finance Companies**

**Pension Funds**

**Mutual Funds**

**Securities Firms**
- Securities brokers and dealers
- Investment banks

so they could serve a customer's banking, insurance, and securities needs. When Congress removed regulatory barriers to affiliations, it provided for the functional regulation of the financial services industry. *Functional regulation* is the principle that a single regulatory body should oversee similar financial activities, regardless of which type of financial institution engages in the activity. As a result, each type of financial service continued to be primarily regulated by the same regulatory agency that was responsible for oversight of that type of financial service before the regulatory barriers were removed.

Because the financial services industry was at the center of the financial crisis of 2007–2010, governments reevaluated how best to regulate the industry. Congress made sweeping changes to regulation of the U.S. financial services industry by enacting the *Dodd-Frank Wall Street Reform and Consumer Protection Act,* commonly known as *Dodd-Frank.*[2] Dodd-Frank was designed to promote the financial stability of the United States by improving accountability and transparency in the financial system and to protect consumers from abusive financial services practices.

Although Dodd-Frank primarily targets banks, it also affects non-bank financial services companies. All financial services companies are subject to new regulatory and reporting requirements. The law created new administrative offices, including the Consumer Financial Protection Bureau (CFPB), which is described in Figure 5.2. Dodd-Frank also charged various administrative agencies with adopting rules and regulations to carry out its many requirements. At the time of this writing, federal officials were still in the process of adopting those rules and regulations. Thus, many of the details had not been set.

---

### Figure 5.2 Consumer Protection Under Dodd-Frank

The Dodd-Frank Act created the *Consumer Financial Protection Bureau (CFPB),* which is an independent bureau within the Federal Reserve System. The CFPB is charged with establishing clear "rules of the road" for banks, mortgage companies, payday lenders, credit card lenders, and other financial services firms. Those rules are designed to ensure that consumers can see clearly the costs and features of financial products and services. The CFPB's responsibilities include

- Enforcing federal consumer financial protection laws

- Restricting unfair, deceptive, or abusive acts or practices

- Taking consumer complaints

- Promoting financial education for consumers

- Researching consumer behavior

- Monitoring financial markets for new risks to consumers

- Enforcing laws that outlaw discrimination and other unfair treatment in consumer finance

---

In the lead-up to the 2007–2010 financial crisis, financial institutions affiliated in new ways that left some of their activities without strict regulatory standards or oversight. In addition, governments had no way to shut down and break apart failing financial firms in a way that did not endanger the rest of the financial system. The interconnectedness of financial institutions means that the failure of one institution can have a ripple effect throughout the industry, endangering the financial stability of other institutions. Some financial institutions are so large and interconnected with other institutions that their failure threatens the nation's financial system. The risk of failure of such a large, interconnected institution is a *systemic risk*, which is a risk that affects the entire financial system.

Dodd-Frank created a new regulatory system to monitor and constrain systemic risk. That system includes the addition of several new federal offices including the *Financial Stability Oversight Council (FSOC)*. The FSOC is an independent agency responsible for monitoring the safety and stability of the nation's financial system, identifying systemic risks, and coordinating regulatory responses to any threats to the system. The FSOC is a collaborative body chaired by the head of the Treasury Department. The Council consists of 10 voting members and 5 nonvoting members, including federal financial regulators, state regulators, and an insurance expert appointed by the President of the United States.

The FSOC has the authority to identify *systemically important financial institutions (SIFIs),* which are institutions—banks and nonbanks—whose failure could potentially pose a risk to the financial system. Firms that are identified as SIFIs will be subject to more stringent regulatory standards than other institutions, including stricter risk management standards, higher capital requirements, and additional regulatory examinations.

# Regulation of Holding Companies

Affiliations among various types of financial services companies have become common. Companies are *affiliates* when they are under the common control of a holding company. A *holding company system* is a corporate ownership structure in which one company—the *holding company*—owns and controls another company (or companies), known as a *subsidiary* of the holding company. In such an arrangement, each company exists as a separate corporate entity. Figure 5.3 gives an example of how companies can be affiliated within a holding company system.

## Insurance Holding Companies

All states have enacted laws to regulate holding company systems that include insurance companies. These laws are designed to protect an insurer's policyowners and to prevent a holding company system from separating an insurer's assets and liabilities from that insurer's control. The following are some of the requirements of state insurance holding company laws:

- Proposed transactions in which one entity will acquire control of an insurer or will merge with an insurer must be approved by the insurance department of the insurer's domiciliary state. Approval generally is granted unless the insurer's financial stability would be threatened, the transaction is unfair to the insurer's policyowners, or competition in insurance would be lessened substantially.

## Figure 5.3 Example of a Holding Company System

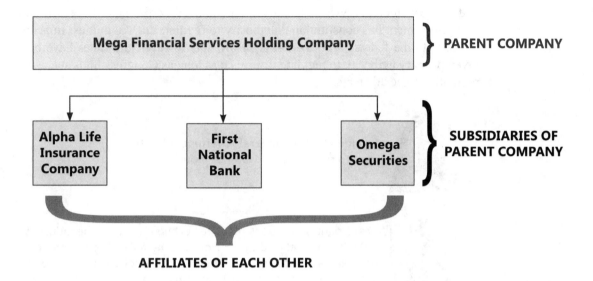

- To protect an insurer's financial stability, the amount that an insurer may invest in subsidiaries is limited.

- Domestic insurers that are part of a holding company system are subject to registration and periodic reporting requirements designed to enable state insurance departments to oversee the operations of insurance holding company systems.

- Transactions between companies affiliated with an insurer must be reported to the insurance department of the insurer's domiciliary state. The insurance department will disapprove a transaction if the terms of the transaction are unreasonable or would threaten the insurer's solvency.

## Financial Holding Companies

A financial institution that wants to provide a full range of financial services must be qualified as a financial holding company. A *financial holding company (FHC)* is a holding company that conducts activities that are financial in nature or incidental to financial activities, such as insurance activities, securities activities, banking, and investment and advisory services. An FHC must include a depository institution, which may be a national bank, state bank, foreign bank, or savings bank. The process to become an FHC is regulated by the Federal Reserve System (the Fed), which we describe later in the chapter. An FHC that includes an insurer also must comply with state insurance holding company laws.

# Regulation of Insurance

The U.S. Constitution gives the federal government the authority to regulate interstate commerce—commerce conducted across state lines. Because insurance and other financial services typically are conducted across state lines, the federal government has constitutional authority to regulate such activities. In accordance with the federal **McCarran-Ferguson Act**, however, the states have been given primary authority to regulate insurance as long as Congress finds such state regulation to be adequate.[3]

So ultimately, the federal government has the right to regulate the insurance industry.

That's right, and it does regulate certain aspects of the industry. But with the McCarran-Ferguson Act, the federal government basically said to the states, "We're going to let you do most of the regulating, and we'll just keep an eye on what you're doing."

So the states are responsible for most of the regulating, but the federal government will get involved if it sees a problem with what the states are doing.

## State Regulation

Each state and U.S. territory has established a system of law to regulate the business of insurance within its geographical borders. State insurance laws can be classified into two broad types of laws:

- **Solvency laws** are designed to ensure that insurance companies are financially able to meet their debts and to pay policy benefits when they come due. Solvency laws, which are fairly uniform across the United States, regulate an insurer's capitalization, policy design, and policy reserves.

- **Market conduct laws** are designed to make sure that insurance companies conduct their businesses fairly and ethically. Market conduct laws regulate most of the nonfinancial operations of insurers, including company management, marketing, sales practices, producer licensing, advertising, underwriting, policyowner service, complaint handling, and claims. Unlike solvency requirements, some aspects of market conduct requirements vary a great deal from state to state.

Although laws vary from state to state, some uniformity exists because many state laws are based on model laws developed by the National Association of Insurance Commissioners (NAIC). In addition to promoting uniformity of state insurance regulation, the NAIC provides various services for state insurance regulators.

These services allow the states to coordinate their regulatory oversight activities and avoid duplication of effort. Figure 5.4 describes some of the services the NAIC provides to state insurance departments.

---

### Figure 5.4 Examples of Services the NAIC Provides to the States

- The NAIC provides several computerized databases to state insurance departments. These databases enable the departments to simplify the producer licensing process, screen insurers that have applied for a certificate of authority, and exchange information about licensed insurers and producers.

- The NAIC's Examination Tracking System enables the state insurance departments to schedule and coordinate on-site examinations of insurers.

- The NAIC maintains a financial database containing information from insurers' Annual Statements and assists state insurance departments in overseeing the solvency of insurers.

---

All of the state insurance regulatory systems contain similar features, including (1) licensing requirements, (2) reporting and filing requirements, (3) periodic examinations of licensed insurers, and (4) the right to take action against licensed companies and producers who violate applicable laws and regulations.

## *Incorporation and Licensing Requirements*

To ensure the long-term stability of insurance companies, state laws require insurers to be organized as corporations. The formation of a corporation that plans to underwrite and issue insurance is basically the same as the formation of all other types of corporations. As part of the incorporation process, the state insurance department typically must approve the formation of such a corporation.

An insurer must select a state in which to incorporate, and that state becomes the insurer's domiciliary state. From the perspective of any given state, an insurer that incorporates in the state is a *domestic insurer*; an insurer that incorporates under the laws of another state in the United States is a *foreign insurer*; and an insurer that incorporates under the laws of a country other than the United States is an *alien insurer*. Each state insurance department has primary responsibility for overseeing the operations of its domestic insurers. By incorporating in a state, an insurer subjects itself to the jurisdiction of that state's insurance department.

All states require that before transacting business within the state, an insurer must obtain a *certificate of authority*, or *license*, which is a document issued by the state insurance department granting the insurer the right to conduct an insurance business in the state. State licensing requirements are designed to (1) make sure that insurers are financially able to meet their obligations to pay policy benefits and (2) enable the states to effectively oversee the operations of insurers.

An insurer must obtain a certificate of authority from each state in which it plans to do business and must conduct business in the state in compliance with all of the state's regulatory requirements. When an insurer receives a certificate of authority from a given state, the insurer becomes subject to the jurisdiction of that state's insurance department. Thus, each state insurance department also is responsible for supervising the operations of foreign and alien insurers that conduct business in the state.

In addition to requiring insurers to be licensed, state insurance laws require that the individuals—known as *insurance producers*—who market and sell insurance products must be properly licensed to sell insurance by each jurisdiction in which they conduct business.

## Reporting and Filing Requirements

To maintain its certificate of authority in a given state, an insurer must file a comprehensive financial report, known as an *Annual Statement*, with the state insurance department and the NAIC and must pay any required renewal fee to the state. Insurers generally must file their Annual Statements by March 1 each year with all states in which they are licensed, and most states require companies to file abbreviated versions of the Statement on a quarterly basis. The Annual Statement must reflect that the insurer has met all the financial requirements imposed by state insurance laws.

Most states also require insurers to file other types of reports as well as materials, such as insurance policy forms, before those materials are used in the state.

## Periodic Examinations of Insurers

Insurance laws in all states authorize and require the state insurance department to periodically examine the condition and affairs of insurers operating in the state to ensure that those companies are financially sound and are conducting business in accordance with applicable regulatory requirements. State insurance departments conduct two types of periodic examinations: financial condition examinations and market conduct examinations.

A *financial condition examination* is a formal investigation of an insurer that is carried out by one or more state insurance departments and is designed to identify and monitor any threats to the insurer's solvency. Most states require each insurer domiciled in the state to undergo such an examination at least every three to five years. Working through the NAIC, the states have developed a zone system of examination to oversee the operations of multistate insurers and thereby avoid duplication of efforts by the various insurance departments in which such insurers operate. Each insurer is domiciled within one of four geographic zones. Examiners representing various states in the zones in which the insurer is licensed participate in examining the insurer.

A *market conduct examination* is a formal investigation of an insurer's nonfinancial operations that is carried out by one or more state insurance departments and is designed to determine whether the insurer's market conduct operations comply with applicable laws and regulations. The states take different approaches to scheduling market conduct examinations. Some states try to periodically examine each licensed insurer. Other states conduct examinations when they identify specific complaints about an insurer's market conduct activities or have some specific concern about an insurer's operations. Despite the variations in state market conduct laws, more and more market conduct examinations are being conducted on a multistate basis.

## Right to Take Action

State insurance departments are authorized to take specified actions when they find that an insurer is not in compliance with applicable regulatory requirements or is in financial difficulty. They also can take actions against licensed insurance producers and agencies that violate applicable state insurance laws. When state insurance departments find that an insurer or licensed producer or agency has violated state laws, they usually impose monetary penalties in the form of fines. In more serious cases, state insurance laws empower the insurance department to suspend or revoke an insurer's certificate of authority.

- When an insurer's certificate is *suspended*, the insurer is required to discontinue operating for a certain period of time. A suspension may be imposed for a stated period of time or may continue until the insurer corrects the violation.

- When an insurer's certificate is *revoked*, the certificate is cancelled and the insurer is not permitted to conduct business within the state until the insurer receives a new certificate from the state insurance department.

A state insurance department, for example, may suspend or revoke an insurer's certificate if the insurer is unsound financially or knowingly fails to comply with state laws or regulations or with an order issued by any state insurance department. Likewise, state insurance departments can suspend or revoke a producer's license if the situation warrants it.

When an insurer becomes financially unsound, state insurance departments are authorized to take a number of actions, depending on the severity of the insurer's difficulties. For example, an insurance department can order an insurer to take specified corrective actions or can place the insurer under the supervision of the department. If the insurance department judges that the insurer's difficulties are so severe that additional action is warranted, the department may ask a court to place the insurer in receivership. When an insurer is placed in **receivership** (sometimes known as *conservatorship*), the state insurance commissioner, acting for a state court, takes control of and administers the insurer's assets and liabilities. The insurance commissioner, or someone acting on the commissioner's behalf, acts as the **receiver** (*conservator*)—the person responsible for formulating a plan to conserve and control the insurer's assets and for making sure that the insurer's obligations to customers are met to the extent possible. An insurance receivership can have two possible outcomes: rehabilitation and liquidation.

- Impaired insurers generally are first placed into *rehabilitation*. The insurer continues to exist as a corporation, and the insurance department assesses more precisely the insurer's financial situation. If it seems possible that an insurer can be rehabilitated, state insurance departments may try to find an investor to invest capital in the insurer. It is rare, however, for an investor to be willing to participate in a rehabilitation.

- If the insurer cannot be rehabilitated, it is placed into liquidation. In a *liquidation*, the receiver either transfers all of the insurer's business—including its reserve liabilities—and assets to other insurers or sells the insurer's assets and terminates the insurer's business. After the business has been liquidated, the insurer ceases to exist.

## Federal Regulation of Insurance

Although the states have primary authority for regulating insurance, insurers are not entirely exempt from federal regulation. The McCarran-Ferguson Act reserves to the federal government certain matters, including national issues such as employer-employee relationships and certain antitrust issues that are not otherwise regulated by the states. As a result, insurance companies are subject to federal regulation on those matters. Insurers also must comply with federal consumer protection laws as described in Chapter 4.

The McCarran-Ferguson Act makes clear that Congress may make any federal law apply to the insurance industry by simply including a provision to that effect in the law. Thus, Congress retains the right to enact insurance laws if it decides that state regulation is inadequate or not in the public interest. Congress has, in fact, enacted many such laws.

One of the primary areas in which life insurers are subject to federal regulation is their sale of investment-type insurance products. Traditional investment products, such as stocks and bonds, are regulated by federal laws that are enforced by the federal Securities and Exchange Commission (SEC). The SEC has determined that some insurance products—notably variable life insurance and variable annuities—contain features of investment products and, thus, are subject to both federal securities laws and state insurance laws. We describe the regulation of securities later in the chapter.

Isn't this the *functional regulation* we learned about earlier in this chapter? If an insurer sells variable products, it is regulated by the SEC because that's the agency that oversees investment products, right?

Great example! Even if the company is primarily an insurance company and subject to state and federal insurance regulation, because it sells some insurance products that are considered investments, it's *also* regulated by the federal securities laws.

Although Dodd-Frank is primarily directed at banks, some provisions affect the insurance industry. The law created the ***Federal Insurance Office (FIO)***, which is an administrative office within the Treasury Department. The FIO has a number of responsibilities, including

- Monitoring the U.S. insurance industry, including all lines of insurance except health insurance, some long-term care insurance, and crop insurance

- Identifying areas where the states are not regulating the industry adequately and consulting with the states on matters of national or international importance

- Helping the FSOC identify systemically risky insurers

- Coordinating federal efforts dealing with international insurance matters and representing the United States in the International Association of Insurance Supervisors (IAIS)

## International Insurance Regulation

Insurance regulation varies a great deal from country to country. Each nation has developed a method for defining which companies are considered insurance companies for regulatory purposes. Companies that fall within the applicable definition are subject to some form of supervision by regulatory authorities. Typically, direct writing companies—that is, companies that underwrite and issue insurance policies—are subject to such regulation.

As a general rule, insurance companies and insurance producers must be licensed by or registered with a specific regulatory agency before conducting business within a country. Figure 5.5 identifies the agencies responsible for insurance regulation in various countries. Each nation has established minimum criteria that insurers must meet in order to be eligible to conduct an insurance business in the jurisdiction.

### Figure 5.5 Insurance Regulatory Bodies in Various Countries

**Argentina:** Superintendency of Insurance

**Australia:** Australian Prudential and Regulatory Authority

**Bermuda:** Bermuda Monetary Authority

**China:** China Insurance Regulatory Commission

**India:** Insurance Regulatory and Development Authority

**Malaysia:** Central Bank of Malaysia

**Mexico:** National Commission of Insurance and Finances

**Philippines:** Insurance Commission

**Singapore:** Monetary Authority of Singapore

**South Korea:** Financial Services Commission

Solvency regulation—referred to as ***prudential regulation*** in many countries—typically is the primary focus of insurance laws and regulatory requirements throughout the world. Most countries impose minimum capital requirements as a prerequisite to an insurer's obtaining a license to conduct an insurance business; a company that is financially unsound is not permitted to receive a license.

In addition, regulatory authorities in most countries continue to monitor and assess the solvency of all licensed insurers on an ongoing basis, and they periodically conduct on-site examinations of insurer operations. Companies are required to file periodic financial reports with insurance regulatory authorities, which apply some type of mathematical model to assess insurer solvency. Many countries require each life insurer to have an *appointed actuary*, who has specified qualifications and who is responsible for making sure that the insurer's operations are mathematically sound. Most countries impose continuing minimum capital requirements, and they impose some type of restrictions on insurers' investments.

As a general rule, when an insurer's financial results fail to meet minimum regulatory requirements, regulators are authorized to intervene in the insurer's operations to protect policyowner interests. The specific actions that regulators are permitted to take when an insurer's solvency is in question vary from country to country. In extreme cases in which an insurer's solvency cannot be restored, however, countries typically have established procedures to liquidate the company. In each case, the protection of policyowner interests is the primary regulatory goal.

Insurance laws in many countries include market conduct requirements designed to ensure that insurers conduct business fairly and to protect the public. However, such laws typically are not as extensive as are the market conduct laws in the United States.

# Regulation of Banking

A **depository institution** is a financial institution that specializes in accepting deposits and making loans. Depository institutions take the following primary forms:

- A **commercial bank** is a depository institution that accepts deposits from people, businesses, and government agencies and uses these deposits to make loans to people, businesses, and government agencies.

- A **thrift institution**, sometimes referred to as a *savings and loan (S&L) association or savings bank*, is a depository institution that receives the majority of its deposits from consumers and makes the majority of its loans as residential mortgage loans.

- A **credit union** is a nonprofit, cooperative financial institution owned and run by its members.

Our focus in this section is on banks. Unless otherwise indicated, we use the term *bank* to refer to both commercial banks and thrift institutions. Insight 5.1 gives a brief overview of how credit unions are regulated.

The specific laws that apply to a bank in a given situation depend on many factors, including how the bank was chartered, the state in which the bank is conducting business, and the product that is being marketed and sold. A bank charter is a document issued by a government agency authorizing a bank to conduct business. Before conducting business, a bank must receive a charter from a federal or state agency; Thus, banks are classified as *national banks* or *state banks* depending on how they are chartered.

## Insight 5.1 Regulation of Credit Unions

Like commercial banks and thrift institutions, a credit union may not begin operations until it receives either a federal charter or a state charter. Federal-chartered credit unions are regulated by the *National Credit Union Administration (NCUA)*, which enforces federal laws that are generally similar to the federal laws that apply to banks.

The NCUA operates the National Credit Union Share Insurance Fund (NCUSIF), which insures federal credit union accounts within specified dollar limits. State-chartered credit unions also may become members of the NCUSIF, if they meet certain financial requirements and their operating policies are safe and sound.

## Federal Banking Laws

All national banks and most state banks are members of the ***Federal Reserve System (the Fed)***, which is a system consisting of 12 regional banks and the state and national banks that are members of the Fed. The Fed's primary functions are to

- Conduct the nation's monetary policy

- Supervise and regulate banking institutions and protect the credit rights of consumers

- Maintain the stability of the nation's financial system

- Provide certain financial services to the U.S. government, the public, and financial institutions

The Fed also has primary authority to supervise state banks that are members of the Fed, and most state banks are Fed members.

The ***Department of the Treasury*** is the federal administrative agency with primary responsibility for administering federal banking laws. The ***Office of the Comptroller of the Currency (OCC)*** is the agency within the Treasury Department that is directly responsible for regulating national banks and most state banks. The OCC is responsible for adopting and enforcing regulations to ensure that banks operate in a safe and sound manner. Like state insurance regulatory requirements, many federal banking requirements are designed to ensure the financial solvency of banks. Banks must periodically file financial reports with regulatory agencies and are subject to periodic examinations by those agencies.

Banks that are members of the Fed are required to protect the funds of their customers by insuring deposit accounts with the Federal Deposit Insurance

Corporation. The *Federal Deposit Insurance Corporation (FDIC)* is a federal agency that guarantees, within stated limits, the funds deposited in member banks. Should an insured bank fail, the FDIC protects each depositor's funds up to the stated dollar amount. The FDIC also takes over the failed bank and can either sell it to another bank or operate it for a time as a federally owned bank.

## State Banking Laws

State banks are governed by the banking laws of the state in which they were chartered. Nevertheless, most states have enacted laws designed to ensure that state banks are able to exercise the same rights and powers and engage in the same activities as national banks, on substantially the same terms and conditions as national banks. As a result, the regulation of banking is fairly uniform across the United States.

In addition, some aspects of the operations of every bank are governed by the laws of the state in which the bank is conducting business. For example, the operation of checking accounts is primarily governed by state laws based on Article 4 of the Uniform Commercial Code (UCC). In addition, checks are negotiable instruments governed by state laws based on Article 3 of the UCC. (We describe negotiable instruments and the UCC in Chapter 9.) Furthermore, banks that market insurance products must comply with state insurance laws.

## International Banking Standards

Banking organizations must comply with the laws of the country in which they are domiciled. Those laws govern a bank's domestic and international operations. In addition, a bank that does business in another country must comply with that country's laws.

The increasing globalization of banking has led to a greater focus on coordinating bank regulations across national borders. Many countries work together through various forums to promote consistency in the regulation of banking. One organization is the *Group of Twenty Finance Ministers and Central Bank Governors*, commonly known as the *G20*. The G20 is a forum for cooperation and consultation among representatives of key countries, the European Union (EU), and a few nongoverning institutions on matters pertaining to the international financial system. The G20 conducts private conferences where members review policy issues and work to support international financial stability.

*The Basel Committee on Banking Supervision* is a cooperative organization with members from all regions of the world. Committee members exchange information on supervision issues and have developed guidelines and supervisory standards that member countries are encouraged to follow. To promote stability in international financial systems, the committee has developed international banking regulations, which are updated periodically as needed. The latest regulations, known as *Basel III*, were created in response to the latest financial crisis. Basel III aims to improve the capital holdings of banks, reduce the amount of risk that banks take on, and increase banks' transparency. The G20 has committed to implementing Basel III bank reforms, and many countries are working to adopt the reforms.

# Regulation of Securities

The U.S. federal government has primary authority to regulate the securities industry and the products that qualify as securities. For regulatory purposes, a *security* is a certificate or electronic record that represents either an ownership interest in a business (for example, a share of stock) or an obligation of indebtedness owed by a business, government, or agency (a bond, for example). Figure 5.6 contains some other examples of securities.

## Figure 5.6 Examples of Securities

**Option:** A contract that gives the owner the right to either buy or sell a specified asset during a limited time period for a stated price.

**Debenture:** An unsecured corporate bond for which the corporate borrower does not pledge any assets or income as security.

**Mutual fund share:** A share in a fund operated by an investment company that raises and pools money from shareholders and invests it in stocks, bonds, and other securities.

**Variable annuity contract:** An annuity contract under which the amount of the accumulated value and of periodic annuity benefit payments fluctuate in accordance with the performance of a specified pool of investments.

**Variable life insurance contract:** A life insurance contract under which the death benefit and the cash value of the policy fluctuate according to the investment performance of a specified pool of investments.

Federal securities laws provide a framework for regulatory oversight of the securities industry. That framework includes (1) registration requirements, (2) reporting and filing requirements, (3) the regulation of the purchase and sale of publicly traded securities, (4) periodic examinations of registered entities and individuals, and (5) the right to take action against those who violate the laws.

The Securities and Exchange Commission (SEC) is the federal agency responsible for administering federal securities laws. The SEC is authorized to make rules and regulations to govern the purchase and sale of securities, including sales that are made publicly through a stock exchange or over the counter. A *stock exchange* is an organized marketplace where specific types of securities, such as common stocks and bonds, are bought and sold by members of the exchange. Sales of stocks that are not traded on a stock exchange are referred to as *over-the-counter (OTC) sales*. For example, the sale of a variable life insurance policy is an over-the-counter sale of a security.

## Registration Requirements

The securities laws impose a range of registration requirements on individuals and firms that offer securities for sale to the public. Investment companies must register with the SEC before conducting business. An *investment company* is a company that issues securities and engages primarily in investing and trading securities. Insurers that sell variable life insurance and variable annuity products maintain separate accounts for those products, and those separate accounts are considered investment companies that must be registered with the SEC. Insight 5.2 describes the basic types of investment companies and explains the registration requirements imposed on insurers that issue variable life insurance and variable annuity products.

## Insight 5.2 Types of U.S. Investment Companies

- An **open-end investment company** is an investment company that establishes a portfolio of securities and issues shares in the portfolio to investors. The public may purchase shares from the investment company at their net asset value, and the investment company will redeem shares upon the owner's request at their current net asset value. Such companies are considered open-end companies because their capitalization is not fixed and they normally issue more shares as people want them. Mutual funds are the primary type of open-end investment company.

- A **closed-end investment company** is an investment company that issues a fixed number of shares to the public and does not redeem shares that are outstanding. Shares typically trade on exchanges or in the over-the-counter market.

- A **unit investment trust** is an investment company that is organized as a trust that buys and holds a portfolio of securities for a predetermined time. The trust sells units in the portfolio to the public for a limited period, and the number of units remains unchanged. At the end of the predetermined time, the trust sells its portfolio of securities and distributes the money to unitholders on a pro rata basis.

Most insurers' separate accounts are registered with the SEC as unit investment trusts, which own and hold assets for the participants in variable life insurance and variable annuity contracts. Each separate account may be divided into subaccounts, and each subaccount may invest in a different open-end investment company. The open-end investment companies in which the separate accounts are invested also must be registered as investment companies. Owners of variable life insurance and variable annuity contracts receive the prospectuses for both the separate account unit investment trust and the open-end investment companies in which they have invested.[4]

Registration requirements also are imposed on individuals and firms that market securities. Sales of securities to the public must be conducted by a securities broker or an individual who acts as an agent for a broker. A *securities broker* is an individual, corporation, or other legal entity engaged in the business of buying and selling securities for the accounts of others. A *securities dealer* is an individual, corporation, or other legal entity that is engaged in the business of buying and selling securities for its own account. Securities brokers often operate as both brokers and dealers, and the term *broker-dealer* is often used to refer to individuals and firms that transact securities businesses. We use the term *broker-dealer* in a broad sense to include persons or companies that engage in securities transactions.

Before entering into securities transactions, securities brokers and dealers must (1) register with the SEC and (2) become members of the Financial Industry Regulatory Authority. The *Financial Industry Regulatory Authority (FINRA)* is a nonprofit organization of member firms responsible for regulating all securities firms doing business in the United States. FINRA is supervised by the SEC.

Individuals who are associated with a FINRA member—including partners, officers, directors, branch managers, and salespeople—and who engage in the securities business must register with FINRA. Generally, the following two levels of qualification and registration are available:

- A *registered representative* is a person who is associated with a FINRA member, engages in the securities business on behalf of the member by soliciting the sale of securities or training securities salespeople, and has passed a special examination administered by FINRA.

- A *principal* is generally an officer and/or manager who is involved in the day-to-day operation and supervision of the securities business, has qualified as a registered representative, and has passed additional examinations administered by FINRA.

We use the term *registered person* to refer to both registered representatives and principals. An individual who solicits the sale of variable life insurance and/or variable annuity products must be licensed as an insurance sales producer and also must be a registered person.

The final registration requirement imposed by the securities laws requires the registration of a security with the SEC before it is advertised or offered for sale to the public. Registration of a security with the SEC does not indicate that the SEC has approved the security or made any judgment as to its merits. Federal laws set strict requirements for the sale of securities, and most such requirements are designed to ensure adequate disclosure of material information about the security to prospective purchasers. Figure 5.7 summarizes the registration requirements that federal securities laws impose on individuals and firms that offer securities for sale to the public.

## Figure 5.7 Securities Registration Requirements in the United States

- Investment companies must register with the SEC.

- Securities brokers and dealers must (1) register with the SEC and (2) become members of FINRA.

- Individuals who are associated with a FINRA member and who engage in the securities business must register with the SEC and FINRA as a registered representative or principal.

- Every security must be registered with the SEC before it is advertised or offered for sale to the public.

# Regulation of the Sale of Securities

The issuers of securities and the broker-dealers and registered persons who buy and sell securities must comply with a range of regulatory requirements. For instance, the issuer of a security is required to provide a *prospectus* to every potential purchaser of the security. A prospectus is a communication, usually written, that offers a security for sale and that must contain detailed information about the issuer of the security and the security itself. The issuer also must provide owners of the security with periodic financial reports on the security and the issuing corporation's financial condition.

## FINRA Conduct Rules

Registered members of FINRA—including broker-dealers and the registered persons who are affiliated with those broker-dealers—must conduct business in accordance with all statutory requirements and in compliance with FINRA rules and regulations. The *FINRA Rules* impose a variety of requirements on how broker-dealers and registered persons must conduct business. The following are examples of such requirements:

- When making an investment recommendation to a customer, the registered person must have reasonable grounds to believe the recommendation is suitable for the customer based on the customer's investment profile.[5] That profile includes the customer's age, other investments, financial situation and needs, tax status, investment objectives, investment experience, investment time horizon, liquidity needs, risk tolerance, and any other information the customer provides.

- Broker-dealers must establish and maintain a system to supervise the activities of the registered persons who work under their control to reasonably ensure that they comply with applicable regulatory requirements.[6] In addition, a principal must directly supervise the activities of each registered representative. A broker-dealer's supervisory system must ensure that registered representatives understand how to conduct business in accordance with regulatory requirements and must provide for meetings at least once a year with each registered representative to discuss regulatory and compliance matters.

- Advertisements, sales literature, correspondence, and other communications that broker-dealers and registered persons use to communicate with the public must meet a number of requirements.[7] For example, materials must not contain promises of specific investment results, exaggerations, or opinions for which there is no reasonable basis. A principal must review and approve advertisements and sales literature before they are used and must initial or sign such materials to indicate that approval. The broker-dealer then must maintain a file of all such materials and must keep materials for at least three years after every use.

- Broker-dealers must submit certain public communication materials to FINRA for its review. During the first year a broker-dealer is a FINRA member, the broker-dealer must submit all such materials to FINRA before using them. After the first year, the broker-dealer must submit certain public communications to FINRA within 10 days of their first use.

These FINRA rules seem pretty specific.

Yes, and with good reason. Anyone who markets investment products—including variable life insurance or variable annuities—is asking consumers to trust her with their money and their future security.

And, investment products *can* be hard to understand.

They are complex products. That's why the laws that govern their marketing and sale are designed to protect consumers from unethical practices.

## Compliance Inspections

FINRA carries out its regulatory responsibilities by conducting periodic compliance inspections of all broker-dealers. The frequency of such inspections varies depending on the nature of the broker-dealer's activities. Examiners review the broker-dealer's books and records to ensure that they are accurate and up-to-date. Sales practices also are reviewed, as is the broker-dealer's financial condition.

### *Dispute Resolution*

Occasionally, a dispute arises between a customer and a broker-dealer or between a broker-dealer and a registered person. FINRA rules require broker-dealers to submit to arbitration when they are involved in disputes with a customer or an affiliated registered person.

# Privacy Protection Laws

As part of conducting business, financial institutions gather a wide range of information about their customers. Advances in technology now enable businesses and government agencies to collect and maintain information about many aspects of an individual's life. Although most consumers understand the needs that businesses and government agencies have for personal information about them, consumers have concerns about how such information is collected and used. These concerns have led many countries to enact laws designed to protect the privacy of consumers.

## U.S. Privacy Laws

Various state and federal laws and regulations are designed to protect consumer privacy. In Chapter 4, we described the federal Fair Credit Reporting Act (FCRA), which regulates the reporting and use of consumer credit information. Financial services companies such as banks and insurance companies must comply with the FCRA when they obtain consumer credit reports. In this section, we describe state insurance laws designed to safeguard the confidentiality of personal information gathered in connection with insurance transactions and federal requirements imposed on all financial institutions.

### *State Insurance Laws*

Many states have enacted laws establishing guidelines that insurers must follow as they collect and use personal information about consumers. Many of these state laws are based on the *NAIC Insurance Information and Privacy Protection Model Act (Model Privacy Act)*, which establishes standards for the collection, use, and disclosure of information gathered in connection with insurance transactions. For purposes of the Model Privacy Act, an *insurance transaction* is a transaction (1) that involves insurance for personal, family, or household needs and (2) in which an insurer either determines an individual's eligibility for insurance coverage or benefits or services a policy. Laws based on the Model Privacy Act apply not only to insurers but also to insurance producers and insurance support organizations that collect information about individuals and provide that information to insurers and insurance producers.

According to the Model Privacy Act, an insurer is required to provide a consumer who has applied for insurance, for a policy renewal, or for a policy reinstatement with a written notice of the insurer's information practices when the insurer (1) intends to collect information about the consumer and (2) will collect that information from sources other than the consumer or public records.

The Model Privacy Act also limits the situations in which an insurer, insurance producer, or insurance support organization has the right to disclose personal or privileged information about consumers.

The Model Privacy Act gives individuals about whom personal information has been collected in connection with an insurance transaction the right to have access to that information and to have the insurer amend or delete from its records information that is incorrect. The Model Privacy Act also imposes requirements on insurers when they make adverse underwriting decisions that affect individual life insurance coverage. For purposes of the Act, an *adverse underwriting decision* is (1) a declination of coverage, (2) a termination of coverage, or (3) an offer to insure at higher than standard premium rates. When an insurer makes an adverse underwriting decision, the insurer must provide the applicant, proposed insured, or policyowner with the reasons for the decision and a summary of the individual's right of access to personal information maintained by the insurer.

As a life insurance underwriter for 10 years, I can tell you that privacy concerns play a large role in my job. Knowing what information I can legally gather, use to make an underwriting decision, and share with others is vital to doing my job well.

That's an excellent point. Underwriting is an area where large amounts of personal information about a potential insured is collected, and we have to make sure that information is handled appropriately and protected from unauthorized distribution.

And I know that sometimes underwriting information is used to help us in handling claims, so we have to know about these privacy laws, too.

Exactly! Now you're starting to see how laws affect many different aspects of our jobs in insurance and financial services. Read on to learn about nonpublic personal information, which is something you both deal with in your jobs.

## Federal Privacy Laws

Federal laws impose privacy requirements on all financial institutions, which must develop privacy policies and procedures for handling *nonpublic personal information* about individuals. **Nonpublic personal information** is personally identifiable information about a consumer that is *not* publicly available. By contrast, publicly available information generally may be shared without restriction.

Information is publicly available if a financial institution reasonably believes the information is available to the general public from government records, widely distributed media, or disclosures required by law. For example, an individual's telephone number usually is widely published in telephone directories that are available to the general public. However, if an individual's telephone number is unlisted, then the number is not publicly available and is protected information. If a consumer can take steps to prevent information from being made publicly available—such as by having an unlisted telephone number—then financial institutions must determine whether the consumer has taken such steps. Thus, each financial institution must establish procedures to identify the nonpublic information it has about consumers and take steps to protect that information.

Subject to several important exceptions, before sharing nonpublic personal information about a consumer with certain nonaffiliated third parties, a financial institution must (1) notify the consumer of the institution's privacy policies and (2) provide the consumer with an opportunity to opt out of information sharing with such third parties. A financial institution also must provide a notice to a consumer about its privacy policies when the institution establishes a customer relationship with the consumer. A customer relationship is established, for example, when a consumer purchases an insurance policy from an insurer. The financial institution must provide additional notices to its customers at least once a year thereafter. Figure 5.8 lists the specific types of information that must be included in such privacy notices.

## Figure 5.8 Required Content of Privacy Notices

- The categories of nonpublic information the institution collects. For example, information may be categorized by sources, such as information from consumers, information from transactions with the institution, and credit report information.

- The categories of nonpublic personal information that the institution may disclose either to affiliated or nonaffiliated parties.

- The categories of affiliated and nonaffiliated parties to whom the institution may disclose nonpublic personal information about consumers.

- The institution's policies about disclosing nonpublic personal information about people who are no longer customers.

- A description of the consumer's right to opt out and the methods by which the consumer may opt out.

- A description of the institution's policies with respect to protecting the confidentiality and security of nonpublic personal information.

Federal laws restrict how a financial institution shares information with *nonaffiliated third parties*, which are entities that are not related by common ownership or control with the financial institution. As a general rule, a financial institution is permitted to disclose nonpublic personal information to a nonaffiliated third party (either directly or through an affiliate) only after the institution has taken the following steps:

- Notified the consumer, in a clear and conspicuous manner, that the information may be disclosed to such a third party. This notice may be given in writing or in an electronic form.

- Given the consumer an opportunity to opt out of the disclosure by directing that the information not be disclosed.

- Explained to the consumer how to opt out of the disclosure.

Under specified conditions, a financial institution is permitted to disclose nonpublic personal information to a nonaffiliated third party without providing customers with an opportunity to opt out if the disclosure is necessary to enable the third party to perform services on behalf of the financial institution. In such cases, the institution must (1) fully disclose to the customer that the information is going to be provided and (2) obtain a contractual commitment from the third party to maintain the confidentiality of the information. For example, an insurer can give information to a nonaffiliated third party to be used in marketing the insurer's own products or services without providing an opportunity for customers to opt out of sharing the information.

## International Privacy Laws

Many countries have adopted laws to regulate how companies collect, use, and disclose personal information about individual consumers. Rules in many countries are less stringent than they are in the United States. For example, many countries require companies to protect personal consumer information but do not impose specific requirements on how companies must fulfill that requirement. By contrast, some countries have adopted requirements that are more stringent than U.S. requirements. Perhaps the most stringent requirements are imposed in the European Union (EU) in its Directive on Privacy and Electronic Communications. As described in Chapter 4, the Directive prohibits the transfer of personal information from the EU to a non-EU country unless the non-EU country provides adequate protection of the information. As the international exchange of information increases, such requirements will influence nations to adopt comparable requirements for protecting personal consumer information.

## Key Terms

functional regulation

Dodd-Frank Wall Street Reform and Consumer Protection Act (Dodd-Frank)

Consumer Financial Protection Bureau (CFPB)

systemic risk

Financial Stability Oversight Council (FSOC)

systemically important financial institution (SIFI)

affiliates

holding company system

holding company

subsidiary

financial holding company (FHC)

McCarran-Ferguson Act

solvency laws

market conduct laws

domestic insurer

foreign insurer

alien insurer

certificate of authority

insurance producer

financial condition examination

market conduct examination

receivership

receiver

Federal Insurance Office (FIO)

prudential regulation

depository institution

commercial bank

thrift institution

credit union

Federal Reserve System (the Fed)

Department of the Treasury

Office of the Comptroller of the Currency (OCC)

Federal Deposit Insurance Corporation (FDIC)

investment company

securities broker

securities dealer

broker-dealer

Financial Industry Regulatory Authority (FINRA)

registered representative

principal

prospectus

FINRA Rules

NAIC Insurance Information and Privacy Protection Model Act (Model Privacy Act)

nonpublic personal information

## Endnotes

1. Gramm-Leach-Bliley Act, 15 U.S.C. §§ 6801 (2011).

2. 12 U.S.C. §§ 5201 et seq. (2011).

3. 15 U.S.C. §§ 1011 et seq. (2011).

4. "Registration Form for Insurance Company Separate Accounts Registered as Unit Investment Trusts that Offer Variable Life Insurance Policies," SEC Release Nos. 33-8088, IC-25522, File No. S7-9-98 (12 April 2002), www.sec.gov/rules/final/33-8088.htm (28 July 2011).

5. FINRA Rules § 2111 (2011).

6. FINRA Rules §§ 3100 et seq. (2011).

7. NASD Rules §§ 2210 et seq. (2011).

10/23/2012 Exam Score 9/14 64% 1,3,4,9,13

Tough Chapter

## Chapter 6

# Contract Law

## Objectives

### *After studying this chapter, you should be able to*

- Describe the sources of contract law and apply conflict of law rules in a given situation to determine which jurisdiction's laws govern a contract
- Distinguish between (1) formal and informal contracts, (2) bilateral and unilateral contracts, (3) commutative and aleatory contracts, and (4) bargaining contracts and contracts of adhesion
- Distinguish among valid contracts, void contracts, and voidable contracts
- Identify and explain the four general requirements for the formation of a valid informal contract in most of the United States
- Identify some of the legal defenses that a defendant may have against a lawsuit for breach of contract
- Identify methods for discharging a contract and describe the remedies available for a breach of contract
- Explain the purpose and effect of the Statute of Frauds
- Describe the rules that the courts follow when interpreting the meaning of a contract
- Explain the purpose of the parol evidence rule and identify situations in which courts permit the use of parol evidence

# Outline

**Sources of Contract Law**

**Types of Contracts**
- Formal and Informal Contracts
- Bilateral and Unilateral Contracts
- Commutative and Aleatory Contracts
- Bargaining Contracts and Contracts of Adhesion

**General Requirements for a Contract**
- Mutual Assent
- Consideration
- Contractual Capacity
- Lawful Purpose
- International Laws

**Defenses to the Formation of a Contract**

**Contract Performance and Breach**

**Form of the Contract**

**Rules of Contract Construction**

**Parol Evidence Rule**

As we described in Chapter 2, a *contract* is a legally enforceable agreement between two or more parties. This agreement consists of a promise or a set of promises. For example, assume that a business agrees to lease office space. The lease agreement is a contract in which the leasing business—the *lessee*—promises to pay a specified amount of rent in exchange for the renting party's—the *lessor's*—promise to provide the office space throughout the term of the lease.

The fact that a contract is legally enforceable means that all of the parties have a legal duty to carry out the promises they made when they entered into the contract. A party breaches a contract by failing to carry out a promise it made when entering into the contract. A breach of contract by one party gives the other party a cause of action. The innocent party then has the right to seek a remedy from the courts for the breach.

People make many promises that they do not expect to be legally enforceable. For example, if you promise to attend a party with a friend, you usually do not expect your promise to have any legal consequences. Most jurisdictions around the world have developed a body of contract law to define which promises are legally enforceable and what remedies are available to enforce those promises. This chapter describes some of the general rules of contract law in the United States and other common law jurisdictions around the world.

Ugh. Contracts must be the most boring documents on the planet.

Well, you may think they're boring, but they're really important to the people who make agreements.

OK, but why do I need to know about contract law?

What if one of our customers doesn't understand that an insurance policy is a contract and that we are bound by the terms of that contract when we evaluate a claim? You might need to know a little bit about contract law to explain the customer's rights under that insurance contract.

# Sources of Contract Law

In the United States and many other common law jurisdictions, the courts have developed a body of common law, known as *case law*, to govern contracts. The common law of contracts includes general principles and rules that govern the formation and legal effect of contracts. We focus on these common law principles in this chapter.

Over time, the common law principles have been modified in some respects by the applicable legislatures. For example, most jurisdictions around the world have enacted statutes that apply to specific types of financial services contracts, such as insurance contracts. In Chapter 10, we describe how such statutes modify the general rules of contract law.

In the United States, the state governments are responsible for enacting laws that govern most contracts. Thus, each state has created its own body of contract law that generally applies to contracts entered into within that state. The basic features of these state laws, however, are fairly uniform, and most features of state contract laws also are found in the laws of many other common law jurisdictions.

As a general rule, the parties to a contract are free to decide which jurisdiction's laws will govern the validity and effect of their contract. Courts typically apply the laws of the place designated by the parties. If the parties did not specify which laws are to govern their contract and both parties are in the same jurisdiction, their contract generally is governed by the laws of that jurisdiction. When parties are in different jurisdictions and have not selected a jurisdiction to govern their contract, the conflict of law rules adopted by the affected jurisdictions determine which jurisdiction's laws govern the contract. Insight 6.1 describes some conflict of law rules that apply to contracts.

# Types of Contracts

The common law of contracts generally recognizes many types of contracts and includes rules that relate to each type of contract. In this section, we identify just a few of the many types of contracts recognized by the common law.

## Insight 6.1 Conflict of Law Rules for Contracts

Conflict of law rules to determine which jurisdiction's laws govern a contract vary from jurisdiction to jurisdiction. Many U.S. states and other common law jurisdictions follow the traditional common law rule, which states that a contract is governed by the law of the place where the contract was created. Typically, that is the place where the last act to create the contract was completed.

**Example.** A person who resides in State A entered into a contract with a person who resides in State B. The contract was completed when the written agreement was signed by the parties in State A. According to the traditional common law rule, the laws of State A govern the contract.

Many jurisdictions, including many states in the United States, follow a more modern conflict of law rule, known as the *center of gravity rule*, which states that the law of the jurisdiction that has the greatest interest in the contract governs the contract.

**Example.** A business in State A entered into a contract with a business in State B to construct an office building in State B. Although the contract was completed in State A, it is to be performed entirely in State B by workers who reside in State B. Following the center of gravity rule, a court could find that the law of State B governs because State B has a greater interest in the contract than does State A.

## Formal and Informal Contracts

Historically, the common law required that all contracts be formal written documents that included a seal, which is a particular mark that attests to the execution of the document. A *formal contract* is a contract that is enforceable because the parties met certain formalities concerning the form of the agreement. These formalities generally require that the contract be expressed in writing and that the written document contain some form of seal to be enforceable. Today, only a few types of contracts remain formal contracts. Many jurisdictions, for example, treat contracts for the sale of real property as formal contracts.

By contrast, most contracts, including life insurance contracts, are informal contracts. An *informal contract* is a contract that is enforceable because the parties met requirements concerning the substance of the agreement rather than requirements concerning the form of the agreement. With certain exceptions, an informal contract may be expressed in either an oral or a written fashion. Informal contracts expressed in writing do not need a seal to be enforceable. By expressing an agreement in writing, however, the parties provide evidence of the specific terms of the contract. Figure 6.1 illustrates the features of formal and informal contracts. This text focuses primarily on informal contracts.

## Bilateral and Unilateral Contracts

Contracts may be either bilateral or unilateral. A *bilateral contract* is a contract under which both parties make legally enforceable promises. For example, contracts for the sale of goods generally are bilateral contracts, because both parties

**Figure 6.1 Features of Formal and Informal Contracts**

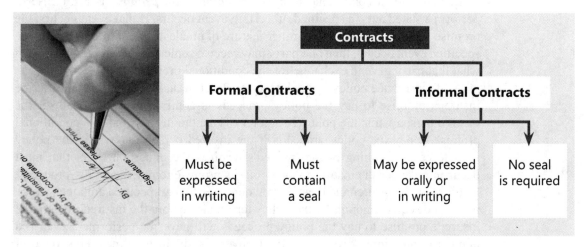

to the contract make an enforceable promise when they enter into the agreement. The purchasing party promises to pay the agreed-upon price, and the selling party agrees to provide the purchaser with specified goods at the agreed-upon price.

A *unilateral contract* is a contract under which only one of the contracting parties makes a legally enforceable promise. A life insurance policy is an example of a unilateral contract. The insurer that issues the policy promises to provide insurance coverage in return for the payment of a stated premium. As long as premiums are paid, the insurer is legally bound by its contractual promises. On the other hand, the purchaser of the policy does not promise to pay the premiums and cannot be compelled by law to pay the premiums. Instead, the policyowner has the right to stop paying premiums and to cancel the policy at any time.

## Commutative and Aleatory Contracts

Contracts also may be classified as either commutative or aleatory. A *commutative contract* is an agreement under which the parties specify in advance the values that they will exchange; moreover, the parties generally exchange items or services that they think are of relatively equal value. For example, contracts often involve the payment of a stated amount in exchange for the provision of specific services. In effect, the parties agree that the services to be provided are worth the payment of the stated price.

An annuity contract is an example of a commutative contract. The owner of an annuity contract pays a premium or premiums to the insurance company that issued the annuity. In exchange, the insurer agrees to make specified payments to a designated person. The amount paid for an annuity has a direct relationship to the amount that the insurer agrees to pay out under the annuity. The total amount of annuity benefit payments that will be made is based on several factors, including the amount paid for the annuity, the length of time over which the insurer will hold and invest those funds, and the length of time over which the insurer will make benefit payments.

In an *aleatory contract*, one party provides something of value to another party in exchange for a conditional promise. A *conditional promise* is a promise to perform a stated act *if* a specified, uncertain event occurs. If that event occurs, the promise must be performed. Another feature of an aleatory contract is that if the specified event occurs, then one party may receive something of greater value than what that party gave in exchange for the conditional promise.

A life insurance policy is an aleatory contract because the performance of the insurer's promise to pay the policy proceeds is contingent on the death of the insured person while the policy is in force. Thus, the insurer makes a conditional promise to pay the policy proceeds if the insured person dies while the policy is in force. The timing of the insured's death is the uncertain event that must occur in order for the insurer to carry out its promise to pay the policy proceeds. In addition, the insurer and the policyowner agree to pay specified amounts, which may not be equal amounts. If the policy terminates before the insured's death, the insurer's promise to pay the policy proceeds will never be performed, even if a number of premiums have been paid. Conversely, the insured may die soon after the policy is issued. In this situation, the death benefit payable may be a much larger amount than the total premiums paid.

**Example:**

Pat Li bought a $150,000 insurance policy on her life. After paying $1,200 in premiums, Ms. Li decided she no longer needed the insurance and terminated the policy. The insurer received $1,200 in premiums and was not obligated to pay any policy benefits.

**Example:**

Norm Key bought a $150,000 insurance policy on his life. Mr. Key died after paying $1,200 in premiums, and the insurer paid the $150,000 death benefit to the policy beneficiary.

So, do you understand why an annuity contract is commutative and a life insurance contract is *aleatory*?

I think so. An annuity is commutative because the owner and the insurer state in advance the values that they will exchange, and those amounts are directly related to each other.

That's right.

And a life insurance contract is *aleatory* because the policyowner gives something of value to the insurer in exchange for a conditional promise. The amounts the insurer and policyowner pay may or may not be equal.

 You've got it!

## Bargaining Contracts and Contracts of Adhesion

Contracts may be further classified as either *bargaining contracts* or *contracts of adhesion*. Most contracts are **bargaining contracts**, which are contracts created when both parties, as equals, set the terms and conditions of the contract. Both parties have the power to negotiate the terms of the contract. In other words, both parties have equal bargaining power.

By contrast, some contracts are **contracts of adhesion**, which are contracts that one party prepares and that the other party must accept or reject as a whole, without any bargaining between the parties as to the terms of the contract. In contracts of adhesion, one party has greater bargaining power than the other party. Only one party is in a position to specify the terms of the contract. Individual life insurance policies and annuities are contracts of adhesion, because the applicant for such a product generally must accept or reject the contract as the insurance company has written it.

# General Requirements for a Contract

The principles of contract law within each jurisdiction determine the legal status of contracts governed by the jurisdiction's laws. Such principles determine whether a given contract is legally enforceable and who has the right to enforce the contract. In describing the legal status of a contract, the words *valid*, *void*, and *voidable* are often used.

- A **valid contract** is a contract that is enforceable by law.

- A **void contract** is an agreement that was never enforceable by law. The term *void contract* is actually a contradiction in terms because it implies that a contract of some kind exists. In reality, *void contract* means that the parties did not create a contract.

- At times, one of the parties to an otherwise enforceable contract has grounds to reject, or *avoid*, the contract. A **voidable contract** is one in which a party has the right to avoid her obligations under the contract without incurring legal liability.

The specific requirements that the contracting parties must meet to create a valid contract vary from jurisdiction to jurisdiction. According to the common law rules in most of the United States, the formation of a valid informal contract involves four general requirements:

1. The parties to the contract must mutually assent (agree) to the terms of the contract.

2. The parties must exchange legally adequate consideration.

3. The parties must have contractual capacity.

4. The contract must be for a lawful purpose.

If any one of these requirements is not present, then one or all of the parties to the contract may have legal grounds to assert that the contract is not enforceable by law. Thus, we examine each of these requirements in detail.

## Mutual Assent

The requirement of mutual assent is sometimes described as a requirement that the parties reach a "meeting of the minds" concerning the terms of their agreement. In order to mutually assent to a contract, all of the parties must intend to be bound by the contract's terms. In addition, each party must clearly manifest the intent to be bound by making some outward expression of that intent.

Whether a party intended to be bound by the terms of a contract is a question of fact. Because outside parties cannot determine a party's subjective intent, the U.S. courts have adopted an objective test to determine whether the parties mutually assented to the terms of a contract. According to this test, the trier of fact must consider the party's actions and determine whether a reasonable person in the other party's place would have understood that those actions manifested assent to the contract and an intent to be legally bound.

> **Example:**
>
> Miguel Hernando alleges that Margaret Miller breached their contract. Ms. Miller maintains that she did not intend to be bound to a contract and did not agree to enter into a contract with Mr. Hernando. Thus, she maintains that no contract was created. In the civil trial, the trier of fact must look at Ms. Miller's actions and decide whether a reasonable person in Mr. Hernando's position would have understood that Ms. Miller assented and intended to be bound to a contract with Mr. Hernando. If Mr. Hernando was reasonable in understanding that Ms. Miller intended to be bound, the court is likely to find that the parties created a valid contract.

The parties typically manifest their mutual intent to be bound to a contract by one party's making an offer to contract, which the other party accepts. Thus, the required elements of mutual assent are an *offer* and an *acceptance*.

## *Offer*

An *offer* is a proposal that, if accepted by another according to its terms, constitutes a binding contract. The party who makes an offer is the *offeror*. The party to whom the offer is made is the *offeree*.

An offer to contract must be definite. An offer is definite when it indicates that the offeror intends to be legally bound if the offeree accepts the offer. The offered terms must be definite enough that any resulting contract can be enforced. Because parties often negotiate before entering into a binding contract, distinguishing between negotiating and making a definite offer is an important concept. Figure 6.2 gives some examples to illustrate the differences between negotiations and a definite offer.

---

## Figure 6.2 Negotiations Distinguished from Offers

Gwendolyn Brook, a homeowner, is having a discussion with Yoshi Morita, who makes general home repairs.

**Statement 1**

- Mrs. Brook says to Mr. Morita, "My roof needs repairs, and I think it should cost about $500 to repair it."

This statement is not an offer, because it does not include any definite terms and does not indicate that Mrs. Brook intends to enter into an agreement with Mr. Morita.

**Statement 2**

- Mrs. Brook says to Mr. Morita, "How much would you charge to repair my roof?"

This statement is not an offer, but rather is a request—known as an *invitation*—for Mr. Morita to make an offer to Mrs. Brook.

**Statement 3**

- Mrs. Brook says to Mr. Morita, "I will pay you $500 if you will repair my roof."

This statement includes a promise to pay a definite amount. It also indicates that Mrs. Brook would like to enter into an agreement with Mr. Morita on her stated terms. The terms of the contract are sufficiently definite that a resulting contract can be enforced. Thus, Mrs. Brook's statement can be considered an offer to contract.

---

Whether one party has made a definite offer is a question of fact. Courts in common law jurisdictions generally apply the objective test we described earlier to the facts of a given situation to determine whether one party made an offer to contract. The trier of fact must decide whether a reasonable person in the offeree's position would have understood that the other party made a definite offer to contract.

## Communication of the Offer

In addition to being definite, an offer is effective only if it is communicated to the offeree. An offer may be communicated orally or in writing, and it may be communicated to one or more people or even to the general public. In order to accept an offer, the offeree must know of the offer. Thus, the offeree must actually receive the offer. For example, if a person mails an offer to another person, the offer is not considered to have been made until that other person actually receives the offer.

## Duration of an Offer

When an offer terminates, the offeree loses the ability to accept the offer. An offer can terminate in several ways. First, an offer can lapse. In every case, the offeror controls the offer and has the right to specify the length of time during which the offer will remain open. If the offeree does not accept the offer within the specified time, the offer terminates—or *lapses*—at the end of the specified time. If the offeror does not specify a time limit, an offer is treated as if it remains open for a reasonable length of time. What constitutes a reasonable time is a question of fact that depends on the circumstances of the particular situation. The subject matter of the transaction, the manner in which an offer was communicated, and customs and trade practices may be relevant to determining what is a reasonable time. For example, an offer to buy a shipment of fresh vegetables, communicated by telephone, probably implies that an immediate reply is requested, because the vegetables are perishable goods. By contrast, an offer to buy a coin collection, communicated to the offeree by mail, does not imply that an immediate reply is expected.

Most offers are *revocable*, meaning the offeror can withdraw or revoke an offer at any time before it has been accepted. When the offeror revokes an offer, the offer terminates and the offeree no longer can accept the offer. An offer generally is revocable unless the offeror made a legally enforceable promise to keep the offer open for a specified time. Unless the parties have entered into a contract in which the offeror promises to keep an offer open for a specified time, an offeror usually can revoke the offer at any time before it is accepted.

An offer also terminates if the offeree rejects the offer in whole or in part. Once an offeree has rejected an offer, the offeree cannot later accept that offer unless the offeror agrees to reopen the offer. This rule is necessary to protect the offeror, whose circumstances may have changed by the time the offeree attempts to accept an offer that has already terminated.

> **Example:**
>
> Carol Wong offered to buy 100 shares of stock from Marvin Staley at its market value of $50 a share, and Mr. Staley rejected the offer. Mr. Staley cannot later accept the offer unless Ms. Wong agrees to reopen that offer. After Mr. Staley rejected her offer, Ms. Wong may have made another investment or the market value of the stock may have changed. It would be unfair to allow Mr. Staley to accept the offer after he had rejected it.

An offer must be accepted without qualification. If an offeree tries to substitute new terms or to modify the terms of the original offer in any way, then the offeree has rejected the offer and has made a **counteroffer**. A counteroffer terminates the original offer, because it constitutes a rejection of the offer. When an offeree makes a counteroffer, the process of forming a contract begins again. The parties, however, switch roles as illustrated in Figure 6.3. Thus, a counteroffer is an offer. The party who makes the counteroffer becomes the offeror, and the party to whom the counteroffer is made is the offeree.

If either party dies or loses contractual capacity after an offer has been made, the offer automatically terminates by operation of law. In such cases, the parties are unable to come to a meeting of the minds, and they cannot enter into an enforceable contract.

## Figure 6.3 Offer and Counteroffer

**Offeror**
**Buddy Inman**

"I'll repair your roof for $700."

Offer

**Offeree**
**Walt Bentley**

"Let me think about it."

**Buddy Inman**
becomes the
**Offeree**

"Okay. I'll do it for $600."

Counteroffer

**Walt Bentley** makes a counteroffer and becomes the **Offeror**

"I'll pay you $600 for those roof repairs."

## *Acceptance*

The *acceptance* of an offer is the offeree's unqualified agreement to be bound to the terms of the offer. Whether an offer was accepted is a question of fact that is evaluated by the objective test described earlier—that is, would a reasonable person in the offeror's position believe that the offeree accepted the offer? As long as all other requirements for a contract are met, a contract is created when an offeree unconditionally accepts an offer.

### Only the Offeree Can Accept

A general principle of contract law in the United States and many other jurisdictions is the principle of freedom of contract. According to the principle of *freedom of contract*, parties have the right to contract with whomever they choose and on whatever lawful terms they choose. The offeror controls the offer and has the right to decide with whom he will contract. The identity of the offeree in any given situation, therefore, is controlled by the terms of the offer. The offeree is that person or persons to whom the offeror intended to make an offer. Generally, only the offeree can accept an offer.

### Manner of Acceptance

The offeree can accept an offer in a variety of ways, depending on the circumstances of the situation. Typically, the nature of the offer controls how the offer must be accepted. For example, when an offeror makes an offer to enter into a bilateral contract, the offeror makes a promise and in exchange seeks a promise from the offeree. To create a contract, the offeree's acceptance must be in the form of a promise and typically would consist of words—oral or written—that indicate that the offeree intends to be bound. Alternatively, when an offeror makes an offer to enter into a unilateral contract, the offeror makes a promise and in return seeks the performance of an act. The offeree can accept the offer and create a contract by performing the requested act. The acceptance of an offer to enter into a unilateral contract, therefore, typically consists of conduct rather than words. Figure 6.4 illustrates the acceptance of an offer.

In any case, the offeree's acceptance must comply with all of the terms of the offer.

- If the terms of an offer require a specific manner of acceptance, the offeree must accept in the specified manner in order to create a contract. For example, if an offer requires acceptance in writing, the offeree must accept in writing.

- If the offer requires the offeree to perform more than one act to accept the offer, the offeree must perform all of the acts. For example, if the offer requires the offeree to sign a contract and send payment of a specified amount, signing the contract alone does not constitute acceptance.

- If the offeror does not specify a particular manner of acceptance, the offeree can accept the offer in any manner that is reasonable under the circumstances. In such cases, the manner of acceptance must clearly indicate that the offeree intends to accept the offer.

## Figure 6.4 Acceptance of an Offer

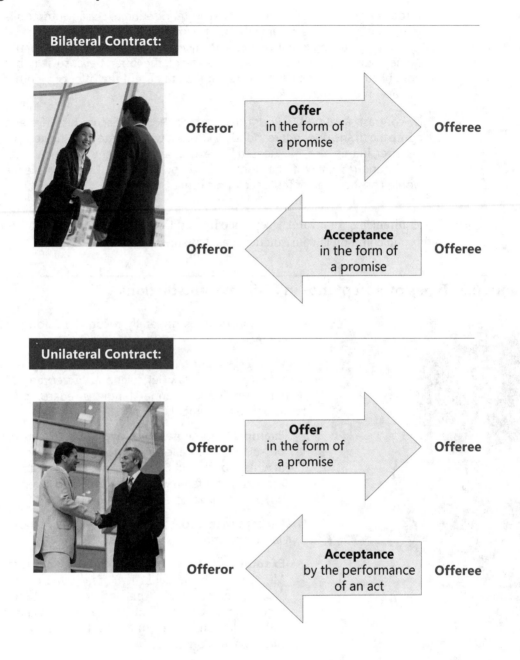

The offeree usually must manifest the intent to accept by making some outward expression of that intent. For example, when the parties put their agreement into writing, they generally all sign the document to show that they intend to be bound to the contract. As a general rule, the offeree's silence—that is, failure to reject an offer—does not constitute an acceptance.

> **Example:**
>
> Jorge Rodriguez sent Barbara Rosetti a letter offering to sell an automobile to her and ended the letter with the statement, "If I do not hear from you by Friday, I will know that you accept my offer." In this case, Ms. Rosetti's silence would *not* constitute acceptance of the offer because it is not possible to determine whether she intends to accept the offer or whether she ever received the offer.
>
> By contrast, assume Mr. Rodriguez and Ms. Rosetti discuss his offer and agree that if she does not respond by Friday it will indicate that she accepts his offer. In this case, Ms. Rosetti has expressed her intent that she will let Mr. Rodriguez know if she does not accept the offer. Thus, her silence would constitute an acceptance of his offer.

Requirements for a valid acceptance in civil law jurisdictions are quite similar to those in common law jurisdictions, as explained in Insight 6.2.

## Insight 6.2 Types of Acceptance in Civil Law Jurisdictions

Civil law jurisdictions generally recognize 3 forms of acceptance:

**Written acceptance** is the most preferred type of acceptance in civil law jurisdictions. Acceptance in written form limits misunderstandings regarding the terms of the agreement.

> **Example.** A furniture store advertised, "All couches on sale for $199 each. Acceptance must be made in writing before 7:00 p.m. on Friday." If a customer accepts that offer in writing before 7:00 p.m. on Friday, he will have accepted the store's offer.

**Oral acceptance** also is a valid form of acceptance in civil law jurisdictions.

> **Example.** While speaking to one of her students, Mrs. Lacita Alvado said, "I will teach you how to play the piano for $50 per lesson." Her student responded, "Great. I will see you Wednesday for my lesson." The student verbally accepted Mrs. Alvado's offer.

**Acceptance by conduct** is generally recognized in civil law jurisdictions.

> **Example.** David Ray visited Japan but could not speak Japanese. He went to a supermarket to purchase groceries, took the desired items from the shelf, and placed them on the counter in front of the cashier. The cashier totaled the price of the items and accepted Mr. Ray's payment in that amount. The cashier, thus, accepted Mr. Ray's offer to purchase the items by her conduct.

An acceptance made orally or in writing is known as an **express acceptance**. An acceptance by conduct is said to be an **implied acceptance**. Like common law jurisdictions, civil law jurisdictions allow the offeror to specify the manner in which the offer must be accepted.

## Consideration

To be enforceable, a contract must be supported by legally adequate consideration. *Consideration* is whatever a promisor asks for and receives in exchange for his contractual promise. As a general rule, consideration is legally adequate if it was bargained for and exchanged between the parties.

Courts in common law jurisdictions typically are not concerned with the actual value of the consideration received for a contract. Instead, the courts generally leave it to the parties to make their own agreement on the terms they choose. If the element of a bargained-for exchange of value exists, the requirement of legally adequate consideration is met.

According to general contract law, consideration can consist of either a promise or an act. Mutual promises, such as those exchanged in a bilateral contract, generally are adequate consideration for each other. Similarly, the performance of an act in exchange for a promise is adequate consideration to support a valid unilateral contract. For example, the act requested in exchange for a promise often is the payment of a specified amount of money. Figure 6.5 discusses the types of promises that do not qualify as adequate consideration.

## Contractual Capacity

*Contractual capacity* means that a person has the legal power to enter into a valid contract. The requirement is designed to ensure that contracting parties are mature enough and have the mental capacity to protect their own interests. As a general rule, everyone is presumed to have contractual capacity. Some persons, however, do not have such capacity, and contracts they enter into may not be valid and binding on all of the parties. The primary groups who have limited contractual capacity are persons who are (1) under the age of majority or (2) mentally incapacitated.

### Minors

Traditional common law rules stated that the age of majority was 21. Anyone younger than 21 was a *minor* who did not have full contractual capacity. Most legislatures, however, have enacted laws that modify the traditional common law rules. Most states now have made 18 the age of majority. Thus, in most states, contracts entered into by 18-year-olds are valid and binding on both parties. Figure 6.6 lists the age of majority in some other countries.

According to the common law, contracts entered into by a minor usually are voidable by the minor. Thus, a minor can enforce a contract against the other party to the contract, but the other party cannot enforce the contract against the minor. This rule protects minors against those who would take advantage of a minor's innocence or lack of experience. Because minors generally can avoid liability for their contracts, competent parties often are hesitant to contract with minors.

To protect competent parties and encourage them to contract with minors when the contract is beneficial to the minor, the common law provides some exceptions to the general rule that a minor's contracts are voidable by the minor. One of the primary common law exceptions states that a contract for necessaries is not voidable by a minor. *Necessaries* are goods and services that a minor or other incapacitated person actually requires to sustain her well-being. Whether specific goods and services are necessaries is a question of fact that must be answered on

## Figure 6.5  Promises that Do Not Qualify as Adequate Consideration

Courts sometimes decide that certain types of promises do not amount to adequate or sufficient consideration.

- A **gratuitous promise** is a promise that is not supported by consideration. A person who makes a promise and asks for nothing in exchange has made a gratuitous promise that is unenforceable.

    **Example.** Marta promised Vinnie that she would give him half of her paycheck. Marta did not bargain for anything in return from Vinnie. Thus, her promise to Vinnie is unenforceable.

- **Past consideration** is a promise made in exchange for actions or events that have already taken place. Consideration requires a bargain or exchange to occur immediately or in the future.

    **Example.** Jack washed the car of his friend, Su Lin, and did not charge her a fee. Two days later, Su Lin told Jack that she would pay him $20 for his kindness. Su Lin's promise to pay Jack $20 is unenforceable because it was made in return for an action that had already taken place.

- A promise to do what one has a legal duty to do is a promise to perform a **preexisting duty** and is, therefore, not sufficient consideration.

    **Example.** The ABC Building Company agreed to build new cabinets for Adam Stokely and entered into a contract with Mr. Stokely to perform the work for $8,000. After 2 weeks, ABC demanded an extra $2,000 to complete the work. Mr. Stokely agreed because he wanted the cabinets completed. However, his agreement to pay the extra $2,000 is unenforceable because ABC was already contractually obligated to build the cabinets for $8,000. Thus, ABC had a preexisting duty to build the cabinets for $8,000.

a case-by-case basis. For example, food, clothing, lodging, and medical attention typically are considered necessaries, but they are not necessaries if the minor does not actually need them. Thus, if a minor lives with his parents, and they provide him with food and clothing, a contract the minor enters into to purchase food or clothing probably is not a contract for necessaries. Although a minor may not avoid a contract for necessaries, the minor is required to pay only the reasonable value of such necessaries. Thus, if the contract price is greater than the reasonable value of the necessaries, the minor cannot be forced to pay the full contract price.

Legislatures have modified the common law rules to make some additional types of contracts valid and binding on minors. For example, many states have enacted laws that authorize minors of a stated age to enter into life and health insurance contracts if specific conditions are met.

## Figure 6.6  Age of Majority in Selected Jurisdictions

| Jurisdiction | Age of Majority |
|---|---|
| Argentina | 21 |
| Brazil | 18 |
| Canada | 18 or 19, depending on the province |
| China | 18 |
| Hong Kong | 18 |
| India | 18 |
| Malaysia | 18 |
| Scotland | 16 |
| Singapore | 21 |
| Taiwan | 20 |

Most other contracts are voidable by a minor. A minor's exercise of his right to avoid a contract is known as ***disaffirmance***. A minor can disaffirm a contract at any time before reaching the age of majority and within a reasonable time *after* attaining the age of majority. If a minor disaffirms a contract, the minor generally must return whatever consideration he received for the contract. If the minor returns the consideration, the minor can recover whatever he gave to the other party as consideration. The parties will be restored as much as possible to the same positions they were in before entering the contract.

## *Mental Incapacity*

To enter into a valid contract, each party must have the mental capacity to clearly understand the nature of the agreement and the effect of entering into the agreement. A party's mental incapacity is a question of fact that must be decided on a case-by-case basis. The effect of a party's mental incapacity on the validity of a contract depends on whether a court has found the person to be incompetent and has appointed a guardian for the person.

A ***guardian*** is an individual or group of individuals who is authorized by a court to take care of a person, known as the ***ward***, and manage the ward's property and affairs. Typical cases involve people who are incapacitated because of mental illness or defect, habitual drunkards, drug addicts, aged persons, and minors. Court proceedings generally are initiated by a family member who asks the court to protect the person from squandering his property or being taken advantage of by another party because he is unable to understand how to protect himself and his property. In such a case, the person's court-appointed guardian has the capacity to enter into contracts on the ward's behalf. Any contract the ward enters into without the consent of the guardian is void. The result is the same regardless of whether the other contracting party knew about the guardianship.

Sometimes a person's mental competence is impaired, but she has not been declared incompetent by a court. For example, a person can be mentally impaired as a result of being drunk, drugged, or mentally ill. The validity of a contract entered into by someone whose competence is impaired at the time of contracting depends on the person's ability to understand the agreement. For example, a mentally challenged person may be able to understand some simple transactions and yet not understand the terms of more complicated agreements.

## Contractual Capacity of Corporations

As a general rule, a corporation is a legal person that has the necessary capacity to enter into contracts. The specific limits placed on the contractual capacity of a corporation are spelled out in the corporation's articles of incorporation, which generally describe the types of activities and the type of business in which the corporation will engage. Statutes in many jurisdictions also place limits on the contractual capacity of corporations. In each case, the capacity of a given corporation to enter into a specific type of contract is an issue of fact that depends on the specific situation.

Applicable laws generally require financial services companies to operate as corporations, and a life insurer's articles of incorporation generally state that the corporation will engage in a life insurance business. To conduct a life insurance business in a given jurisdiction, the insurer generally must be licensed by that jurisdiction to conduct such a business. Thus, the insurer's capacity to issue life insurance contracts within a given jurisdiction depends both on the insurer's articles of incorporation and on whether the insurer has obtained a license to offer life insurance contracts in that jurisdiction.

According to laws in most jurisdictions, corporations also have certain implied powers to conduct their businesses. They generally have the power to enter into any kind of contract that would allow them to conduct normal operations. For example, corporations can contract for the office space, supplies, and services needed to operate their businesses.

## Lawful Purpose

When the purpose of an agreement is illegal, the agreement is illegal and void. The courts will not enforce such an agreement. Some agreements are illegal because they are agreements to commit an act that has been declared illegal by a statute. All jurisdictions have enacted laws that make certain acts punishable as crimes. An agreement to commit a crime is unenforceable in the courts. Likewise, an agreement to commit a tort is unenforceable in the courts.

An agreement also is illegal if it violates public policy or violates a principle of common law. Agreements that are contrary to public policy include agreements that unreasonably restrain a person's right to marry and agreements that unreasonably restrain competition. Insight 6.3 describes agreements that restrain competition.

## Insight 6.3 Agreements that Restrain Competition

The common law seeks to protect competition by prohibiting agreements that unreasonably restrain competition. Generally, an agreement not to compete with another party is void if the only purpose of the agreement is to restrain competition. However, an agreement that contains a noncompetition clause may be enforceable if it meets certain requirements. Such clauses sometimes are included in employment contracts, contracts for the sale of a business, and partnership agreements. The courts generally enforce a noncompetition clause if the following requirements are met:

- **The clause serves a legitimate business purpose.** For example, consider a case involving the sale of a business that has developed valuable relationships with its existing customers. The buyer has a legitimate business purpose for wanting to include a noncompetition clause under which the seller agrees not to operate a competing business to which the buyer's customers would defect. Other business interests that parties may try to protect are trade secrets or customer lists.

- **The restriction is reasonable in terms of its time limits, its geographic limits, and its scope.** For example, assume that Rupert Marvin is a salesperson for the Beta Manufacturing Company. Mr. Marvin's employment contract includes a noncompetition clause that prohibits him from competing with Beta in any activities within the United States for a period of 20 years after leaving employment with Beta. It is likely that such a clause would be unenforceable because the restrictions are unreasonably broad in time and geographic scope. In contrast, a more reasonable restriction would prohibit Mr. Marvin from contacting Beta's customers within his assigned sales territory for a period of one year after leaving employment with Beta.

- **The restraint does not impose an undue hardship.** For example, if a noncompetition clause would prevent a person from earning a living, the courts are not likely to enforce the clause.

Some aleatory contracts are illegal. The primary example of such an illegal contract is a *wagering contract* in which either party may gain or lose depending on the outcome of an uncertain event, such as a sporting event. Private wagering agreements are illegal and unenforceable. Recall that insurance contracts are aleatory contracts. State laws impose an insurable interest requirement to guard against insurance contracts being purchased as wagering contracts. An *insurable interest* exists when a person is likely to suffer a genuine loss or detriment should the event insured against occur. If the insurable interest requirement is met when a policy is purchased, the contract is not an illegal wagering agreement. We describe the insurable interest requirement in Chapter 10.

## International Laws

Although the specific requirements for the formation of a contract vary from jurisdiction to jurisdiction, the general requirements are similar. As a general rule, all jurisdictions require that the parties mutually agree to the contract. Typically, mutual agreement is established when one party makes an offer that the other party accepts. Insight 6.4 describes the requirements to form a valid contract in some civil law jurisdictions.

---

### Insight 6.4 Contract Formation in Civil Law Jurisdictions

In civil law jurisdictions, the basics of contract law typically are a part of a jurisdiction's **law of obligations.** Many obligations are imposed by applicable laws, such as obligations that arise when one's negligence harms another. An obligation also may arise as the result of a contract. A person, for example, who enters into a contract to hire another person becomes obligated to pay the agreed-upon wages in exchange for the other party's performance of the work. Civil law jurisdictions often impose the following requirements for the formation of a valid contract:

- **The parties must consent by means of an offer and an acceptance.** Certain persons, such as minors and mentally incompetent people, cannot consent to a contract. Note that this requirement is similar to the common law requirements of mutual assent and contractual capacity.

- **The subject matter of the contract must be certain.** Generally, anything that can be identified with certainty can be the subject of a contract. Services that are not illegal or against public policy also generally can be the subject of a contract. This requirement is similar to the common law requirement that contracts must be for a lawful purpose.

- **An obligation created by the contract must have a cause.** In other words, a party who becomes obligated under a contract must have an adequate cause for entering into the obligation. Generally, a party who becomes obligated receives something in exchange, such as the other party's promise or performance of an act. This requirement is similar to the common law requirement that the parties to a contract must exchange legally adequate consideration.

---

# Defenses to the Formation of a Contract

Although most contracts are carried out with few problems, when a dispute arises, the parties may resort to the courts. A breach of contract that results in damage to the innocent party gives the innocent party a cause of action against the breaching party. When a lawsuit is filed concerning a contract breach, the defendant may have any number of legal defenses to the lawsuit. If any requirement for the formation of a contract was not met, for example, the defendant has a defense to the lawsuit. Thus, assume that the defendant proves that he lacked the legal capacity to enter into the contract. Because the defendant lacked the necessary capacity to contract, the contract is void or voidable by the defendant and the plaintiff's action for breach of contract will fail. A number of other defenses are available, including duress, undue influence, misrepresentation, and fraud.

For a contract to be valid, the parties all must freely enter into the contract. Therefore, if one party enters a contract under duress, the contract generally is voidable by that party. **Duress** exists when a person acts wrongfully or threateningly to overpower the will of another so as to force that person to enter into a contract against her own free will. Duress can take a number of forms, such as threats or physical or mental coercion. When a person enters into a contract under duress such that a reasonable person would have been compelled to enter into the contract against her will, then the contract generally is voidable by the person.

Similarly, a contract created by the use of undue influence is voidable by the party who was the subject of the undue influence. **Undue influence** generally involves the misuse by one person of a position of trust or confidence to overcome the free will of another person. For example, a party may—because of weakness, trust, or dependence—unreasonably rely on the advice of another. The potential for undue influence exists in relationships between lawyer and client, doctor and patient, guardian and ward, and parent and child. The stronger party exerts undue influence by using his position to persuade the weaker party to act for the benefit of the stronger party rather than the weaker party.

A **misrepresentation** is an untrue statement of a fact. As a general rule, when one party makes a **material misrepresentation**—that is, a misrepresentation that induces the other party to enter into a contract that it would not have entered had it known the truth—the contract is voidable by the innocent party. Such a contract is voidable even if the misrepresentation was made in good faith with the belief that it was true. A fraudulent misrepresentation made with knowledge and the intent to deceive the other party also makes a contract voidable by the innocent party. Material misrepresentation is an important defense for insurers because they must be able to rely on representations of fact provided by applicants for insurance. We describe material misrepresentation in the formation of life insurance contracts in Chapter 13.

## Contract Performance and Breach

A contract is performed when each party has satisfactorily carried out her contractual obligations. For example, a contract for the sale of goods is performed when the goods have been delivered to the buyer, who pays for the goods in full. When a party carries out her obligations, she is discharged and has no further obligations under the contract. Insight 6.5 describes some other ways in which a party can be discharged from further contractual obligations.

## Insight 6.5 Methods for Discharging a Contract

Typically, a party is discharged from further contractual obligations after he performs his contractual obligations. Contracting parties also can be discharged in the following situations:

- The parties can discharge a contract by mutual agreement.

- The parties can discharge a contract by entering into an agreement known as an ***accord and satisfaction***, in which one party agrees to accept something other than what he was entitled to receive under the original contract.

- A party can waive his right to require another party's performance of a contract. A ***waiver*** is the voluntary relinquishment of a known right. Such a waiver discharges the other party's obligation to perform the contract.

As a general rule, the effect on a contract of a breach of that contract depends on whether the breach is a *minor breach* or a *substantial breach*. After a minor breach, the contract typically remains valid and enforceable. Parties continue to have a duty to perform their remaining contractual obligations. The innocent party, however, may have the right to have the breach remedied.

> **Example:**
>
> Ellen Cain entered into a contract with the Acme Construction Company. Acme promised to build Ms. Cain a house, for which she agreed to pay a specified amount. Acme completed the house but failed to install a kitchen oven in accordance with the terms of the contract. Acme substantially performed its part of the contract by building the house, so Ms. Cain is required to pay Acme the purchase price. However, Ms. Cain also has the right to have the breach remedied; Acme must either install the oven or be liable for the damages that result from its failure to install the oven. The amount of those damages would include, for example, the cost of having someone else install the oven.

By contrast, when one party substantially breaches a contract, the innocent party has two possible courses of action. She can affirm the contract and treat it as if it were valid and binding. Alternatively, the innocent party can treat the contract as if it were terminated. This option excuses her from performing any remaining contractual obligations. In addition, the innocent party has a right to a remedy for the damages that resulted from the breach.

Whether a contract has been performed and whether a party has breached a contract are questions of fact. In deciding such questions of fact, the courts are likely to consider all of the circumstances surrounding the transaction. For example, the trier of fact will consider whether the innocent party received the benefit he bargained for and the extent to which the breaching party performed the contract.

# Form of the Contract

As a general rule, informal contracts may be entirely oral, partly oral and partly written, or entirely written. Unless a statute requires an informal contract to be in writing, an oral informal contract is valid. However, for a number of practical reasons, contracting parties often seek to protect their interests by putting their agreements in writing. A written agreement provides evidence that the contract exists and evidence as to the terms of the contract. If a lawsuit concerns an oral contract, the parties not only must prove that a contract was formed, but they also must prove the terms of the contract. Proving these facts is often difficult. If there is no written evidence of the contract, the court must base its decision solely on the conflicting testimony of the parties to the contract.

A number of statutes require certain kinds of contracts to be in writing. Most U.S. states and other common law jurisdictions have enacted some form of the common law Statute of Frauds. The **Statute of Frauds** is a law that declares certain types of contracts to be unenforceable unless they are evidenced by a written document signed by the party to be charged with performing the contract.

> **Example:**
>
> Myra Baxter filed a lawsuit in which she alleges that Carl Chen breached their contract. The contract is governed by the Statute of Frauds. To prevail in her action, Ms. Baxter must provide evidence in the form of a written document that contains the contract's terms and is signed by Mr. Chen. If Ms. Baxter cannot produce such evidence, then the Statute of Frauds provides Mr. Chen with a legal defense to the lawsuit, and the contract will be unenforceable.

The Statute of Frauds typically governs the following types of contracts, which must be in writing to be enforceable:

- A promise by the executor or administrator of a deceased person's estate to answer for a debt of the deceased out of the executor's or administrator's own funds.

- A promise to be responsible for the debt or default of another.

- An agreement made in consideration of marriage.

- A contract concerning an interest in land.

- An agreement that cannot be performed according to its terms within one year after the contract is completed. Thus, if it is at all possible for the parties to perform a contract within one year, then the contract is not subject to the Statute of Frauds and need not be in writing to be enforceable. Insurance contracts generally can be performed within one year. Thus, they are not required to be in writing by the Statute of Frauds. By contrast, an agreement to enter into a partnership to last for 10 years cannot be performed according to its terms within one year and must be in writing in order to be enforceable.

The Statute's requirement of a written document usually is met if the plaintiff in a lawsuit produces a writing that contains the essential terms of the agreement. This writing must be signed by the party to be charged with performing the contract—that is, the defendant. The other party need not have signed the document. In addition, the writing may consist of more than one document as long as the documents refer to each other and are clearly connected with one transaction.

Keep in mind that the Statute of Frauds is only one law that may require a specific type of contract to be in writing. Figure 6.7 lists several types of agreements for which states and other common law jurisdictions have imposed a writing requirement.

## Figure 6.7 Additional Writing Requirements

Several states and other common law jurisdictions have imposed a writing requirement for the following types of agreements:

- Insurance contracts
- Promises to pay debts discharged in bankruptcy
- Agreements to pay commissions to real estate agents
- Agreements that cannot be performed during the lifetime of the promisor

Be sure you're clear on this issue. Although the Statute of Frauds does *not* require insurance contracts to be in writing, many states and other common law jurisdictions have passed additional laws that *do* require insurance contracts to be in written form.

# Rules of Contract Construction

Disputes between the parties to a contract often concern the meaning of the contract's terms, and courts often are called on to interpret the meaning of those terms. When the terms of a contract are clear and unambiguous, no interpretation is needed. The terms of the contract will be given effect in accordance with their clear meaning. A court cannot rewrite a contract for the parties. The court must enforce the contract as the parties wrote it.

If the terms of a contract are not clear, however, the court must follow established rules of contract construction to interpret the meaning of the contract. In common law jurisdictions, these rules of contract construction typically are found in the jurisdiction's case law. In civil law jurisdictions, rules of contract construction typically are found in the jurisdiction's statutory law.

A court's primary goal in interpreting a contract is to determine what the parties intended when they entered into the contract. The court must look to the words that the parties used in the contract as the basic source of the parties' intent. Generally, courts try to determine the most reasonable meaning of the contract given the circumstances of the situation. The question the courts try to answer is, "What would a reasonable person in the position of the parties have understood the contract to mean?"

In interpreting the meaning of a contract, a court must consider the entire contract. It must consider all of the words included in the contract and construe all of the contract's provisions together to determine the purpose and intent of the contract. The court must construe the contract so that all of its provisions are given effect in a consistent and reasonable manner.

Courts generally give words their plain, ordinary meaning. Nevertheless, the intent of the parties controls the meaning of words used in a contract. For example, if the parties seem to have intended a word to have a technical meaning, the court will construe the contract by giving the word its technical meaning.

Occasionally, a contract consists of a preprinted form on which the parties have handwritten or typed additions or changes to the form. In interpreting such a contract, the courts generally place more importance on the handwritten or typed portions of the contract. The rationale for this practice is that handwritten or typed portions are more likely than the preprinted portions to represent the parties' intent. Thus, if a preprinted portion conflicts with a handwritten or typed portion, the handwritten or typed portion generally is given effect. If a handwritten portion conflicts with a typed portion, the handwritten portion generally is given effect.

Courts typically construe unclear or ambiguous language against the party who drafted or prepared the written contract, unless the use of the unclear language was required by law. This rule, known as the *rule of contra proferentem*, is applied most often to contracts of adhesion such as insurance policies. If an insurance policy is found to contain ambiguous terms, the courts will construe the contract against the insurer and in favor of the policyowner or beneficiary.

## Parol Evidence Rule

As noted in Chapter 2, the parties to a lawsuit must prove their side of a lawsuit by producing evidence. The courts have developed procedural rules that govern the evidence that may be produced at trial. One such procedural rule, known as the ***parol evidence rule***, states that parol evidence is *not* admissible to add to, vary, or contradict the terms of a written contract. ***Parol evidence*** is evidence that is extrinsic to—that is, outside of—a written agreement. Parol evidence may be oral evidence, such as the testimony of witnesses concerning the negotiations leading up to the contract, or it may be written evidence, such as letters or memoranda.

The common law courts developed the parol evidence rule to allow contracting parties to rely on the certainty of a written contract and to prevent one party from subsequently trying to change the terms of the agreement to her advantage. The rule applies only when the parties entered into a valid written contract and intended the writing to contain their entire agreement. In other words, if the writing is clear, definite, and complete, the law presumes that the parties reduced their entire agreement to that writing. Thus, parol evidence is not admissible to add to, vary, or contradict the writing. The rule, however, does not prevent the introduction of evidence that is intended to prove that no contract was formed. For example, the defendant has the right to introduce evidence that the contract was illegal and void or was entered into under duress.

The parol evidence rule also applies only when the written contract is clear and unambiguous. In such cases, the courts will enforce the contract as written and will exclude parol evidence that contradicts the written contract. Parol evidence, however, is admissible to aid a court in interpreting a written contract that is unclear. For example, the parties are allowed to introduce evidence to explain the meaning of technical terms and terms that have a special trade meaning or a special meaning in the locality where the contract was completed.

As with most procedural rules, the parol evidence rule has a number of exceptions. The following are some specific situations in which courts permit the use of parol evidence:

■  When it is reasonably certain that the written contract does not contain all of the terms that the parties intended to include in their agreement, the courts permit parol evidence to prove the omitted terms.

■  When the parties made an oral agreement after they reduced their original agreement to writing, the courts permit parol evidence concerning the subsequent oral agreement.

■  When the written contract does not express the true intent of the parties, the courts permit parol evidence concerning the actual intent of the parties. For example, assume that the parties agreed on a contract price of $10,000 but mistakenly drafted the written contract to state a price of $100,000. The parties are permitted to introduce parol evidence concerning the contract price.

# Key Terms

| | |
|---|---|
| center of gravity rule | gratuitous promise |
| formal contract | past consideration |
| informal contract | preexisting duty |
| bilateral contract | contractual capacity |
| unilateral contract | minor |
| commutative contract | necessaries |
| aleatory contract | disaffirmance |
| conditional promise | guardian |
| bargaining contract | ward |
| contract of adhesion | wagering contract |
| valid contract | insurable interest |
| void contract | duress |
| voidable contract | undue influence |
| offer | misrepresentation |
| offeror | material misrepresentation |
| offeree | accord and satisfaction |
| counteroffer | waiver |
| acceptance | Statute of Frauds |
| freedom of contract | parol evidence rule |
| consideration | parol evidence |

## Chapter 7

# Agency Law

## Objectives

---

### *After studying this chapter, you should be able to*

■ Describe the agency relationship between a principal and an agent

■ Identify the various types of authority an agent may possess to act on behalf of a principal

■ Describe an agent's duties to the principal and the principal's duties to the agent, and identify the remedies available if either party breaches the agency agreement

■ Identify situations in which a principal is liable to a third party with whom an agent deals on the principal's behalf

■ Identify situations in which an agent acting on behalf of a principal is liable to a third party

■ Describe the four methods by which an agency relationship can terminate, and explain when a principal has a duty to notify third parties of the termination

# Outline

### The Agency Relationship
- Agency Agreement
- Effect of Agency Relationship
- Capacity of the Parties

### Agent's Duties to the Principal
- Loyalty and Good Faith
- Obedience
- Competence
- Accounting
- Principal's Remedies

### Principal's Duties to the Agent
- Compensation
- Reimbursement
- Indemnification
- Agent's Remedies

### Principal's Liabilities to Third Parties
- Principal's Contract Liability
- Principal's Tort Liability

### Agent's Liabilities to Third Parties
- Agent's Contract Liability
- Agent's Warranty of Authority
- Agent's Tort Liability

### Termination of an Agency Relationship
- Termination by Act of a Party
- Termination by Mutual Agreement
- Termination by Performance of Agreement
- Termination by Operation of Law
- Principal's Duty to Notify Third Parties

The law defines an *agent* as a party who is authorized by another party, the *principal*, to act on the principal's behalf. *Agency* is the legal relationship between these parties. The rights, duties, and liabilities that arise among the parties when an agent represents a principal in dealings with third parties are the subject of the *law of agency*. This chapter describes some of the basic rules of agency law in the United States and most common law jurisdictions. The specifics of agency law vary somewhat from jurisdiction to jurisdiction, but the basic rules are similar in most common law jurisdictions.

We refer to our insurance sales force as agents.

That's true, and they usually have an agency relationship with the company. But other employees also act as agents for the company.

# The Agency Relationship

An agency relationship can take many forms, and an agent may hold broad authority to act on behalf of the principal. Alternatively, an agency relationship may be created for a limited purpose or one specified transaction. Agency relationships also can vary in duration. These relationships may be ongoing, or they may be created for a specified duration of time. The scope of an agent's authority and the duration of the agency relationship often depend on the type of transactions in which the agent and principal are involved. Figure 7.1 lists transactions that often involve agency relationships.

## Figure 7.1 Transactions that Often Involve Agency Relationships

**Real estate transactions.**

A buyer may select a salesperson to act as her real estate agent in buying a home. Conversely, a seller may select a salesperson to act as his real estate agent in selling a home.

**Financial services transactions.**

A person may select a stockbroker to purchase stock on his behalf. An insurance company often appoints people to act on its behalf in selling its insurance and annuity products.

**Contract negotiations.**

An athlete may select an individual to act as his agent in contract negotiations.

## Agency Agreement

Typically, an agency relationship is created by an agreement between the principal and agent. As part of an agency agreement, the principal confers actual authority on the agent. *Actual authority* is the authority to act on behalf of the principal that the principal intentionally confers on the agent and that the agent reasonably believes is conferred. Actual authority can be either express or implied. *Express authority* is the authority that a principal explicitly confers on an agent. *Implied authority* is the authority that a principal intends an agent to have and that arises incidentally from an express grant of authority. For example, a corporation's board of directors typically confers express authority on the corporation's officers to perform certain acts to carry out the corporation's business. In addition, the officers have implied authority to do all other acts that are reasonably necessary to carry out their express duties.

As a general rule, a principal may do anything through an agent that the principal can legally do for himself. Some acts, however, are of such a personal nature that they cannot be delegated to an agent. For example, an individual cannot vote in a government election through an agent. The law requires individuals to perform such an act themselves.

The scope of an agent's actual authority is a question of fact. The courts typically use an objective test to determine the scope of that authority. In applying this objective test, the trier of fact must determine what authority a reasonable person in the position of the agent would understand the principal to have conferred on the agent.

No formalities are required to create an agency relationship. The parties generally may consent either orally or in writing. Some agency agreements, however, must be in writing to be enforceable. For example, the Statute of Frauds requires an agency agreement that is to last for more than one year to be in writing in order to be enforceable by the courts.

## Effect of Agency Relationship

When an agent acts within the scope of her authority, the agent's acts typically are considered to be the acts of the principal.

> **Example:**
>
> Tony Gallagher owed money to a creditor and repaid the money to an agent who had authority to accept such a payment on behalf of the creditor. Mr. Gallagher's payment to an agent who was authorized to accept the payment on the principal's behalf is considered to be payment to the principal. If the agent does not give the money to the principal, the principal cannot seek to recover the money from Mr. Gallagher.

Likewise, contracts entered into by an agent within the scope of her authority are binding on the principal.

The knowledge an agent gains while carrying out the principal's business typically is considered to be the knowledge of the principal. Regardless of whether the agent actually communicates the information to the principal, the principal is deemed to have the information.

> **Example:**
>
> Saul Schwartz authorized his agent, Paula Takedo, to purchase land to be developed as residential property. Ms. Takedo discovered that the land was suitable for residential development but that the costs of residential development would be excessive compared to the costs to develop other nearby sites. Nevertheless, Ms. Takedo completed a contract to purchase the land without communicating her knowledge about the land to Mr. Schwartz. As a general rule, Mr. Schwartz will be deemed to have Ms. Takedo's knowledge about the transaction and will be bound to the contract to purchase the land.

## Capacity of the Parties

The legal effect of a contract entered into by an agent on behalf of the principal depends in part on the contractual capacity of the principal. For a contract entered into by an agent to be valid and binding on the principal, the principal must have contractual capacity. For example, if a minor appoints an agent who enters into a contract for non-necessaries on the minor's behalf, the contract is voidable by the minor. Likewise, a principal who has been judicially declared to be insane lacks contractual capacity. Any contracts that an agent tries to create on behalf of such a principal generally are void.

An agent who enters into a contract on his principal's behalf is not a party to that contract. Thus, the agent generally does not need to have contractual capacity to form a contract that binds the principal. In appointing an agent, however, the principal assumes the risks of being represented by the agent. For example, assume that a competent principal appoints a minor as her agent. Any contract the minor enters into within the scope of his authority as an agent is binding on the principal. Because the agent is a minor, however, the agency agreement between the agent and principal is voidable by the minor.

# Agent's Duties to the Principal

The terms of the agreement between a principal and agent determine the parties' rights and duties. In addition, the common law imposes a number of duties on agents. By empowering an agent to act on her behalf, a principal places her trust in the agent. Thus, the agent is a fiduciary, who must meet her fiduciary duties. Figure 7.2 summarizes these duties.

## Figure 7.2 Agent's Duties to the Principal

**Duty of loyalty and good faith:**

An agent must act primarily for the principal's benefit.

**Duty of obedience:**

An agent must obey the principal's lawful instructions.

**Duty of competence:**

An agent must use reasonable care, skill, and diligence in carrying out the agency duties.

**Duty of an accounting:**

An agent must account to the principal for all money that comes into the agent's possession as a result of the agency relationship.

## Loyalty and Good Faith

Because an agent acts in a fiduciary capacity, he owes a duty of undivided loyalty and good faith to the principal. This duty requires an agent acting within the scope of his authority to act primarily for the principal's benefit. An agent, therefore, must put the interests of the principal above all other interests, including the agent's own interests.

An agent's duty of loyalty and good faith requires the agent to provide the principal with all material information that relates to the principal's business. In addition, an agent may not engage in any business that interferes with or competes with the principal's business. In some circumstances, however, an agent may have a financial interest in a transaction that involves the principal. In such a case, the agent has a duty to fully disclose all material facts to the principal. The agent may deal on his own behalf in such a transaction only when the principal, with full knowledge of the material facts, consents to the transaction.

The duty of loyalty and good faith prohibits an agent from making secret profits from the agency relationship.

**Example:**

A principal authorized her agent to purchase certain property for her and to pay no more than $100,000. The agent purchased the property for himself for $80,000 and then resold the property to the principal for $100,000. By acting on his own behalf and profiting from the transaction, the agent violated his duty of loyalty to the principal. The $20,000 profit the agent realized actually belonged to the principal, who should have been the one to benefit from the $80,000 purchase price.

An agent also may not receive secret commissions or other secret payments from third parties. An agent who secretly profits from the agency relationship must turn over those profits to the principal.

## Obedience

An agent has a duty to obey the principal's instructions. Because an agent is acting for the principal, the agent must carry out her duties according to the principal's wishes. An agent, however, has no duty to obey instructions that are unlawful or unreasonable. For example, if an agent would be physically endangered by following the principal's instructions, the agent has no duty to follow the instructions. When an agent commits an unlawful act on the instructions of the principal, as a general rule both the agent and the principal are liable for the unlawful act.

## Competence

An agent has a duty to use reasonable care, skill, and diligence in carrying out her agency duties. The level of care required of an agent is that of a reasonably prudent person who has the same skills as the agent. Thus, an agent must use the degree of care that a reasonably prudent person with the same skills would use in the same or similar circumstances. An agent who fails to use reasonable care in carrying out her agency duties has breached a fiduciary duty owed to the principal.

## Accounting

An agent has a duty to account to the principal for all money that comes into the agent's possession as a result of the agency relationship. An agent also must keep proper records and account to the principal within a reasonable time after receiving money, as well as when the agency relationship terminates. Additionally, most states and other common law jurisdictions require that the principal's money be kept in a separate account.

## Principal's Remedies

An agent who fails to carry out the terms of the agency agreement is in breach of the agreement. For example, if an agent exceeds his actual authority and binds the principal to a contract with a third party, the agent has breached the agency agreement. Similarly, if an agent fails to carry out a fiduciary duty owed to the principal, the principal generally may consider the failure to be a breach of the agency agreement.

An agent's breach of the agency agreement provides the principal with legal justification for terminating the agency relationship. In addition, such a breach gives the principal the right to recover damages for the losses that resulted from the breach.

## Principal's Duties to the Agent

As a party to an agency agreement, a principal is obligated to carry out the agreement according to its terms. Unlike agents, principals are not fiduciaries. Nevertheless, the law imposes certain duties on principals. For example, when an agent is an employee of the principal, the principal must comply with applicable employment laws. The principal's duties are summarized in Figure 7.3.

## Figure 7.3 Principal's Duties to the Agent

**Compensation:**

A principal generally has a duty to pay an agent the reasonable value of the agent's services, unless the parties have agreed otherwise.

**Reimbursement:**

A principal generally has a duty to reimburse an agent for all reasonable expenses incurred in performing the agency duties, unless the parties have agreed otherwise.

**Indemnification:**

A principal generally has a duty to compensate an agent for any losses the agent incurs while performing the agency duties.

## Compensation

The principal and agent typically agree on how the agent is to be paid for his services. When the parties do not agree on compensation in advance, however, the principal has a duty to pay the agent the reasonable value of his services. What constitutes a reasonable value for services is a question of fact that depends on the circumstances surrounding the situation. Factors that might be considered in determining the reasonable value of an agent's services include the

- Types of services the agent provided

- Prior dealings between the parties

- Customs and trade practices of the business

A principal has no duty to pay an agent who agrees to provide services without compensation.

## Reimbursement

The parties may agree as to whether the principal will reimburse the agent for expenses she incurs in carrying out her agency duties. A principal generally has a duty to reimburse an agent for all reasonable expenses incurred in performing her agency duties unless the agency agreement provides otherwise. Whether an expense is reasonable is a question of fact.

## Indemnification

A principal generally has a duty to indemnify an agent for any losses the agent incurs while performing his duties as long as the loss was not the result of the agent's negligence or misconduct. *Indemnification* means the compensation or reimbursement of another person's loss. A principal's duty to indemnify an agent usually arises in situations in which the agent's liability results from no fault of his own and while he was following the principal's instructions.

> **Example:**
> An agent followed his principal's instructions and entered into a contract with a third party. The agent was held personally liable on the contract and was forced to pay money to the third party. The principal has a duty to indemnify the agent for the amount the agent had to pay out under the contract.

## Agent's Remedies

If the principal breaches the agency agreement, the agent typically can terminate the contract. In addition, the agent has a legal cause of action against the principal for breach of contract. For example, if the principal fails to compensate the agent, the agent may bring a civil lawsuit to recover the amount owed.

# Principal's Liabilities to Third Parties

As noted, when an agent acts on behalf of a principal in dealings with a third party, legal issues sometimes arise between the third party and the principal. In this section, we describe some of these issues.

## Principal's Contract Liability

Whether a principal is bound to a contract made by an agent depends on whether (1) the principal was disclosed, partially disclosed, or undisclosed and (2) the agent was acting within the scope of his actual or apparent authority.

### Disclosed, Partially Disclosed, and Undisclosed Principal

When an agent enters into a contract with a third party on behalf of a named principal, the principal is known as a *disclosed principal*. When the named parties to a contract are the disclosed principal and the third party, the principal is personally liable under the contract.

Occasionally, an agent contracts in her own name with a third party on behalf of a partially disclosed or an undisclosed principal.

■ When an agent contracts on behalf of a principal but does not identify the principal, the principal is known as a *partially disclosed principal*. In such a case, the agent discloses that he is acting on behalf of a principal, but the principal is not named as a party to the contract.

■ When an agent purports to act on his own behalf and does not mention the existence of a principal, the principal is known as an *undisclosed principal*.

In the foregoing cases, the third party may enforce the contract against the partially disclosed or undisclosed principal. However, the principal may enforce the contract against the third party only if the agent acted within the scope of her actual authority.

## *Actual and Apparent Authority*

An agent's authority to bind the principal may be actual authority or apparent authority. We described an agent's actual authority earlier in the chapter. ***Apparent authority*** is authority that is not expressly conferred on an agent but is authority that the principal either intentionally or negligently allows a third party to believe the agent possesses. When a principal allows a third party to reasonably believe that an agent has authority to bind the principal and the third party relies on the appearance of that authority, the agent is deemed to have had apparent authority. The principal is then bound by the agent's act.

An agent's apparent authority is created by intentional or negligent acts of the principal. Although it is sometimes difficult for a third party to know the scope of an agent's actual authority, third parties must act reasonably and prudently to protect themselves. A third party, therefore, cannot rely solely on the appearances created by an agent and has a duty to use reasonable care to determine the scope of the agent's actual authority. Whether an agent had actual or apparent authority to bind a principal is a question of fact. The third party bears the burden of proving that the agent had actual or apparent authority to act on behalf of the principal. While actual authority is created by a principal's representations to an agent, apparent authority is created by a principal's representations to a third party. Figure 7.4 discusses the basic elements of proving apparent authority.

So *actual* authority is something a principal intentionally gives to an agent.

Whereas *apparent* authority is something the principal communicates–on purpose or otherwise–to a third party about an agent.

You're both correct. And if an agent is found to have had either actual *or* apparent authority, the principal is bound by that agent's act.

## Figure 7.4 Proving Apparent Authority

Most common law jurisdictions require a showing of the following three elements to prove apparent authority:

- A representation by the principal to a third party
- A reliance on that representation by a third party
- A change in position by a third party in reliance on that representation

When an agent enters into a contract on the principal's behalf without actual or apparent authority to bind the principal, the contract generally is not binding on the principal. In this situation, a principal may reject or accept the contract. A principal accepts such a contract by ratifying the agent's unauthorized actions. *Ratification* is the adoption by a principal of an act that was taken on the principal's behalf but without the principal's authorization. By ratifying a contract, the principal affirms that he is a party to the contract. The contract is then effective as of the date it was originally entered into by the agent and the third party. A principal may ratify an unauthorized act even if there was no agency relationship with the purported agent. In such a case, ratification of the unauthorized action creates an agency relationship known as *agency by ratification*.

For a ratification to be effective, the following requirements must be met:

- A principal can ratify only those contracts that she could have authorized. A principal, for example, cannot ratify an illegal contract.

- The agent must have purported to act on behalf of a principal. If an agent purported to act on his own behalf without disclosing the existence of the principal, the principal cannot ratify the agent's unauthorized acts.

- Before ratifying such a contract, the principal must have full knowledge of all of the material facts surrounding the transaction.

- The principal must ratify the entire contract. She must accept both the favorable and unfavorable terms of the contract.

- The principal must ratify the contract within a reasonable time. Furthermore, the third party may withdraw from the contract at any time before it is ratified. Thus, if the third party withdraws from the contract before it is ratified, any subsequent attempt at ratification by the principal is ineffective.

Depending on the circumstances, a principal's ratification may be either express or implied and may consist of words or conduct. For example, if the principal begins to perform the contract according to its terms, that performance indicates that the principal has ratified the contract. The principal's silence may be ratification if the facts are such that the principal would be expected to object if she did not intend to ratify the contract. Whether a principal ratified an unauthorized act is a question of fact.

## Principal's Tort Liability

As we discussed earlier in this text, the law distinguishes between employees and independent contractors. An agent may be an employee of the principal or an independent contractor. For example, a business owner might appoint one of his employees as an agent, who is authorized to contract on behalf of the business. Alternatively, the owner might appoint someone other than an employee as an agent who is authorized to contract on behalf of the business. The principal's duties and liabilities with respect to an agent vary depending on whether the agent is the principal's employee or an independent contractor. Employers must comply with the applicable jurisdiction's employment laws. If an agent is considered an employee under a given employment law, the principal-agent relationship must comply with that law. In addition, the extent of a principal's vicarious liability depends on whether an agent acted in a given situation as an employee or independent contractor.

*Vicarious liability* is indirect liability. As a general rule, every person is responsible for his own acts. Thus, everyone is personally liable for the torts he commits. When an employee commits a tort while in the course of his employment, the employer also is liable for the tort. In other words, the employer is vicariously liable for the harm that resulted from the tort even though the employer may not have been directly at fault. In contrast, an employer generally has no vicarious liability for the torts of an independent contractor. Insight 7.1 describes vicarious liability in more detail.

## Insight 7.1 Vicarious Liability

The legal concept of vicarious liability grew out of a common law doctrine known as *respondeat superior*, which means "let the master answer." Although employees are personally liable for their own torts, employees often do not have the financial resources to compensate the individuals they injure. In addition, because the employer profits from the employee's employment, the employer is liable to a third party who is injured as a result of that employment.

A person injured as a result of another's tortious conduct faces several legal hurdles in winning a lawsuit against the wrongdoer's employer. First, the employer generally will have vicarious liability only if the wrongdoer was its employee. If the individual was an employee, the injured party also must prove that when the injury occurred, the wrongdoer was acting within the course of his employment. For example, assume that Katherine Hartwell was employed by the Farmington Company. While on vacation, Ms. Hartwell negligently caused an automobile accident and injured another person. Because the accident and resulting injuries had nothing to do with Ms. Hartwell's employment, the Farmington Company is not vicariously liable to the injured person. By contrast, if the accident had occurred while Ms. Hartwell was carrying out her job duties, the Farmington Company would likely have vicarious liability.

The question of whether an individual was acting in the course of her employment can become quite complicated. Courts typically consider the following factors:

- Whether the employee's conduct was the kind of conduct she was hired to perform

- Whether the tortious event occurred within the employee's normal work time

- Whether the event occurred at a place where the employee was authorized to be as a part of her employment

In most states, a person who is injured as a result of a tortious act committed by an employee acting within the course of her employment may file a lawsuit against both the employee and employer or may file separate lawsuits against them. The liability of the employer and employee in such cases is known as *joint and several liability*, which means that each defendant is independently liable for the entire amount of damages awarded to a plaintiff regardless of a defendant's share of responsibility for the losses. The total amount the plaintiff can recover is limited to the amount of damages awarded by the court.

OK, suppose a delivery driver is making a work delivery and she causes a car accident that injures another person. Who is responsible for paying damages to the injured person—the driver or the company she works for?

Under joint and several liability, both the driver and the company are liable for paying damages. The plaintiff has the right to recover damages from either one, or from both.

Regardless of their role in the accident? If the driver caused the accident, it's not the company's fault!

Yes, but that is part of the employer's vicarious liability—the employer is liable for torts an employee commits in the course of her work. Businesses typically carry insurance to protect them against that risk.

So I guess the company has to be very careful about who they hire!

Exactly.

## Agent's Liabilities to Third Parties

Although an agent typically is not a party to the contracts he enters into on behalf of a principal, an agent sometimes is personally liable under such a contract. An agent may be liable to a third party for breach of the warranty of authority or may have tort liability to a third party.

## Agent's Contract Liability

Whether an agent is personally liable under a contract to a third party generally depends on whether the agent contracted in her own name. When an agent contracts on behalf of a disclosed principal and the principal and third party are the named parties to the contract, the agent has no personal liability under the contract.

When an agent contracts in her own name on behalf of a partially disclosed or an undisclosed principal, the third party can enforce the contract against the agent and/or the principal. Likewise, the agent and the principal typically can enforce the contract against the third party. If an agent acted within the scope of her actual authority and was held personally liable on a contract entered into on behalf of a partially disclosed or an undisclosed principal, the agent is entitled to be indemnified by the principal for any losses the agent incurred.

## Agent's Warranty of Authority

An agent who acts, or purports to act, on behalf of a principal is deemed to warrant that she has authority to act for the principal and that she is acting within the scope of that authority. A *warranty* is a promise or guarantee recognized by law that a statement of fact is true. A *warranty of authority* is a guarantee recognized by law that an agent is acting on behalf of a principal who has contractual capacity and that the agent has authority to act for the principal.

If an agent does not have actual authority to act on behalf of the principal, the third party has a cause of action against the agent for breach of the warranty of authority. For example, if an agent enters into an unauthorized contract on behalf of the principal, the principal is not bound by the agent's acts. If the principal rejects the contract and chooses not to ratify it, the third party has a cause of action against the agent for breach of the warranty of authority. Figure 7.5 discusses the elements for proving a breach of warranty of authority in most common law jurisdictions.

### Figure 7.5 How to Prove Breach of Warranty of Authority

Most common law jurisdictions require a showing of the following three elements to prove a breach of warranty of authority:

- An agent represents that he has authority to act on behalf of a principal

- No such authority actually exists

- A third party relies on that misrepresentation to his detriment

## Agent's Tort Liability

As noted, every person is personally liable for his own torts. As a result, an agent who commits a tort while carrying out his agency duties is liable for the harm caused by the tort. For example, if an agent makes material misrepresentations and the third party is injured as a result, the third party may recover from the agent for the damages caused by the misrepresentations.

The relationships among principals, agents, and third parties are summarized in Figure 7.6.

### Figure 7.6 Principal and Agent Relationships with Third Parties

| Transaction with Third Party | Effect on Principal | Effect on Agent |
|---|---|---|
| An agent acts on behalf of a disclosed principal | The principal and the third party are bound to the contract | The third party has no cause of action against the agent |
| An agent contracts in his own name on behalf of a partially disclosed or undisclosed principal | The third party may enforce the contract against the principal | The third party may enforce the contract against the agent |
| An agent commits a tort while carrying out his agency duties | The third party has a cause of action against the principal only if the agent is an employee acting within the course of her employment when the tort is committed (vicarious liability) | The third party has a cause of action against the agent for harm that results from the tort |
| An agent acts on behalf of a principal but does not possess authority to do so | The principal is not bound by the agent's act | The third party has a cause of action against the agent for breach of the warranty of authority |

# Termination of an Agency Relationship

When an agency relationship terminates, the agent's actual authority to bind the principal is extinguished. In some situations, however, an agent continues to have apparent authority to bind the principal even after the agency relationship terminates. An agency relationship can terminate by (1) an act of one of the parties, (2) mutual agreement of the parties, (3) performance of the agency agreement, or (4) operation of law. The method by which an agency relationship ends affects the rights and liabilities of the principal, the agent, and any third parties who deal with the agent after termination of the agency relationship.

As discussed earlier, an agent may or may not be the principal's employee. The termination of an employment relationship must be distinguished from the termination of an agency relationship. Employment relationships are governed by a number of federal and state laws, such as antidiscrimination laws. Thus, termination of an agency relationship when the agent is an employee is governed by employment laws in addition to the law of agency.

## Termination by Act of a Party

Because agency is a relationship requiring the consent of both parties, either party has the power to end the relationship at any time. A party, however, may have the *power* to end the relationship but not the *legal right* to do so. For example, assume that a principal and agent enter into an agency agreement that is for a term of one year. Either the agent or principal has the power to end the relationship at any time during that year, but neither has the legal right to do so without the other's agreement. A party who ends an agency relationship without the legal right to do so is in breach of the agency agreement and is liable to the other party for any damages that result from the breach.

As we have noted, if an agent breaches a fiduciary duty, the principal has the right to terminate the agency relationship without liability to the agent. Similarly, when an agent has the legal right to terminate the agency relationship, the agent may do so without further liability to the principal. For example, an agent typically has a legal right to end the agency relationship when the principal refuses to compensate the agent in accordance with the agency agreement.

## Termination by Mutual Agreement

An agent and principal have the legal right to agree to end the agency relationship at any time without incurring further legal liability to each other. This is true whether or not the agency agreement included a termination provision. As long as both parties agree, they have the legal right to end their relationship at any time and on any terms they desire.

## Termination by Performance of Agreement

Many agency agreements state that they are to continue until a specified date or until a specified purpose is accomplished. When an agency agreement contains a specific termination provision, the agreement terminates upon the occurrence of the specified condition. Neither party has a duty to notify the other party of the termination or to take any action for the termination to be effective. When an agency agreement has been performed, the parties have no further liabilities or duties to each other.

When an agency agreement does not contain a specific termination provision, the relationship terminates after a reasonable time. What constitutes a reasonable time is a question of fact that depends on the circumstances surrounding the agency relationship. An agency relationship that is to continue for an unspecified amount of time is known as an ***agency at will***. Either the principal or agent has the legal right to terminate an agency at will at any time and for any reason by giving the other party notice of termination of the relationship. If the amount of notice required is not stated in the agency agreement, the terminating party must give a reasonable amount of notice. What is reasonable notice is a question of fact that may be affected by a number of factors, such as the customs and trade practices of the industry.

## Termination by Operation of Law

The occurrence of certain events results in the termination of an agency relationship by operation of law. Termination by operation of law means that an agent's authority to bind the principal automatically terminates as a result of the operation of law rather than as the result of an action of the agent or of the principal. The following are some of the events that terminate an agency relationship by operation of law:

- **Either the principal or the agent dies.**

- **The principal loses his contractual capacity.**

- **An event makes it impossible for the agency agreement to be performed.** For example, if a principal hires an agent to sell a house and the house is destroyed in a storm, the agency agreement can no longer be performed because its subject matter is gone.

- **The agent loses the capacity to perform the agency agreement.** For example, if the agent is required to have a license to perform the agency agreement and the agent loses her license, then the agent has lost the capacity to perform the agency agreement.

Upon the occurrence of such an event, the agency relationship is terminated by operation of law and the acts of the agent are no longer binding on the principal.

## Principal's Duty to Notify Third Parties

When an agency relationship terminates by operation of law, the agent's authority—actual and apparent—to bind the principal also is terminated by operation of law. Because the agent's authority automatically terminates in such cases, the principal generally has no duty to notify third parties of the termination. A third party who contracted with an agent on behalf of a principal after the agency terminated cannot enforce the contract against the principal. Likewise, the principal cannot enforce the contract against the third party. The third party's only recourse is against the agent, who may be held liable for breach of the warranty of authority.

When an agency relationship terminates for reasons other than by operation of law, the agent may continue to have apparent authority even though her actual authority to bind the principal has ended. Because apparent authority is created by the principal's actions, such authority continues until the principal takes action to revoke it. Any third party who is unaware that the agency relationship ended and who enters into a contract with the agent on behalf of the principal can enforce the contract against the principal. Consequently, the principal must take steps to revoke the agent's apparent authority by providing actual notice of the end of the agent's authority to third parties who dealt with the agent during the agency relationship.

The principal also must take steps to notify third parties who did not deal with the agent but who knew of the agency relationship. The principal must take whatever steps are reasonable to notify such third parties. What steps are reasonable is a question of fact that depends on the circumstances of the case. For example, if the agent has business cards, stationery, and other supplies that contain the name of the principal's business, the principal should recover those materials.

So, if a principal isn't careful, he could be bound to a contract entered into by someone who is no longer his agent.

That's right. It's up to the principal to make it known that the agency relationship has ended.

## Key Terms

agent
principal
agency
law of agency
actual authority
express authority
implied authority
indemnification
disclosed principal
partially disclosed principal
undisclosed principal
apparent authority
ratification
agency by ratification
vicarious liability
joint and several liability
warranty
warranty of authority
agency at will

## Chapter 8

# Property Law

## Objectives

### After studying this chapter, you should be able to

- Distinguish between real property and personal property
- Describe common methods of acquiring property and identify the various forms of property ownership
- Identify restrictions that may be placed on property ownership rights
- Explain how a property owner transfers ownership rights in real property through real estate sales and leases
- Explain how property is distributed when the property owner dies with a valid will and when the property owner dies without a valid will
- Describe the probate process and identify the roles that people play in administering an estate
- Distinguish between copyrights, patents, and trademarks or service marks, and explain how the owner of intellectual property can protect his rights in the property

## Outline

**Types of Property**

**Property Ownership**
- Acquiring Property Ownership
- Forms of Property Ownership
- Restrictions on Ownership

**Transfers of Ownership Rights**
- Real Estate Sales
- Real Estate Leases
- Testamentary Transfers

**Intellectual Property**
- Copyrights
- Patents
- Trademarks

The law of property governs all of the rights that a person has with respect to something. In legal terminology, ***property*** is anything tangible or intangible that is capable of being owned by someone. In the United States, property laws generally are a matter of state and local law, with some federal regulation of how people use their property. For the most part, however, U.S. property owners face only limited restrictions on property use. Other countries, however, place more extensive restrictions on property use.

What's the connection between property law and insurance? Isn't property law about real estate?

You're right that property law applies to real estate, or *real property*. There's another type of property, called *personal property*. Read on.

# Types of Property

In most countries, including the United States, property is characterized as either *real property* or *personal property*. **Real property**, sometimes referred to as *real estate*, consists of land and whatever is growing on or affixed to the land. Examples of real property include trees, buildings, and fences that are attached to the land. Some jurisdictions refer to real property as *immovable property*.

All property other than real property is characterized as **personal property,** or *movable property*. As illustrated in Figure 8.1, personal property can be further categorized as either *tangible property* or *intangible property*.

- ***Tangible property*** means an object or thing that can be physically possessed and that has value as an object. For example, the value of books, furniture, clothing, and other such physical objects typically consists of their usefulness or desirability as objects.

- **Intangible property** is property that consists of one or more intangible legal rights that have value because, if necessary, the rights can be enforced by the courts. Shares of stock, insurance policies, bonds, and interests in a trust fund are intangible property. For example, although a share of stock is evidenced by a piece of paper, the intangible property rights represented by the paper are what make the stock valuable. The shareholder has a number of property rights, such as the right to receive any dividends declared by the issuing corporation's board of directors and the right to vote in elections of the board.

## Figure 8.1 Types of Property

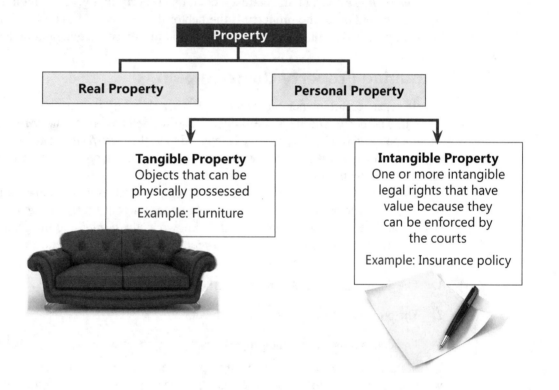

The character of property can change over time. Sometimes, for example, an item of personal property is attached to real property and, thus, becomes a *fixture* that is part of the real property. For example, a furnace is personal property. If it is installed into a house, the furnace becomes a fixture and is considered to have become part of the house, which is real property. Ownership of the house includes ownership of the furnace. If the owner removes the furnace from the house, it becomes personal property again.

Property also can be characterized as either *public property* or *private property*. Property that is owned by a government entity is classified as **public property**. Property that is owned by anyone other than a government entity is classified as **private property**. Jurisdictions around the world take various approaches to allocating property between public and private ownership. In the United States, for example, a person who owns land owns the right to whatever minerals are found on the land and can sell or give away those mineral rights. By contrast, in other countries—China, for example—the government owns all mineral rights within the country.

Business Law for Financial Services Professionals

# Property Ownership

Ownership of property means that the owner has a bundle of rights in the property, and the law recognizes and protects those rights. This bundle of ownership rights generally includes (1) the right to enjoy and use the property and (2) the right to dispose of the property. For example, assume that you own a silver bracelet. Your ownership of the bracelet includes the legal right to possess and wear the bracelet. You have the right to lend it to a friend, rent it, or use it yourself. Because you have the right to dispose of the property, you can sell it to anyone at any time on whatever terms you choose or give it away as a gift. You also can use the bracelet as security for a loan by giving a creditor a security interest in the bracelet. A *security interest* is a claim against a debtor's property that gives a creditor the right to possession of the property if the debtor defaults on the underlying loan. In the event of a default, the property can be sold to satisfy the outstanding debt.

## Acquiring Property Ownership

People often acquire ownership of property when they buy it from the party who owns it. The party who buys the property is often referred to as the *transferee*, and the party who sells the property is referred to as the *transferor*. In any transfer of property ownership, the new owner generally can receive only those ownership interests that the prior owner had to transfer.

Sometimes a person receives property as a *gift*, which is a voluntary transfer of property ownership from one person to another without the exchange of consideration. The person who makes a gift is known as the *donor*, and the person to whom a gift is made is known as the *donee*. State laws typically require that the following three elements be present to complete a valid gift:

1. The donor must intend to make a gift.

2. The property must be delivered to the donee.

3. The donee must accept the property as a gift.

Another common method of acquiring property is referred to as *accession*, which means "to add to." In other words, a person generally has the right to all that his property produces and all that is added to or united with the property. Thus, the owner of land usually owns all crops that grow on the land. The owner of a bank account owns the interest that his money earns.

Sometimes, property is abandoned, lost, or stolen. In these cases, determining who has the right to claim title to the property can be difficult. In this context, *title* is a person's claim to ownership of property that is superior to anyone else's ownership claim. The following general rules govern abandoned and lost property:

- When someone *abandons* property and no longer intends to possess it, whoever claims the property becomes the owner.

- When someone *loses* property by negligently or accidentally misplacing it, that person continues to own the property. Anyone who finds the property has the right to keep it until the rightful owner is located. The finder in such a case has a superior claim to the property over anyone other than the rightful owner.

- When someone receives or buys property that was *stolen*, the transferee receives no title because the transferor did not have title to transfer. Such goods remain the property of the original owner.

Sometimes, a buyer obtains more rights and better title in property than the seller had in the property. For example, a *good faith purchaser for value* generally takes property free of an unknown lien or interest in the property held by another party. A ***lien*** is a generic term used to describe a claim against property resulting from a debt or other obligation. Two elements are necessary for a buyer to qualify as a good faith purchaser for value:

1. The buyer must make the purchase in good faith with no knowledge that anyone other than the seller has an ownership interest in the property. For example, if a buyer could have discovered such an interest by exercising reasonable care, then the buyer does not qualify as a good faith purchaser.

2. The buyer must pay a valuable consideration in exchange for the property. Thus, someone who receives property as a gift does not qualify as a good faith purchaser for value.

> **Example:**
>
> Samuel Chu borrowed money from Vera Schuman. To secure the debt, Mr. Chu gave Ms. Schuman a lien on a piece of property he owned. Mr. Chu later sold the property to Pilar Gomez. Because Ms. Gomez was a good faith purchaser for value, Ms. Schuman's lien on the property terminated. Although Ms. Schuman may seek repayment of the loan from Mr. Chu, she has no claim against the property after Mr. Chu sold the property to a good faith purchaser for value.

## Forms of Property Ownership

As a general rule, any individual, business, or government entity can own property. Special rules apply to property that is owned by more than one person. In most states, property can be held by more than one individual in the following forms:

- *Tenants in common* are two or more parties who each own an undivided portion of the property. Assume, for example, that two sisters own land as tenants in common. One sister has a one-third interest and the other has a two-thirds interest in the land. Each tenant has an equal right to possess and use the property, and each has the right to sell or otherwise transfer ownership of her undivided interest in the property. Each tenant also has the right to decide who will receive her interest in the property following her death.

- In a *joint tenancy*, two or more individuals own equal shares in property and have a right of survivorship. A ***right of survivorship*** means that, when one joint tenant dies, his share automatically passes to the surviving joint tenant or tenants. Like tenants in common, joint tenants each have the right to possess and use the property, and a joint tenant may transfer his ownership interest to a third party. Such a transfer ends the joint tenancy, however, and a tenancy in common is created. Thus, the remaining owner and the new owner become tenants in common.

As part of their laws governing marriages, most countries have enacted laws that govern the ownership of property by married couples. In the United States, many states recognize a form of property ownership, known as a *tenancy by the entirety*, in which both spouses have the right to possess and use the property and ownership includes the right of survivorship. Neither spouse can transfer ownership of the property without the consent of the other. If the parties divorce, then the tenancy by the entirety is dissolved and the parties usually own the property as tenants in common.

I've heard that in some states married people jointly own property once they get married. How does that work?

There are states that treat property owned by a married couple as jointly owned property; each person has an undivided half interest in the property. It's called *community property*.

That doesn't seem fair. My grandmother left me some antique jewelry that is worth quite a bit of money. Does that mean that if I get married, my spouse would automatically own half of it?

Not exactly. There are exceptions for property owned separately before the marriage. Keep reading.

A few states have enacted *community property laws* that govern property ownership between spouses. In a community property state, a married couple is treated as a community. **Community property** is certain property owned by a married couple in which each spouse has an undivided half interest. For example, assume that a husband is employed outside the home and the wife stays at home to raise their children. The income the husband earns during the marriage is community property. Any property, such as a house and automobiles, that the couple buys with community property during the marriage becomes community property also.

By contrast, some property is considered a married person's **separate property** and belongs entirely to the individual. The following general rules apply to such separate property:

- Property an individual obtained before marriage remains that person's separate property.

- Property acquired during a marriage with separate property is that spouse's separate property. For example, assume that a wife had money in savings when she married. That money is her separate property, and anything she buys during the marriage with that money also is her separate property.

■ Property acquired by one spouse during a marriage as a gift or inheritance is the separate property of that spouse.

As a general rule, both spouses must agree before ownership of community property may be transferred to a third party. When one spouse dies, the surviving spouse is entitled to half of the community property. The other half generally belongs to the estate of the deceased spouse. Figure 8.2 gives some examples of the operation of community property laws.

## Figure 8.2 Community Property Laws

- When he married, Mr. Bingham owned a paid-up insurance policy on his own life. After he married, he named his sister as the beneficiary of the policy. Because he owned the policy before the marriage, the policy is Mr. Bingham's separate property in which his wife has no ownership rights.

- After their marriage, Mr. and Mrs. Zarcati opened a mutual fund account, and they set up an automatic payment plan under which funds were periodically withdrawn from their joint checking account to purchase shares in the mutual fund. Because they used community funds to purchase the mutual fund shares, the mutual fund account is community property.

A husband-wife community ends upon (1) the death of either spouse, (2) the divorce of the parties, or (3) the annulment of the marriage. When a community ends, the couple's community property is divided equally between the parties.

## Restrictions on Ownership

A person who holds all of the legal rights that exist in certain property is the absolute owner of the property. An owner's rights in property, however, are not always absolute, because property rights may be subject to some governmental restrictions. In the United States, most state legislatures have delegated to cities and other local governments the *police power*, which is the power to enact laws to promote the public health, safety, and welfare. As part of their police power, local governments typically enact zoning laws that regulate how land within the jurisdiction may be used. For example, property that is zoned residential may be used only for residential purposes, and property zoned commercial may be used only for commercial purposes. Most local governments in the United States also have enacted building codes that prescribe minimum construction requirements for new buildings. Many other countries also have building codes that place requirements on new building construction.

Some countries, however, place even more restrictions on the ownership rights of property owners. For example, Indonesian property owners cannot draw from the natural resources of the land. In Indonesia, only government banks and social and religious organizations may pull natural resources from the land. In China, the government restricts the quantity of land that can be used for construction purposes and does not allow private ownership of land.

An owner's right to property may be restricted in other ways, such as by an easement. An *easement* is the right to make specific uses of another person's property—known as an *affirmative easement*—or the right to prevent another from making specific uses of his own property—a *negative easement*. In many locations, for example, local governments and utility companies are granted affirmative easements over private property to install water, sewer, and utility connections. When someone owns a negative easement, the easement owner may prohibit a neighbor from placing buildings or other structures on her own property if the structures would affect the easement owner's property in a specific way. For example, a negative easement might prohibit someone from building something that would block the flow of light or air to the easement owner's property.

Real property owners sometimes enter into agreements, known as *restrictive covenants*, which place restrictions on how owners may use their property. Many residential subdivisions in the United States are subject to restrictive covenants that place a range of restrictions on property within the subdivision. Restrictive covenants, for example, often restrict the size and type of houses that may be built within a subdivision.

An owner's rights also may be limited if another person has rights in the same property. Because property is a bundle of rights, the owner may transfer any or all of those rights to others. For example, when a property owner uses the property as collateral for a loan, he gives the creditor an interest in the property. We describe creditor rights later in this text.

 A lot of these property ownership rules seem to apply to real estate. What do they have to do with insurance and financial services products?

 Well, these laws apply to all types of property, real estate as well as personal property.

 And I guess we just learned that insurance and other financial products like stocks are a type of intangible personal property.

Correct. Right now, we're learning the basics about property laws, and using examples about real estate and tangible personal property helps illustrate these laws clearly. But be patient, in Chapter 11 we'll get into a lot more detail about owning insurance and financial services products. For example, you'll see how the concepts of tenants in common and joint tenancy apply to mutual funds.

In that case, I better make sure I understand these basic property laws first!

Forms of property ownership and restrictions on ownership vary greatly among different jurisdictions. Insight 8.1 discusses property ownership rights in China.

---

## Insight 8.1 Property Ownership Rights in China

In 2007, China passed the Property Rights Law of the People's Republic of China (the New Property Law), which outlined significant changes in Chinese property ownership. The law does not change the Chinese system of land tenure by which the state owns all land. The New Property Law, however, provides that private persons have the right to occupy, utilize, and enjoy the fruits of the land. Thus, the law grants private persons certain land use rights along with ownership rights in buildings and fixtures located on the land.

The majority of urban Chinese people live in multi-family structures. The New Property Law provides the first legal framework for the private ownership of condominiums. As a result of the law, China has experienced a substantial increase in the private ownership of condominium units that were formerly owned by the state.

Basic rights of condominium owners in China are similar to those of owners in the United States. Chinese condominium owners generally hold the following rights:

- Individual ownership rights in the specific dwelling unit and any parking space assigned to that unit

- Common ownership rights in the common areas of the building

- The ability to actively participate in the condominium management association and to vote in general meetings

Because China's condominium ownership structure is so new, the government has the authority to assist in forming the condominium management association. After an adequate management association has been established, however, the government cannot interfere with the affairs of the condominium owners.

**Source:** Property Rights Law of the People's Republic of China (People's Republic of China) National People's Congress, Order No. 62, 16 March 2007, www.lehmanlaw.com/resource-centre/lawsand-regulations/general/property-rights-law-of-the-peoples-republic-of-china.html (23 September 2011).

# Transfers of Ownership Rights

Ownership of property includes the basic right to transfer some or all ownership rights to another. We begin this section by discussing how an owner transfers all of her ownership rights in real estate by selling the property. We then discuss how an owner of real estate transfers the right to possess the property by leasing the property to another. Real estate sales and leases are types of *inter vivos transfers*, meaning that they are transfers made during a property owner's life.[1] We end the section by describing *testamentary transfers* of property, which are transfers that occur after a property owner's death. We describe the laws that govern another type of property transfer—the sale of goods—in the next chapter.

Although the states have primary authority for regulating property located within their geographic jurisdictions, inter vivos transfers of real property interests are governed by both state and federal laws. The primary federal law affecting such transactions is the *Fair Housing Act*, which prohibits discrimination in the sale, rental, and financing of dwellings, and in other housing-related transactions, based on race, color, national origin, religion, sex, familial status, and handicap or disability.[2]

## Real Estate Sales

The agreement between the seller and the buyer of real estate is a contract that is governed by the general rules of contract law. Real estate sales contracts generally are subject to a great deal of negotiation between the buyer and seller. In the United States, buyers and sellers often hire real estate professionals to represent them and help them in negotiating real estate transactions.

When a buyer and seller reach an agreement for the sale of real property, they must execute a written contract that complies with the Statute of Frauds. The sales contract usually specifies a future date on which the transaction will be completed. During the interim, the buyer can finalize the financing arrangements, and the parties have time to comply with any conditions that they included in their sales contract. For example, the buyer may have conditioned his purchase on the seller making certain repairs to the property.

On the specified future date, the parties close their transaction. A *closing* is the conclusion of a real estate transaction when the parties fulfill all of the terms of their sales contract. Among other things, the buyer pays the promised consideration in exchange for a deed to the property. In the next section, we describe mortgages and real property deeds.

### Mortgages

The most common method of financing the purchase of real estate is through a mortgage. A *mortgage* is an agreement under which a borrower, the *mortgagor*, transfers its interest in property to another party as security for a loan or other obligation. The party to whom the interest is transferred, the *mortgagee*, usually is a financial institution such as a bank. In exchange for the security interest, the mortgagee provides the funds the mortgagor needs to purchase the property. The mortgagor usually repays the mortgage in equal monthly installments over a stated number of years.

If a mortgagor fails to repay a mortgage loan according to its terms, the mortgagee has the right to foreclose on the loan. *Foreclosure* is a process by which a mortgagee may put mortgaged property up for sale to raise funds to pay off a mortgagor's debt. The foreclosure process differs from state to state.

## Deeds and Recording Statutes

In order to complete a valid transfer of real property ownership, the seller generally must provide the buyer with a *deed*, which is a written instrument that transfers title to real property from one person, the *grantor*, to another person, the *grantee*. The following types of deeds are recognized in most states:

- A *warranty deed* conveys clear title to the property and contains warranties that the grantor has clear title to the property. The terms *clear title*, *good title*, and *marketable title* are used somewhat interchangeably to refer to title that has no known defects. As we previously noted, a warranty is a promise that a specific statement of fact is true. If the grantee under a warranty deed does not receive clear title, she has a cause of action against the grantor for breach of the warranties contained in the deed.

- A *quitclaim deed* conveys whatever ownership rights the grantor had in the property when the deed was executed. Unlike a warranty deed, a quitclaim deed does not contain warranties of title. The grantor does not claim to have title to the property, and the grantee has no cause of action against the grantor if the grantee does not receive clear title. Quitclaim deeds often are used to correct technical defects in the chain of title to property.

State laws generally require a valid deed to include specific information, including (1) the grantee's name, (2) a statement of the consideration paid in exchange for the deed, (3) a complete description of the property being conveyed, and (4) the grantor's signature. When the seller delivers a valid deed to the buyer of real property, title to the property is transferred from the seller to the buyer. The rights that property deeds convey to property owners often depend on the country in which the land lies. Insight 8.2 lists examples of common property deeds in Thailand and Indonesia.

A person who buys property and receives a valid deed can fully protect his ownership interests by recording the deed. Each U.S. state has enacted a *recording statute* that establishes an administrative system for recording all transactions that affect real property in the state. These statutes create a way for conflicting claims to real property to be resolved. To record a deed, the grantee must file a copy of the deed with the appropriate governmental agency and pay a recording fee. These administrative systems provide evidence of the chain of title of all property located in the applicable jurisdiction. Potential buyers of real property can review the governmental records to determine who has ownership rights in the property. Insight 8.3 describes how conflicting claims to title are resolved under various types of recording statutes.

## Insight 8.2 Common Property Deeds of Thailand and Indonesia

**Thailand**

- **Sor Kor 1 (SK1):** Conveys the right to occupy and use land for an indefinite period of time.

- **Nor Sor 2 (NS2):** Conveys the right to occupy and use land for a temporary period of time not to exceed three years.

- **Nor Sor 3 (NS3):** Conveys the right to possess land that has not been surveyed and has no official boundaries. The land must be confirmed by neighbors and a ground survey.

- **Nor Sor 3 Gor (NS3G):** Conveys the right to possess land that has identifiable boundaries confirmed by an aerial survey.

- **Nor Sor 4 (NS4) or Chanote:** Conveys full rights over the land. This type of title is the strongest and most preferred title in Thailand.

**Indonesia**

- **Hak Milik (HM):** Conveys full rights over the land. This type of title is the strongest and most preferred title in Indonesia.

- **Hak Pakai (HP):** Conveys the right to use land for any purpose for a period of 25 years and can be extended for another 20 years.

- **Hak Guna Usaha (HGU):** Conveys the right to use state-owned land for agricultural purposes.

- **Hak Guna Bangunan (HGB):** Conveys the right to construct buildings on a piece of land that is owned by someone else.

## Real Estate Leases

A *lease* is a contract under which the owner of real property, the ***landlord*** or *lessor*, conveys to another party, the ***tenant*** or *lessee*, the exclusive right to possess the property for a period of time. As a general rule, the relationship between the parties is governed by the terms of the lease, and the lease is governed by the rules of contract law of the jurisdiction in which the property is located. A lease may be for either residential or commercial purposes. The following are some common types of commercial leases:

- Nonretail businesses often lease space in commercial office buildings. Depending on the availability of office space in the geographic area, owners of office space may or may not be willing to negotiate the terms of the lease with potential tenants. Typically, the amount of rent a tenant pays depends on the amount of space the tenant leases.

- Leases for property that will be used for retail purposes are structured somewhat differently than are leases for nonretail office space. The amount a retailer pays in rent often includes both a flat monthly fee plus a percentage of the retailer's gross monthly sales.

## Insight 8.3 Conflicting Claims to Real Property

The states have established various systems for recording interests in real property. Let's look at an example to illustrate some of the common types of recording statutes. Assume that Ruth Williams owned land, which she sold to her neighbor, David Morton, in 2010. In 2011, Ms. Williams sold the same land to Wendy Sakamoto.

The states have enacted the following three types of recording statutes:

- Under a **race statute**, the party who first records a deed to property gains a superior claim to that property over any party who later records a deed to the property. Thus, the party who wins the race and is first to record his deed gets the superior claim. In our example, if Ms. Sakamoto records her deed before Mr. Morton records his deed, she will have the superior claim to the property, even though Mr. Morton purchased the property first.

- Under a **pure notice statute**, a later grantee of property has superior title to that property if she acquired the interest without knowing of an earlier grantee's claim under an unrecorded deed. In our example, assume that when Ms. Sakamoto bought the property, Mr. Morton had not yet recorded his deed. If Ms. Sakamoto did not know of Mr. Morton's earlier deed, she would have a superior right to the property even if Mr. Morton ultimately records his deed before Ms. Sakamoto records her deed. However, if Ms. Sakamoto knew of Mr. Morton's earlier deed, she would not have a superior claim even if she records her deed first.

- Under a **race-notice statute**, to have priority to property, a grantee must have no knowledge of an earlier grantee's claim and must record her deed first. Such statutes protect a party who buys property in good faith and without notice of another buyer but only if the subsequent good faith purchaser is the first to record her deed. In our example, if Ms. Sakamoto is a good faith purchaser *and* if she records her deed first, she will have the superior claim to the property. However, if Ms. Sakamoto knew of Mr. Morton's earlier deed, she will not have a superior claim to the property, even if she records her deed before Mr. Morton records his deed.

- Under a ground lease, a tenant leases undeveloped land for a relatively long term and erects whatever buildings it wishes. The tenant benefits because it does not have to incur the cost of buying the land, and the landowner retains ownership of the land without incurring the cost of improving the land.

The length of time a tenant has the right to possess the property depends on the type of tenancy established by the lease. The following types of tenancies are common in most states:

- Under a *tenancy for a term*, the tenant has the right to possess the property until a specified date. On that date, the tenancy automatically ends, unless the parties have agreed otherwise. Often, the parties agree to renew the lease for another specified term.

- Under a *periodic tenancy*, the tenancy continues from month to month, year to year, or some other specified period until one of the parties terminates the lease by giving notice to the other party. The amount of notice required varies from state to state, and typically is at least one month.

- A *tenancy at will* has no fixed time period, and it can be terminated by either party at any time by giving notice to the other party as required by state law.

When a tenant does not vacate the property at the end of a lease term, a *tenancy at sufferance* is created. In such a case, the landlord has two options: (1) bring a legal action to evict the tenant, who has become a trespasser, or (2) allow the tenant to remain and pay rent. **Eviction** is a legal process by which a trespasser is removed from real property. If the landlord decides to let the tenant remain, a new tenancy is created. Depending on the facts of the case, the new tenancy generally is either a tenancy for a term or a periodic tenancy.

In addition to being governed by the terms of a lease, the landlord-tenant relationship is governed by state and local laws that modify the general rules of contract law as it applies to leases. For example, most jurisdictions impose specific rights and duties on landlords and tenants. To protect individual consumers who are at more of a disadvantage in negotiating the terms of a lease than are businesses, many such state laws often govern only residential leases.

## Testamentary Transfers

An important right of property ownership is the owner's right to decide who will receive the property when the owner dies. An individual who dies is referred to as a *decedent*. A decedent's **estate** includes all of the property that the individual owned at her death. Ownership of some property in that estate automatically passes by operation of law. For example, when property is owned jointly with a right of survivorship, ownership passes automatically to the joint owner. Any property owned by a decedent that does not pass at her death automatically by operation of law forms the person's **probate estate**.

### Wills

A person can determine who will receive the property in his probate estate by executing a **will**, which is a legal document that directs how the person's property is to be distributed after his death. The person who makes a will is known as the **testator**, and a person who dies with a valid will is said to die **testate**.

Laws in each state set out the requirements that must be met in order for a will to be valid. Typically, a person's will must be *executed*—signed—in accordance with the requirements of the applicable laws in the state in which the person is domiciled. A person's **domicile** is that place where the person has her true, fixed, and permanent home.

Although the specific requirements vary from state to state, a will must be executed in accordance with certain formalities in order to be valid. The following formalities are required in most states:

- A will must be in writing.

- The testator must have the legal capacity to make a will, referred to as ***testamentary capacity***. As a general rule, anyone who has attained a stated age, typically 18, and is of sound mind has testamentary capacity. For purposes of making a will, a person is considered to be of sound mind if he (1) understands the nature and character of the property he owns, (2) understands that he is making a will, and (3) recognizes the people who would be expected to be provided for in his will.

- The will must be signed by the testator or by someone else who signs on behalf of the testator, at the testator's direction, and in the testator's presence.

- The testator must sign the will in the presence of competent witnesses or must attest to the witnesses that it is his signature. Witnesses generally are competent if they have attained a specified age, usually 18, and if they are disinterested parties who are not beneficiaries of the will.

- The witnesses must sign the will in the presence of the testator.

A number of states recognize some wills that are not executed with the required formalities. Some states, for example, recognize oral wills that are made in very limited circumstances, such as when sailors are at sea and are unable to execute a formal will. Typically, an oral will can transfer ownership of only a limited amount of a testator's property. Some states recognize a ***holographic will***, which is a will that is handwritten and signed by the testator.

Because a will does not become effective until the testator's death, a testator may revoke a will at any time before her death. For example, a testator may revoke a will by executing a subsequent valid will. A testator also may revise a valid will by executing a ***codicil***, which is a testamentary document that supplements a will. Because it is a testamentary document, a codicil must be executed with the same formalities that are required to execute a valid will. A codicil can be used to add to the provisions of a will, to revoke or alter provisions, and to explain or qualify provisions. For example, a testator may use a codicil to dispose of property she acquired after she executed her will.

The types of wills and the formalities required for wills vary from country to country. Insight 8.4 describes the most common types of wills recognized in Thailand.

## *Intestate Succession*

A person who dies without a valid will is said to die ***intestate***, and that person is known as an intestate. Intestate succession laws in each state specify the individuals who are entitled to the probate estate of individuals who die intestate. In addition, if a person dies testate but fails to dispose of all of his property in a valid will, then the remaining property is distributed in accordance with the intestate succession law. For conflict of laws purposes, the distribution of an intestate's real property is governed by the laws of the state in which the property is located. The distribution of an intestate's personal property is governed by the laws of the jurisdiction in which the person was domiciled at the time of his death.

## Insight 8.4 Types of Wills in Thailand

- A **customary witnessed** will is a will that is required to be made in writing and signed and dated by the testator in the presence of at least two witnesses. The witnesses must also sign the will to certify the authenticity of the testator's signature.

- A **will made through a public document** is a will in which the testator declares the content of his will in the presence of two witnesses and the Kromakarn Amphoe, a Thai public official. The Kromakarn summarizes the content of the will in a formal note. After confirming that the note reflects the intent of the testator, the witnesses and testator sign the note. After the Kromakarn signs and seals the note, it becomes the official will of the testator.

- A **holographic** will must be dated and signed by the testator. In Thailand, holographic wills do not require the presence of a witness.

- A **secret will** is a will in which the testator writes his intent in a signed and dated document. The testator then submits the document to the Kromakarn Amphoe and at least two witnesses. The Kromakarn must sign and seal the document, and the two witnesses must also sign the document.

THAILAND

- An **oral will** is recognized under Thai law when circumstances make it impossible for the testator to create any other type of will. Such circumstances include periods of epidemic, war, or imminent danger. The testator must orally recite the will's content before at least two witnesses. The witnesses then recite the content of the will to the Kromakarn Amphoe, who then summarizes the content of the will in a formal note. After the Kromakarn and the witnesses sign the note, it becomes the official will of the testator. An oral will is automatically invalidated after one month when the testator has an opportunity to make another will.

Most countries have intestate succession laws which provide that property passes to a person's close family members—including surviving spouse, children and other descendants, and parents—in a specified order of priority. For example, in the United States, most states have adopted laws based on the Uniform Probate Code. The purpose of intestate succession laws is to distribute the intestate's property in a manner that closely represents how the average person would have passed on his property had that person created a will. However, the laws are inflexible, and they vary greatly from jurisdiction to jurisdiction. As a result, an intestate's property often is not passed on as the person would have wished. To illustrate how these laws can affect the distribution of a decedent's property, Insight 8.5 compares typical intestate succession laws in the United States to those in Malaysia.

---

## Insight 8.5 Comparisons of Intestate Succession Laws in the United States and Malaysia

**Example 1:** Victoria Caldwell was survived by her husband and their son and left an estate valued at $300,000.

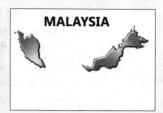

**Laws in most U.S. states:** The entire estate will pass to her husband.

**Malaysia Distribution Act\*:** Her husband will be entitled to one-third of the estate, or $100,000, and her son will be entitled to two-thirds of the estate, or $200,000.

---

**Example 2:** William Achiari was survived by his wife and his parents and left an estate valued at $500,000.

**Laws in most U.S. states:** His wife will be entitled to the first $300,000 of the estate plus three-quarters of the remaining estate, which brings her total to $450,000. His parents will receive the remaining $50,000.

**Malaysia Distribution Act:** His wife will be entitled to one-half of the estate, or $250,000, and his parents will be entitled to one-half of the estate, or $250,000.

---

**Example 3:** Harry Grayson was survived by his daughter and his parents and left an estate valued at $300,000.

**Laws in most U.S. states:** The entire estate will pass to his daughter.

**Malaysia Distribution Act:** His parents will be entitled to one-third of the estate, or $100,000, and his daughter will be entitled to two-thirds of the estate, or $200,000.

\*The Malaysia Distribution Act applies only to Peninsular Malaysia and does not govern estates of Muslims.

**Source:** Uniform Probate Code § 2–102 (2008); Distribution Act of 1958 (Malaysia) s. 6, http://202.75.6.111/Akta/Vol.%206/Act%20300.pdf (26 September 2011).

---

So, when you get home tonight, are you going to review your will to make sure you didn't leave anything out?

Are you kidding? I don't even have a will, but now that I know what can happen if I die without one, believe me, I'm going to make a will!

### Estate Administration

Each state has established procedures for handling the distribution of the estates of deceased persons. That process, referred to as the *probate process*, typically is conducted under the supervision of a local court, which usually is known as a *probate court*. Typically, the probate court that has authority to oversee the probate of a will is the probate court of the jurisdiction in which the decedent was domiciled at the time of her death.

In each case, a *personal representative* is appointed by the court as the person who is responsible for settling the decedent's estate. A will typically names the person the testator wants the court to appoint as the personal representative. The personal representative is known as an *executor* when a decedent dies with a valid will. In the case of an intestate decedent, the personal representative who is appointed by the court typically is known as the *administrator* of the decedent's estate. The personal representative is responsible for collecting and completing an inventory of the decedent's property. The representative is also responsible for filing any required income tax returns, collecting all debts owed to the decedent, and paying all outstanding debts owed by the decedent. The personal representative then distributes any remaining property to the people who are determined by the probate court to be entitled to it in accordance with either the terms of the decedent's will or the applicable laws of intestate succession.

You know, with a life insurance policy the beneficiary designation is crucial to making sure proceeds go where the insured intended.

Yes, in certain cases, proceeds may be paid to a deceased's estate instead of to the person whom the insured intended.

So then the policy proceeds get lumped in with the rest of the estate and might go to creditors or other people with claims on the estate? How could that happen?

Well, let's not get ahead of ourselves. For now, just make sure you understand the concepts of intestate succession and probate; we'll get into specifics about life insurance beneficiary designations in Chapter 11.

# Intellectual Property

Businesses often have rights in intellectual property such as inventions, drawings, photographs, books, and magazine articles. We use the term *intellectual property* to refer to intangible personal property that is a product of the human intellect and in which the creator has ownership rights. Individuals and businesses that express ideas in some tangible or artistic form have specific ownership rights in that intellectual property. Most countries have enacted laws that protect specific ownership rights that individuals and businesses have in intellectual property. Such laws generally include copyright laws, patent laws, and trademark laws.

## Copyrights

A *copyright* is a right that is granted by statute to the author or originator of an original literary or artistic work and that gives the copyright holder the exclusive right to publish, produce, or perform the work for a specified time. Copyrights are granted for works such as novels, fine and graphic arts, music, records, photography, software, video, cinema, and choreography.

In the United States, copyrights are governed by federal law, which provides that copyright protection attaches to a work when it is first created.[3] For works created after January 1, 1978, an author or originator has copyright protection in the work for his lifetime and for 70 years thereafter. Figure 8.3 gives some examples of the length of copyright protection in other countries. In each case, a copyright granted under a given jurisdiction's laws is enforceable only within that jurisdiction. Thus, for example, an author who publishes a novel in the United States and several other countries is granted a separate copyright in each country.

### Figure 8.3 Copyright Laws Around the World

**Brazil:** For authors' works, a copyright lasts for the author's lifetime plus 70 years measured from January 1 of the year after the author's death.[4]

**Hong Kong:** With certain exceptions, a copyright is protected during the author's life and for 50 years measured from the end of the calendar year in which the author dies.[5]

**India:** With certain exceptions, an author's copyright continues in a work for the lifetime of the author and for 60 years following the author's death.[6]

**Philippines:** A copyright generally is protected during the life of the author and for 50 years after the author's death.[7]

**Singapore:** For authors' works, a copyright lasts 50 years after either the death of the author or the first publication of the work, whichever is later.[8]

Because U.S. copyright protection attaches when a work is created, no special action is required for an author or originator to protect the work. Copyright holders typically include a copyright notice on their works to put others on notice of the copyright, and they are permitted, but not required, to register their copyright with the U.S. Copyright Office at any time during the time of copyright protection.

Any violation of an author's exclusive rights in a work constitutes an infringement of the author's copyright. *Infringement* means any violation of the exclusive rights belonging to the owner of intellectual property. If a third party infringes a copyright, the copyright holder has a cause of action against the infringer under the federal copyright law. That law, however, requires the copyright holder to register her copyright before she can file a lawsuit against the infringer. By registering a copyright with the U.S. Copyright Office, the owner also gains the following benefits:

- If someone infringes a copyright after it has been registered, the copyright holder is entitled to recover damages from the infringer and can elect to receive either her actual damages or statutory damages. If a work was not registered at the time of the infringement, the copyright holder generally is entitled to recover only her actual damages, including all profits the infringer earned as a result of the infringement.

- A certificate of registration, obtained before or within five years after publication of the work, constitutes prima facie evidence that the copyright is valid. By having such evidence, the copyright holder is not required to produce evidence at trial to prove the validity of the copyright.

In addition to awarding damages, the courts may issue an injunction that prohibits further infringements of the plaintiff's copyright.

The rights granted by a copyright are not unlimited. The primary limitation on those rights is the *fair use doctrine*, which is a legal doctrine that permits others to use limited portions of a copyrighted work for purposes such as criticism, comment, news reporting, teaching, scholarship, or research.

I wonder how copyright laws keep up with all the changes in technology?

It's not easy! Original copyright laws predate computers and information technology, so they have to be amended and new laws created to deal with issues arising from the new ways we create, use, and share information.

## Patents

A *patent* is a governmental grant of property rights to the inventor or creator of an original process, machine, manufactured article, or chemical compound. In the United States, the federal government has authority to issue patents, and federal laws specify the requirements an invention must meet to receive a patent. Unlike copyrights, which attach upon the creation of a work, a patent is effective only after the applicable government agency acts on an application for a patent.

To get a U.S. patent, an inventor must file an application with the U.S. Patent and Trademark Office (USPTO). The information provided in the application should demonstrate in detail that the invention meets the requirements for a patent. For example, an invention must be something new, which means that it must add to existing knowledge. Obtaining a patent is an expensive and time-consuming process that usually takes several years. Insight 8.6 describes who has ownership rights in a copyright or patented invention.

---

### Insight 8.6 Who Owns a Copyright or Patent?

A copyrightable work or a patentable invention is created by an individual or group of individuals. But often, those individuals are hired by a business to create the work or invention. In such cases, who is entitled to ownership of the work—the individual creators or the businesses that funded the work?

Under U.S. federal copyright laws, the author or creator of a work owns the work unless it was created as a work for hire. A **work for hire** is a work prepared (1) by an employee within the course of his employment or (2) as the result of an agreement of the parties that it is a work for hire. The employer, not the employee, is the owner of the copyright of a work for hire.

U.S. federal patent laws approach the issue somewhat differently. Only the inventor or inventors may apply for a patent on their invention. However, an inventor may assign ownership of the patent to another party. A business that employs an inventor typically obtains ownership of patent rights in an invention when the individual inventor assigns ownership of those rights to the business.

---

Like copyrights, a patent generally is effective only within the country that granted the patent. To eliminate the potential time and expense of having to file multiple patent applications in several different countries, the *Patent Cooperation Treaty (PCT)* provides a method of obtaining international patent protection. Under the PCT, a person can file one application and pay one filing fee and can request patents from any or all of the more than 110 countries that have signed the PCT. Applications generally can be filed with the inventor's national patent office. Each country retains the right to evaluate the application and issue a patent that is effective within its jurisdiction.

When a patent application is filed under the PCT, one of the patent offices participating in the Treaty conducts an international search to learn whether other patents already exist that would affect the patentability of the invention. The search helps the applicant decide whether it is likely that his invention is patentable and whether to continue the patent process.

A patent gives its owner the right to exclude others from making, using, selling, offering to sell, or importing the patented invention in the applicable jurisdiction during the term of the patent. A U.S. patent typically is granted for a period of 20 years from the date the patent application was filed. Anyone who makes, uses, sells, offers to sell, or imports a patented invention within the United States during the term of the patent without permission from the patent owner has infringed the patent.

When a valid patent is infringed, the patent holder is entitled to various remedies. The court may issue an injunction that prohibits the infringer from continuing the infringement. The patent holder also is entitled to damages, and the court may award treble damages if the infringement was intentional or willful. Court costs and attorneys' fees also may be awarded to a successful plaintiff.

## Trademarks

A *trademark* is a word, phrase, symbol, design, or combination thereof that identifies and distinguishes the source of one party's goods from those of other parties. A *service mark* is the same as a trademark, except that it identifies and distinguishes the source of a service rather than goods. The term *mark* is used to refer to both trademarks and service marks.

In the United States, individuals and businesses may use any mark they choose to identify the source of their goods and services, as long as it does not infringe another's mark. By using a mark to identify goods or services, a person or business establishes property rights in the mark. To further protect their property rights in a mark, however, individuals and businesses generally register their marks with the USPTO.

A person who wants to register a mark must file an application with the USPTO, which evaluates the information in the application to determine whether the applicant meets the statutory requirements for registering a mark. The primary consideration is whether the mark is so similar to an existing mark that it is likely to cause confusion as to the source of the goods or services. If confusion is likely, the application will be rejected. Figure 8.4 identifies some of the advantages of federal registration of a trademark.

## Figure 8.4 Advantages of U.S. Trademark Registration

- A legal presumption is created that the registrant owns the mark and has the exclusive right to use the mark nationwide on or in connection with the goods and/or services listed in the registration.

- The registrant gains the ability to bring an action in federal court concerning the mark.

- The U.S registration can be used as a basis to obtain registration in foreign countries.

- The U.S. registration can be filed with the U.S. Customs Service to prevent the importation of foreign goods bearing an infringing mark.

A U.S. trademark or service mark registration generally remains in force for 10 years. Registrations can be renewed for additional 10-year periods by paying the applicable fee and filing with the USPTO an affidavit attesting to the registrant's continuing use of the mark.

A person who claims rights in a mark can use the TM (trademark) or SM (service mark) designation to alert the public to his claim, regardless of whether he has filed an application with the USPTO. After a mark has been registered, the registrant can give notice to others of its ownership claim by displaying with the mark the words *Registered in U.S. Patent and Trademark Office, or Reg. U.S. Pat. & Tm. Off.*, or the letter R enclosed within a circle: ®.

A mark is infringed when someone, without the consent of the mark's owner, uses a copy or imitation of a mark to sell, distribute, or advertise a product or service and such use is likely to cause confusion, cause mistake, or deceive the public. If the mark has been registered, the registrant may file a lawsuit in federal court and may be entitled to an injunction to prevent further use of the infringing mark. If the infringing acts were committed with knowledge that use of the imitation is likely to cause confusion, mistake, or deception, then the registrant is entitled to recover money damages.

# Key Terms

| | |
|---|---|
| property | grantee |
| real property | warranty deed |
| personal property | quitclaim deed |
| tangible property | recording statute |
| intangible property | lease |
| fixture | landlord |
| public property | tenant |
| private property | eviction |
| security interest | estate |
| transferee | probate estate |
| transferor | will |
| gift | testator |
| donor | testate |
| donee | domicile |
| accession | testamentary capacity |
| title | holographic will |
| lien | codicil |
| right of survivorship | intestate |
| community property | probate process |
| separate property | probate court |
| police power | personal representative |
| easement | executor |
| restrictive covenant | administrator |
| inter vivos transfer | intellectual property |
| testamentary transfer | copyright |
| closing | infringement |
| mortgage | fair use doctrine |
| mortgagor | patent |
| mortgagee | work for hire |
| foreclosure | trademark |
| deed | service mark |
| grantor | |

# Endnotes

1. *Inter vivos* is a Latin term that means "during lifetime."

2. 42 U.S.C. § 3601 et seq. (2011).

3. 17 U.S.C. §§ 101 et seq. (2011).

4. Lei 9.610/98, article 41, http://entertainmentlawbrazil.com.br/brazilian-copyright-act-law-no-961098/ (19 March 2012).

5. Copyright Ordinance (Hong Kong), cap 528, s 17, http://www.legislation.gov.hk/eng/home.htm?SearchTerm=copyright%20ordinance (26 September 2011).

6. S. 22, Indian Copyright Act, 1957, <http://copyright.gov.in/Documents/CopyrightRules1957.pdf (19> March 2012).

7. Rep. Act No. 8293 (1998) (Philippines), sec. 17, <http://portal.unesco.org/culture/en/files/39609/12505084093ph_IPCode_1998_en.pdf/ph_IPCode_1998_en.pdf (26> September 2011).

8. Copyright Act (Singapore, cap 63, 2006 rev ed), http://statutes.agc.gov.sg/aol/search/display/view.w3p;page=0;query=CompId%3A2fb5de3e-0ec7-457a-a12e-6d84023041d4;rec=0;resUrl=http%3A%2F%2Fstatutes.agc.gov.sg%2Faol%2Fbrowse%2FtitleResults.w3p%3Bletter%3DC%3Btype%3DactsAll (19 March 2012).

*Chapter 9*

# Commercial Transactions and Bankruptcy

## Objectives

### After studying this chapter, you should be able to

■ Describe how Article 2 of the Uniform Commercial Code governs the sale of goods and explain how Article 2 rules of contract formation differ from the common law rules of contracts

■ Identify remedies that Article 2 of the Uniform Commercial Code provides for the breach of a sales contract

■ Describe common types of negotiable instruments and identify the four requirements to qualify as a negotiable instrument

■ Identify ways in which an instrument can be indorsed in the United States

■ Describe the requirements that qualify the holder of a negotiable instrument as a holder in due course

■ Identify the parties who have liability under a negotiable instrument in a given situation

■ Distinguish between unsecured and secured credit transactions and describe the two basic requirements that must be met to gain a security interest in personal property

■ Identify the three primary methods of perfecting a security interest and describe the rights that the debtor and the secured party have in a property that is subject to a security interest

■ Distinguish among the various types of bankruptcy proceedings that are available under the U.S. Bankruptcy Act

# Outline

**Sales of Goods**
- Contract Formation
- Remedies for Contract Breach

**Negotiable Instruments**
- Required Formalities
- Indorsements
- Holder in Due Course
- Liabilities of the Parties

**Credit and Secured Transactions**
- Perfecting a Security Interest
- Rights of the Parties

**Bankruptcy**
- Liquidation Proceedings
- Rehabilitation Proceedings

In this chapter, we complete our discussion of general business law topics by describing some common types of commercial transactions. In the United States, state laws govern these types of transactions, many of which occur across jurisdictional lines. To create uniformity in commercial transactions and enable the flow of commerce across jurisdictional lines, all states have enacted statutes based on the *Uniform Commercial Code (UCC)*, which is a model law created by the American Law Institute and the National Conference of Commissioners on Uniform State Laws to govern commercial transactions. Figure 9.1 describes the UCC.

---

## Figure 9.1 The Uniform Commercial Code (UCC)

**The UCC is divided into the following nine articles:**

**Article 1** contains definitions of commercial law terms and general rules of construction that apply to transactions under most of the provisions of the UCC.

**Article 2** governs contracts for the sale of goods.

**Article 3** governs negotiable instruments.

**Article 4** governs bank collections of checks and drafts.

**Article 5** governs letters of credit. A **letter of credit** is a document written by one party who (1) asks a second party to give credit to a third party and (2) agrees to repay the second party for the amount given in credit.

**Article 6** governs bulk sales, such as the sale of the entire inventory of a business.

**Article 7** governs domestic documents of title, which include bills of lading in shipment transactions as well as warehouse receipts and other evidences of bailments. A **bailment** is the delivery of goods to another person for a particular use. For example, the Baxter Rental Company is in the business of renting trucks to the public. Before renting out a truck, Baxter enters into a contract with the individual renting the truck. This contract creates a bailment under which the individual agrees to return the truck in good condition at a stated time and place.

**Article 8** governs transactions in investment securities.

**Article 9** governs secured transactions.

---

We begin the chapter by describing the rules that govern the sale of goods. Then we describe negotiable instruments and secured transactions. The chapter concludes with a description of bankruptcy laws in the United States and other countries.

## Sales of Goods

In Chapter 6, we described the basic common law rules of contracts. Statutes have been enacted in all states to modify the common law rules governing certain types of contracts. In this section, we describe the laws that have been enacted to govern contracts involving the sale of goods. By *sale of goods*, we mean the transfer of ownership of tangible personal property in exchange for some other property, money, or services. Contracts for the sale of goods often are referred to as *sales contracts*.

In the United States, Article 2 of the UCC governs contracts for the sale of goods, but it does *not* apply to contracts involving the sale of services, real estate, or intangible property. Intangible property includes stock certificates, bonds, promissory notes, and insurance policies. The sale of such property is governed by general contract law principles, other Articles of the UCC, or other state and federal laws.

But if the sale of insurance policies is not governed by this part of the UCC, then why do I need to know about this?

These laws are important because insurers have to buy all types of goods just to conduct business. Look around. There's office furniture, computer equipment, even coffee in the breakroom that the company bought.

I see. So entering into sales contracts is just a part of doing business.

Article 2 provisions tend to follow established customs of trade generally used by merchants. Unlike consumers, who usually are not familiar with commercial transactions, merchants are familiar with such transactions and are held to a higher standard of conduct. As a result, many Article 2 provisions apply only to merchants or to transactions between merchants.

To remove legal barriers and promote the development of international trade, more than 70 countries, accounting for a significant portion of world trade, have ratified the *United Nations Convention on Contracts for the International Sale of Goods (CISG)*. Contracts for the sale of goods between parties located in countries that have signed the Convention are governed by the CISG, which establishes rules for the formation and performance of sales contracts that are similar to the rules established by Article 2 of the UCC.

**Example:**

Yardley Metal, a U.S. company, entered into a contract to sell goods to a Canadian merchant. Because the United States and Canada both have ratified the CISG, the sales contract will be governed by the CISG. In contrast, sales contracts that Yardley Metal enters into with other U.S. merchants are governed by provisions of the UCC.

## Contract Formation

Under Article 2, parties generally are free to contract on whatever terms they choose and in whatever manner they choose. Some limits, however, are imposed. For example, the courts will not enforce contract terms that are unconscionable, that is, terms that are grossly unfair or one-sided.

Recall that to create a contract under the common law, one party must make a definite offer and the other party must accept that offer unconditionally. By contrast, Article 2 provides that a sales contract is formed when it is clear that the parties intend to make a contract. Thus, the intent of the parties determines whether a contract has been created.

Under the common law, an agreement that omits a material term—such as the contract price—is not definite and, thus, is not an enforceable contract. By contrast, a sales contract can be created even though the parties have not agreed on all of the terms to include in the contract. For example, the parties may agree that they will set the price of the goods at a later date. If the parties fail to include all of the terms in their contract, the terms can be supplied by the UCC.

**Example:**

Two parties entered into a contract for the sale of goods but failed to agree on the price of the goods. When the seller delivered the goods, a dispute arose between the parties as to the price to be paid, and a lawsuit was filed. Because the parties failed to agree on the price of the goods, an issue of fact exists as to the price. The court will look to the UCC, which states that the price of the goods is whatever amount is considered reasonable when the goods were delivered to the buyer. The parties will have the opportunity to present evidence as to what would have been a reasonable price when the goods were delivered, and the trier of fact will weigh the evidence and determine the price.

Sometimes, an acceptance of an offer to enter into a sales contract is effective even if it contains additional or different terms. According to the UCC, an acceptance that contains new terms results in the creation of a contract *unless* the acceptance was conditioned on the offeror's agreement to the additional terms. If the acceptance was conditional, then no contract is created until the offeror agrees to the additional terms contained in the acceptance. In contrast, under the common law, an acceptance that contains additional or different terms is a counteroffer that does *not* result in the creation of a contract. Figure 9.2 contains some examples to illustrate when an acceptance creates a valid contract under the UCC.

## Figure 9.2 When Does an Acceptance Create a Contract Under the UCC?

- Trudy's Pet Shop offered to purchase 100 pet cages from one of its regular suppliers at a stated price. The supplier had only 50 cages in stock and accepted Trudy's offer to purchase the 50 cages. According to Article 2 of the UCC, even though the supplier's acceptance changed the terms of the contract from 100 cages to 50 cages, it is sufficient to create a contract between the parties.

- The Good Value Manufacturing Company offered to sell 500 completed items to one of its regular distributors at a stated price. The distributor needed 700 completed items, and it accepted Good Value's offer on condition that Good Value supply 700 items. The distributor also required Good Value to accept the change in terms within a reasonable time. According to Article 2 of the UCC, no contract will be created unless Good Value accepts the change in terms within a reasonable time.

## Remedies for Contract Breach

As under any contract, the parties to a sales contract are obligated to perform the contract according to its terms. In the case of a breach of contract, Article 2 provides various remedies to the injured party. As a general rule, these remedies are designed to put the injured party in the position she would have been in had the contract been performed.

The parties to a sales contract may agree on the remedy that will be available should a party breach the contract. For example, the parties may include a term in the contract that specifies the amount of damages that will be paid to the injured party. When the parties agree in advance to the amount of damages that will be paid by a breaching party, the damages are known as *liquidated damages*. Article 2 permits the enforcement of a liquidated damages provision if (1) the amount of damages specified is reasonable and (2) it would be difficult to prove the amount of actual damages that would result from a breach.

A buyer may breach a sales contract in a number of ways. For example, a buyer may refuse to accept the goods, may fail to pay for the goods according to the contract's terms, or may otherwise be unwilling to perform the contract. Among other things, when a buyer has breached a sales contract, Article 2 permits the seller of the goods to

- Cancel the contract

- Withhold or stop delivery of the goods

- Sell the goods to another party

- Recover damages from the buyer

Likewise a seller may breach a contract by failing to deliver goods as promised, delivering goods that do not conform to the terms of the contract, or otherwise refusing to perform the contract according to its terms. In such cases, Article 2 provides the buyer of goods with the following options:

- The buyer can cancel the contract.

- The buyer can *cover*, which means the buyer can purchase substitute goods from another seller and recover from the original seller damages equal to the difference between the cost of cover and the contract price.

- The buyer can ask the court for specific performance of the contract. Recall from Chapter 2 that specific performance is a remedy that requires a party to a contract, the seller in this case, to perform the contract according to its terms. Courts generally order specific performance of a sales contract only if the goods are unique or if the circumstances of the case are such that fairness requires such performance.

# Negotiable Instruments

Commerce and trade require the transfer of money from buyers to sellers. Because trade often crosses state and national borders, individuals and businesses need to be able to complete transactions without having to pay cash. Negotiable instruments were developed as a substitute for cash. A *negotiable instrument* is a written document that represents an unconditional promise or order to pay a specified amount of money upon the demand of the owner of the instrument. *Negotiability* means that possession of an instrument can be transferred—or negotiated—from person to person, and the instrument generally is accepted as a substitute for cash. As noted, a negotiable instrument can take one of two forms:

1. An instrument that is a *promise* to pay a sum of money is referred to as a *note*. By executing a note, a debtor provides a creditor with a document that can be enforced in the courts.

2. An instrument that is an *order,* or an instruction, to pay a sum of money is referred to as a *draft*. For example, a check is a draft that instructs a financial institution, such as a bank, to pay money from a specific account to a third person. The bank from which the money is to be withdrawn is referred to as the *drawee*. The person who writes the check is known as the *maker* or *drawer*. The third person who is specified to receive the money is the *payee*.

Figure 9.3 describes common types of negotiable instruments in the United States. Many other countries have set similar statutory requirements for negotiable instruments.

To negotiate—or transfer—an instrument, a person must be the holder of the instrument. A person is the *holder* of a negotiable instrument if (1) he has possession of the instrument and (2) the instrument is payable to the person or "to bearer." For example, if you have possession of a check that is payable to another person, you do not qualify as the holder of the instrument and cannot negotiate it. We describe instruments payable "to bearer" later in this section.

## Figure 9.3 Examples of Negotiable Instruments in the United States

**Cashier's check:**

A check issued on a financial institution's own account and backed by the creditworthiness of the institution. Cashier's checks typically are used for large transactions between a consumer and a third party when the third party demands cash or its equivalent and the consumer does not want to carry a large amount of cash.

**Money order:**

A type of check that is issued by a financial institution, the U.S. Postal Service, and some retail stores that allows the party named on the order to receive the face amount in cash on demand. Money orders enable a consumer who does not have a checking account to make a payment with a check while avoiding the risks of using cash.

**Traveler's check:**

A check purchased from a financial institution by a consumer, typically to use as a substitute for cash while traveling. At the time of purchase, the consumer signs the checks in the presence of the financial institution's representative. The consumer can negotiate the checks by cashing them at a financial institution or using them to purchase goods or services. The consumer must countersign the checks in the presence of the institution or retailer that is accepting the checks.

**Certificate of deposit:**

An instrument containing (1) an acknowledgment by a bank that a sum of money has been received by the bank and (2) a promise by the bank to repay the sum of money. A certificate of deposit is a note of the bank.

**Source:** Uniform Commercial Code § 3–104.

## Required Formalities

To be negotiable, an instrument must meet four basic requirements as summarized in Figure 9.4. First, the instrument must be in writing and must be signed by its maker. The document may be handwritten, typed, or printed, and the signature may be handwritten, typed, or stamped onto the writing. As a general rule, any type of signature is acceptable as long as it shows the maker's intent to validate the instrument. In addition, the signature must be that of the maker or someone authorized to sign on the maker's behalf. For example, businesses authorize specific individuals to sign negotiable instruments, such as checks, on their behalf.

## Figure 9.4 Requirements to Qualify as a Negotiable Instrument

1. The instrument must be in writing and signed by its maker.

2. The instrument must contain an unconditional promise to pay or an unconditional order to pay.

3. The amount promised or ordered to be paid must be a fixed amount of money.

4. The instrument must be payable on demand or at a definite time.

The second requirement for a negotiable instrument is that it must contain an unconditional promise to pay or an unconditional order to pay. A note that says "I owe you $100" is not negotiable because it does not include a promise to pay the amount owed. Likewise, a note that says "I promise to pay you $100 if you paint my house" is not negotiable because it contains a condition that must be met before the promise is enforceable.

The third requirement is that the amount promised or ordered to be paid must be a fixed amount of money. This requirement is met whether the instrument is payable with or without interest. Thus, as long as the principal amount owed is clearly stated, the amount of interest payable may be stated as a fixed or variable amount or rate.

The fourth requirement is that the instrument must be payable on demand or at a definite time. If an instrument does not state when it is payable, then it is payable on demand. A check, for example, typically is payable whenever the payee chooses to present it for payment; thus, a check is negotiable. A note that is dated and states on its face that it is payable "30 days after date" is payable at a definite time and, thus, is negotiable. By contrast, an instrument that is payable "30 days after my death" is not negotiable because the date of the person's death is unknown. Thus, the instrument is not payable at a definite time.

As a general rule, negotiable instruments must be "payable to bearer" or "payable to order." An instrument that is payable to bearer, known as *bearer paper*, is negotiable by the holder without having to be signed by a specific payee. A signed check that is payable "to cash" is considered to be payable to the bearer who can negotiate it simply by transferring its possession to another person.

An instrument that is payable to the order of a specific payee, known as ***order paper***, can be negotiated if it is *indorsed*—that is, signed on the back of the document—by the named payee and transferred to another. For example, an instrument that is "payable to the order of Nancy Wright" is negotiable if it is indorsed by Nancy Wright and transferred to another party. Checks typically are payable to the order of a specific payee. Figure 9.5 shows an example of bearer paper and order paper.

## Figure 9.5 Order Paper and Bearer Paper

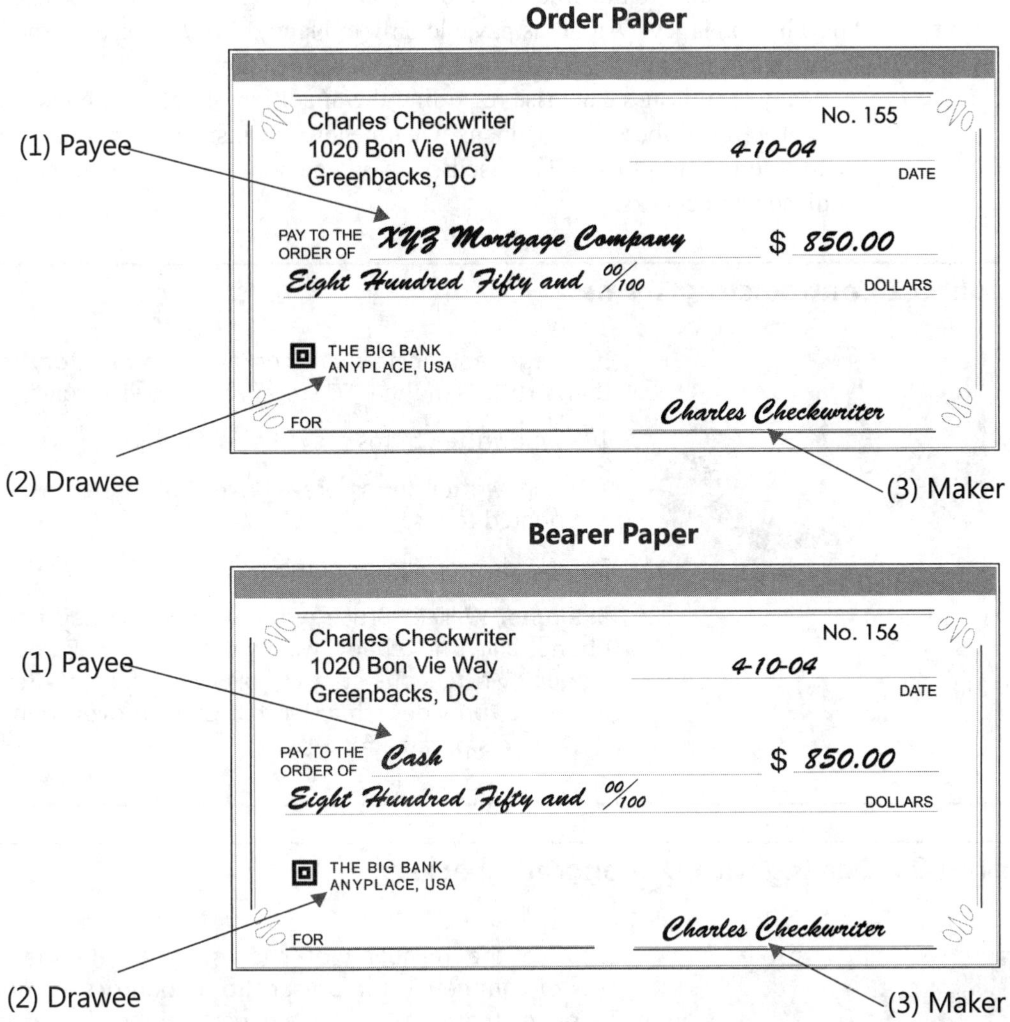

### Order Paper

(1) Payee →

Charles Checkwriter
1020 Bon Vie Way
Greenbacks, DC

No. 155

4-10-04

DATE

PAY TO THE
ORDER OF  *XYZ Mortgage Company*   $ *850.00*

*Eight Hundred Fifty and* 00/100    DOLLARS

THE BIG BANK
ANYPLACE, USA

FOR    *Charles Checkwriter*

(2) Drawee

(3) Maker

### Bearer Paper

(1) Payee →

Charles Checkwriter
1020 Bon Vie Way
Greenbacks, DC

No. 156

4-10-04

DATE

PAY TO THE
ORDER OF  *Cash*    $ *850.00*

*Eight Hundred Fifty and* 00/100    DOLLARS

THE BIG BANK
ANYPLACE, USA

FOR    *Charles Checkwriter*

(2) Drawee

(3) Maker

Wait a minute. Is *indorsed* spelled correctly here?

Yes, it is, although I can see why you'd be confused. The term *endorsement* is sometimes used instead, but generally, statutes and legal writings use the term *indorsement*.

Okay, I'll remember that!

An instrument that is payable to a named person without specifically stating that it is "payable to the order of" the person is *not* negotiable. For example, a note "payable to Nancy Wright" is payable only to Nancy Wright. Because the instrument cannot be transferred, it is not a negotiable instrument.

Many legal issues can arise regarding the operation of negotiable instruments. Insight 9.1 describes what happens when negotiable instruments contain contradictory terms, and Insight 9.2 discusses how one country deals with the problem of dishonored checks.

---

## Insight 9.1 Contradictory Terms

If a negotiable instrument contains contradictory terms, then Article 3 of the UCC states the following rules:

1 Typewritten terms prevail over printed terms

2 Handwritten terms prevail over both typewritten and printed terms

3 Words prevail over numbers

**Example.** William Bruce wrote a check to pay his telephone bill. The check was written for $35, but the amount written out stated "forty-five dollars." Because the UCC provides that words prevail over numbers, the check is payable for $45.

---

## Insight 9.2 Dealing with Dishonored Checks

Ensuring the reliability of checks to enable the free flow of commerce is important to a country's economy. To prevent dishonesty on the part of the drawer of a check, many countries have enacted laws that make it a criminal offense to write a dishonored, or bad, check.

As just one example, in India this offense is punishable by up to one year in prison with fines of up to double the amount of the check. Under Indian law, if a check is dishonored, a payee must give notice in writing to the drawer of the check demanding payment for the amount of the check. The drawer then has 15 days after receipt of the notice to honor the check. If he fails to do so, he is subject to criminal, as well as civil, penalties. Providing proper notice to the drawer of a dishonored check is important because only a drawer who has been given such notice can be held liable.

---

## Indorsements

A holder negotiates an instrument by indorsing it with his signature and transferring the instrument to another person.

> **Example:**
>
> Samuel Forkner receives his monthly salary from his employer in the form of a check made payable to the order of Samuel Forkner. When Mr. Forkner gets a salary check, he becomes the holder of the check. He can negotiate the check by indorsing it on the back and depositing the funds into his own bank account, or he can indorse the check and give it to someone else as payment for an amount he owes that person.

As noted earlier, a holder typically indorses an instrument by signing it on the back side of the instrument. The signature generally must match the holder's name as it appears on the instrument. If an instrument is payable to two or more people jointly, then all of the named people must sign the instrument in order to negotiate it. Thus, an instrument made payable to "John and Jane Doe" must be signed by both John and Jane. By contrast, an instrument made payable to "John or Jane Doe" may be negotiated if it is indorsed by either John or Jane. An instrument that is made payable to a firm or organization may be signed by any individual authorized to act on behalf of the named firm or organization.

The way in which an instrument is indorsed determines how the instrument can be negotiated. The following are some of the various ways that an instrument can be indorsed in the United States:

- A *special indorsement* is an indorsement by a signature along with words indicating to whom the instrument should be paid.

> **Example:**
>
> Peter Wang was the holder of a check made payable to him. He indorsed the check with his signature and the notation "payable to the order of the Silver Star Bank." Thereafter, only the Silver Star Bank is entitled to negotiate the check.

- A *blank indorsement* is an indorsement by signature only, with no additional wording. When an instrument contains a blank indorsement, the instrument becomes bearer paper and any subsequent holder is entitled to negotiate it.

> **Example:**
>
> Charlotte Dempsey was the holder of a check made payable to her. She indorsed the check by signing it with no other notations and later the check fell out of her pocket. Because the check became bearer paper when Charlotte indorsed it, anyone who happens to find the check can negotiate it.

- A *restrictive indorsement* is an indorsement by signature with instructions as to how the instrument can be used. Instruments may be indorsed with notations such as "for deposit only" or "payable to ABC Bank as trustee for the Jamison Trust." Anyone who receives an instrument with a restrictive indorsement must apply the value represented by the instrument consistently with the indorsement. A party who does not apply the value as indorsed is guilty of conversion. Recall from Chapter 2 that conversion is a wrong that occurs when someone exercises unauthorized control over a person's property.

**Example:**

A bank accepted a $50 check indorsed "for deposit only" and in exchange gave the depositor $50 in cash. The bank failed to apply the funds as instructed and, thus, converted the funds. It will be liable for any losses that result from its action. If nothing else, it will have to deposit $50 into an account as instructed by the indorsement.

So you should never sign a check with a *blank* indorsement until you are at the bank. Otherwise, if you lose it, you could be out of luck!

If it is signed with just your signature, anyone who finds it might be able to cash it.

But that doesn't apply to special or restricted indorsements, right?

Generally, that's right. A *special* indorsement gives specific instructions for *who* can negotiate an instrument such as a check.

And a *restrictive* indorsement gives specific instructions for how an instrument like a check must be negotiated, or used, right?

You've got it!

## Holder in Due Course

As we noted in Chapter 8, a person to whom property is transferred generally can receive only those ownership rights that the transferor had in the property. However, a holder in due course obtains special rights that the transferee of an instrument usually does not have. A ***holder in due course*** is the holder of a negotiable instrument who (1) paid value for the instrument, (2) obtained it in good faith, and (3) obtained it without knowledge of defenses or claims against its payment.

- **Paying value.** A holder may pay value in various ways. For example, he can take an instrument in payment of an outstanding debt or can exchange one instrument for another negotiable instrument. By contrast, someone who receives a negotiable instrument as a gift has not paid value for it and is not a holder in due course.

- **Good faith.** A holder acts in good faith by observing reasonable commercial standards of fair dealing.

- **Without notice.** To qualify as a holder in due course, a person must not have notice that the instrument has been dishonored or that anyone has a claim against the maker of the instrument. Also, if an instrument shows any signs of forgery or contains any other irregularities that would call its authenticity into question, then the holder does not qualify as a holder in due course.

If all of the requirements to be a holder in due course are met, the holder obtains the instrument free of such defenses or claims against its payment. Figure 9.6 provides two examples to illustrate the special rights of a holder in due course by contrasting them with the rights of an assignee. An *assignment* is the transfer of ownership rights in property from the property owner, known as the *assignor*, to another party, known as the *assignee*. Assignments usually are used to transfer ownership rights in intangible personal property, such as a life insurance policy as we discuss in Chapter 12. As illustrated in the examples, an assignee obtains only those rights in the property that the assignor had.

## Figure 9.6 Rights of a Holder in Due Course

- A manufacturer and retailer entered into a contract under which the manufacturer agreed to supply goods to the retailer within six months of the contract date. The retailer agreed to pay for the goods in a lump sum when it received all of the goods. The manufacturer then assigned the right to collect under the contract to one of its suppliers. When all of the goods were delivered, the retailer refused to pay for the goods because they were defective. As an assignee, the supplier is subject to all claims and defenses that the retailer has against the manufacturer and may not be able to require the retailer to pay the agreed-upon amount.

- Using the same facts, assume that as part of the contract the retailer gave the manufacturer a negotiable promissory note guaranteeing payment for the goods when they were delivered to the retailer. The manufacturer transferred the note to one of its suppliers, which became a holder in due course. Because the supplier is a holder in due course, the retailer is obligated to pay the note and must pursue any claims it has against the manufacturer in a separate action.

## Liabilities of the Parties

The maker of a negotiable instrument is contractually liable under the instrument. Anyone who signs a negotiable instrument becomes contractually liable to pay the instrument. A person's liability, however, varies depending on the capacity in which she signed the instrument and on whether the instrument was a note or a draft. The following parties have primary liability to pay a negotiable instrument:

- The maker of a note has primary liability to pay the note. Thus, if you sign a note, you have assumed primary liability to pay the note.

- The acceptor of a draft has primary liability to pay the draft. A draft is accepted when the drawee signs it and thus agrees to pay it.

> **Example:**
>
> The holder of a check presents it to the drawee bank for payment. If there are sufficient funds in the account on which the check was written, then the bank will accept the check, note its acceptance by signing the front of the check, and pay the stated amount to the holder. If the account does not have sufficient funds to pay the check, the bank will not accept the check. By accepting a check, the bank becomes liable to pay the stated amount.

Other parties who sign a negotiable instrument have secondary liability to pay it. The maker of a draft has secondary liability—after the drawee—for payment of the draft. If the drawee accepts the draft, then the maker's liability is extinguished. However, if the drawee does not accept the draft, then the maker remains liable to pay the draft.

> **Example:**
>
> John Landry wrote a check to pay a monthly bill, but he did not have sufficient funds in his bank account to cover the check. The drawee bank will refuse to accept the check, and Mr. Landry will remain liable to pay the creditor the amount of the unpaid bill.

A person who indorses a negotiable instrument also has secondary liability to pay it. If the instrument is dishonored, then a person who indorsed the instrument is liable to pay the instrument according to its terms.

> **Example:**
>
> A debtor signed a note agreeing to pay a stated amount on a stated date and gave the note to a creditor. The creditor indorsed the note and transferred it to the Green Bank, which held it until it came due. If the debtor does not pay the note when it comes due, then the creditor is secondarily liable because it indorsed the note. Thus, the Green Bank can require the creditor to pay the note. As the maker of the note, the debtor has primary liability for the note, and the creditor can try to collect on the note from the debtor.

As illustrated in Figure 9.7, when several people indorse a negotiable instrument, they are liable to each other in the reverse order in which they indorsed the instrument, from the last person to indorse it back to the first person to indorse it.

## Figure 9.7 The Liability of Indorsers of a Negotiable Instrument

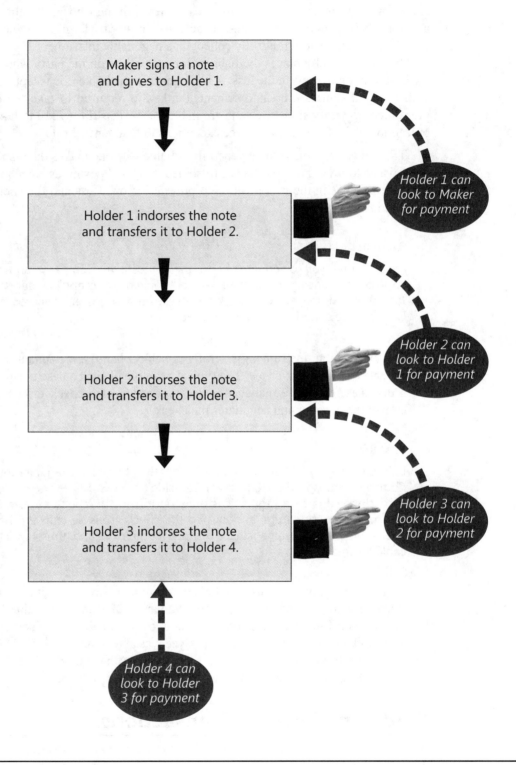

As a general rule, the forgery of a signature on a negotiable instrument makes the instrument nonnegotiable. However, people do not always detect a forged signature. Article 3 of the UCC contains rules for determining who has liability under a negotiable instrument when someone acts dishonestly by forging a signature or taking other actions to wrongfully collect on a negotiable instrument.

The UCC typically places the liability for such a loss on the party who was in the best position to prevent the loss. A bank generally is liable if it accepts a check with a forged signature or indorsement. Banks are required to take reasonable precautions to verify signatures and are liable for the loss if they fail to take such precautions. The following are some exceptions to that general rule:

- The maker of an instrument generally is liable when he makes the instrument payable to an imposter—that is, to someone who is posing as someone else. The maker is in the best position to prevent his own loss and thus bears the loss in such cases.

> **Example:**
>
> Assume that you owed money to the Jamestown Company, and an imposter convinced you that he was authorized to accept payment for Jamestown. If you make a check payable to the imposter, then you are liable for the stated amount of the check.

- The maker of an instrument generally is liable when the instrument is made payable to a fictitious payee. The typical example of such a case occurs when a dishonest employee manages to get possession of a check drawn on the employer's account and negotiates the check.

> **Example:**
>
> Mildred Wagner is an accountant for the Ironside Manufacturing Company and is authorized to sign Ironside's checks. Ms. Wagner drew a check payable to a regular customer, indorsed the check by forging the customer's signature, and cashed the check. Ironside is in the best position to protect itself against a dishonest employee and, thus, it will be liable for the check.

The maker of a note or draft who fails to use proper care in writing or signing the instrument so that another person could alter the instrument is liable for any losses that result from the alteration. For example, assume that the maker writes a check for $50, but he wrote it so that the payee was able to alter it to read $150 by adding the number 1 before the "50." As a general rule, the maker will be liable for the $150 and can try to recover the $100 overpayment from the payee.

# Credit and Secured Transactions

Individuals and businesses often purchase goods and services and agree to pay for them at a later date. Such credit transactions are common throughout the world, and most jurisdictions have established legal rules to govern the operation of various types of credit transactions. Credit transactions can be either unsecured or secured.

■ An ***unsecured transaction*** is a credit transaction in which a creditor extends credit and receives only the debtor's promise to pay the debt. Should a debtor fail to repay an unsecured debt, the creditor must sue the debtor and obtain a judgment to recover the unpaid amount.

■ A ***secured transaction*** is a credit transaction in which a creditor extends credit and receives a security interest in the debtor's property as a way to guarantee that the creditor will be protected if the debtor defaults on the loan. For example, automobiles are often purchased by means of a secured transaction in which the debtor agrees to repay the borrowed amount plus interest; the creditor obtains a security interest in the purchased vehicle and can repossess the vehicle if the debtor fails to repay the loan. A creditor who obtains a security interest in a debtor's property is referred to as a ***secured party***.

The rules governing security interests vary depending on the type of property that is involved in the transaction. In Chapter 8, we described security interests in real property. Here, we describe security interests in personal property. As a general rule, the laws of the state where the personal property is located govern the operation of a security interest in that property. In the United States, Article 9 of the UCC governs security interests in personal property.

## Perfecting a Security Interest

In order to gain the full benefits and protections of a security interest, the secured party must comply with all requirements of the applicable state laws. Two basic requirements generally must be met to gain a security interest in personal property: (1) the interest must be attached to specific property and (2) the interest must be perfected.

The security interest must *attach* to specific property so that it is clear to anyone who is interested that the property is subject to a security interest. In order for a security interest to attach to specific property, the following requirements must be met:

■ The parties must enter into a contractual agreement—known as a ***security agreement***—in which the debtor gives the creditor a security interest in specific property that is identifiable.

■ The debtor must have ownership rights in the attached property.

■ The creditor must give value to the debtor in exchange for the security interest. In other words, there must be a debt between the parties.

Requirements for *perfecting* an interest vary somewhat from state to state, and they vary depending on the type of property that is attached. The primary methods of perfecting a security interest are (1) the filing of a financing statement, (2) perfection by taking possession of property, and (3) perfection by operation of law.

I'm still not sure I understand what "perfecting" means.

Perfecting an interest basically refers to extra steps a creditor takes to protect its interest in a debtor's property.

So when a creditor has perfected its security interest in a debtor's property, nothing can take away that interest?

Well, generally speaking, yes. Of course, as with all legal matters, there are other factors to consider.

Why doesn't that surprise me?

But those are beyond the scope of our discussion here. For now, just focus on the three ways to perfect a security interest and you'll do fine.

Sounds good to me!

Under the most common method of perfecting a security interest, the secured party must file a document known as a ***financing statement*** with a specified state or local official. In some states, the secretary of state is the administrative official who is responsible for handling such document filings. In many states, local governments are responsible for handling filings concerning personal property. The financing statement, which must be signed by the debtor, contains the names and addresses of the debtor and creditor and a description or other identification of the property that has been attached to secure the debt.

The states have established administrative systems to handle financing statement filings. The filings become a part of the public record, and anyone can search the records to determine whether a given piece of property is subject to a security interest. Thus, these filings serve as notice to the public of property that is subject to a security interest. Figure 9.8 gives an example of a financing statement.

## Figure 9.8 Financing Statement

**UCC FINANCING STATEMENT**
FOLLOW INSTRUCTIONS (front and back) CAREFULLY

A. NAME & PHONE OF CONTACT AT FILER [optional]

B. SEND ACKNOWLEDGMENT TO:   (Name and Address)

THE ABOVE SPACE IS FOR FILING OFFICE USE ONLY

1. DEBTOR'S EXACT FULL LEGAL NAME - insert only one debtor name (1a or 1b) - do not abbreviate or combine names

| 1a. ORGANIZATION'S NAME | | | |
|---|---|---|---|
| OR 1b. INDIVIDUAL'S LAST NAME | FIRST NAME | MIDDLE NAME | SUFFIX |
| 1c. MAILING ADDRESS | CITY | STATE | POSTAL CODE | COUNTRY |

| 1d. **SEE INSTRUCTIONS** | ADD'L INFO RE ORGANIZATION DEBTOR | 1e. TYPE OF ORGANIZATION | 1f. JURISDICTION OF ORGANIZATION | 1g. ORGANIZATIONAL ID #, if any | NONE |

2. ADDITIONAL DEBTOR'S EXACT FULL LEGAL NAME - insert only one debtor name (2a or 2b) - do not abbreviate or combine names

| 2a. ORGANIZATION'S NAME | | | |
|---|---|---|---|
| OR 2b. INDIVIDUAL'S LAST NAME | FIRST NAME | MIDDLE NAME | SUFFIX |
| 2c. MAILING ADDRESS | CITY | STATE | POSTAL CODE | COUNTRY |

| 2d. **SEE INSTRUCTIONS** | ADD'L INFO RE ORGANIZATION DEBTOR | 2e. TYPE OF ORGANIZATION | 2f. JURISDICTION OF ORGANIZATION | 2g. ORGANIZATIONAL ID #, if any | NONE |

3. SECURED PARTY'S NAME (or NAME of TOTAL ASSIGNEE of ASSIGNOR S/P) - insert only one secured party name (3a or 3b)

| 3a. ORGANIZATION'S NAME | | | |
|---|---|---|---|
| OR 3b. INDIVIDUAL'S LAST NAME | FIRST NAME | MIDDLE NAME | SUFFIX |
| 3c. MAILING ADDRESS | CITY | STATE | POSTAL CODE | COUNTRY |

4. This FINANCING STATEMENT covers the following collateral:

| 5. ALTERNATIVE DESIGNATION [if applicable]: | LESSEE/LESSOR | CONSIGNEE/CONSIGNOR | BAILEE/BAILOR | SELLER/BUYER | AG. LIEN | NON-UCC FILING |
|---|---|---|---|---|---|---|

| 6. ☐ This FINANCING STATEMENT is to be filed [for record] (or recorded) in the REAL ESTATE RECORDS.     Attach Addendum     [if applicable] | 7. Check to REQUEST SEARCH REPORT(S) on Debtor(s) [ADDITIONAL FEE]    [optional] | All Debtors | Debtor 1 | Debtor 2 |
|---|---|---|---|---|

8. OPTIONAL FILER REFERENCE DATA

**FILING OFFICE COPY** — UCC FINANCING STATEMENT (FORM UCC1) (REV. 05/22/02)

A financing statement filing is valid for a specified period of time, typically five years. If a debt has not been repaid and the secured party wants to continue its security interest, it can file a ***continuation statement***, which amends the initial financing statement and continues the effectiveness of that financing statement for a specified number of years. Additional continuation statements may be filed if necessary, and a ***termination statement*** is filed when the debt is repaid and the creditor no longer has a security interest in the debtor's property.

A secured party can perfect a security interest in certain types of property by taking possession of the property that serves as collateral for a debt. Typically, a secured party perfects a security interest in negotiable instruments and money by taking possession of the property. A secured party also can take possession of goods and thereby perfect a security interest in the goods. In such cases, possession serves as notice to third parties of the security interest.

For certain limited types of collateral, a security interest is perfected by operation of law when the security interest attaches to the property. For example, when a consumer borrows money to purchase consumer goods and the creditor takes a security interest in those goods, the security interest is perfected automatically when the interest attaches to the goods.

## Rights of the Parties

When a security interest has been perfected in identified property, both the debtor and the secured party have rights in the property. Typically, the debtor has the right to possess and use the property. If the debtor sells or otherwise disposes of the property, the creditor's security interest nevertheless continues in the property. Thus, the creditor continues to have a perfected security interest and its rights are protected.

> **Example:**
>
> Marie Chung purchased farm equipment. She paid for the equipment by obtaining a secured loan from the Forest Green Bank, which perfected its security interest in the equipment. Before she repaid the loan, Ms. Chung sold the equipment to a neighbor. Because Forest Green Bank had perfected its security interest in the equipment, the bank's security interest continues in the equipment until Ms. Chung repays the loan.

If a debtor defaults on the debt, then the secured party has the right to foreclose by taking possession of the property and disposing of it at a public or private sale. The proceeds from the sale of the property are used to pay the expenses incurred in the foreclosure proceeding and to satisfy the debtor's obligation to the creditor. If any proceeds remain, they may be used to pay other creditors that have a security interest in the property. When several creditors have a security interest in the same property, the order in which they perfected their security interests determines which of them has priority to the proceeds from the sale of the property. The first creditor to perfect a security interest has priority over all other creditors.

> **Example:**
>
> On January 10, the Hillenburg Manufacturing Company obtained a loan from Stateland Bank and gave the bank a security interest in some of its machinery. Stateland perfected its security interest on January 20. On April 1, Hillenburg borrowed money from Northside Bank and gave Northside a security interest in the same machinery. Northside Bank perfected its security interest on April 10. When Hillenburg defaulted on both loans, it owed $5,000 to Stateland Bank and $2,500 to Northside Bank. Stateland Bank foreclosed on the machinery, which it sold for $6,000, and incurred costs of $200 in the foreclosure proceedings. Because Stateland Bank perfected its security interest first, it has priority over Northside Bank. Thus, Stateland Bank is entitled to recoup the $5,000 debt owed by Hillenburg and the $200 foreclosure costs. The remaining $800 received from the machinery's sale is payable to Northside Bank.

# Bankruptcy

Sometimes an individual or a business is unable to pay its debts as they come due. To protect themselves, creditors may file lawsuits and may begin to compete for access to the debtor's assets. When a number of creditors are involved, a debtor may need protection from an onslaught of lawsuits. In the United States, the federal **Bankruptcy Act** provides a procedure, known as a **bankruptcy proceeding**, for dealing with insolvent debtors under the supervision of a federal bankruptcy court.[1]

The Bankruptcy Act provides two basic types of bankruptcy proceedings:

- In a **liquidation proceeding**, the bankrupt debtor's assets are liquidated and the proceeds are used to pay the creditors. These proceedings sometimes are referred to as straight bankruptcies.

- In a **rehabilitation proceeding**, the bankrupt debtor can work out a plan for paying its creditors over a period of time.

Every bankruptcy proceeding begins when a bankruptcy petition is filed with the federal bankruptcy court. A petition may be filed by a debtor, in which case it is known as a **voluntary petition**. Alternatively, some types of petitions, known as **involuntary petitions**, can be filed by a creditor or creditors of an insolvent debtor. As described in Insight 9.3, certain types of businesses, including many financial services companies, are not eligible to file a petition with the bankruptcy courts.

The filing of a bankruptcy petition acts as an automatic stay. A *stay* is a suspension of a court case or specified proceedings within a case. An automatic stay in a bankruptcy proceeding protects the debtor by prohibiting creditors from taking certain actions against the debtor. For example, creditors cannot file an action against the debtor, and any existing lawsuits also are stayed. In some situations, however, creditors are not subject to the automatic stay.

The process for initiating bankruptcy proceedings varies among different countries. Insight 9.4 discusses bankruptcy proceedings in Singapore.

## Insight 9.3 Some Organizations Not Eligible for Federal Bankruptcy Proceedings

Insurance companies, municipal corporations, railroads, banks, and savings and loan companies are not permitted to file a bankruptcy petition with the federal bankruptcy courts. Instead, when these types of organizations are unable to pay their debts as they come due, each type of organization is subject to specific types of regulatory requirements. For example, the solvency of insurance companies is one of the primary objects of state insurance regulation. Laws in each state establish procedures for state insurance departments to follow in monitoring the solvency of insurers and taking action to either rehabilitate or liquidate insurers that become insolvent.

## Insight 9.4 Bankruptcy Proceedings in Singapore

In Singapore, creditors may initiate bankruptcy proceedings against a debtor if the debtor is unable to pay debts of $10,000 or more. Upon the issuance of a bankruptcy order, a public official called the Official Assignee is appointed to administer the estate of the debtor. The duties of the Official Assignee include

- Making a formal accounting for all of the debtor's assets

- Monitoring the debtor's conduct while the debtor remains in bankruptcy

- Assisting the debtor in obtaining a discharge from bankruptcy when possible

Singapore law does not provide any type of automatic discharge from bankruptcy. Generally, debtors can escape bankruptcy in only one of three ways:

- Annulment of a bankruptcy is possible if all debts are fully repaid.

- The court can discharge a bankruptcy under certain circumstances. The court will consider the debtor's age, earning capacity, money repaid to creditors, and cooperation with the Official Assignee.

- The Official Assignee may discharge a debtor from bankruptcy if the debt is below $500,000 after three years.

In Singapore, debtors can self petition or voluntarily seek bankruptcy. Debtors in Singapore, however, choose this alternative far less frequently than debtors in the United States. Singapore places severe travel restrictions on individuals in bankruptcy and also requires a regular accounting of income and expenses, both of which make voluntary bankruptcy an option of last resort for Singapore debtors.

## Liquidation Proceedings

When a debtor has so much debt that he is unlikely to be able to work out a way to repay his creditors, he can be relieved from those debts by obtaining a discharge under Chapter 7 of the Bankruptcy Act. Under rules passed in 2005, a debtor must meet certain criteria to file for Chapter 7 bankruptcy. To file for Chapter 7 bankruptcy, a debtor's current monthly income must be less than or equal to the median income of a household of the debtor's same size in the debtor's state of residence. If the debtor's income is greater than the median, the court will examine whether the debtor qualifies for a Chapter 13 bankruptcy filing. We discuss Chapter 13 bankruptcy proceedings later in this chapter.

At the beginning of the liquidation proceeding, the debtor must disclose all of his debts to the court and, with certain exceptions, turn over all of his property to a trustee appointed by the court. Only those debts that the debtor discloses can be discharged by the court. Some debts, however, cannot be discharged. For example, taxes owed to a state or federal government and alimony and child support payments cannot be discharged in bankruptcy. When a debtor owes a debt that is not discharged by a bankruptcy proceeding, the debtor still must pay the debt.

Some of the debtor's property is exempt from bankruptcy proceedings, which means that the debtor can keep that property. Exempt property includes, within stated dollar limits, the debtor's primary residence, automobile, clothing, and other personal property used for household purposes. The Bankruptcy Act enables debtors to keep some of their property as part of the Act's goal to give debtors a fresh start after the bankruptcy proceeding. Thus, debtors are allowed to keep a minimum amount of property so that they are able to live and continue working to earn a living. Insight 9.5 describes property exemptions in more detail.

The trustee liquidates the debtor's property and uses the funds to pay the creditors. Creditors are paid in a specific order of priority. For example, if a creditor has a security interest in an item of the debtor's property, then that creditor has priority to the proceeds of the sale of that item. If money remains from the sale of such an item, then those remaining funds are distributed to other creditors.

When the debtor complies with all requirements of the bankruptcy proceeding, he receives a discharge from the court. A *discharge* is a court order that relieves the debtor from any further obligation to pay the debts that were included in the bankruptcy proceeding.

## Rehabilitation Proceedings

Sometimes a debtor may be able to repay her debts if her creditors are willing to give her more time. The Bankruptcy Act provides for three types of rehabilitation proceedings designed to give debtors time to solve their financial problems by relieving them from immediate pressure from their creditors. The following types of such proceedings are provided by the Bankruptcy Act:

- Chapter 11 of the Act provides for a *reorganization proceeding* under which a debtor can work out a plan for paying its creditors. Because of the complexities of Chapter 11 proceedings, individuals generally do not file under Chapter 11. Instead, such proceedings typically are used by businesses that have become insolvent.

- Chapter 12 of the Act provides a proceeding under which a debtor involved in a family farming business can work out a plan for paying creditors.

- Chapter 13 of the Act provides a proceeding under which an individual who has a regular income can work out a plan for paying creditors.

After a bankruptcy petition is filed for a rehabilitation proceeding, the debtor submits to the court a repayment plan that details how she intends to repay her creditors over a period, such as from three to five years. Creditors often are willing to accept such a plan, because they likely will receive a larger portion of the amounts they are owed than they would receive under a liquidation proceeding. When the debtor is a business, the creditors may be willing to restructure the way in which the debt will be repaid. For example, in exchange for forgiveness of part of a debt, a creditor might be issued stock in the debtor corporation.

If the creditors and the bankruptcy court accept the debtor's plan, the debtor is responsible for carrying out that plan. When the debtor has repaid the debts according to the plan, the debtor receives a discharge from the bankruptcy court.

## Insight 9.5 Property Exempt from Bankruptcy Proceedings

Under the U.S. federal Bankruptcy Act, specific property belonging to a debtor is exempt from a bankruptcy proceeding. The following are some examples of the types of property that the federal law permits a debtor to keep:

- An interest in property used as the debtor's primary residence, but not to exceed a value of $15,000

- An interest in one motor vehicle, but not to exceed a value of $2,400

- An interest in household furnishings, clothing, appliances, books, and animals that are owned primarily for personal, family, or household use, but not to exceed a value of $400 in any one item or $8,000 in aggregate value

- An interest in jewelry held primarily for personal, family, or household use not to exceed a value of $1,000

- Life insurance policies owned by the debtor

- Professionally prescribed health aids

- Social Security, disability, alimony, and other benefits that are reasonably necessary for the support of the debtor or her dependents

The Bankruptcy Act gives debtors a choice of law regarding which property is exempt from creditors. A debtor may choose the federal law, which provides the foregoing exemptions. Alternatively, a debtor may choose the laws of the state in which the debtor resides. Some states provide exemptions from bankruptcy proceedings that are more favorable to debtors than the federal law exemptions.

**Source:** 11 U.S.C. § 522 (2011).

# Key Terms

| | |
|---|---|
| Uniform Commercial Code (UCC) | assignment |
| sale of goods | assignor |
| liquidated damages | assignee |
| cover | unsecured transaction |
| negotiable instrument | secured transaction |
| negotiability | secured party |
| note | security agreement |
| draft | financing statement |
| drawee | continuation statement |
| maker | termination statement |
| payee | Bankruptcy Act |
| holder | bankruptcy proceeding |
| bearer paper | liquidation proceeding |
| order paper | rehabilitation proceeding |
| special indorsement | voluntary petition |
| blank indorsement | involuntary petition |
| restrictive indorsement | discharge |
| holder in due course | reorganization proceeding |

# Endnote

1. 11 U.S.C. §§ 101 et seq. (2011).

*Chapter 10*

# Sale of Financial Services Products

## Objectives

### *After studying this chapter, you should be able to*

■ Describe the process of offer and acceptance and identify other requirements the parties must meet to form a valid life insurance contract

■ Explain the significance of the insurable interest requirement and the consent requirement, and describe how these requirements are met

■ Determine in a given situation whether an insurance policy would be considered to have been delivered to the policyowner

■ Distinguish between a closed contract and an open contract, and identify the documents that constitute the entire contract between the insurer and the policyowner

■ Distinguish among the various types of temporary insurance agreements, and explain how courts apply the doctrine of reasonable expectations to interpret premium receipts

■ Identify the types of activities that agency agreements typically authorize insurance producers to perform on behalf of an insurer

■ Describe common regulatory requirements with which insurance producers must comply

■ Identify steps involved in the formation of annuity contracts and in mutual fund sales

# Outline

Life insurance policies and many other products marketed by financial services companies involve a contractual relationship between the companies and their customers. In this chapter, we describe the legal issues that surround the formation of individual life insurance contracts and individual annuity contracts. Then we describe the role of insurance producers in the sale of these contracts. We conclude the chapter by describing mutual fund sales.

# Life Insurance Contract Formation

The parties to an individual life insurance contract are the insurer that issued the policy and the policyowner. As noted in Chapter 6, individual life insurance contracts are informal contracts that require no special formalities to be valid. (Figure 10.1 lists some other characteristics of individual life insurance contracts.) Like other informal contracts, life insurance contracts are not required by the general rules of contract law to be written to be valid. However, laws in many states require insurance contracts to be in writing. Insurance contracts typically are expressed in written form—whether required by law or not—for practical reasons. Putting the contract in writing helps prevent misunderstandings between the parties as to the terms of their agreement, and a written contract provides a permanent record of the agreement, which may remain in force for many years.

As with the formation of other informal contracts, the parties must meet four requirements to form a valid life insurance contract: (1) the parties must mutually assent to the contract, (2) they must exchange legally adequate consideration, (3) they must have contractual capacity, and (4) the contract must be for a lawful purpose.

## Mutual Assent

The parties manifest their mutual assent to a life insurance contract when one party makes a definite offer to contract and the other party accepts that offer unconditionally.

## Figure 10.1 Features of Life Insurance Contracts

Individual life insurance contracts can be characterized as

- **Informal contracts** that require no special formalities to be valid

- **Unilateral contracts** under which only one party—the insurer—makes legally enforceable promises

- **Aleatory contracts** under which one party—the policyowner—provides something of value to another party—the insurer—in exchange for a conditional promise

- **Contracts of adhesion** that one party—the insurer—prepares and that the other party—the applicant—must accept or reject as a whole without any bargaining between the parties

## *Offer and Acceptance*

As a general rule, applicants for insurance make an offer to enter into an insurance contract by completing an application for insurance and submitting it to an insurer along with payment of the initial premium for the applied-for policy. The insurer can accept an applicant's offer by (1) issuing a policy that contains the same terms as those stated in the applicant's offer and (2) delivering the policy to the applicant. When a valid contract is created, the applicant becomes the policyowner.

If an applicant does not pay the initial premium when she submits an application for insurance, then she has not made an offer. In such a case, the applicant has invited the insurer to make an offer. The insurer can make an offer to contract by issuing a policy and delivering it to the applicant. Note that the policy the insurer issues and delivers need not be the same policy the applicant applied for. The applicant can accept the insurer's offer by accepting the policy and paying the initial premium.

## *Counteroffers*

Insurers often issue a policy that contains terms different from those stated in an applicant's offer.

> **Example:**
> Joel Schwartz applied for a life insurance policy at a standard premium rate and paid the initial premium based on that standard rate. The insurer classified Mr. Schwartz as a substandard risk, issued a policy at a higher-than-standard premium rate, and delivered the policy to Mr. Schwartz. Because the insurer issued a policy on terms other than those applied for, the insurer rejected Mr. Schwartz's offer and made a counteroffer. Figure 10.2 illustrates this example.

An applicant can accept an insurer's counteroffer by accepting delivery of the policy and agreeing to the new contract terms that the insurer proposed. In our example, Mr. Schwartz can accept the insurer's offer by paying the additional premium—that is, the difference between the standard premium he already paid and the higher premium that the insurer actually charged.

## Figure 10.2 Counteroffer Example

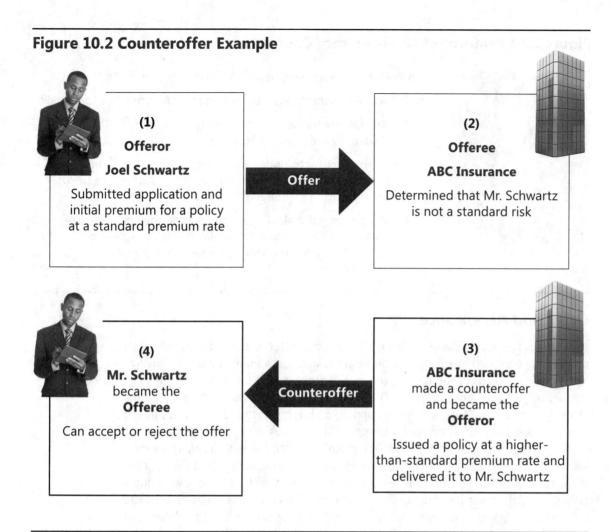

### Withdrawing an Offer

According to the general common law rules governing contracts, an offeror usually can withdraw an offer at any time before the offeree has accepted the offer. Thus, an applicant who has applied for an insurance policy and paid the initial premium has the right to withdraw that offer at any time before the insurer accepts the offer. If an applicant withdraws an offer, then the insurer generally must return the premium the applicant paid.

> **Example:**
>
> Lyle Cobb applied for an insurance policy on his life from the ABC Insurance Company and paid the initial premium. The next day, he spoke to an insurance producer who represented the XYZ Insurance Company. Mr. Cobb decided that he could purchase a policy more suited to his needs from XYZ. Mr. Cobb then completed an application for a policy from XYZ and submitted the application to XYZ. In this situation, Mr. Cobb has the right to withdraw his application from ABC and receive a refund of the premium he paid to ABC.

Although insurers also have the right to withdraw an offer to enter into an insurance contract, they usually do not exercise that right.

## *Rejecting an Offer*

Because a contract is a consensual relationship, either party can reject an offer from the other party. An applicant for insurance has the right to reject any offer made by an insurer and to receive a refund of the initial premium she paid.

> **Example:**
>
> Mae Chen applied for a policy at standard premium rates. The insurer rejected that offer and made a counteroffer by issuing a policy at a higher-than-standard premium rate. If Ms. Chen does not want to pay the higher premiums, she can reject the insurer's counteroffer and receive a refund of the initial premium she paid.

Within certain limits, insurers also have the right to reject offers to contract. For example, insurers reject the applications of proposed insureds when the insurers' underwriters find the proposed insureds present too great a risk to be eligible for insurance. In such instances, the insurers are rejecting offers to contract. State insurance laws, however, prohibit insurers from unfairly discriminating against proposed insureds because of factors such as race, national origin, marital status, sex, sexual orientation, and certain physical and mental impairments.

We underwriters follow strict guidelines when evaluating a proposed insured's risk to ensure we classify risks fairly.

That's right. If an insurer rejects an offer to contract, that decision must be based on recognized actuarial principles or actual or reasonably anticipated experience.

For example, a proposed insured with a terminal illness would likely be declined life insurance coverage because her condition prevents the insurer from providing coverage at an affordable cost for her.

Right. But insurers usually don't reject offers to contract; they generally try to offer coverage on some basis to as many proposed insureds as possible.

## Adequate Consideration

As an informal contract, a life insurance contract must be supported by legally adequate consideration in order to be valid. Life insurance contracts are unilateral contracts in which only the insurer makes an enforceable promise—that it will pay policy benefits upon the occurrence of the events insured against. Thus, the applicant for insurance must pay adequate consideration in exchange for the insurer's contractual promises. Legally adequate consideration for a life insurance contract consists of the applicant's submission of an application for insurance and payment of the initial premium.

## Contractual Capacity

For an insurance contract to be valid, the parties to the contract must have contractual capacity. Insurers that are licensed to conduct business within the applicable state have the legal capacity to enter into insurance contracts in the state. Applicants for insurance who are competent adults have the capacity to enter into an insurance contract.

Because insurance is not considered a necessity, insurance contracts entered into by a minor generally are voidable by the minor. When a minor decides to avoid an insurance contract, he is entitled to a refund of the premiums he paid. As a result, the minor benefits from the insurance coverage and pays nothing for it.

To modify this common law rule, most states have enacted laws that enable minors of a stated minimum age to enter into enforceable life insurance contracts. As a result, minors are able to enter into valid insurance contracts, and insurers that provide coverage to minors are protected against a minor's ability to avoid such a contract. The following are some of the limitations that state laws place on minors' purchases of life insurance:

- The age at which minors may enter into valid and binding insurance contracts varies from age 14 to age 16, depending on the state.

- Laws vary as to the types of insurance that minors may purchase. Some states permit minors to purchase life and health insurance on their own lives, and other states permit minors to purchase life and health insurance on any individual in whose life or health the minor has an insurable interest.

- Laws vary as to the individuals who may be named as the beneficiary of a life insurance policy purchased by a minor on her own life. Many states, for example, require the beneficiary of such a policy to be the minor's parent or legal guardian, spouse, child, brother, or sister.

Many other jurisdictions around the world have enacted laws to enable minors of a specified age to purchase insurance. Figure 10.3 lists the ages at which individuals generally are able to purchase life insurance in a few jurisdictions around the world.

## Lawful Purpose: Insurable Interest

To be valid, an informal contract must have a lawful purpose. The lawful purpose requirement is met in the formation of a life insurance contract by the presence of an insurable interest. Many early life insurance policies were purchased as wagers

## Figure 10.3 Age at Which Minors Can Purchase Insurance

**Canada:**

In the common law provinces of Canada, a minor who has attained age 16 has the capacity to enter into an enforceable life insurance contract on his own life or on the life of another as if the minor had attained the age of majority.[1]

**Singapore:**

A minor who has attained age 16 has the capacity to enter into an insurance contract without the consent of his parents or guardian. A minor between the ages of 10 and 16 has the capacity to enter into an insurance contract if he has the written consent of his parents or guardian.[2]

**Malaysia:**

A minor who has attained age 16 may enter into a life insurance policy on his own life and on the life of another person if the minor has an insurable interest in the insured's life. A minor between the ages of 10 and 16 may enter into a life insurance contract on his own life or the life of another person in whose life the minor has an insurable interest if the minor has the written consent of his parent or guardian.[3]

by individuals who had no relationship at all with the insured. In addition, the ability to gain substantial profits from an insured's death creates the danger of someone insuring another person with the intent of killing the insured and collecting policy proceeds. The insurable interest requirement is intended to prevent such situations and provides assurance that the insurance contract is being made for the lawful purpose of providing protection against financial loss, rather than for an unlawful purpose. Most countries around the world impose an insurable interest requirement on the formation of life insurance contracts. The specific requirements, however, vary from country to country. Insight 10.1 describes the insurable interest requirement in a few countries to illustrate the types of differences that exist in the requirements.

Insurable interest requirements were first developed by the common law courts and have been enacted into statutes in most U.S. states. As with most rules of law, insurable interest requirements vary somewhat from state to state. In all states, for the contract to be valid, a policyowner must have an insurable interest in the insured person when the life insurance policy is issued. Generally, an insurable interest exists when a person is likely to benefit if the insured continues to live and is likely to suffer some loss or detriment if the insured dies. Whether the requirement is met in a given case is a question of fact. Note that the insurable interest must exist only at the time of contracting and is not required to continue throughout the life of the policy.

In most cases, individual life insurance policies are applied for and owned by the person who is insured by the policy. Some policies, however, are issued to persons other than the insured. Insurable interest requirements vary depending on whether a policy insures the policyowner or someone other than the policyowner.

## Insight 10.1 Insurable Interest Requirements in Various Countries

### Australia

The Insurance Contracts Act was amended in 2005 to end the insurable interest requirement for the formation of a valid life insurance contract. The Act now states that a life insurance contract is not void for lack of insurable interest when the contract is created.[4]

### Canada

All provinces require an applicant to have an insurable interest in the person insured by a life insurance policy when the contract is formed. However, if the proposed insured consents in writing to the issuance of a policy on his life, then the insurance contract is valid even if the applicant has no insurable interest in the proposed insured.[5]

An insurable interest is presumed to exist between certain family members. In the common law provinces, an insurable interest exists between a person and (1) his children and grandchildren, (2) his spouse, and (3) anyone who contributes to his support or education. In Quebec, an insurable interest exists between a person and (1) his spouse, (2) his descendants and his spouse's descendants, and (3) anyone who contributes to his support or education.

### Malaysia

An insurable interest is deemed to exist between a person and (1) his spouse and his child or ward who is under the age of majority at the time the insurance is effected, (2) his employee, or (3) a person on whom he is wholly or partly dependent when the insurance is effected.[6]

### Policyowner Insures His Own Life

In all states, a person is considered to have an unlimited insurable interest in his own life. In other words, a person can buy as much insurance on his own life as insurers are willing to issue. An applicant who seeks to insure his own life meets the insurable interest requirement and generally may name anyone he wishes as beneficiary. Thus, state laws do not require the beneficiary of such a policy to have an insurable interest in the proposed insured's life.

### Policyowner Insures Another Person's Life

When someone applies for insurance on another person's life, the applicant generally must provide the insurer with evidence that she has an insurable interest in the insured's life. In most states, an insurable interest is presumed to exist between certain close family members. Thus, an insured's spouse, mother, father, child, grandparent, grandchild, brother, and sister are presumed to have an insurable interest in the life of the insured. The bonds of love and loyalty that exist in such family relationships are deemed sufficient to protect the insured. State laws do not presume an insurable interest in the case of more distant relatives, such as cousins, aunts and uncles, and stepchildren.

Anyone other than a close relative must demonstrate that she has a financial interest in the continued life of the insured to satisfy the insurable interest requirement. For example, an individual who is not a close relative of an insured may be financially dependent on the insured and, thus, would be harmed if the insured died. Business relationships also may give someone a financial interest in another's continued life. Figure 10.4 describes business relationships that create an insurable interest.

### Figure 10.4 Insurable Interest and Business Relationships

The following are some of the business relationships that create an insurable interest:

- Partners are each considered to have an insurable interest in the lives of the other partners

- An employer has an insurable interest in the lives of its key employees

- A creditor has an insurable interest in the lives of its debtors

Typically, a person who purchases insurance on another person's life names himself as the policy beneficiary. Thus, the person who will benefit from the policy after the insured's death is also the policyowner, who has an insurable interest in the insured's life. When a person purchases insurance on another person's life and names a third person as the policy beneficiary, the possibility of policy proceeds becoming payable to someone with no insurable interest in the insured's life arises. To prevent such a situation, statutes in many states require that when a person purchases a policy on another person's life, the person named as the policy beneficiary must have an insurable interest in the insured's life.

### Consent Requirement

In addition to the insurable interest requirement, most states require a proposed insured to consent to the issuance of a policy on her life. Without such consent, a policy taken out on the life of another person is void. The consent requirement is designed to protect insureds from another person profiting from their deaths without their knowledge. State insurance laws include exceptions that allow an insurance policy to be issued without the insured's consent. For example,

- A parent generally is permitted to insure the life of a minor child without the child's consent.

- A few states permit one spouse to insure the life of the other spouse without the insured's consent.

- A few states permit employers to purchase insurance on the lives of their employees without the employees' consent.

### *Insurers' Duty of Care*

Insurers are careful to make sure that the insurable interest requirement is met before they issue a policy. In addition, many insurers' underwriting guidelines impose more stringent insurable interest requirements than the requirements imposed by state laws. An insurer that fails to exercise reasonable care in evaluating whether the insurable interest requirement is met for a given policy could be subject to tort liability for any harm that befalls an insured who did not consent to the policy. Insight 10.2 describes a case in which an insurer was held liable for damages following an insured's death because the insurer failed to use reasonable care when it issued a life insurance policy.

So it is the underwriter's responsibility to determine if insurable interest exists?

Yes, we have to follow legally established guidelines and examine the facts in each case to determine whether the beneficiary has an insurable interest in the life of the proposed insured.

That's an important job, and it sounds like there are a lot of laws and rules to follow.

Exactly. So companies make sure their underwriters are kept up to date on new laws and changes to existing laws.

---

## Insight 10.2 Insurers' Tort Liability

Although insurers are careful to ensure that the insurable interest requirement is met for every life insurance policy they issue, cases have arisen in which the lack of insurable interest contributed to an insured's death. In one case, a young child's aunt purchased several insurance policies on the child's life and named herself as the beneficiary.[7] The child did not live with the aunt and was not financially dependent on the aunt, who had no insurable interest in the child's life. The child's parents were unaware that the policies had been issued on the child's life. The aunt poisoned the child and was convicted of murdering the child so that she could collect the insurance policy proceeds. The child's father then sued the insurer, alleging that the insurer failed to use reasonable care when it issued the policies. The court found that the insurer had failed in its duty to use reasonable care and that the insurer's failure had resulted in the child's death. The insurer was required to pay damages for the child's wrongful death.

## Policy Delivery

An individual life insurance policy typically states that the policy does not become effective until (1) it is delivered to the policyowner and (2) the initial premium is paid. Both requirements must be met during the continued good health of the insured in order for the contract to be effective. If an insurance producer helped the applicant complete the application for insurance, the insurer typically mails the newly issued policy to the producer, who delivers the policy to the policyowner. If no insurance producer is involved in the sale, then the insurer generally mails the policy directly to the policyowner.

Sometimes, a policy is considered to have been delivered even though it never actually reached the policyowner. Delivery in such cases is referred to as *constructive delivery* because although there was no actual delivery, the courts would consider the policy to have been delivered. As a general rule, a policy is considered to have been constructively delivered when the insurer parts with control of the policy and intends to be bound to the terms of the contract.

> **Example:**
>
> On May 1, June Sun applied for a policy on her life and paid the initial premium. On May 10, the insurer issued the policy as applied for. On May 11, the insurer mailed the policy to the insurance producer for delivery to Ms. Sun. Ms. Sun died on May 14 before the producer was able to actually deliver the policy to her. Courts generally would consider that, because the insurer parted with control of the policy and intended to be bound to it on May 11, the policy had been constructively delivered to Ms. Sun at the time of her death. Thus, the policy would be considered effective, and the insurer would be liable to pay the policy death benefit.

Most states have enacted laws that spell out the required wording of standard provisions that insurers must include in individual life insurance policies, and most states require policies to include a free look provision. The *free look provision* gives the policyowner a specified period—usually 10 days—following delivery of the policy within which to cancel the policy and receive a refund of the premium paid. The free look period allows the policyowner time to review the policy and evaluate whether it is the policy applied for and is the product best suited to the policyowner's needs. During the free look period, the policy and the coverage it provides are effective and binding on the insurer. Figure 10.5 lists the provisions that most states require individual life insurance policies to include. We describe these provisions throughout the remainder of the text.

## Entire Contract

Individual life insurance policies generally must include an *entire contract provision*, which defines the documents that constitute the contract between the insurer and the policyowner. The specific wording of the entire contract provision varies depending on whether the policy is a closed contract or an open contract.

With the exception of fraternal insurers, U.S. insurers issue individual life insurance policies that are closed contracts. A *closed contract* is a contract for which only those terms and conditions that are printed in—or attached to—the contract are considered to be part of the contract. In a closed life insurance contract, the

## Figure 10.5 Required Life Insurance Policy Provisions

**Individual life insurance policies** typically must include the following provisions:

- Free look provision
- Entire contract provision
- Grace period provision
- Incontestability provision
- Misstatement of age provision
- Reinstatement provision

**Participating policies** also must include a dividend provision.

**Permanent policies** also must include a nonforfeiture provision and a policy loan provision.

entire contract provision states that the contract consists of the policy, any attached riders and endorsements, and the attached copy of the application. In Chapter 13, we describe the importance of the insurer attaching a copy of the application to the policy when it is delivered to the policyowner.

Fraternal insurers issue life insurance coverage in the form of an ***open contract***, which is a contract that identifies the documents that constitute the contract between the parties, but the enumerated documents are not all attached to the contract. Typically, policies issued by fraternal insurers state that the entire contract between the parties consists of the following documents:

- The policy and any attached riders and endorsements
- The fraternal society's charter, constitution, and bylaws
- The application for membership in the fraternal society
- The declaration of insurability, if any, signed by the applicant

Typically, a fraternal insurer attaches a copy of the application for membership and the declaration of insurability to the policy delivered to an insured member. Although the fraternal's charter, constitution, and bylaws are not attached to the policy, these documents are available to society members, and the terms of these documents are enforceable by the parties as part of their contractual agreement.

## Temporary Insurance Agreements

Most applicants for life insurance pay the initial premium when they complete their application for insurance. The applicant, the insurer, and the insurance producer benefit when the initial premium is submitted along with the application. The advantage to the applicant is that, under certain circumstances, insurance coverage may exist before the policy itself is effective. The underwriting process can take several weeks, and many applicants pay the initial premium so that their coverage can begin before the underwriting and policy issue processes are completed. The advantage to the insurer and the insurance producer is that an applicant who has paid the initial premium is more likely to accept the policy when it is delivered than is an applicant who has not paid the initial premium.

When an applicant pays the initial premium with the application, the insurance producer gives the applicant a premium receipt that acknowledges the premium payment and often includes a temporary insurance agreement. Such an agreement provides insurance coverage on the proposed insured before a policy is issued and delivered, although such coverage may be subject to certain conditions. A temporary insurance agreement is a contract between the insurer and the life insurance applicant. The contract is formed when the insurance producer—who is acting as an authorized agent of the insurer—makes an offer to provide temporary insurance coverage if the applicant pays the initial premium. The applicant accepts the insurer's offer by paying that premium, and the temporary insurance agreement is then effective.

A premium receipt that provides temporary insurance coverage states (1) when that coverage becomes effective, (2) the conditions that must be met for the coverage to become effective, and (3) when the coverage will end. Premium receipts also usually state that the temporary insurance coverage is provided subject to the terms of the insurance policy for which the applicant applied.

> **Example:**
>
> If the policy applied for contains a suicide exclusion provision, then the temporary insurance agreement also contains that suicide exclusion provision even if the premium receipt is silent concerning suicide.

When the terms of a premium receipt conflict with the terms of the policy applied for, then the terms of the premium receipt control.

> **Example:**
>
> Premium receipts often limit the life insurance benefits available to a stated dollar amount, which is often less than the amount of insurance that the applicant applied for. If the proposed insured dies while insured under a temporary insurance agreement, the amount of the death benefit payable is limited to the amount specified in the premium receipt.

## Types of Temporary Insurance Agreements

Although the terms of premium receipts vary widely, two basic types of receipts are issued: conditional premium receipts and binding premium receipts. Both types of receipts are subject to conditions. In contract law, a *condition* is an uncertain event, the occurrence or nonoccurrence of which either creates or extinguishes a party's duty to perform a contractual promise. Thus, a condition is a contractual term that limits a party's promise. Conditions can be categorized as either conditions precedent or conditions subsequent.

■ A *condition precedent* is a condition that must occur in order to give rise to one party's duty to perform a promise. For example, an insurer's promise to pay a life insurance policy death benefit is subject to a condition precedent—the contract must be in force when the event insured against occurs. If the contract is not in force at the insured's death, then the condition precedent is not met, and the insurer is not liable to pay the policy death benefit.

■ A *condition subsequent* is a condition that, if it occurs, cancels one party's duty to perform a promise. For example, some insurance policies provide that, unless a claimant furnishes the insurer with proof of a covered loss within a stated time after the occurrence of the loss, the insurer has no liability to pay for the loss. The claimant's failure to provide the insurer with proof of a covered loss within the required period, when the claimant could have done so, is a condition subsequent that relieves the insurer of its duty to pay for the loss.

## Conditional Premium Receipts

A *conditional premium receipt* provides temporary insurance coverage only if specified conditions are met. One kind of conditional premium receipt is an *insurability premium receipt*, which provides temporary insurance coverage on condition that the insurer finds the proposed insured to be insurable as a standard or preferred risk. The insurer's contractual promise to pay a benefit if the proposed insured dies while the agreement is in force is subject to the condition precedent that the insurer find the proposed insured to be insurable as a standard risk on a specified date according to the insurer's standard underwriting guidelines. The premium receipt states the date on which the insured's insurability must be determined. That date typically is either the date of the premium receipt, the date of the application, or the date of a required medical examination.

### Example:

Jose Alvarado completed an application for insurance and paid the initial premium on May 1. He received an insurability premium receipt that provided temporary insurance coverage if the insurer found him to be an insurable risk on the date of a required medical examination. Mr. Alvarado underwent the examination on May 10, and the physician submitted his report to the insurer. After reviewing the application and medical examination, the insurer's underwriter approved Mr. Alvarado as a standard risk on May 17. Before it issued the policy, the insurer learned that Mr. Alvarado died in an accident on May 16. Because the insurer found that Mr. Alvarado was insurable on the date of his medical examination, the condition precedent to insurance coverage under the temporary insurance agreement was met. The insurance on Mr. Alvarado became effective on the date of the medical examination, and the insurer was liable to pay the benefit specified in the premium receipt.

**Example:**

Marisa Bolinger completed an application for insurance and paid the initial premium on April 1. She received an insurability premium receipt that provided temporary insurance coverage if the insurer found her to be an insurable risk on the date of a required medical examination. Ms. Bolinger died on April 5 before the medical examination was completed. The condition precedent to the insurer's duty to pay a death benefit was not met, and Ms. Bolinger was not insured under the temporary insurance agreement.

**Example:**

Ricky Larson completed an application for insurance and paid the initial premium on August 15. He received an insurability premium receipt that provided temporary insurance coverage if the insurer found him to be an insurable risk on the date of a required medical examination. Mr. Larson underwent the examination on August 20, and the physician submitted his report to the insurer. Mr. Larson, however, died before the insurer evaluated his application for insurance. The insurer was required to complete the underwriting process to make a good faith determination as to whether Mr. Larson was insurable on the day of the medical examination. If the insurer determined that Mr. Larson was insurable on the date of the medical examination, then it would be liable to pay the benefit specified in the premium receipt.

Another type of conditional receipt is an ***approval premium receipt***, which provides temporary insurance coverage only when the insurer approves the proposed insured as a standard or better-than-average risk. Insurance coverage under an approval premium receipt is subject to the condition precedent that the insurer must in fact approve the insured as a standard risk. If the condition precedent is met and the insurer approves the risk, then insurance coverage is effective on the date of the insurer's approval. However, if the proposed insured dies before the application is approved, then the insurer is not liable to pay a death benefit. U.S. insurers rarely issue approval premium receipts.

To protect consumers, some states prohibit insurers and producers from describing a conditional premium receipt as a *temporary insurance agreement*. Lawmakers in these states think that the term temporary insurance agreement may cause confusion and some applicants could think that coverage is in force when it is not.

## Binding Premium Receipts

A ***binding premium receipt*** provides temporary insurance coverage that becomes effective on the date specified in the receipt. Unlike conditional premium receipts, binding premium receipts provide temporary insurance coverage without requiring that specified conditions be met. Compared to the terms of other types of premium receipts, the terms of binding premium receipts are more advantageous to applicants and less advantageous to insurers. Under a binding receipt, the insurer provides insurance coverage before it has the opportunity to evaluate whether the proposed insured is insurable. A sample binding premium receipt is shown in Figure 10.6.

## Figure 10.6 Sample Binding Premium Receipt

| | | |
|---|---|---|
| **XYZ** Life Insurance | **TEMPORARY LIFE INSURANCE AGREEMENT** | XYZ LIFE INSURANCE COMPANY PO Box 1234 Anywhere, USA 12345-1234 |

Subject to the terms of this Agreement, this Agreement provides a limited amount of life insurance protection for the Proposed Insured, for a limited period of time.

                                                                       Yes  No

1.  Has the Proposed Insured:
    a.  Within the past 6 months, been admitted to a hospital or other medical facility, or been advised to be admitted by a physician or other medical practitioner; or had surgery performed or recommended by a physician or other medical practitioner? ☐ ☐
    b.  Within the past 2 years, been treated for heart trouble, stroke, acquired immunodeficiency syndrome (AIDS), AIDS-related complex (ARC), or cancer; or had such treatment recommended by a physician or other medical practitioner? ☐ ☐
    c.  Within the past 2 years, been declined or offered life or health insurance at higher than standard premiums by any company? ☐ ☐
2.  Is the Proposed Insured younger than 15 days of age or older than age 65 (age last birthday)? ☐ ☐

**No temporary insurance will be provided under this Agreement if any of the above questions are answered YES or LEFT BLANK. However, the application should still be submitted for evaluation WITHOUT PAYMENT; no insurance will result from such application until the policy is accepted by the applicant, and the first modal premium has been paid to XYZ Life Insurance Company (hereinafter known as "XYZ Life" or "Company").**

### TERMS AND CONDITIONS

**DATE COVERAGE BEGINS**

Temporary life insurance begins on the date that your application, first modal payment and this Agreement are **received and accepted** by XYZ Life.

**AMOUNT OF COVERAGE** — $500,000 MAXIMUM FOR ALL APPLICATIONS OR AGREEMENTS

If the Proposed Insured dies while this temporary insurance is in effect, XYZ Life will pay to the designated beneficiary the lesser of: (a) the amount of all applicable death benefits applied for in the application; or (b) $500,000. This total benefit limit applies to all insurance applied for under any current applications to the Company, and to any other Temporary Life Insurance Agreements issued by XYZ Life and still in effect.

**DATE COVERAGE TERMINATES — 90-DAY MAXIMUM PERIOD**

Temporary life insurance under this Agreement will terminate automatically on the earliest of:
    a.  90 days from the effective date of this Agreement; or
    b.  the date the policy applied for becomes effective; or,
    c.  the date the Company mails notice of termination of coverage to the Applicant's last known mailing address. XYZ Life may terminate coverage at any time before the policy is issued.

**SPECIAL LIMITATIONS**

- This Agreement does not provide benefits for disability.
- Fraud or material misrepresentations in either the application or this Agreement invalidate this Agreement; the Company's only liability is to refund any payment made.
- If the Proposed Insured dies by suicide, the Company's liability under this Agreement is limited to a refund of any payment made.
- There is no coverage under this Agreement if the check or draft submitted as payment is not honored by your bank.
- No one is authorized to waive or modify any of the provisions of this Agreement.

*(continued on next page)*

## Figure 10.6 Sample Binding Premium Receipt *continued...*

$ _____

Please indicate the amount of first modal payment you are submitting. Consult with your XYZ Life Representative if you need assistance in determining the correct amount. **Send no money if any of the above questions are answered YES or LEFT BLANK.**

I (WE) HAVE READ THIS AGREEMENT AND DECLARE THAT THE ANSWERS ARE TRUE TO THE BEST OF MY (OUR) KNOWLEDGE AND BELIEF. I (WE) UNDERSTAND AND AGREE TO ALL ITS TERMS.

X_____    _____ XX _____    _____
Signature of Proposed Insured                              Date                    Signature of Proposed Owner/Applicant        Date
                                                                                   (If Owner/Applicant other than
                                                                                   Proposed Insured)

FOR COMPANY USE ONLY

_____

_____

NOTICE: When this Agreement becomes effective, a copy of it (signed by an authorized XYZ Life Representative) will be returned to the Applicant.

TIA-EFT01-01

Unlike the temporary insurance coverage provided by conditional premium receipts, which is subject to a condition precedent, the coverage provided by a binding premium receipt is subject to a condition subsequent because the insurer has the right to cancel the temporary insurance coverage if certain circumstances occur. Temporary coverage under a binding premium receipt typically remains effective until the earliest of the following occurrences: (1) the insurer issues the applicant a policy, (2) the insurer declines the application, (3) the insurer terminates or suspends coverage under the receipt, or (4) a specified time—usually 45 to 60 days—expires.

## Courts' Interpretations of Premium Receipts

Historically, U.S. courts enforced the various types of conditional premium receipts in accordance with the stated terms of those receipts, and many courts continue to enforce the terms of insurability and approval premium receipts. More recently, however, courts in many states have enforced conditional premium receipts as if they were binding premium receipts that provided coverage whether or not a specified condition precedent was met. Courts have followed various types of reasoning to arrive at their decisions:

- Some courts have found that the terms of conditional premium receipts were ambiguous. When the terms of a contract of adhesion such as an insurance contract are ambiguous, the rules of contract construction require the court to interpret the contract in a way that is most favorable to the policyowner or claimant.

- Other courts have based their decisions on a legal doctrine known as the *doctrine of reasonable expectations*. According to this doctrine, an applicant who pays the initial premium in advance and receives a premium receipt that provides temporary insurance coverage can reasonably assume that he is covered immediately unless it is clearly brought to his attention that coverage is not immediate. Insight 10.3 describes the doctrine of reasonable expectations.

- A few courts have refused to enforce the terms of conditional premium receipts because those terms are unfair to applicants who expect the receipt to provide coverage without being subject to specified conditions.

---

### Insight 10.3 The Doctrine of Reasonable Expectations

Although it is not used often, courts in most states have adopted the doctrine of reasonable expectations for purposes of interpreting the meaning of insurance contracts.[8] The doctrine grew out of the common law rules governing how courts interpret the meaning of contracts. As a contract of adhesion, an insurance contract that contains an ambiguity is construed against the insurer that drafted the contract. Thus, if an insurance contract contains terms that are ambiguous, courts sometimes base their decision as to the meaning of the ambiguous terms by interpreting the contract so as to enforce the policyowner's reasonable expectations. In other words, if an insurance contract contains language that can reasonably be interpreted in more than one way, then the court will interpret the language as the average policyowner would have reasonably interpreted the language.

The doctrine typically is used only in narrow circumstances, but predicting with any certainty when courts will apply the doctrine is difficult. In many states, the doctrine is applied only if the terms of an insurance contract are ambiguous or a policy contains exclusions that are written in technical language that the average policyowner would not understand. Courts in some states, however, have applied the doctrine even when they found that the contract was not ambiguous.[9]

---

## Formation of an Annuity Contract

Like individual life insurance contracts, individual annuity contracts are informal contracts. The parties to an individual annuity contract are the insurer that issued the annuity and the person who purchased the annuity, commonly referred to as the *contract owner*.

The parties create a valid annuity contract by meeting the same four requirements as do the parties to any informal contract:

- **Mutual assent:** Typically, the process of offer and acceptance is uncomplicated. The applicant completes an application for the type of annuity he wants and the insurer generally issues the contract as applied for. The application typically does not contain questions relating to the insurability of the applicant, and the insurer does not evaluate the insurability of the applicant.

- **Adequate consideration:** The applicant for an annuity usually pays all or a part of the consideration required to pay for the annuity when he submits the application. Amounts paid for an annuity often are referred to as *annuity considerations* as well as premiums.

- **Contractual capacity:** Both parties must have contractual capacity.

- **Lawful purpose:** Unlike a life insurance policy, an annuity usually does not present the opportunity for the applicant to wager on someone's life or for someone to benefit from another's death. Thus, insurable interest requirements are not imposed. As long as no illegal purposes are involved, the creation of an annuity contract meets the lawful purpose requirement. Annuities usually are purchased for the purpose of managing the customer's need for asset accumulation during the annuity's accumulation period and income distribution during retirement or another period of similar financial need.

A contract is created between the parties when the insurer issues the contract and delivers it to the contract owner and the contract owner pays the amount required as the first annuity consideration. In the case of a single-premium annuity, for example, the required single premium must be paid.

State insurance laws generally require individual annuity contracts to include some of the same provisions that must be included in individual life insurance policies. The following are some of the provisions that individual annuity contracts typically must include:

- An *entire contract provision*, which usually states that the entire contract between the parties consists of the annuity contract, the application if it is attached to the contract, and any attached riders and endorsements.

- A *free look provision*, which gives the contract owner a specified period, usually from 10 to 30 days, within which to return the contract and receive a full refund of all consideration paid for the contract. The contract is effective throughout the free look period.

# Insurance Producers' Role

To market life insurance in the United States, an insurance producer first must be licensed to sell insurance by each state in which he conducts business. Licensing requirements seek to ensure that insurance producers are of good character. Thus, an individual who has been convicted of a felony or who has violated state insurance laws may not qualify for a producer's license. Licensing requirements also seek to ensure that insurance producers are knowledgeable about the products they sell. A candidate for a license must pass a written examination in each line of insurance that he plans to sell, and the license he receives identifies the lines of insurance he is authorized to sell. Most states consider annuities to be a type of life insurance; thus, a producer's license to sell life insurance usually includes the right to sell annuities. In addition to obtaining a state insurance license, a producer who plans to sell variable products must be a registered representative associated with a FINRA member.

## Agency Agreement

An insurance producer who markets and sells life insurance products on behalf of an insurance company acts as an agent of the insurer. Typically, insurers enter into a written contract, known as an ***agency agreement*** or *agency contract*, with each of their producers. The terms of such an agency agreement spell out the rights and duties of the principal (the insurer) and the agent (the producer). Figure 10.7 lists some of the terms that commonly are included in agency agreements.

---

## Figure 10.7 Common Terms in an Agency Agreement

- A statement that the producer is an independent contractor and not an employee of the insurance company, if such is the case

- A description of the producer's authority to represent the company, solicit and take applications, arrange medical examinations, collect initial premiums, and issue premium receipts

- Limitations on the producer's authority, specifying that the producer cannot change premium rates, alter contracts, incur debts on behalf of the company, or otherwise act outside the scope of granted authority

- Performance requirements, particularly with respect to adherence to company rules and the prompt remittance of premiums to the company

- A compensation schedule, stating the rate of commissions, service fees, bonuses, and other compensation

- Termination provisions, stating (1) justifiable causes for termination, (2) the length of time required for notice of termination by either the producer or the company, and (3) the obligations of each party after the agency agreement is terminated

---

As the principal in an agency relationship, an insurer has the right to determine the scope of the agent's authority, and the scope of that authority is spelled out in the agency agreement. Because an agent who acts within the scope of his authority has the power to bind his principal, insurers generally are interested in limiting the scope of such authority.

Producers typically are authorized to issue a premium receipt to an applicant who completes an application and pays the initial premium. Depending on the terms of the receipt, the insurer may be contractually bound to provide temporary insurance coverage under the receipt. With the exception of binding an insurer to providing temporary coverage under a premium receipt, a producer is not authorized to enter into binding life insurance contracts on an insurer's behalf. Only specified employees—usually in the insurer's home office—have actual authority to approve an application and issue a life insurance policy that is binding on the insurer. An application for life insurance generally includes a notice to the applicant stating that no policy will become effective unless the application is approved and a policy is issued by the insurer's home office. By signing the application, the applicant acknowledges he is aware that the insurance producer is not authorized to complete an insurance contract on the insurer's behalf.

Life insurance producers typically have actual authority to accept *initial* premium payments on behalf of an insurer. Payment of an initial premium to such an agent is legally considered payment to the insurer. Life insurance producers, however, generally do not have actual authority to accept *renewal* premium payments.

Sometimes an agent acts outside the scope of his authority and the principal is bound by the act. In these cases, the principal generally is bound because the agent had apparent authority to act on behalf of the principal. For example, assume that a life insurance producer repeatedly accepts renewal premium payments from one of his clients and remits the payments to the insurer. If the insurer establishes a pattern of accepting the payments from the producer, then the insurer has in effect agreed to the producer's actions and probably has conferred apparent authority on the producer to accept future renewal premium payments from this client. Payment of a renewal premium to a producer who has apparent authority to accept it is payment to the insurer even if the producer does not promptly remit the payment to the insurer. The scope of an agent's authority is a question of fact that depends on the circumstances of the situation.

Because an insurance producer is an agent of an insurer, the knowledge an insurance producer has concerning the business he has transacted on behalf of the insurer is considered to be the knowledge of the insurer. We describe such situations in detail in Chapter 13.

## Regulatory Requirements

In addition to conducting business in accordance with the terms of their agency agreements, life insurance producers must comply with applicable regulatory requirements. An agent who conducts business within a state must comply with that state's insurance laws and regulations. The primary goal of such regulation is to protect the interests of consumers to ensure that they receive accurate and complete information on which to base purchase decisions. In this section, we describe some of the regulatory requirements that states impose on insurance producers.

Most states have enacted as part of their insurance laws an ***Unfair Trade Practices Act*** that defines certain practices as unfair and prohibits those practices in the business of insurance if they are committed flagrantly in conscious disregard of the Act or so frequently as to indicate a general business practice. State Unfair Trade Practices Acts generally apply to all individuals and legal entities that engage in the business of insurance, including insurers and insurance producers. Activities that are prohibited by most state Unfair Trade Practices Acts include

- Defamation

- False statements and entries

- Unfair discrimination

- ***Rebating***, which is a sales practice in which a producer offers a prospect an inducement to purchase a policy from the producer and the inducement is not offered to all applicants in similar situations and is not stated in the policy itself

Because of the complexity of life insurance policies, consumers often rely on insurance producers to explain the features of insurance policies and the costs of various policies and coverages. Therefore, to ensure that consumers can trust the information given to them by producers, the states have enacted insurance laws that prohibit producers from misrepresenting to consumers any feature or aspect of an insurance policy. Figure 10.8 describes some specific misrepresentations the states typically prohibit.

## Figure 10.8 Specific Misrepresentations Prohibited by the States

- Life insurance and annuity policies must not be misrepresented as "investments" or "savings" vehicles.

- Premiums must not be misrepresented as "deposits" or "premium deposits."

- Policy dividends must not be misrepresented as "earnings" or "savings," and no guarantees may be implied.

- Life insurance producers may not imply that the beneficiary of a permanent life insurance policy will receive both the policy death benefit and the policy cash value following the death of the insured, unless this is in fact the case.

A variety of state laws and regulations govern insurance advertising by both insurers and insurance producers. In addition to state insurance laws, most states have general consumer protection statutes that regulate all types of advertisements, and these laws often govern life insurance advertisements. In all states, insurers and insurance producers are prohibited from placing before the public any advertisements that are untrue, deceptive, or misleading.

When a licensed producer violates state regulatory requirements, the producer is subject to being sanctioned by the applicable state insurance department. In addition, when a producer's actions cause harm to a customer, the producer and the insurer for which the producer is acting as an agent may be liable to pay damages caused by the injury.

## Mutual Fund Sales

Insurance is primarily intended to compensate an individual or business for a financial loss, not to provide an opportunity for financial gains. Other products marketed by financial services companies are investment products that provide customers with the potential for financial gains. Transactions for the purchase of financial products other than insurance do not involve any underwriting. Thus, the purchase of these other financial products does not create the legal issues that surround the formation of a life insurance contract.

Stocks and bonds issued by corporations have long been popular investment vehicles. Investors also can diversify their stock and bond investments by purchasing shares in a mutual fund, and many financial services companies market mutual funds. Investors generally can purchase mutual fund shares from various sources. Some funds permit investors to purchase shares directly from the fund without an intermediary. An investor also may purchase shares through a registered representative who is affiliated with a broker-dealer, is a bank employee, or is an insurance producer.

To open a mutual fund account, an investor typically must complete an application that the mutual fund prepares. A fund's prospectus includes the appropriate application. Depending on the fund, the investor may be required to invest a stated minimum amount to open the account. The person who will be the owner of the account must sign the application, and the investor's initial investment must accompany the application. When the fund receives the application and the initial investment, it establishes the account and then mails to the investor a confirmation of the transaction.

## Key Terms

constructive delivery
free look provision
entire contract provision
closed contract
open contract
condition
condition precedent
condition subsequent
conditional premium receipt
insurability premium receipt
approval premium receipt
binding premium receipt
agency agreement
Unfair Trade Practices Act
rebating

*What is the difference?*

## Endnotes

1. Insurance Act of Ontario, R.S.O., ch. I-8, s. 202 (1990) (Can.).

2. Insurance Act (Singapore, cap 142, 2002 rev ed), http://statutes.agc.gov.sg/aol/search/display/view.w3p ;page=0;query=CompId%3A4268296e-5b49-407e-9869-66a8bc27e1f1;rec=0;resUrl=http%3A%2F% 2Fstatutes.agc.gov.sg%2Faol%2Fbrowse%2FtitleResults.w3p%3Bletter%3DI%3BpNum%3D1%3Bty pe%3DactsAll (19 March 2012).

3. Insurance Act 1996 (Malaysia) s. 153, <http://www.pytheas.net/docs/malaysia/InsuranceAct1996.pdf (19> March 2012).

4. Insurance Contracts Act 1984 (Cth.) s. 16(1)[54].

5. Insurance Act of Ontario, R.S.O., ch. I-8, s. 178(2) (1990) (Can.); C.C.Q., ch. 64, art. 2148 (1991) (Can.).

6. Insurance Act 1996 (Malaysia) s. 152, <http://www.pytheas.net/docs/malaysia/InsuranceAct1996.pdf (19> March 2012).

7. Liberty National Life Insurance Co. v. Weldon, 267 Ala. 171 (1957).

8. Max True Plastering Co. v. United States Fidelity & Guaranty Co.,. 912 P.2d 861 (Okla. 1996).

9. National Mutual Insurance Co. v. McMahon & Sons, Inc., 177 W.Va. 734 (1987).

## Chapter 11

# Ownership of Financial Services Products

## Objectives

### After studying this chapter, you should be able to

- Describe a policyowner's rights to name and change the beneficiary of a life insurance policy

- In a given situation, identify the party to whom life insurance policy proceeds are payable following the insured's death

- Identify in a given situation whether a life insurance policy premium has been paid and describe the insurer's rights in such situations

- Distinguish among the various nonforfeiture options that insurers provide to owners of cash value life insurance policies

- Describe the policy loan provision and the policy withdrawal provision in a life insurance policy, and distinguish between a policy loan and a commercial loan

- Identify and explain the requirements for the reinstatement of a life insurance policy

- Identify the ownership rights that a contract owner has in an annuity

- Describe the requirements that qualify a mutual fund as an individual retirement arrangement (IRA), and identify the ownership rights that a shareholder has in a mutual fund

# Outline

A financial product is a type of intangible personal property that consists of a bundle of property rights. Most of the property rights in such a product vest in the owner. A *vested right* is a right that cannot be altered or changed without the consent of the person who owns the right. Persons other than the owner may have, or may be specifically granted, certain rights in such personal property. In this chapter, we discuss property rights as they relate to individual life insurance, annuity, and mutual fund products.

# Ownership of Individual Life Insurance

Most of a life insurance policyowner's rights in the policy vest when the policy is issued. In this section, we discuss the policyowner's rights in regard to beneficiary designations, premium payments, nonforfeiture benefits, policy loans and withdrawals, and reinstatements.

## Right to Name the Beneficiary

One of the most important contractual rights a policyowner has in an individual life insurance policy is the right to name the beneficiary who will receive the policy proceeds. The beneficiary may be a named individual, the policyowner's estate, a corporation, a charitable organization, or any other entity. We describe the naming of a trustee as beneficiary in the next chapter.

The *primary beneficiary* is the party who, if still living, will receive the life insurance policy proceeds after the insured's death. The policyowner may name more than one primary beneficiary and may indicate how the proceeds are to be divided among the beneficiaries. Following the insured's death, the insurer will pay the policy proceeds in accordance with the policyowner's wishes as stated in the beneficiary designation, assuming that the designation is valid and clearly stated.

A policyowner also has the right to name a *contingent beneficiary* who will receive the policy proceeds if the primary beneficiary dies before the insured. A contingent beneficiary, sometimes referred to as a *secondary* or *successor beneficiary*, is entitled to the policy proceeds only if all designated primary beneficiaries have predeceased the insured. The policyowner may name more than one contingent beneficiary and may indicate how the proceeds are to be divided among the beneficiaries. Figure 11.1 presents some examples that illustrate the payment of policy proceeds to beneficiaries.

## Figure 11.1 Payment of Policy Proceeds to the Beneficiary

**Example 1:**

Anna Rousseau purchased a $500,000 policy insuring her life. She named her husband, Victor, as primary beneficiary and her children, Marie and Jean, as equal contingent beneficiaries. Victor survived Anna and, thus, was entitled to receive the $500,000 death benefit.

**Example 2:**

Barry Wilder purchased a $500,000 policy insuring his life. He named his mother, Sadie, as primary beneficiary and his brothers, Elton and Hal, as equal contingent beneficiaries. Only Elton and Hal survived Barry and, thus, they were each entitled to receive $250,000 of the policy death benefit.

**Example 3:**

Celia Bartholomew purchased a $500,000 policy insuring her life. She named her husband, Sal, as primary beneficiary and her children, Martha, Mary, and Matt, as equal contingent beneficiaries. Only Martha and Matt survived Celia and, thus, they were each entitled to receive $250,000 of the policy death benefit.

Most insurers permit policyowners to designate additional levels of contingent beneficiaries. For example, a policyowner-insured might name his wife as the primary beneficiary, his child as contingent beneficiary, and his grandchild as a second-level contingent beneficiary. The grandchild would be entitled to receive the policy proceeds only if both the insured's wife and child predeceased him.

As we described in Chapter 10, the following limits may be placed on a policyowner's right to name the beneficiary:

- Minors lack contractual capacity and are limited in their right to purchase insurance. Although most states permit minors of a stated age to enter into life insurance contracts if specific conditions are met, many states limit a minor's right to name the beneficiary by requiring that the beneficiary be the minor herself or one of her close family members, such as a parent or guardian.

- When a person purchases insurance on her own life, she generally may name anyone as beneficiary. Recall from Chapter 10 that when a person purchases insurance on another person's life, the beneficiary generally must have an insurable interest in the insured's life when the contract is formed.

## Class Designations

A policyowner may name a group of people as life insurance policy beneficiaries. A beneficiary designation that identifies a certain group of people, rather than naming each person individually, is called a *class designation*. The designations "to my children," "to my brothers and sisters," and "to my grandchildren" are class designations. The advantage to the policyowner of making a class designation is that the members of the class who will share in the policy proceeds are not determined until the insured dies. Persons who are born or adopted after the designation is made are automatically included as beneficiaries without the policyowner's execution of a new beneficiary designation. The disadvantage of a class designation is that, before any proceeds are paid, the insurer must identify and locate all members of the beneficiary class. Locating all of the class members after the insured's death may be difficult and, thus, could delay payment of the policy proceeds.

As noted, the members of the class who are entitled to share in the policy proceeds are determined after the insured's death. Class members who survive the insured are entitled to share in the policy proceeds equally.

> **Example:**
>
> Donna Groover named "my children" as the beneficiaries of a policy insuring her life. When she purchased the policy and named the beneficiaries, Mrs. Groover was newly married and had no children. During the marriage, the Groovers had four sons and one adopted daughter. If all five children survive Mrs. Groover, then they are each entitled to one-fifth of the policy proceeds. If only three children survive Mrs. Groover, they are each entitled to one-third of the proceeds.

As the example illustrates, adopted children share in policy proceeds on the same basis as biological children. By contrast, a stepchild whom an insured did not legally adopt is not entitled to share in the policy proceeds under such a class designation.

Class designations can be classified as either per capita designations or per stirpes designations. A *per capita beneficiary designation* is a class designation in which the class members all stand in the same relationship to the policyowner, and the class members who survive the insured share the policy proceeds equally. The designation described in the previous example is a per capita beneficiary designation. Only those children who survive the insured share the policy proceeds, and each survivor receives an equal share of the proceeds. No descendants or heirs of a deceased class member share in the distribution.

Oh boy, here we go with the legal jargon again!

I know these terms might sound funny, but their Latin meanings are actually very clear; "per capita" literally means "by the head."

So a per capita class designation refers to individual people within a group, like a policyowner's children.

Exactly, and policy proceeds only go to those individuals in that group. And "per stirpes" literally means "by the branch."

So a per stirpes class designation refers to a group of people who make up various branches of a family.

That's a good way to look at it. It separates the family into branches, and policy proceeds are distributed through the branches, according to who is alive at the time of the insured's death.

A ***per stirpes beneficiary designation*** is a class designation in which the descendants of a deceased class member take the decedent's share of the policy proceeds by representation. A typical per stirpes beneficiary designation is stated as "to my children in equal shares with the share of any deceased child to the children of such child per stirpes." A per stirpes designation can be described as a method of dividing policy proceeds by family branches.

**Example:**

Ollie Freeman owned a $600,000 policy on his life. He named as beneficiary his children in equal shares with the share of any deceased child to the children of such child per stirpes. Mr. Freeman had five children: Jane, Jack, Kevin, Mike, and Keith.

- Assume that all five children survived Mr. Freeman. Because he was survived by five family branches, each child was entitled to one-fifth of the policy proceeds ($120,000).

- Assume that Mr. Freeman was survived by (1) Jane, (2) Jack, (3) Kevin, and (4) Keith's two sons. Because he was survived by four family branches, each branch is entitled to one-fourth of the policy proceeds. Jane, Jack, and Kevin each receive one-fourth ($150,000). Keith's two sons share one-fourth of the proceeds equally ($75,000 each).

- Assume that Mr. Freeman outlived all of his children. He was survived by (1) Jane's two children, (2) Jack's child, and (3) Keith's two children. Because he was survived by three family branches, each branch is entitled to one-third of the policy proceeds. Jane's two children share one-third equally ($100,000 each); Jack's child is entitled to one-third ($200,000); and Keith's two children share one-third equally ($100,000 each).

Figure 11.2 illustrates how a per capita designation differs from a per stirpes designation.

---

## Figure 11.2 Comparison of a Per Capita Designation and a Per Stirpes Designation

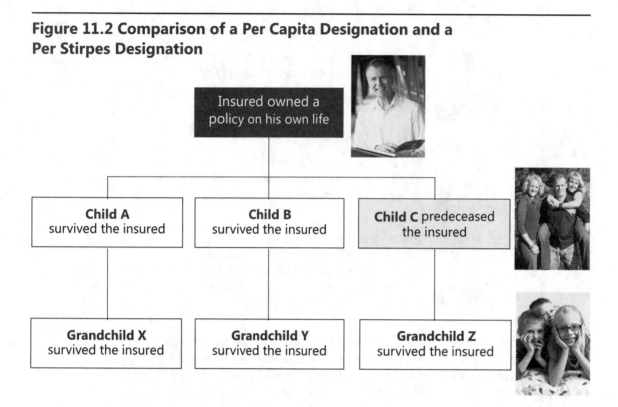

- **Per Capita Designation:** "To my children in equal shares."

The insured's surviving two children—Child A and Child B—will each receive one-half of the policy proceeds.

- **Per Stirpes Designation:** "To my children in equal shares with the share of any deceased child to the children of such child per stirpes."

The insured's surviving two children—Child A and Child B—will each receive one-third of the policy proceeds, and Grandchild Z will receive one-third by representation of his deceased parent.

---

### Changing the Beneficiary

A life insurance policy typically gives the policyowner the contractual right to change a policy's beneficiary designation whenever he wants during the lifetime of the insured. When a policyowner names a new beneficiary, the prior beneficiary's right to receive the policy proceeds is revoked. A beneficiary designation is revocable if the policyowner has the unrestricted right to change the designation during the insured's lifetime; such a beneficiary is known as a **revocable beneficiary**.

A revocable beneficiary's interest in life insurance policy proceeds vests when the insured dies. Until that time, a revocable beneficiary generally has neither a legal interest in the proceeds nor any involvement with the policy. During the insured's lifetime, a revocable beneficiary cannot make a claim against any policy values, and a revocable beneficiary usually cannot prohibit the policyowner from exercising any policy ownership rights. Thus, during the insured's lifetime, a revocable beneficiary's interest in the life insurance policy is said to be a *mere expectancy*. Although a revocable beneficiary expects to receive the policy proceeds following the insured's death, that expectation may not be met because, as long as the insured is alive, the policyowner has the right to change the beneficiary designation without obtaining the beneficiary's consent.

Beneficiary changes can be made only during the lifetime of the insured. When an insured dies, the right to receive the policy proceeds vests in the designated beneficiary.

## Limitations on Beneficiary Changes

A beneficiary designation generally is considered to be revocable unless the policyowner voluntarily gives up the right to change the beneficiary. A policyowner gives up the right to change the beneficiary when she designates the beneficiary as an irrevocable beneficiary. An *irrevocable beneficiary* is a beneficiary whose rights to policy proceeds are vested when the beneficiary designation is made. An irrevocable beneficiary's vested interest in the policy proceeds usually continues as long as the policy remains in force or until the beneficiary (1) consents in writing to a change of beneficiary or (2) predeceases the insured.

> **Example:**
>
> Max Cho purchased an insurance policy on his life and named his wife, Amanda, as the irrevocable beneficiary. He named his children as revocable contingent beneficiaries. After Max and Amanda divorced, Amanda would not consent to Max's request to change the beneficiary; thus, she remained the irrevocable beneficiary. Ten years later, Amanda died and her vested interest in the policy proceeds was extinguished. Max then had the right to name another primary beneficiary as either a revocable or irrevocable beneficiary.

Because an irrevocable beneficiary has a vested interest in the policy proceeds, policies typically limit the policyowner's right to deal with policy values in certain ways unless the irrevocable beneficiary consents in writing. For example, a policyowner typically cannot obtain a policy loan or surrender the policy for cash without the irrevocable beneficiary's consent.

To make an effective beneficiary change, a policyowner must have legal capacity. In addition, an irrevocable beneficiary must have the legal capacity to consent to a beneficiary change for the change to be effective. A person generally has the required legal capacity if she has attained the age of majority and is mentally competent. As noted in Chapter 6, the age of majority in most states is 18. Whether a person is mentally competent is a question of fact that depends on whether the person understood what he was doing at the time. The question of whether a person was mentally competent to make a beneficiary change typically arises when an earlier-named beneficiary claims the policy proceeds and alleges that a later beneficiary designation was ineffective because the policyowner was incompetent at the time. A party to a lawsuit who alleges that a person was not mentally competent to make a beneficiary change or to agree to such a change has the burden of proving that fact.

An irrevocable beneficiary who is a minor does not have the legal capacity to consent to a policyowner's exercising her rights under a life insurance policy. As a result, if an irrevocable beneficiary has not attained the age of majority, the policyowner cannot obtain the beneficiary's consent to any policy transaction. Furthermore, a minor's guardian typically cannot consent on the minor's behalf. The guardian has a duty to protect the interests of the minor and, thus, usually cannot consent to a transaction that would reduce the minor's interest in a policy. Therefore, when a minor is designated irrevocably, the policyowner generally is unable to deal with the policy in any way that would require the beneficiary's consent until the beneficiary reaches the age of majority and gives consent.

In most states, the divorce of a married couple does not automatically affect their rights in a life insurance policy. For example, assume that at the time of their divorce, a man owned a policy on his life and the wife was the revocable beneficiary. The fact that the parties divorce does not affect the husband's ownership of the policy, and the wife remains the beneficiary until the policyowner changes the beneficiary designation. In granting a couple a divorce, however, the court may include an order that one party keep a life insurance policy in force and keep the former spouse as the policy beneficiary. Such a court order limits the policyowner's right to change the beneficiary of the policy.

Laws in some places impose different limitations on beneficiary designations than the general U.S. rules described here. For example, in the Canadian province of Quebec,

- The designation of a policyowner's spouse is presumed to be an irrevocable designation unless the policyowner specifically makes the designation revocable.[1]

- The divorce or annulment of a marriage extinguishes the designation of the former spouse as irrevocable beneficiary.[2]

## Methods of Beneficiary Changes

If a policyowner has retained the right to change the beneficiary, the procedure to make such a change is straightforward. To make an effective change of beneficiary, a policyowner must comply with any contractual requirement found in the insurance policy. Most policies issued today specify the ***recording method*** for a beneficiary change. Such policies require the policyowner to provide the insurer a written and signed notification of the change. After the insurer receives such a written notification, it updates its policy records to reflect the name of the new beneficiary. Some insurers also require a change of beneficiary request to be signed by disinterested witnesses.

Some older life insurance policies specify the ***endorsement method*** for changing the beneficiary. An ***endorsement*** is a document that is attached to a policy and that becomes a part of the contract. When a policy requires the endorsement method, the policyowner must submit his policy to the insurer along with the beneficiary change request. The insurer adds to the policy the endorsement that specifies the name of the new beneficiary and returns the policy to the policyowner. This method of changing a policy beneficiary is rarely used today.

As noted, a policyowner must comply with the beneficiary change method required by his policy to make an effective change. Courts in most states, however, allow an exception to this general rule under the equitable doctrine of substantial compliance. According to the ***doctrine of substantial compliance***, when a policyowner has done everything possible to comply with the beneficiary change procedure set forth in the policy, but has failed because of circumstances beyond his control, the change will be considered effective.

> **Example:**
>
> Blair Fagan owned an insurance policy on his life and wanted to change the beneficiary from his brother to his daughter. His policy stated the recording method for making a beneficiary change. As required by the policy, Mr. Fagan completed a signed notification of the desired beneficiary change and mailed it to the insurer. The written notification was delayed in the mail because of bad weather, and Mr. Fagan died several days before the insurer received and processed the beneficiary change. Mr. Fagan's brother and his daughter both claimed the policy proceeds. Courts in states that apply the doctrine of substantial compliance are likely to find the beneficiary change to be effective because Mr. Fagan did everything he could to change the beneficiary before his death. Thus, the policy proceeds would be payable to Mr. Fagan's daughter.

Courts apply the doctrine of substantial compliance only if it is clear that the policyowner intended to change the beneficiary, and they consider all of the surrounding circumstances to determine the policyowner's intent.

If a life insurance policy does not specify a method for changing the named beneficiary, then any method the policyowner uses to change the beneficiary is effective as long as the method selected clearly indicates the policyowner's intent to change the beneficiary. In such cases, some states even permit a policyowner to make an effective beneficiary change by means of the policyowner's will.

## Death of the Beneficiary

If the primary and all contingent beneficiaries predecease the insured, then the policy proceeds are payable to the policyowner, if she is alive; otherwise, the proceeds usually are payable to the policyowner's estate.

A beneficiary sometimes survives the insured but dies before the insurer has paid the policy proceeds. In such a case, the proceeds are paid in accordance with the terms of the policy and the beneficiary designation. Some policies contain a ***survivorship clause*** or *time clause* that requires the beneficiary to survive the insured for a stated number of days to be entitled to the policy proceeds. A policyowner also has the right to require that the beneficiary survive the insured by a specified amount of time in order to receive the policy proceeds.

> **Example:**
>
> Roger Lavelle owned two insurance policies on his life. The beneficiary designation of a $750,000 policy was "to my wife, Pamela Lavelle, if living on the thirtieth day after the death of the insured; otherwise to my daughter, Martha Lavelle." The beneficiary designation of a $100,000 policy was "to my wife, Pamela Lavelle." Roger's brother, Sam, was the contingent beneficiary of the second policy. Roger and Pamela were involved in an automobile accident. Roger died instantly. Pamela died 5 days later.
>
> Because Pamela did not survive Roger by 30 days, the proceeds of the $750,000 policy with the survivorship clause are payable to Martha as the contingent beneficiary. Because Pamela did survive Roger, the proceeds of the $100,000 policy with no survivorship clause are payable to Pamela's estate.

## Designation of the Policyowner's Estate

As noted, a policyowner-insured may make life insurance policy proceeds payable to his own estate. The designation of a policyowner's estate is always considered to be a revocable beneficiary designation. The policyowner has the right to change such a beneficiary designation at any time during the insured's life.

When policy proceeds are payable to an estate, the decedent's personal representative is responsible for distributing the proceeds in accordance with (1) the terms of the decedent's will or (2) the provisions of the applicable intestate succession laws. (See Chapter 8 for a discussion of how a decedent's estate is distributed.) Policy proceeds that are paid to a decedent's estate become part of the decedent's probate estate and, therefore, become subject to claims of the decedent's creditors. As a result, the people whom a policyowner-insured wanted to receive the policy proceeds may not in fact receive the money. In addition, the amount the decedent's heirs ultimately receive may be reduced due to taxes and other estate expenses. By contrast, life insurance policy proceeds that are paid to a named beneficiary pass outside a decedent's will and do not become part of the decedent's probate estate. A policyowner can seek to ensure that policy proceeds are paid to a named beneficiary rather than to her estate by naming several levels of contingent beneficiaries.

## Premium Payments

When an insurer issues a life insurance policy, the insurer makes a contractual promise to pay a stated death benefit if the insured dies while the policy is in force. The insurer's promise is a conditional promise; the death benefit is payable only if the policy is in force at the insured's death. A policyowner must pay policy premiums as they come due to keep a policy in force.

Whether a premium was paid when due is a question of fact. The burden of proof concerning this fact rests on the party who claims that the premium was paid. For example, assume an insurer denied a claim for policy proceeds on the ground that the policy was not in force when the insured died. The claimant to the policy proceeds sued the insurer claiming that premiums were paid when due and, thus, the policy was in force at the insured's death. The claimant has the burden to prove that premiums were paid when due.

## *Initial Premium*

The initial premium forms part of the consideration an applicant for life insurance pays in exchange for the insurer's contractual promise. The insurance contract does not take effect until this essential part of the consideration is paid. Typically, an applicant pays the initial premium when she completes the application for insurance. If the parties do not enter into a life insurance contract, the insurer must refund the premium to the applicant. Likewise, if a policyowner rejects a life insurance contract during the contract's free look period, the insurer must return the initial premium to the policyowner. Recall from Chapter 10 that the insurance policy and the coverage it provides are effective during the free look period.

## *Renewal Premiums*

Individual life insurance policies state the dates on which renewal premiums are due. We use the term *renewal premiums* to refer to all premiums payable after the initial premium. Although a renewal premium must be paid when due to keep a policy in force, the policyowner has no legal obligation to pay a renewal premium. Policyowners have the right to discontinue premium payments at any time without incurring liability to the insurer.

 Does some of this remind you of what we learned about contract law back in Chapter 6?

 Yes! A life insurance policy is a *unilateral contract* because only one party—the insurer—makes a legally enforceable promise. The policyowner does not promise to pay premiums, so she is not legally bound to do so.

 And I remember that a life insurance policy is an *aleatory contract* because the insurer's promise to pay benefits is conditional on the death of the insured while the policy is in force.

 Good! So even though a policyowner is not legally obligated to pay life insurance premiums, if she does not pay them and the policy lapses, the insurer is no longer legally bound to its promise to pay benefits.

State laws require life insurance policies to include a **grace period provision**, which allows a policyowner to pay a renewal premium within a stated time following a premium due date. For term and whole life insurance policies, the grace period usually is 31 days; universal life policies usually include a 61-day grace period. Life insurance coverage continues in force throughout the policy's grace period, regardless of whether the premium is ever paid. If the insured dies during the grace period but before the premium is paid, the insurer is obligated to pay the policy proceeds. The insurer, however, is entitled to deduct the amount of the unpaid premium from the policy proceeds before paying those proceeds.

The grace period begins on the day following a premium due date. For example, if a premium that is due on April 1 is unpaid on that date, then April 2 is the first day of the policy's grace period. If the policy provides a 31-day grace period, then the last day of the grace period is May 2. The insurer must receive payment no later than midnight of the last day of the grace period in order for the premium to be considered paid when due. However, if the last day of the grace period falls on a nonbusiness day, such as a Saturday, Sunday, or a legal holiday, then the premium can be paid on the next business day.

## Premium Payment Methods

An insurer has the right to incorporate into a policy any reasonable terms the company wants concerning the method of premium payment. For example, an insurer can demand payment in cash or can agree to accept payment by check, promissory note, money order, or any other method it chooses.

### Payment by Personal Check

Policyowners often pay premiums by mailing a personal check to the insurer. In such cases, the premium is not considered paid until the insurer receives the check. An insurer's acceptance of a check in such cases is conditioned on the bank's honoring the check. If the account on which the check was drawn does not contain sufficient funds to cover the amount of the check, then the bank will not honor the check. If the check is not honored, then the premium has not been paid.

When a check is dishonored and the grace period has expired, an insurer has two choices. First, it can lapse the policy for nonpayment of premium. Alternatively, the insurer can try to collect on the dishonored check. In either case, the insurer must act promptly because an unreasonable delay may subject it to liability to pay policy proceeds. In cases in which an insurer unreasonably delays in acting when a check is dishonored, a court is likely to find that the insurer waived its right to lapse the policy for nonpayment of premium.

### Payment by Promissory Note

Insurers sometimes accept a promissory note—a written and signed promise to pay money owed—in payment of premiums. If an insurer accepts a promissory note unconditionally, then the premium is deemed paid and the policy remains in force even if the promissory note is not paid according to its terms. An insurer can protect itself by accepting the note with conditions. Thus, an insurer can accept a promissory note in payment of a premium on the condition that the note is paid when due. In such a case, if the note is not paid when due, then the insurer can treat the policy as having lapsed for nonpayment of premium as of the date the note was made.

### Policy Dividends

State insurance laws generally prohibit an insurer from lapsing a policy for non-payment of premium if the insurer has policy dividends on deposit sufficient to pay a renewal premium *and* the policyowner has not elected another method of using policy dividends. Note that this general rule contains two qualifications:

■   The insurer must apply policy dividends to pay a renewal premium only if the amount of dividends the insurer has is large enough to cover the full amount of the renewal premium that is due.

■   The insurer must apply policy dividends to pay a renewal premium only if the policyowner has not chosen another policy dividend option.

The policyowner has the contractual right to select one of the dividend options specified in her policy. Typically, a policyowner selects an option when she completes the application for insurance, but she may change the option at any time during the life of the policy. However, to change to the additional term insurance option, the policyowner usually is required to provide the insurer with evidence of the insured's insurability. Policies also specify an automatic dividend option that the insurer will apply if the policyowner for some reason does not choose a dividend option.

## Who May Pay the Premium

Insurers typically accept payment of a premium from anyone who tenders the payment. A beneficiary who pays a premium generally does so to keep the policy in force and protect her own interest in the policy. As a general rule, however, payment of a premium by a beneficiary does not give the beneficiary any contractual rights in the policy.

> **Example:**
>
> A revocable beneficiary voluntarily paid a number of premiums for the policyowner, who later changed the beneficiary designation. Even though the original beneficiary paid premiums, she has no right to receive any part of the policy proceeds.

## Premium Notices

Policyowners who do not receive premium notices may not remember to pay premiums when they are due. To help policyowners remember to pay premiums, insurers generally send premium due notices to all policyowners. As a general rule, however, insurers are not legally obligated to send premium due notices to life insurance policyowners unless a statute requires them to do so. Some states have enacted statutes requiring insurers to send premium due notices, and those states limit an insurer's right to lapse a policy for nonpayment of premium if the insurer failed to send a premium due notice to the policyowner as required by the statute.

When an insurer has established a pattern of sending premium notices over a period of time, courts in most states limit the insurer's right to lapse a policy for nonpayment of premium if the insurer stops sending premium due notices and does not notify the policyowner that it will no longer send notices.

> **Example:**
>
> An insurer consistently sent quarterly premium due notices to a policyowner for many years, but failed to send one notice. The policyowner-insured did not pay that renewal premium and died shortly after the end of the policy grace period. The insurer denied the beneficiary's claim on the ground that the policy had lapsed for nonpayment of premium. Courts in most states would find in favor of the beneficiary and would require the insurer to pay the policy proceeds, less the amount of the unpaid premium.

Courts reach this result using a doctrine known as estoppel. *Estoppel* is an equitable doctrine by which someone is restrained—or *estopped*—from acting in a manner that contradicts her previous conduct. Estoppel is invoked when (1) one party's conduct has misled an innocent party and (2) inconsistent actions by the first party would harm the innocent party. Estoppel is based on a moral principle that seeks to prevent an injustice to an innocent party. Figure 11.3 describes the doctrine of estoppel in more detail. In the foregoing example, it would be unfair to allow the insurer to avoid its liability under the policy because it had led the policyowner-insured to believe that he would receive a premium notice. When an insurer has established a pattern of sending premium due notices, the insurer has the legal right to stop sending such notices only if it notifies policyowners that it will no longer send such notices.

## Figure 11.3 The Doctrine of Estoppel

The following elements typically are necessary to create an estoppel:

- The first party has knowledge of the facts but communicates something in a misleading way, either by words, conduct, or silence.

- The second party does not have knowledge of the facts and reasonably relies on the first party's words, conduct, or silence.

- The second party would be harmed if the first party were allowed to assert a claim that is inconsistent with his earlier words, conduct, or silence.

Insurers also have a duty to send premium due notices to policyowners when the policyowners would not otherwise know the amount of the premium that is due. For example, the owner of a flexible-premium policy may not know the amount of premium required to keep the policy in force.

## *Late Payment Offers*

Although insurers have the right to require timely payment of premiums, they sometimes extend a late payment offer to a policyowner who has not paid a premium by the end of the grace period. A *late payment offer* is an example of an insurer's conditional offer to waive its right to require timely payment of a premium. The policyowner can accept the insurer's offer by paying the overdue premium within the time specified in the insurer's offer—usually 30 to 90 days after the end of the grace period. Late payment offers typically require that the unpaid premium be paid during the lifetime of the insured. Upon receipt of the premium during the specified time, the insurer must put the policy back into force.

By extending a late payment offer, an insurer does *not* extend the policy's grace period. Instead, the insurer has offered to waive its right to require timely payment. The insurer does not actually waive that right until the policyowner meets the terms of the conditional offer. A late payment offer applies only to the then unpaid renewal premium; the offer does not include a waiver of the insurer's right to require timely payment of future premiums.

# Nonforfeiture Benefits

The effect on a policy of a premium's being unpaid when due depends on the type of policy, the terms of the policy, and the wishes of the policyowner. When a premium is unpaid for a policy that provides no cash values, the policy terminates without value; that is, the policy and coverage under the policy terminate.

In contrast, insurance laws in all states require insurers to provide a cash surrender value after a cash value life insurance policy has been in force for a specified minimum time, typically three years. The states also impose requirements as to how insurers must calculate a policy's minimum cash surrender value. The nonforfeiture provision usually gives the policyowner the right to select from among several nonforfeiture options if a premium is unpaid when the grace period ends. Most policies provide three types of nonforfeiture benefits: a cash payment benefit, continued insurance coverage benefits, and an automatic nonforfeiture benefit.

## *Cash Surrender*

The *cash surrender value nonforfeiture option* or *cash payment nonforfeiture option* specifies that a policyowner who discontinues premium payments can surrender the policy and receive the policy's cash surrender value in a lump-sum payment. When a policy is surrendered, the life insurance contract and all coverage under the contract terminate. The parties have no further contractual rights or obligations. If the beneficiary is an irrevocable beneficiary, the policyowner must obtain the beneficiary's consent to surrender the policy.

The amount of cash value actually available to a policyowner upon surrender of the policy may not be the exact cash surrender value amount described in the policy. Dividend additions, advance premium payments, policy loans (including unpaid interest), surrender charges, and policy withdrawals result in additions to and subtractions from the cash surrender value. The amount the policyowner actually receives after such adjustments have been made is called the *net cash surrender value*. *Dividend additions*, also known as *paid-up additions*, are additional amounts of insurance purchased using policy dividends. Because dividend additions represent paid-up insurance, they also have cash values that the policyowner can collect upon surrender of the policy.

The laws of most states require life insurance policies to include a provision that gives the insurer the right to defer payment of the policy's cash surrender value for up to six months after the request for payment is made. This right to defer payment is designed to relieve the pressure on the insurer's cash reserves should there be a rush of surrenders occurring over a short period. Insurers rarely invoke this right.

## Continued Insurance Coverage Benefits

Many cash value policies give the policyowner the option of discontinuing premium payments and continuing insurance coverage as either reduced paid-up insurance or extended term insurance.

### Reduced Paid-Up Insurance

Under the *reduced paid-up insurance nonforfeiture option*, the net cash surrender value of the policy is used as a net single premium to purchase paid-up life insurance of the same plan as the original policy. The premium charged for the paid-up insurance is based on the age the insured has attained when the option is exercised. The amount of paid-up insurance that can be purchased under this option is smaller than the face amount of the policy—hence the name *reduced* paid-up insurance.

The coverage issued under this option continues to have and to build a cash value. In addition, the policyowner continues to have the rights available to the owner of any life insurance policy, including the right to surrender the policy for its cash value and the right to receive policy dividends if the original policy was issued on a participating basis.

### Extended Term Insurance

Under the *extended term insurance nonforfeiture option*, the policy's net cash surrender value is used as a net single premium to purchase term insurance for the full face amount provided under the original policy—less the amount of any outstanding policy loans and unpaid interest—for as long a term as that net cash surrender value can provide. The length of the term for which coverage is provided depends on the amount of the coverage, the amount of the net cash surrender value, and the insured's attained age when the option is exercised. In most states, the length of the term also depends on the sex of the insured. A policy providing this nonforfeiture option usually includes a schedule that shows the length of time the original face amount of the policy will be continued in force under the extended term option for each of the first 20 policy years.

Most policies specify that, when the policy is continued on an extended term insurance basis, the policyowner cannot exercise the policy loan privilege or receive policy dividends. However, the policyowner has the right to cancel the extended term insurance at any time and surrender the policy for its remaining cash value.

## *Automatic Nonforfeiture Benefits*

Individual life insurance policies that accumulate a cash value typically provide an *automatic nonforfeiture benefit*, which is a specified nonforfeiture benefit that becomes effective automatically when a renewal premium is not paid by the end of the grace period and the policyowner has not elected another nonforfeiture option. Note that the automatic benefit becomes effective only if the policyowner has not elected another nonforfeiture option.

Policies typically state that the automatic nonforfeiture benefit is either the extended term or reduced paid-up insurance benefit described earlier or an automatic premium loan benefit. Under an *automatic premium loan (APL) benefit*, the insurer automatically pays an overdue premium by making a loan against the policy's cash value if the cash value equals or exceeds the amount of the premium due. The use of the automatic premium loan keeps the policy in force for the full amount of coverage. An automatic premium loan is a form of policy loan. Once the APL benefit becomes effective, the policy remains in force until all funds held by the insurer in connection with the policy have been used.

## Policy Loans and Policy Withdrawals

An individual life insurance policy that accumulates a cash value typically gives the policyowner the right to borrow money from the insurer by using the cash value of the policy as security for the loan. The *policy loan provision* gives the policyowner the right to take out a loan for an amount that does not exceed the policy's cash value less one year's interest on the loan. Laws in most states permit insurers to defer granting policy loans—except for loans made for the purpose of paying premiums—for a specified period, usually up to six months. This deferral option, which insurers rarely enforce, is intended to protect insurers from suffering significant financial losses if large numbers of policyowners request policy loans.

A policy loan differs from a commercial loan in that a policyowner is not legally obligated to repay a policy loan, although the policyowner has the right to repay any part or all of the loan any time during the lifetime of the insured. If a policy loan has not been repaid when the insured dies, the insurer deducts the amount of the unpaid loan plus interest from the policy benefit that is payable. Similarly, if a policy loan is not repaid when the policyowner surrenders the policy for its cash value, the insurer deducts the amount of the unpaid loan and interest from the cash value paid to the policyowner. In contrast, a commercial loan creates a debtor-creditor relationship between the borrower and the lender. The borrower is legally obligated to repay the loan, and if he does not, the lender may seek the help of the courts to recover the debt.

Insurers charge interest on each policy loan, and interest usually is charged annually. Any interest charges that are unpaid become part of the policy loan. If the amount of a policy loan plus unpaid interest increases to the point at which the total indebtedness is greater than the amount of the policy's cash value, the policy terminates without further value. An insurer must notify a policyowner at least 30 days in advance of such a policy termination. Such a notification gives the policyowner the chance to repay part or all of the loan to avoid the policy's termination.

Some life insurance policies, such as universal life policies, permit the policyowner to make withdrawals from the policy's cash value. A ***policy withdrawal provision***, which is often called a *partial surrender provision*, permits the policyowner to reduce the amount in the policy's cash value by withdrawing up to the amount of that value in cash. Because the amount of benefit payments to be made under such policies depends on the amount of the cash value, some policies specify that a withdrawal also reduces the benefit payment amounts. For example, universal life policies sometimes provide that a withdrawal reduces both the cash value and the face amount (death benefit) of the policy by the amount of the withdrawal.

Policies usually place limits on the amount that may be withdrawn and on the number of withdrawals that are permitted each year. Many policies also impose a fee on each withdrawal, but policies typically do not impose interest charges on withdrawals. Most policies do not allow a policyowner to repay a withdrawal; the reduction in the amount of the death benefit payable as a result of a withdrawal is permanent.

Policy loans and policy withdrawals seem similar.

Well, both are advance payments of the amount an insurer eventually must pay out under the policy, that's true.

One big difference seems to be that loans can be repaid but withdrawals generally cannot.

Right. And because a policy withdrawal usually is permanent, it can permanently reduce the policy's benefit payments. On the other hand, a policy loan can be repaid—and as long as it is repaid during the insured's lifetime, it will not affect the policy's benefit payments.

And both loans and withdrawals are available only on policies that accumulate a cash value, right?

Exactly!

## Reinstatement

Individual life insurance policies typically include a ***reinstatement provision*** that describes the conditions the policyowner must meet to reinstate a policy. ***Reinstatement*** is the process by which an insurer puts back into force a life insurance policy that has either (1) been terminated for nonpayment of premium or (2) been continued under the extended term or reduced paid-up insurance nonforfeiture option. Most insurers do not permit reinstatement if the owner has surrendered the policy for its cash value.

Most states require individual life insurance policies to include a reinstatement provision. Laws in these states require policies to provide at least a three-year period during which the policyowner may reinstate a policy that has lapsed. Most U.S. insurers include a reinstatement provision in all individual life insurance policies as a matter of practice. Some insurers also provide a reinstatement period that is longer than the required three-year period. Insurers are free to include such provisions that are more favorable to policyowners than those required by law.

### *Reinstatement Requirements*

To reinstate a policy, a policyowner must meet certain conditions, which are spelled out in the policy. Reinstatement provisions typically require the policyowner to

- Complete a reinstatement application within the time frame stated in the reinstatement provision.

- Provide the insurer with satisfactory evidence of the insured's continued insurability.

- Pay a specified amount of money; the amount required depends on the type of policy being reinstated. For a fixed-premium policy, the policyowner must pay all unpaid back premiums plus interest on those premiums. For a flexible-premium policy, the policyowner must pay an amount sufficient to cover the policy's mortality and expense charges for at least two months. Some flexible-premium policies also require the policyowner to pay mortality and expense charges for the period between the date of lapse and the date of reinstatement.

- Pay any outstanding policy loan or have the policy loan reinstated when the policy is reinstated.

### *Effect of Reinstatement*

When a policy is reinstated, the original policy is put back into full force and effect as if it had never lapsed; no new policy is issued. The beneficiary designated to receive the policy proceeds remains the beneficiary. If the beneficiary was designated irrevocably, then the designation remains irrevocable. To protect the insurer against antiselection, a new contestable period begins on the date the policy is reinstated. The length of the contestable period is the same as the original contestable period provided by the policy. However, the new contestable period applies only to statements made in the reinstatement application. Insurers generally are not permitted to impose a new suicide exclusion period when a policy is reinstated. We describe the contestable period in Chapter 13.

# Ownership of Annuities

For regulatory purposes, annuities are treated as a form of life insurance, and they have some of the same qualities as life insurance. Like a life insurance policy, an annuity contract is intangible personal property that consists of a bundle of property rights. Most of those property rights vest in the contract owner when the contract is issued. The specific rights a contract owner has depend on the terms of the annuity contract.

The owner of an annuity has the right to designate the payee who will receive the periodic income payments. The owner also has the right to decide when those payments will begin. Annuities include a ***payout options provision*** or *settlement options provision* that identifies each of the payout options from which the contract owner may select.

The owner of a deferred annuity has additional ownership rights that exist during the contract's accumulation period. During the accumulation period, the contract owner has the right to deal with the contract in a number of ways. State insurance laws require deferred annuities to provide nonforfeiture values. During the accumulation period, the contract owner has the right to withdraw all or part of the annuity's accumulated value. The contract owner also has the right to surrender the annuity for its cash surrender value.

Deferred annuities typically provide a death benefit, known as a survivor benefit, that is payable to a beneficiary named by the contract owner. The survivor benefit is a determinable amount that is payable if the contract owner dies during the contract's accumulation period. Unless the beneficiary is an irrevocable beneficiary, the contract owner has the right to change the beneficiary designation at any time during the accumulation period. At the contract's maturity date, survivor benefits are no longer payable, and any rights the designated beneficiary had in the contract end.

The owner of an annuity may have the right to transfer ownership of the contract by means of an assignment. Whether the contract owner has that right depends on whether the annuity qualifies as an individual retirement arrangement (IRA), which we describe in Figure 11.4.

To satisfy requirements of the federal tax laws, an individual retirement annuity must be nontransferable by the contract owner. Thus, the contract owner cannot assign her interest in the contract, and individual retirement annuity contracts must contain a provision that spells out this limitation. We describe assignments in Chapter 12.

# Ownership of Mutual Fund Shares

A mutual fund is a corporation or trust that is owned by all of the individuals and businesses who purchase shares in the fund, who are referred to as *shareholders*. When a customer decides to invest in a mutual fund, the fund creates an account for the shareholder. A mutual fund account is personal property in which the shareholder has a number of ownership rights. U.S. federal income tax laws permit certain individuals to open a mutual fund account that qualifies as an IRA.

## Figure 11.4 U.S. Individual Retirement Arrangements (IRAs)

An ***individual retirement arrangement (IRA)*** is a retirement savings plan that allows individuals with taxable compensation to deposit a stated amount of that income into a savings arrangement that meets certain requirements specified in the federal tax laws and, thus, receives favorable federal tax treatment. The tax laws specify which taxpayers are eligible to contribute to an IRA and place maximum limits on the annual contributions a taxpayer may make to an IRA. An individual retirement arrangement may take one of two forms:

- An ***individual retirement account*** is an IRA that takes the form of a trust or custodial account set up in the United States for the exclusive benefit of a taxpayer and his beneficiaries. The trustee must be a bank, brokerage firm, mutual fund company, or similar financial institution.

- An ***individual retirement annuity*** is an IRA that takes the form of an individual annuity issued by an insurance company.

## Account Registration

When a person opens a mutual fund account, she has the right to determine how the mutual fund registers the account. The account registration denotes who owns the account. Registration requirements differ depending on whether the mutual fund account is established as an IRA.

### *Mutual Funds that Are Not IRAs*

A mutual fund account that is not established as an IRA may be owned by one or more individuals. When such a mutual fund account is registered in one individual's name, that individual is the only person who has the right to deal with the account. Thus, the individual owner may purchase more shares for the account, make withdrawals from the account, or close the account. The shareholder also may transfer ownership of all or part of the account by notifying the fund, which changes the registration of the account into the name of the new owner.

At a shareholder's death, the mutual fund account becomes part of the shareholder's probate estate. To ensure that the account passes to the person the shareholder wishes, the shareholder must provide for that disposition in her will.

A mutual fund account also may be registered in the names of two or more individuals. Joint ownership can take two forms: a tenancy in common or a joint tenancy with rights of survivorship. When an account is owned by *tenants in common*, the tenants must specify what percentage of the total shares in the account each tenant owns. Each owner has an undivided interest in her part of the account, which means that each owner can deal with her part of the account as she wishes. For example, a tenant in common can transfer ownership of her share of the account during her lifetime. A tenant in common also can direct how her ownership interest will pass after her death by including a provision to that effect in her will. Otherwise, ownership of the tenant's interest in the account will be determined by the applicable state's laws of intestate succession.

An account also may be owned by *joint tenants with rights of survivorship*. The advantage of this form of ownership is that, at the death of one owner, the surviving owner automatically obtains full rights to the deceased owner's interest in the account. Such an ownership transfer occurs automatically at one owner's death, and the deceased owner's interest in the account does not become part of his probate estate. During their lifetimes, joint tenants who have survivorship rights each have the ability to deal with the entire account without obtaining the other tenant's consent.

## Mutual Funds that Qualify as IRAs

Most mutual fund companies allow investors to open a mutual fund account that qualifies as an IRA. To qualify as an IRA, such a mutual fund account must be owned by only one individual. So, for example, a married couple who both qualify to contribute to an IRA must each establish their own mutual fund account. Unlike other mutual fund accounts, a mutual fund that qualifies as an IRA allows the shareholder to name beneficiaries who will automatically own the account if the shareholder dies while owning the account. If the account owner dies, ownership of the IRA automatically transfers to the primary beneficiary or to the secondary beneficiary if the primary beneficiary does not survive the account owner.

# Ownership Rights

Mutual fund shareholders have a number of specific rights, which are similar to the rights of those who own common stock in a corporation. Federal securities laws require mutual funds to provide shareholders with financial statements at least twice every year. Shareholders in a mutual fund have the right to vote on the following matters:

- Elections of the fund's directors

- Approval of changes to the fund's investment policies and practices

- Approval of the fund's investment adviser

Shareholders each receive one vote for each share they own in the fund. A fund must hold an annual meeting at which shareholders have the right to vote on the foregoing matters. The fund must provide each shareholder with a proxy so that shareholders can cast their votes by proxy without having to attend a shareholder meeting in person.

Mutual fund shareholders have the right to sell their shares back to the fund; such a sale is known as a **redemption**. When an owner redeems shares, the fund pays the owner the net asset value (NAV) of the redeemed shares. Figure 11.5 describes how funds calculate the NAV of fund shares. A shareholder can liquidate his account by redeeming all of his shares, or he can redeem a specific portion of his shares. Mutual funds also permit account shareholders to make systematic redemptions. For example, a shareholder may want to liquidate his account over a 10-year period by periodically redeeming a stated number of shares or taking out a stated dollar amount from his account.

## Figure 11.5 The Net Asset Value of a Mutual Fund Share

When individuals purchase and redeem shares in a mutual fund, the price they pay and receive for each share is referred to as the share's *net asset value (NAV)*. Mutual funds typically calculate the NAV of their shares on a daily basis. The NAV of a fund share is calculated as follows:

(Total asset value of the fund ÷ Total number of shares outstanding)

The **total asset value** of the fund is calculated as follows:

Total value of all securities that the fund owns

+ All other assets of the fund

− The fund's total liabilities

Shareholders can earn money from their mutual fund investment in three ways:

1. **Distributions from net investment income.** A fund may earn income in the form of dividends and interest on the securities in its portfolio. The fund then pays its shareholders the income, minus expenses, it has earned.

2. **Capital gains distributions.** The prices of the securities a fund owns may increase. When a fund sells a security that has increased in price, the fund realizes a capital gain. At the end of the year, most funds distribute these capital gains, minus any capital losses, to investors.

3. **Increased NAV.** If the market value of a fund's portfolio increases after deduction of expenses and liabilities, then the NAV of the fund and its shares increases. The higher NAV reflects the higher value of a shareholder's investment.

Funds usually give shareholders a choice as to how they want to receive income payments and capital gains distributions. A shareholder can receive a check or other form of payment or can have her dividends or distributions reinvested in the fund to buy more shares.

## Key Terms

vested right
primary beneficiary
contingent beneficiary
class designation
per capita beneficiary designation
per stirpes beneficiary designation
revocable beneficiary
irrevocable beneficiary
recording method
endorsement method
endorsement
doctrine of substantial compliance
survivorship clause
grace period provision
estoppel      ?
late payment offer
cash surrender value nonforfeiture option
net cash surrender value
dividend additions
reduced paid-up insurance nonforfeiture option
extended term insurance nonforfeiture option
automatic nonforfeiture benefit
automatic premium loan (APL) benefit
policy loan provision
policy withdrawal provision
reinstatement provision
reinstatement
payout options provision
individual retirement arrangement (IRA)
individual retirement account
individual retirement annuity
redemption

## Endnotes

1. C.C.Q., ch. 64, art. 2449 (1991) (Can.); C.C.Q. ch. 6, s. 56 (2002) (Can.).

2. C.C.Q., ch. 64, art. 2459 (1991) (Can.); C.C.Q. ch.6, s. 58 (2002) (Can.).

*Chapter 12*

# Rights of Third Parties

## Objectives

### *After studying this chapter, you should be able to*

- Identify ways in which the owner of a life insurance policy can transfer ownership of the policy to another person

- Distinguish between an assignee's rights under an absolute assignment and a collateral assignment

- Describe how the rights of a policy beneficiary under an assignment vary according to the type of assignment and the type of beneficiary designation

- Explain the rights that creditors of a life insurance policyowner or beneficiary have in the policy

- Identify the parties to a trust agreement and describe the duties of the trustee and the rights of the trust beneficiary

- Distinguish among various types of trusts and describe reasons for establishing a trust

- Identify the typical settlement options that a life insurance policy provides and describe the rights of beneficiaries and payees in regard to settlement options

# Outline

**Ownership Transfers**
- Assignments
- Change of Ownership Provision

**Creditors' Rights in Life Insurance**
- Judgment Creditors
- Creditor as Policyowner or Beneficiary

**Trust Agreements**
- Types of Trusts
- Reasons for Establishing a Trust

**Life Insurance Policy Settlement Options**

The bundle of rights in a life insurance policy can be shared among many people. As described in Chapter 11, when a policy is issued, most of the rights in the policy belong to the policyowner. Over time, additional parties may gain an interest in the policy. In this chapter, we describe some of the ways in which people can gain rights in a life insurance policy.

# Ownership Transfers

The owner of a life insurance policy has the right to transfer ownership of some or all of her rights in the policy. In this section, we discuss ownership transfers accomplished by assignments and in accordance with a policy's change of ownership provision.

## Assignments

The owner of personal property may give away or sell his ownership rights in the property by assigning the rights to another. Similarly, a property owner can, by means of an assignment, pledge his rights in personal property as security for a debt.

Two methods of transferring life insurance policy ownership rights during the lifetime of the insured are through an absolute assignment and a collateral assignment. An ***absolute assignment*** is the irrevocable transfer of all of a policyowner's ownership rights in a life insurance policy to another.

> **Example:**
> Cassie Lawson bought an insurance policy on her son's life when he was 2 years old. When her son reached age 21, Ms. Lawson gave him the policy by absolutely assigning it to him.

 So after an absolute assignment of a policy, who's the policyowner?

 The assignee becomes the policyowner. After that, the original owner has no rights in the policy.

A *collateral assignment* is the transfer of some of a policyowner's ownership rights in a life insurance policy, usually to provide security for a debt. A collateral assignment gives the assignee the right to share in the policy proceeds to the extent of the policyowner's outstanding debt at the insured's death. When a policyowner repays the debt owed to a collateral assignee during the lifetime of the insured, the assignee's interest in the policy ends. All of the assignee's interest in the policy then reverts to the policyowner.

> **Example:**
> Gordon Bailey owned a $100,000 insurance policy on his life. He collaterally assigned the policy to the Dover Bank as security for a $50,000 loan. When Mr. Bailey died, he still owed the bank $30,000. Dover Bank will be entitled to receive $30,000 from the policy proceeds, and the remaining $70,000 is payable to the named beneficiary.

## Assignment Agreement

The right to assign property, including a life insurance policy, is given to the property owner by general property law. Property is assigned by means of a contractual agreement between the assignor and the assignee, and the terms of that agreement determine the rights and interests of the assignor and the assignee in the property. An assignment of a life insurance policy is not required to be in writing unless a statute or the policy requires it. To protect the parties, however, it is common for assignments to be put into a written agreement.

Under the terms of an absolute assignment of a life insurance policy, the assignee obtains all of the policyowner's rights and interests in the policy; the absolute assignee thereby becomes the policyowner. The assignor has no further interest in the policy. Thus, the assignee becomes responsible for premium payments and is entitled to receive policy dividends (if applicable), surrender the policy, or deal with the policy as she wishes.

The terms of a collateral assignment usually restrict the policyowner from dealing with the policy in ways that would affect the collateral assignee's interest. Collateral assignment agreements usually transfer to the assignee the right to

- Obtain a policy loan

- Surrender the policy for its cash surrender value

- Exercise nonforfeiture options

- Receive policy dividends

In practice, assignees do not exercise the foregoing rights unless the assignor fails to repay the loan as required. Collateral assignments usually state that the policyowner retains the right to designate and change the policy beneficiary and the right to select a settlement option.

A collateral assignment agreement typically does not require the collateral assignee to pay the policy's renewal premiums. If the assignee does pay such premiums, however, the assignee has the right to recover the amount paid from the policy proceeds. Thus, the amount of premiums the assignee pays is in effect added to the debt the policyowner owes the assignee.

> **Example:**
>
> Isaac Schonberg owned a $500,000 insurance policy on his life. When Mr. Schonberg took out a $50,000 loan from the New Bank, he collaterally assigned his policy to the bank. At the time of his death, Mr. Schonberg owed $25,000 on the loan, and the New Bank had paid $2,500 in premiums on his policy. The bank is entitled to receive $27,500 of the policy proceeds, and the remainder of proceeds are payable to the named beneficiary.

According to conflict of laws rules, the validity and effect of an assignment agreement are governed by the law of the state in which the assignment was made—that is, where it was executed by the assignor. In other words, any questions concerning the validity of an assignment or the interpretation of the assignment's terms are to be determined according to the law of the state in which the assignor signed the assignment agreement. As in the case of other contractual agreements, the parties to an assignment must have contractual capacity for the agreement to be valid and binding on the parties.

Can parties to a contract decide which state's laws will govern their agreement?

Yes, they can put a conflict of laws provision in their contract. Life insurance policies, assignments, and other contracts usually state which laws will govern the agreement. But if a contract *doesn't* say which laws will govern, then the court applies conflict of laws rules.

## Beneficiary's Rights

When a life insurance policy is assigned, the rights of the policy beneficiary vary depending on the type of assignment and on whether the beneficiary is revocable or irrevocable.

### Revocable Beneficiaries

When a policy that has a revocable beneficiary is absolutely assigned, courts' decisions concerning the beneficiary designation vary. Some courts hold that the absolute assignment of a policy revokes the beneficiary designation. Other courts have found that the designation remains in effect, but the absolute assignee has the right to change that designation.

Regardless of whether a revocable beneficiary consents to the collateral assignment of a policy, the collateral assignee's rights in the policy are superior to the beneficiary's rights. Thus, the collateral assignee is entitled to be repaid from the policy proceeds even if the revocable beneficiary did not consent to the assignment.

Remember that a revocable beneficiary has no legal interest or involvement in a policy during the insured's lifetime.

So that's why a collateral assignee's claims to policy proceeds override a revocable beneficiary's claims.

Exactly. But, as you'll see, the situation is different with an *irrevocable* beneficiary.

## Irrevocable Beneficiaries

An irrevocable beneficiary's vested interest in a life insurance policy cannot be revoked without the beneficiary's consent. According to the terms of most policies, when a beneficiary is designated irrevocably, the policyowner cannot transfer ownership of the policy without obtaining the beneficiary's consent.

When a policy that has an irrevocable beneficiary is absolutely assigned, the beneficiary remains the irrevocable beneficiary unless she consents to a change of beneficiary. In addition, the assignee cannot take out a policy loan or surrender the policy for cash without the irrevocable beneficiary's consent.

An irrevocable beneficiary who does not consent to a collateral assignment generally has a superior right to the policy proceeds than does the assignee. Thus, in order for a collateral assignee to be repaid from the policy proceeds following the insured's death, an irrevocable beneficiary must consent to the assignment. Figure 12.1 gives examples of the rights of beneficiaries when a policy is collaterally assigned.

## *Policy Provisions*

Because an owner's right to assign her property is granted by general property law, an insurer is not required to give policyowners notice of their right to assign their policies. Most individual life insurance policies, however, do include an **assignment provision**, which describes the roles of the insurer and the policyowner when the policy is assigned. Policies typically state that an assignment is not binding on the insurer unless the insurer is notified in writing of the assignment. Consider, for example, a situation in which an insurer is not notified that a policy has been assigned. If the insured dies, the insurer will pay the policy proceeds to the designated beneficiary in accordance with the terms of the policy. Because the insurer did not know of the assignment and paid the policy proceeds in good faith, the insurer would have no further liability under the policy; the assignee will not be able to enforce a claim against the insurer.

## Figure 12.1 Beneficiary's Rights in a Collateral Assignment

**Example 1:** Edgar Hampton owned a $100,000 policy insuring his life. His wife was the irrevocable beneficiary. Mr. Hampton borrowed $50,000 from his brother, Jack, and collaterally assigned the policy to Jack as security for the loan. A week later, Edgar died without having told his wife about the assignment.

Because Mrs. Hampton was the policy's irrevocable beneficiary, her vested interest in the policy proceeds could not be assigned without her consent. Mrs. Hampton did not consent to the assignment, and thus the $100,000 policy proceeds are payable to Mrs. Hampton.

**Example 2:** Heather Jefferson purchased a $100,000 policy insuring her life and named her husband as the revocable beneficiary. She collaterally assigned the policy to the Brown Bank as security for a $10,000 loan without obtaining her husband's consent. When Mrs. Jefferson died, she owed the Brown Bank $5,000.

Because Mr. Jefferson was the policy's revocable beneficiary, his wife was not required to obtain his consent to the collateral assignment. As a result, the Brown Bank is entitled to receive $5,000 of the policy proceeds, and the remaining $95,000 is payable to Mr. Jefferson.

The typical assignment provision in individual life insurance policies states that the insurer is not responsible for the validity of an assignment of the policy. Because the insurer is not a party to an assignment, the insurer has no control over the validity of such an agreement. If a properly written notice of an assignment has been sent to the insurer, then the insurer usually presumes that the assignment is valid. The insurer typically cannot be held liable if it acts in good faith and in accordance with an assignment that is later declared invalid. In other words, if an insurer pays policy proceeds to an assignee who appears entitled to them but the assignment is subsequently determined to be invalid, then the insurer cannot be required to pay the proceeds again to the person who was in fact entitled to them. However, if the insurer had knowledge of circumstances that should have made it question the validity of an assignment, then the insurer may be liable if it acts in accordance with an invalid assignment.

Assignment provisions also usually state that the rights of the insurer take precedence over the rights of an assignee with regard to the policy proceeds. Such a statement highlights the fact that an assignee cannot receive an amount greater than the amount of the *net policy proceeds*—that is, the proceeds remaining after any overdue premiums and any outstanding policy loans and interest have been deducted. An insurer is never obligated to pay any claimant an amount greater than the net policy proceeds, regardless of whether this fact is explained in the policy.

## *Multiple Assignments*

Questions sometimes arise as to who is entitled to policy proceeds when a policy-owner has assigned a policy to more than one assignee. The states have adopted two different rules to determine which assignee has a superior claim to the proceeds when both assignees have notified the insurer of their assignments. Let's look at an example to illustrate the operation of these two rules.

> **Example:**
>
> Peggy Vincenzo owned a $100,000 policy on her life. She assigned the policy to the Black Bank as security for a $75,000 loan, and then later assigned the same policy to the Orange Bank as security for a second $75,000 loan. Although both banks notified the insurer of their assignments, the Orange Bank notified the insurer before the Black Bank did. When Ms. Vincenzo died she had not repaid either loan, and she owed each bank $70,000.
>
> - In states that follow what is known as the American rule, the first assignment has priority over a later assignment. Thus, in this example, the Black Bank has the superior claim and is entitled to $70,000 of the policy proceeds. The remaining $30,000 is payable to the Orange Bank.
>
> - In states that follow what is known as the English rule, the first assignee to notify the insurer of its assignment has priority over other assignees. Thus, in our example, the Orange Bank has the superior claim and is entitled to $70,000 of the policy proceeds. The remaining $30,000 is payable to the Black Bank.

## Change of Ownership Provision

Many individual life insurance policies issued in the United States include a *change of ownership provision*, which specifies a simple, direct method of transferring all the policy's ownership rights. Under this method, policy ownership can be transferred without requiring the policyowner to enter into a separate assignment agreement. According to a typical change of ownership provision, the policyowner can change ownership of the policy by notifying the insurer, in writing, of the change. When the insurer records the ownership change in its records, the change generally becomes effective as of the date the policyowner signed the written notification.

The change of ownership provision typically gives the insurer the right to require that the ownership change be endorsed in the policy. In such a case, the policyowner must send the policy to the insurer, which adds an endorsement to the policy stating the name of the new owner. As in the case of a beneficiary change that must be endorsed on a policy, many courts apply the substantial compliance rule to situations in which an ownership change must be endorsed in the policy. If a policyowner has done everything possible to comply with the ownership change procedure set forth in the policy but has failed because of circumstances beyond her control, then such courts would consider the change to be effective.

# Creditors' Rights in Life Insurance

In addition to obtaining rights in a debtor's life insurance policy by means of an assignment, creditors also can gain rights in insurance policies in much the same way that they gain rights to other valuable property owned by a debtor, although insurance policy values sometimes are granted special exemptions from creditors' claims.

## Judgment Creditors

We described the distinction between secured creditors and unsecured creditors in Chapter 9. A creditor who obtains a security interest in the debtor's property is protected if the debtor defaults on the loan. By contrast, if a debtor defaults on an unsecured loan, the creditor must sue the debtor and obtain a judgment to recover the unpaid amount. A creditor who has obtained such a judgment against a debtor is referred to as a *judgment creditor.*

Each state has enacted laws that govern how a judgment creditor may enforce that judgment by looking to property owned by the debtor. For example, if a debtor has money in a bank account, a judgment creditor can satisfy all or part of the judgment from the funds in the bank account. State laws provide exemptions for certain types of property that a judgment creditor cannot reach. The goal of such laws is to enable the debtor to continue to earn a living and provide for himself and his dependents.

Public policy seeks to encourage people to purchase life insurance to provide for their families and other dependents. Thus, laws in all states provide exemptions for life insurance policies, although the specific exemptions vary a great deal from state to state. Figure 12.2 provides a few examples of how state exemption laws vary. The exemption laws in most states protect life insurance policy death benefits, cash values, and accrued dividends from the reach of judgment creditors. While a policy is in force, most such values are exempt from the claims of judgment creditors of the policyowner and of the beneficiary.

## Figure 12.2 Examples of State Exemption Laws

**Colorado:** The cash surrender value of a life insurance policy is exempt from claims of an insured's creditors, but only up to a maximum of $100,000. All life insurance policy proceeds paid to a named beneficiary are exempt from claims of the insured's creditors.[1]

**Florida:** Policy proceeds payable upon the death of a Florida resident are exempt from claims of the decedent's creditors. Likewise, the cash surrender value of an insurance policy issued on the life of a Florida resident is exempt from claims of the insured's creditors.[2]

**Minnesota:** Insurance proceeds payable to a surviving spouse or child following the death of a spouse or parent are exempt up to a maximum of $20,000. If a surviving spouse or child has dependents, then the $20,000 limitation is increased by $5,000 for each dependent. When a debtor owns an in-force life insurance policy on her own life, the policy values are exempt up to a limit of $4,000.[3]

The situation changes, however, if the policyowner exercises his ownership rights and the insurer pays money to the policyowner. For example, assume a policyowner-insured surrenders his policy for its cash surrender value. Once the insurer pays the cash surrender value to the policyowner, that money held by the policyowner generally loses its exemption from his creditors' claims.

Similarly, a beneficiary's creditors are not able to claim the policy death benefit while the policy is in force. Upon the insured's death, however, the policy proceeds are payable to the beneficiary and may be subject to claims of the beneficiary's creditors. The applicable state's exemption law determines the rights of the beneficiary's creditors, and statutes vary a great deal.

Exemption laws in some states protect life insurance policy proceeds from claims of creditors of the policyowner but do not protect proceeds from claims of the beneficiary's creditors. Laws in other states protect policy proceeds from creditors of both the policyowner and beneficiary. When proceeds are not exempt from claims by a beneficiary's creditors, as soon as the beneficiary's right to the policy proceeds vests, then the beneficiary's creditors may follow the applicable state's procedures to obtain repayment while the insurer has the money. Typically, a creditor in such a case uses the state's garnishment procedure, which we described in Chapter 4. Later in the chapter, we describe a special type of trust that can be established to protect policy proceeds from the claims of a beneficiary's creditors.

## Creditor as Policyowner or Beneficiary

Sometimes a creditor seeks to protect himself by taking out a policy on his debtor's life and naming himself as the beneficiary. When a creditor purchases such a policy and pays the policy premiums, the creditor is entitled to receive the full policy proceeds after the insured's death even if those proceeds are more than the amount of the unpaid debt.

Other times a debtor who owns a policy on her own life names the creditor as the policy beneficiary.

> **Example:**
>
> When Irene Durham purchased a $25,000 policy on her life, she owed $25,000 to Matt Jergen. To ensure that the debt would be repaid, Ms. Durham named Mr. Jergen as the policy beneficiary. When Ms. Durham died, the $25,000 debt remained unpaid. In most states, Mr. Jergen would be entitled to receive the entire policy proceeds, because they equaled the amount of the unpaid debt.

 What happens if the amount of the policy proceeds is more than the amount of the unpaid debt?

 In most states, the creditor can recover only the amount of the unpaid debt. If the creditor paid any premiums for the policy, he can recover those premiums plus interest. Any policy proceeds remaining after the creditor is repaid are payable to the policyowner-insured's estate.

# Trust Agreements

A *trust* is an arrangement in which one person, the *trustee*, holds title to property for the benefit of another, the *trust beneficiary*. A trust is created when one person, the *settlor* or *grantor*, transfers ownership of property to a trustee, who has a duty to manage the property for the trust beneficiary's benefit. Real and personal property can be deposited into a trust.

Ownership of trust property is split between the trustee and the trust beneficiary. The trustee has formal *legal title* to the property and, thus, is the legal owner of the property. The trust beneficiary has *equitable title* to the trust property, which means that the beneficiary has ownership rights based on considerations of fairness and equity. Insight 12.1 describes this division of ownership interests between legal title and equitable title.

## Insight 12.1 Legal and Equitable Title

Ownership of trust property is divided into two components: equitable title and legal title. All property has these two ownership interests, although one person may be both the legal and equitable owner of property. An everyday example of this division of interests is when someone purchases an automobile and finances the purchase with a loan from a bank, finance company, or other lender. The lender may physically hold the automobile's title documentation, or the title documentation may list the lender as a lien holder on the title. In both situations, the lender controls the legal title to the automobile. However, the person who purchased the automobile and borrowed the money to purchase the automobile has an equitable interest in the automobile and gets the economic benefit from it—possession of the vehicle.

If the purchaser wants to dispose of the automobile, the two parties have to cooperate; the purchaser has to convey his economic interest, and the lender has to convey legal title. Neither party can sell the vehicle without the other. When the purchaser repays the lender, the lender's interest in the vehicle ends, and the purchaser thereafter owns both legal title and equitable title.

Ownership rights in a trust are similar to the ownership rights in the automobile. The trustee who holds legal title to trust property may control the timing and the amounts of the property distributions to the trust beneficiaries. Eventually, however, the trust beneficiaries will receive the assets in the trust.

So, if I pay cash for a car, then I have both legal and equitable title to the car?

That's right. But if you borrow money to buy a car, then the lender has legal title to it. Your interest is an equitable interest.

A trustee is a fiduciary and, therefore, is obligated to act solely for the benefit of the trust beneficiary. A trustee's fiduciary duties include

- The duty to manage the trust property by exercising the degree of care that a reasonably prudent person would exercise in managing his own affairs.

- A duty of loyalty to the trust beneficiary. The trustee must not allow his own personal interests to conflict with the interests of the beneficiary.

A trustee will be liable to a trust beneficiary for any losses caused by a breach of the trustee's fiduciary duties. If the trustee does not follow the settlor's instructions in handling the trust property, then the beneficiaries have the right to ask a court to enforce the terms of the trust agreement. The court can then force the trustee to act in accordance with the settlor's instructions.

Anyone who has the legal capacity to transfer property ownership may create a trust of that property. Thus, minors typically do not have the legal capacity to create a trust. In the past, a settlor was not permitted to be both the trustee and the sole trust beneficiary. Today, most states permit the settlor to be both the trustee and the trust beneficiary of a trust as long as specific requirements are met.

## Types of Trusts

A trust that takes effect during the settlor's lifetime is known as an ***inter vivos trust*** or a living trust. No specific formalities such as signing a written document are required to create a living trust, unless the trust property includes real property. However, the settlor usually drafts and signs a written document, known as a ***trust agreement***, that spells out the terms of the trust, including instructions as to how the trustee is to handle the trust property. The trust agreement may name one or more trustees, and it may name a bank or trust company to serve as trustee. The trust agreement also may name a *successor trustee*, who will assume the position of trustee if the original trustee can no longer serve that function.

In contrast to a living trust, a ***testamentary trust*** is a trust that takes effect at the settlor's death. A testamentary trust must comply with the applicable wills statute to be valid. Typically, the terms of a testamentary trust are included in the settlor's will.

A settlor may establish a trust as a revocable trust or an irrevocable trust. When a trust is *revocable*, the settlor retains the right to change the terms of the trust or to dissolve the trust. When a trust is *irrevocable*, the settlor may not change or revoke the trust.

An ***insurance trust*** is an irrevocable trust in which the trust property consists of insurance policies on the life of the settlor or the proceeds of such policies. Upon the insured's death, life insurance policy proceeds held in trust are not included in the insured's taxable estate. Thus, the insured can both reduce the amount of estate taxes owed and provide funds to pay estate taxes. Figure 12.3 identifies and describes some other types of trusts.

## Figure 12.3 Examples of Various Types of Trusts

**Discretionary trust:** A trust in which the trustees have discretion as to how to invest trust assets and as to the timing and amounts of distributions to make to the trust beneficiaries.

**Nondiscretionary trust:** A trust in which the trustees are given no discretion as to the timing and amount of distributions to make to the trust beneficiaries. Instead, the trust agreement includes specific instructions as to such distributions.

**Annuity trust:** A trust from which the trustee is required to pay a specified sum each year to each trust beneficiary for the beneficiary's lifetime or for a stated number of years.

**Bond trust:** A trust in which the trust property consists of bonds.

**Express trust:** A trust created in express terms, usually in a written document.

**Constructive trust:** A trust that is created by operation of law as distinguished from an express trust. Constructive trusts are imposed by courts on equitable grounds in situations in which the legal owner of property cannot also benefit from the property without violating principles of equity.

---

A *spendthrift trust* is a trust that is designed to keep trust property out of the hands of creditors of the trust beneficiary. The primary difference between a spendthrift trust and other trusts is that the beneficiary of a spendthrift trust is prohibited from assigning or otherwise transferring her interest in the trust. By contrast, most states permit the beneficiaries of other types of trusts to assign their interest in the trust. Thus, for example, a trust beneficiary can assign her interest in a trust as collateral for a loan. By prohibiting such assignments or other transfers of an interest in spendthrift trust property, a spendthrift trust protects the trust property from the trust beneficiary's actions. In addition, state laws generally prohibit creditors from seizing the property in a spendthrift trust. After trust assets are transferred to the trust beneficiary, however, those assets can be seized by the beneficiary's creditors. Later in the chapter, we describe how life insurance policyowners can use a spendthrift trust to protect a policy's beneficiary.

To effectively protect the trust beneficiary, a spendthrift trust typically must be established as an irrevocable trust. In addition, the trustee generally is given full discretion in handling the trust assets. In most states, the settlor of a spendthrift trust cannot also be a trust beneficiary. A few states, however, now permit a person to establish a spendthrift trust and name himself as the trust beneficiary if certain requirements are met.

## Reasons for Establishing a Trust

A trust generally can be created for any lawful purpose. When the purpose of a trust is illegal or against public policy, the trust is void and unenforceable. Thus, for example, a settlor may not transfer property as a way to defraud his creditors.

Trusts are often created to ensure that the settlor's dependents are provided for over a period of time. For example, a person with young children or children who are not capable of handling large sums of money may establish a trust and instruct the trustee to transfer trust assets to the trust beneficiaries only when they reach a specified age or only for specified purposes. Children that are mentally or physically incapacitated can be cared for throughout their lifetimes by means of a trust.

A trust also can be a useful estate planning tool. In the United States, when someone dies owning a probate estate valued at more than a specified dollar amount, the decedent's estate is required to pay federal taxes known as *estate taxes*. Life insurance trusts often are established to provide funds to pay estate taxes. In such a case, the life insurance policies that are held in trust become payable at the settlor's death, and those funds can be used to pay any estate taxes payable at the settlor's death. In addition, if the settlor transferred ownership of the life insurance policies to the trustee, then the policy proceeds payable are not included in the settlor's taxable estate; thus, the amount of estate taxes owed is reduced.

With proper planning, transferring assets into an irrevocable living trust can reduce the assets in a decedent's estate and, thus, can reduce the amount of estate taxes payable. In addition, assets that are not part of the settlor's probate estate are available immediately to provide for the decedent's dependents without going through the probate process.

A trust also can be used for charitable purposes. For example, people sometimes transfer ownership of property into a trust that is established for the benefit of an educational or charitable organization. In such a case, the settlor can retain possession of the property during her lifetime; at the settlor's death, possession of the property is transferred to the designated charity. By establishing a charitable trust, the settlor reduces the amount of her taxable estate.

## Life Insurance Policy Settlement Options

Although life insurance policy proceeds usually are paid in a single lump sum following the insured's death, policies provide other methods of payment. Most states require individual life insurance policies to include a *settlement options provision*, which grants the policyowner or beneficiary several choices as to how the insurer will pay the policy proceeds. The settlement options that insurers commonly offer in individual life insurance policies are identified in Figure 12.4.

A policyowner may select one of the settlement options at the time of application or at any time while the policy is in force. The policyowner also has the right to change to another settlement option at any time during the insured's life. When the policyowner selects a settlement option while the policy is in force, the terms of the settlement usually are incorporated into a *settlement agreement*, which is a contractual agreement between the policyowner and the insurer governing the rights and obligations of the parties after the insured's death. The settlement agreement then becomes part of the life insurance contract.

A policyowner who selects a settlement option for the beneficiary may choose to make the settlement mode irrevocable. In such a case, the beneficiary will not be able to change to another option when the policy proceeds become payable. If the settlement agreement does not state that the settlement mode is irrevocable, then the mode is considered to be revocable and the beneficiary has the right to select another settlement option when the proceeds become payable. Thus, the

## Figure 12.4 Common Settlement Options

- The **interest option**, under which the proceeds are temporarily left on deposit with the insurer and the interest earned is paid out annually, semiannually, quarterly, or monthly

- The **fixed period option**, under which the insurer pays the proceeds and interest in a series of annual or more frequent installments for a preselected period

- The **fixed amount option**, under which the insurer uses the proceeds and interest to pay a preselected sum in a series of annual or more frequent installments for as long as the proceeds and interest last

- The **life income option**, under which the insurer uses the proceeds and interest to pay a series of annual or more frequent installments over the entire lifetime of the person designated to receive the policy benefit

beneficiary can elect to receive the proceeds in a lump sum or can elect another settlement option provided by the policy.

If the policyowner has not selected a settlement option when the policy proceeds become payable, then the beneficiary has the right to select a settlement option. In such a case, the life insurance contract matures at the insured's death, and the beneficiary and the insurer enter into a new contract governing how the policy proceeds will be paid. Such a settlement agreement between an insurer and a policy beneficiary sometimes is referred to as a *supplementary contract*.

The person who will receive policy proceeds under a settlement agreement generally is referred to as a *payee* rather than as a beneficiary. Although the payee usually is the named beneficiary, the different terminology results from the fact that a payee under a settlement agreement may not have been the policy beneficiary. A policyowner often has the right to name a *contingent payee* or *successor payee*, who will receive any proceeds still payable at the time of the payee's death; the contingent payee may or may not have been designated as the contingent beneficiary of the policy.

So if a policyowner does not choose a specific settlement option, the policy proceeds are simply paid to the beneficiary according to the terms of the policy.

Correct. But if a specific settlement option is chosen—either by the policyowner or by the beneficiary—that's called a *settlement agreement*. The person who receives proceeds under that agreement is known as the payee.

And usually the payee is the same person as the beneficiary, but not always

That's right. There may also be a contingent payee, who may or may not be the same person as the contingent beneficiary.

Although neither contingent payees nor contingent beneficiaries have any vested rights to policy proceeds during the insured's lifetime, the rights of a contingent payee and of a contingent beneficiary differ after the death of the insured. If a primary beneficiary survives the insured, then the expectancy of the contingent beneficiary is extinguished. By contrast, a contingent payee's expectancy continues beyond the death of the insured. The examples in Figure 12.5 illustrate the different rights of contingent beneficiaries and contingent payees.

## Figure 12.5 Rights of Contingent Beneficiaries and Contingent Payees

Bryan Bell owned a policy insuring his life and named his brother, Neal, as the primary beneficiary and his cousin, Maggie, as the contingent beneficiary.

**Example 1:** Assume that Neal and Maggie survived Bryan, and thus, Neal was entitled to the policy proceeds. Maggie's interest was extinguished. Neal elected to receive the proceeds under an optional mode of settlement and thereby became the payee of the settlement agreement. He named his wife, Ginny, as the contingent payee. Ginny will receive any proceeds remaining at Neal's death.

**Example 2:** Assume that Bryan elected an optional mode of settlement and named Maggie as the contingent payee. When Bryan died, the insurer began to pay the policy proceeds to Neal in accordance with the terms of the settlement agreement. If Neal dies before all proceeds are paid, then the remaining proceeds will be paid to Maggie as the contingent payee.

**Example 3:** Assume that Bryan elected an optional mode of settlement and named Neal's wife, Ginny, as the contingent payee. Neal died several months before Bryan, and thus, the policy proceeds were payable to Maggie as the contingent beneficiary. The insurer will pay the policy proceeds to Maggie in accordance with the terms of the settlement agreement. Any proceeds remaining at Maggie's death will be paid to Ginny, the contingent payee.

Life insurance policyowners also can include a spendthrift clause in their policies to protect a beneficiary. A **spendthrift clause** or *spendthrift trust clause* is a provision that may be included in a life insurance policy or a settlement agreement to protect the policy proceeds from being seized by the beneficiary's creditors. A policyowner can ask the insurer to add such a clause to a policy by adding a rider or endorsement to the policy or can enter into a settlement agreement that includes a spendthrift clause.

When a policy or settlement agreement includes a spendthrift clause, the beneficiary's creditors cannot reach any money that is held by the insurer. In addition, the beneficiary is prohibited from assigning or otherwise transferring her interest in the policy proceeds. The beneficiary also is prohibited from changing the terms on which the policy proceeds are payable. For example, assume that $250,000 in policy proceeds became payable at the insured's death. Under the terms of the settlement agreement, the insurer agreed to pay out only a specified sum each month to the beneficiary. The beneficiary cannot change the terms of the settlement agreement. After the insurer pays money to the beneficiary, however, those funds can be reached by the beneficiary's creditors.

Although a few states permit a person to establish a spendthrift trust and name himself as the trust beneficiary, a life insurance policyowner cannot try to protect himself with a spendthrift clause. Such a clause may be included only for the benefit of someone other than the policyowner. This requirement is imposed to prevent a policyowner from trying to defraud his own creditors.

## Key Terms

| | |
|---|---|
| absolute assignment | trust agreement |
| collateral assignment | testamentary trust |
| assignment provision | insurance trust |
| net policy proceeds | spendthrift trust |
| change of ownership provision | estate taxes |
| judgment creditor | settlement options provision |
| trust | settlement agreement |
| trustee | supplementary contract |
| trust beneficiary | payee |
| settlor | contingent payee |
| equitable title | spendthrift clause |
| inter vivos trust | |

## Endnotes

1. Colo. Rev. Stat. § 13-54-102 (2011).

2. Fla. Stat. Ann. § 222.13 (2011).

3. Minn. Stat. Ann. § 550.37 (2010).

*Chapter 13*

# Policy Contests and Civil Remedies

## Objectives

### *After studying this chapter, you should be able to*

- Distinguish between situations in which an insurer performs a life insurance contract and situations in which it contests the validity of a life insurance contract
- Describe the grounds on which an insurer may contest the validity of a life insurance contract
- Describe the three elements of a material misrepresentation, and explain the actions an insurer may take when there is a misrepresentation of the insured's age or sex
- Explain how the incontestability provision limits an insurer's right to contest the validity of a life insurance contract, and identify other barriers to a policy contest
- Distinguish among the types of mistakes that can affect the validity of a life insurance contract
- Define common legal and equitable remedies available to the parties to a life insurance contract

# Outline

**What Is a Policy Contest?**

**Elements of a Material Misrepresentation**
- Duty to Disclose
- Known Facts
- Material to the Insurance

**Barriers to a Contest on the Grounds of Material Misrepresentation**
- Incontestability Provision
- Knowledge of the Agent
- Delay by the Insurer
- Failure to Inquire
- Copy of the Application

**Other Grounds for Contesting a Contract**
- Defect in the Formation of the Contract
- Mistake
- Beneficiary Wrongfully Kills the Insured

**Remedies**
- Legal Remedies
- Equitable Remedies

Most individual life insurance contracts are valid and enforceable because the parties met the prerequisites to the formation of a valid contract discussed earlier in this text. In some cases, however, parties fail to meet the prerequisites to the formation of a valid contract, and the contract is void or voidable. If the contract is void, no contract was ever formed between the parties. If the contract is voidable by one of the parties, that party has the option of avoiding the contract, and if that party does so, the contract is terminated. In this chapter, we discuss the grounds on which the validity of an individual life insurance policy may be challenged and the remedies that are available to the parties to civil lawsuits involving life insurance policies.

# What Is a Policy Contest?

By *policy contest*, we mean a court action to determine the validity of a life insurance contract. According to the rules of general contract law, when parties fail to enter into a valid contract, all parties must be returned as much as possible to the positions that they occupied before they attempted to enter into the contract. Therefore, when an insurer is successful in contesting the validity of an individual life insurance contract, the insurer generally must return to the policyowner all premiums paid plus any interest less any withdrawals.

Whether a policy contest arises before or after the insured's death often determines the parties to the contest and what remedy a party seeks. When an insurer learns that it has grounds for a policy contest during the insured's lifetime, the insurer notifies the policyowner that it has elected to rescind the life insurance contract, and it returns all premiums paid for the contract plus any interest. If the policyowner refuses to accept the premium refund, the insurer initiates an action in court for rescission of the contract. We discuss rescission in more detail later in this chapter.

When an insurer learns that it has grounds to avoid a contract after the death of the insured, it denies payment of policy proceeds and returns all premiums paid plus any interest less any withdrawals. A claimant to life insurance proceeds who wishes to challenge such an action may file an action in court to enforce the contract. The insurer's defense to such an action is that the policy was invalid.

Not every court action involving a life insurance policy is a policy contest. Sometimes, an insurer denies a claim or takes other actions for reasons other than a challenge of a contract's validity. For example, an insurer may deny a claim because the insured died as a result of a cause that a policy provision excludes from coverage. When an insurer denies a claim based on a provision in the life insurance policy, the insurer is performing the contract according to its terms. Such an action acknowledges the validity of the contract and is not a policy contest. We discuss performance of the life insurance contract in more detail in Chapter 14. Figure 13.1 provides examples of performing a contract and contesting a contract.

## Figure 13.1 Performing Versus Contesting a Life Insurance Contract

**Performing the contract:**

Peggy Moon was insured by an individual life insurance policy that contained an aviation exclusion provision, which excluded from coverage death caused by aviation-related activities performed while in the military. Ms. Moon died while piloting an airplane during military service. The insurer denied the claim, because the cause of the insured's death was not covered by her policy.

**Contesting the contract:**

Herb Wood died during the contestable period of his individual life insurance policy. While evaluating the death claim, the insurer discovered material misrepresentations on Mr. Wood's application for insurance. The insurer denied payment of the claim, notified the claimant that the policy was invalid, and returned all premiums paid. The claimant filed an action in court to enforce the contract. The insurer defended the lawsuit on the grounds that the policy was invalid as a result of material misrepresentation in the application.

# Elements of a Material Misrepresentation

A material misrepresentation is the most common reason insurers rescind life insurance contracts and deny payment of policy proceeds. As a general rule, when one party makes a material misrepresentation—that is, a misrepresentation that induces the other party to enter into a contract that it would not have entered into had it known the truth—the contract is voidable by the innocent party. Thus, when an applicant makes a misrepresentation that induces an insurer to enter into a life insurance contract that it would not have entered into had it known the true facts, the contract is voidable by the insurer.

Each jurisdiction has its own requirements that insurers must meet to successfully challenge the validity of a life insurance contract based on a misrepresentation in the application for insurance. Most jurisdictions require that an insurer prove the following three elements:

- The applicant or proposed insured failed to disclose or misrepresented a fact.

- The fact was within the person's knowledge at the time the misrepresentation was made.

- The fact was material—or relevant—to the insurer's acceptance of the risk.

As a general rule, when the validity of a contract is contested in court, the party who seeks to avoid the contract bears the burden of proof. Thus, when an insurer seeks to avoid a life insurance contract on the grounds of material misrepresentation, the insurer has the burden of proving these three elements. How an insurer meets its burden of proving a material misrepresentation varies depending on the facts of a particular case.

## Duty to Disclose

When deciding whether to issue an insurance contract, the insurer must determine if the proposed insured is an insurable risk according to the insurer's underwriting standards; if so, the insurer must decide what premium rate it should charge to provide the requested coverage. In the case of an individual life insurance policy, the information the insurer needs to make these determinations is provided by the applicant for insurance or the proposed insured. The insurer, therefore, must be able to rely on the truth of the statements in the application.

The duty to disclose requires applicants and proposed insureds to disclose to the insurer any fact that is within their knowledge and that is material to the insurance. The applicant and the proposed insured must answer truthfully and completely any questions contained in the application for insurance, asked during a medical examination, or included in any other written statements or answers furnished to the insurer as evidence of insurability.

Note that an applicant or proposed insured must disclose any material facts to the insurer, and this duty to disclose is breached when an applicant or proposed insured *conceals* a material fact.

> **Example:**
>
> An application for life insurance asked the applicant to list the names of every physician she had consulted in the last five years and explain the reason for each consultation. The applicant revealed that she had consulted one physician on four occasions for three routine physicals and for treatment of a cold on a fourth visit. In fact, the applicant had three routine physicals, but the fourth visit was for treatment of a respiratory disorder. The applicant's primary physician then referred her to a respiratory specialist who treated her for emphysema.
>
> The applicant failed to meet her duty to disclose by misstating the reason for the fourth visit to her primary physician and concealing the fact that another physician treated her for emphysema.

As this example shows, both a concealment and a material misrepresentation can provide grounds for the insurer to contest the life insurance policy during the time limit specified in the incontestability provision.

The incontestability provision?

That's a life insurance contract provision that sets a time limit in which the insurer can contest a life insurance policy on the ground of material misrepresentation in the application. Keep reading to make sure you understand the elements of material misrepresentation first, and then we'll explain more about the incontestability provision.

## Known Facts

In providing an insurer with evidence of insurability, an applicant or a proposed insured is required to disclose only those facts that are within the applicant's or proposed insured's knowledge. They are not required to speculate on the proposed insured's health status.

> **Example:**
>
> Juan Araya underwent a series of routine medical tests after experiencing periods of extreme fatigue. After undergoing the tests, Mr. Araya's physician assured him that he was in good health and that the tests were a precautionary measure. Ten days later, the results of Mr. Araya's medical tests revealed that he had diabetes. The physician, however, never discussed these results with Mr. Araya.
>
> Soon after completing the medical tests, Mr. Araya completed an application for life insurance. In the application, Mr. Araya disclosed that he had experienced periods of fatigue and had undergone medical tests. By disclosing these facts, Mr. Araya met his duty to disclose because he revealed the facts that were within his knowledge.

## Material to the Insurance

According to the traditional rules of contract law, statements made by parties when they enter into a contract can be classified as either warranties or representations. As explained in Chapter 6, a *warranty* is a statement made by a contracting party that becomes part of the contract. A warranty that is not *literally* true gives an injured party grounds to avoid the contract. In the past, the technical enforcement of the doctrine of warranties often resulted in unjust and harsh results when applied to life insurance. For example, assume that an applicant for life insurance stated that she had visited a physician one time in two years for treatment for an infected toe on her left foot. In reality, the visit was for treatment for an infected toe on the applicant's right foot. Under the doctrine of warranties, the insurer had grounds to rescind the contract even though the misrepresentation would not have affected the insurer's decision to issue the policy. Because of this potential unfairness, laws throughout the United States now make it clear that, in the absence of fraud, statements made in life insurance applications are representations rather than warranties.

A *representation* is a statement made by a contracting party that can be used to invalidate the contract if the statement is not *substantially* true and the statement induced the other party to enter into the contract. In other words, if a party misrepresents a fact that is relevant—that is, material—to the insurance, the contract is voidable by the other party. A misrepresentation is considered to be material to the insurance when the insurer, if it had known the truth, would have evaluated the proposed risk differently. Generally, a misrepresentation is material if an insurer that knew the true facts would have either (1) declined to issue the policy, (2) increased the premium rate charged for the policy, or (3) excluded coverage for certain risks.

The question of whether a misrepresented or concealed fact was material to the insurance is a question of fact that must be answered from the point of view of the insurer. The answer does *not* depend on what a reasonable person in the applicant's position would have considered to be material to the insurance.

A few states permit an insurer to avoid a life insurance contract on the grounds of material misrepresentation *only if* the cause of the insured's death was directly related to the misrepresentation. In most states, however, an insurer can avoid a life insurance contract on the grounds of material misrepresentation even if the cause of the insured's death was not related to the fact that was misrepresented.

When a proposed insured misrepresents his medical history on the application for insurance, an insurer may seek to avoid the life insurance contract on the grounds of a material misrepresentation. However, the actions an insurer may take because of misrepresentations regarding a proposed insured's age or sex usually are determined by the provisions of the life insurance policy. Insight 13.1 discusses these types of misrepresentations.

## Insight 13.1 Misrepresentation of the Insured's Age or Sex

In most jurisdictions, misrepresentations regarding an insured's age or sex affect the premium rate that an insurer charges for life insurance. A misstatement of the insured's age or sex is, therefore, a significant error. In the United States and many other countries, life insurance policies typically include a **misstatement of age or sex provision** that describes the action an insurer will take to adjust the amount of the policy benefit in the event that the age or sex of the insured is incorrectly stated. The provision states that if the age or sex of the insured is misstated and the misstatement resulted in an incorrect premium amount for the amount of insurance purchased, the insurer will adjust the face amount of the policy to the amount the premium actually paid would have purchased if the insured's age or sex had been stated correctly.

Insurers follow this procedure whenever the misstatement of age or sex is discovered *after* the death of the insured. If the insurer discovers the misstatement *before* the death of the insured, the insurer may grant the policyowner the option to pay, or receive as a refund, any premium amount difference caused by the misstatement instead of having the policy's face amount adjusted.

Note that when an insurer adjusts a life insurance policy's face amount because of a misstatement of age or sex, the insurer is enforcing the misstatement of age or sex provision of the contract. Such an action by the insurer is not considered a contest to the validity of the contract and is not prohibited by the incontestability provision.

# Barriers to a Contest on the Grounds of Material Misrepresentation

Sometimes an insurer is prevented from contesting the validity of a life insurance contract even after the insurer discovers that a material fact was misrepresented. An insurer's primary barrier to contesting the validity of a life insurance contract is the incontestability provision. Other barriers arise when

- An agent's knowledge of a misrepresentation is imputed to the insurer

- The insurer delays in acting on its knowledge of a misrepresentation

- The insurer fails to inquire about ambiguous answers provided on the application for insurance

- The insurer does not provide the policyowner with a copy of the insurance application

## Incontestability Provision

As explained earlier, the rules of contract law give an insurer the right to avoid an otherwise enforceable insurance contract if the applicant misrepresented material facts in the application for insurance. Laws in most jurisdictions, however, limit the time within which an insurer has such a right. The *incontestability provision* is a life insurance policy provision that denies the insurer the right to avoid the contract on the grounds of a material misrepresentation in the application after the contract has been in force for a specified period of time. The *contestable period* is the time period within which the insurer has the right to avoid a life insurance policy on the grounds of a material misrepresentation in the application. A typical incontestability provision found in individual life insurance contracts reads as follows:

> ### Incontestability
>
> We will not contest the validity of this policy after it has been in force during the lifetime of the insured for two years from the date of issue.

The incontestability provision limits the period during which the insurer can avoid the contract to two years from the date the policy was issued. A two-year contestable period is the maximum period allowed by most states. Some life insurers include a one-year contestable period in the policies they issue. Such a shorter period is permitted because the shorter period is more favorable to policyowners.

The phrase *during the lifetime of the insured* is an important part of an incontestability provision because this phrase ensures that the policy never becomes incontestable if the person whose life is insured dies during the stated contestable period. As a result, the insurer has the opportunity to investigate for material misrepresentation when a death claim arises within the contestable period of the policy. If the phrase *during the lifetime of the insured* was not included and the insured died during the contestable period, a claimant could delay making a death claim until after the contestable period expired. Because the policy's contestable period had expired when the insurer received the death claim, the insurer could not contest the validity of the contract even if it discovered a material misrepresentation on the application for insurance. Figure 13.2 provides an example of how this phrase affects an insurer's ability to contest a policy when the insured dies during the contestable period.

---

## Figure 13.2 Death of the Insured During the Contestable Period

Raman Mattipalli completed an application for insurance and submitted it to the Euphoric Life Insurance Company. Mr. Mattipalli made material misrepresentations on the application. Euphoric issued Mr. Mattipalli a life insurance policy containing a two-year contestable period. Mr. Mattipalli died one year and nine months after Euphoric issued the policy. Euphoric received the death claim two years and one month after it issued the policy. During its review of the death claim, Euphoric discovered the material misrepresentation in the application.

| | | |
|---|---|---|
| If the incontestability provision did not include the phrase "during the lifetime of the insured" |  | The policy became incontestable two years after it was issued. Because Euphoric discovered the material misrepresentations after the contestable period expired, it cannot contest the validity of the policy based on the misrepresentations. |
| If the incontestability provision included the phrase "during the lifetime of the insured" |  | Because Mr. Mattipalli died during the contestable period, the policy will never become incontestable. Euphoric can contest the validity of the contract based on material misrepresentations in Mr. Mattipalli's application. |

---

The incontestability provision allows policyowners and beneficiaries to know with certainty that if all required premiums are paid and the policy has been in force during the insured's lifetime for at least the stated contestable period, the insurer cannot contest the policy's validity and usually must pay policy proceeds following the insured's death.

So now do you see how the incontestability provision relates to material misrepresentations?

I think so. It means that the insurer can contest a policy on the grounds of material misrepresentation only during a certain amount of time after the policy went into force.

And that time is called the contestable period, and it is usually two years.

Right! And can you see how it affects both insurers and policyowners?

Well, it means we underwriters have to do our jobs thoroughly! After a policy is in force, insurers have only a limited amount of time to contest it based on any factual errors in the application.

That's true. And remember: if the insured dies during the contestable period, then the insurer can contest the policy at any time.

And the provision protects policyowners and beneficiaries because it gives them peace of mind. They'll know that after the contestable period, if all premiums are paid, the insurer can't avoid the policy.

## *Date from Which the Contestable Period Runs*

Most individual life insurance policies contain a date of issue and an effective date, which is the date insurance coverage begins. Life insurance policies typically specify that the contestable period begins on the date of issue. Sometimes, however, the policy does not specify the date on which the contestable period begins to run. When this situation occurs and the date of issue and the effective date are not the same, an ambiguity arises as to which date should be used to determine the start of the contestable period. Under traditional rules of contract construction, ambiguities in a contract are construed against the party that drafted the contract. In such a situation, a court would interpret the terms of the contract in a manner that is more favorable to the policyowner. Thus, a court would likely choose the date that allows the contestable period to expire as early as possible. Figure 13.3 provides an example of such a situation.

## Figure 13.3 Determining When the Contestable Period Runs

**Example:** The ABC Insurance Company issued an individual life insurance policy to Victor Bothwell. The policy's issue date was August 10, 2012, but ABC backdated the policy's effective date to August 1, 2012. The policy did not specify the date on which the contestable period would begin.

**Analysis:** Because the policy did not specify the date on which the contestable period began, an ambiguity arose as to which date should be used to determine the start of the contestable period. ABC drafted the contract; therefore, under traditional rules of contract construction, a court would construe the ambiguity against ABC, the insurer, and in favor of Mr. Bothwell, the policyowner. In this case, the court would likely determine that the contestable period started on the effective date of August 1, because that date allows the contestable period to expire as early as possible.

## Effect of Reinstatement

We noted in Chapter 11 that, when a life insurance policy is reinstated, a new contestable period typically begins on the date the policy is reinstated. The length of that new contestable period is the same as the original period provided by the policy. During the new contestable period following reinstatement of a policy, the insurer may contest the policy based only on misrepresentations in the reinstatement application. If the policy's original contestable period has not expired, the insurer may contest the policy based on misrepresentations in the original application.

**Example:**

Helen Kalafut was the policyowner-insured of a policy that contained a two-year contestable period. One year after the policy became effective, Ms. Kalafut failed to pay a premium when due and the policy lapsed. Two months later, Ms. Kalafut reinstated the policy. The reinstated policy became contestable for two years from the reinstatement date based on misrepresentations in the reinstatement application. The original contestable period, which had not expired when the policy lapsed, also was revived upon reinstatement; thus, the insurer also had the right to contest the policy based on misrepresentations in the original application until two years after the policy first became effective. Figure 13.4 illustrates this example.

## Figure 13.4 Effect of Reinstatement

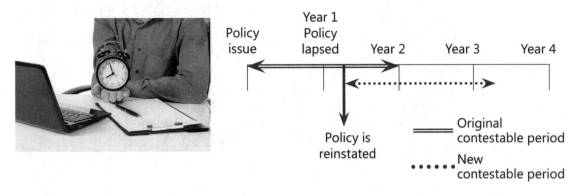

## Knowledge of the Agent

An insurance producer who helps an applicant complete an application for life insurance is acting as an agent of the insurer. Likewise, a physician who conducts a medical examination of a proposed insured on behalf of an insurer is acting as the insurer's agent. Recall that, according to the general rules of agency law, the knowledge that an agent gains while acting in his capacity as an agent is considered to be the knowledge of the principal. Based on that rule, if an insurance producer or physician has knowledge of facts about a proposed insured, then the insurer is considered to have that knowledge.

> **Example:**
>
> An insurance producer helped Vera Yip complete an application for an insurance policy on her life. Ms. Yip told the producer that she had been treated for a respiratory disease the previous year. The producer incorrectly recorded that information on the application, making it appear that Ms. Yip had not revealed the information. The insurer issued the policy as applied for. Ms. Yip died during the contestable period, and the insurer discovered the misrepresentation on the application.

Whether the insurer is able to contest the validity of such a policy on the basis of the misrepresentation varies from state to state. Courts in most states hold that the insurer is considered to have the agent's knowledge if the agent recorded false answers without the knowledge of the applicant. In a minority of states, however, the courts do not consider the insurer to have the knowledge of the agent in such a case. In these states, the applicant for insurance has a duty to read the application and ensure that the information it contains is accurate before signing the application.

Sometimes an agent of an insurer and an applicant engage in *collusion*, which is an agreement between two or more people to defraud another person of his rights. When an agent and an applicant engage in collusion, the agent's knowledge is *not* considered to be the knowledge of the insurer.

> **Example:**
>
> An applicant for insurance had a serious health impairment that made her uninsurable. The applicant told the insurance producer about her health condition, and the producer agreed to falsify the application to conceal the problem from the insurer to ensure that a life insurance policy would be issued to the applicant. The insurer issued a policy at a standard premium rate, and several months later the insured died. Because of the collusion between the applicant and the insurer's agent, the agent's knowledge of the insured's health impairment would not be attributed to the insurer. Thus, the insurer has the right to avoid the contract because of material misrepresentation.

## Delay by the Insurer

An insurer may be prevented from contesting the validity of a life insurance contract if the insurer learns of—or has a sufficient reason to suspect—a misrepresentation but fails to act on that information within a reasonable time. By failing to take action to contest the contract on a timely basis, the insurer is deemed to have waived its right to contest the contract's validity.

> **Example:**
>
> Joseph Rodriguez failed to disclose material information on an application for life insurance. Shortly after issuing a policy to Mr. Rodriguez, the insurer learned of the misrepresentation. The insurer, however, failed to investigate further or take action to contest the contract until it received a death claim 20 months later. In this case, the insurer would likely be barred from contesting the validity of the contract because it failed to act within a reasonable time and thus waived its right to contest the policy.

What constitutes a reasonable time within which an insurer must act is a question of fact that depends on the circumstances of a particular case.

## Failure to Inquire

Sometimes, the answers on an application for life insurance are ambiguous, conflicting, or missing altogether. In such cases, the insurer has received information that should cause it to question the truth or completeness of representations on the application. When the insurer has information that would cause a prudent person to investigate further, and the insurer fails to do so, the insurer may be unsuccessful in later contesting the validity of the contract on the basis of a material misrepresentation in the application.

**Example:**

An applicant stated in the application that he was taking prescription medication but failed to explain what the medication was or why he was taking it. The insurer issued the policy without investigating further and without knowing why the applicant had been taking the medication. The insured died shortly thereafter as a result of a chronic disease for which he had been taking the medication. Although the insured concealed the fact that he was suffering from a disease, the insurer likely would have discovered the truth had it further investigated the application. As a result, the insurer may be unsuccessful in contesting the contract on the grounds of material misrepresentation.

Note that when an insurer investigates an application and issues a policy, the insurer is not prevented from avoiding the policy if the application contains material misrepresentations. In responding to an insurer's inquiries, the proposed insured has a duty to disclose all facts material to the insurance. Figure 13.5 illustrates a proposed insured's duty to disclose when an insurer inquires about facts material to the insurance.

## Figure 13.5 The Duty to Disclose

**Example:** Before approving an application for life insurance, an underwriter for the Rightway Life Insurance Company conducted an investigation of the proposed insured. The underwriter asked the proposed insured several questions about her health history. The underwriter concluded that the insured was an insurable risk, and Rightway issued a policy. The insured died during the policy's contestable period, and Rightway discovered that the application for insurance contained a number of material misrepresentations.

**Analysis:** Although the insurer conducted its own investigation and concluded that the insured was an insurable risk, the applicant's duty of disclosure remained. As long as the insurer had no reasonable grounds to inquire further about specific representations, it most likely can avoid the contract because of the applicant's material misrepresentations.

## Copy of the Application

In the United States, the insurance policy and the attached application usually constitute the entire life insurance contract. In most states, an insurer has the right to use a material misrepresentation in the life insurance application as a basis for avoiding a life insurance contract *only* when a copy of the application is attached to the policy when it is delivered to the applicant. The application for insurance is not considered a part of the contract unless it is attached to the policy when the policy is issued. The only exception is when a policy is issued electronically. In such a case, the insurer must provide the policyowner with a copy of the application, but the application does not have to be physically attached to the policy.

Requiring that the application for life insurance be attached to the life insurance contract ensures that the owner of the policy receives every document that may affect his rights or benefits under the contract.

# Other Grounds for Contesting a Contract

In the previous section, we described factors that limit an insurer's right to contest the validity of a life insurance contract on the grounds of material misrepresentation. However, an insurer has the right to contest the validity of a contract on other grounds at any time while the contract is in force. (Note that, once the contract terminates, the parties may no longer contest the validity of the contract. For example, after an insurer pays policy proceeds, the contract terminates and can no longer be contested.) In this section, we discuss some of these grounds for contesting a contract.

## Defect in the Formation of the Contract

As noted in Chapter 6, the formation of a valid informal contract, such as a life insurance contract, involves four requirements: mutual assent, adequate consideration, contractual capacity, and lawful purpose. If any one of these requirements is missing, the parties never entered into a valid contract. A party has the right to contest a contract's validity at any time if any requirement was not met.

Recall that state insurance laws impose an insurable interest requirement on individual life insurance contracts to guard against these policies being purchased as wagering contracts. Requiring the policyowner to have had an insurable interest when the policy was issued ensures that the lawful purpose requirement for forming a contract is met. If no insurable interest existed at the time of contracting, the contract is void. The incontestability provision, therefore, does not prohibit a contest based on lack of an insurable interest. The insurer may contest a contract's validity based on lack of an insurable interest at any time while the contract is in force.

## Mistake

A contract is sometimes void or voidable because one or both parties made a mistake when entering the contract. Only certain types of mistakes, however, affect the validity of a contract. For example, if one party to a contract makes an error in judgment and later realizes that he made a bad bargain, that party must honor the contract. The courts will not remedy a bad bargain. The types of mistakes that make a contract void or voidable are mistakes that prevent the parties from mutually assenting to the terms of the agreement. Without mutual assent to the terms of the agreement, no contract is formed.

Mistakes can be characterized as either mistakes of law or mistakes of fact. A *mistake of law* occurs when, with full knowledge of the facts, the parties make a mistake as to the legal effect of those facts. A mistake of law has no effect on the validity of the contract.

> **Example:**
>
> An applicant applied for an individual life insurance policy from an insurer. Both the applicant and the insurer were aware that, if the insurer issued the policy, it would contain a required free look provision, which would give the applicant a certain period of time after the policy was issued to return the policy to the insurer and receive a full refund of the initial premium. The applicant, however, believed that the law in his state required individual life insurance contracts to contain a 30-day free look provision. The law, in fact, required such contracts to contain a 10-day free look provision. The insurer issued a policy that contained a 10-day free look provision. Thus, the applicant made a mistake of law, but this mistake has no effect on the validity of the contract.

By contrast, mistakes of fact can render a contract void or voidable. A *mistake of fact* occurs when one or both parties is mistaken as to the existence of something or as to the identity of something or someone. The incontestability provision does not prohibit a contest of the policy on the grounds of a mistake of fact. Either party can contest a contract's validity on the grounds of mistake of fact at any time, even after the contestable period has expired.

A *unilateral mistake* is a mistake made by only one of the parties to the contract. The effect of a unilateral mistake of fact depends on the type of mistake and the circumstances of the particular situation. For example, assume that the offeror mistakenly misstates the price of the contract. If the offeree reasonably relied on the price as it was stated and entered into a contract, the contract is valid and binding. In contrast, if a reasonable person in the position of the offeree would have known that the offeror made a mistake in stating the price, then the contract generally is voidable by the offeror. In such a case, the party who made the unilateral mistake may avoid the contract after discovering the mistake.

A *bilateral mistake* occurs when both parties are mistaken when they enter into a contract. Bilateral mistakes can be either common mistakes or mutual mistakes. The parties to a contract make a *common mistake* when they both make the same mistake. When the parties make a common mistake as to the identity or existence of the subject matter of the contract, the contract is void.

> **Example:**
>
> An applicant for life insurance and the insurer were both unaware that the proposed insured died before the policy was issued. The contracting parties thus made a mistake of fact because they were mistaken as to the existence of the proposed insured. As a result of a common mistake of fact, the life insurance contract is void.

When parties make a common mistake about a general characteristic concerning the subject matter of the contract, the contract usually is valid.

> **Example:**
>
> Two parties entered into a contract for the sale of a building. One party believed that the building was 10 years old. The other party believed that the building was 15 years old. In fact, the building was 20 years old. The parties made a common mistake about a general characteristic of the subject matter—that is, the building's age. In most jurisdictions, the contract is valid.

A **mutual mistake** occurs when both parties to a contract make a mistake, but they make different mistakes. If the parties are unaware of a mutual mistake as to the subject matter of the contract and are at cross-purposes when entering the contract, then the contract usually is void. This type of mutual mistake involves a misunderstanding between the parties.

Note that some mutual mistakes may not render a contract void if both parties are in agreement as to what the terms of the agreement *should* have been. For example, when both parties make mutual mistakes in drafting a contract, a common remedy is to permit reformation of the contract to reflect the actual intent of the parties. Figure 13.6 illustrates the distinctions between the various types of mistakes.

## Figure 13.6 Types of Mistakes

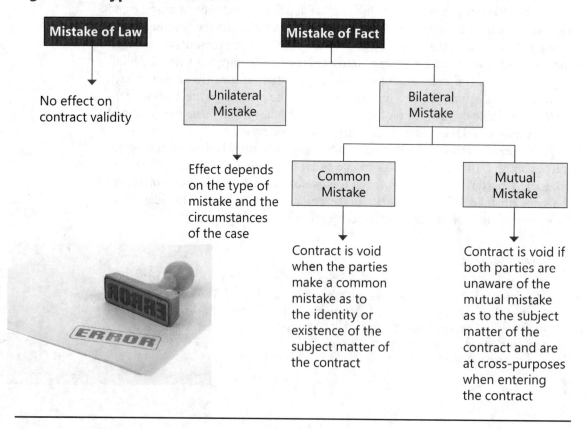

## Beneficiary Wrongfully Kills the Insured

In the United States and other common law jurisdictions, laws exist to prevent individuals from profiting from criminal acts. For this reason, when a person purchases a life insurance policy with the intention of killing the insured to collect policy proceeds, the insurance contract is void. The insurer is not liable to pay the policy proceeds and is responsible only for returning premiums paid, plus any interest, less any withdrawals to the policyowner. In this situation, the incontestability provision does not prohibit a contest of the policy, and the insurer can contest the contract's validity at any time.

If, on the other hand, the policy was not purchased with the intention of killing the insured, but a beneficiary later is convicted in a civil or criminal court of wrongfully killing the insured, the contract is valid. The beneficiary, however, is disqualified from receiving policy proceeds. In this situation, the insurer must pay the policy proceeds to someone—usually another beneficiary. If no other beneficiary exists, the insurer usually pays the proceeds to the policyowner or the policyowner's estate. We discuss disqualification of a beneficiary in more detail in Chapter 14.

# Remedies

As we discussed in Chapter 2, remedies are typically classified as either legal or equitable. Legal remedies primarily involve the payment of money damages to injured parties. Equitable remedies are based on moral rights and concepts of justice. Common law courts are empowered to grant both types of remedies. In this section, we focus on the primary remedies available to the parties to a life insurance contract.

## Legal Remedies

Most litigation involving life insurance policies begins after an insurer denies a claim for life insurance policy proceeds. A claimant who disagrees with the insurer's decision may file a civil action against the insurer alleging that the insurer breached the life insurance contract by refusing to pay policy proceeds. If a claimant is successful, a court typically orders the insurer to pay damages, which is the basic legal remedy for most civil wrongs.

As we discussed in Chapter 2, civil damage awards generally provide a plaintiff with compensatory damages that reimburse an injured party for the monetary losses that resulted from the defendant's wrongful conduct. In an action for breach of contract, compensatory damages usually are measured as the benefit of the bargain—that is, the amount that restores the plaintiff to the financial position he would have been in if the contract had been performed. For a claimant to life insurance policy proceeds, the benefit of the bargain is the amount of policy proceeds payable by the insurer.

Punitive damages are awarded in addition to compensatory damages when a defendant's conduct was malicious or willful. Punitive damages generally are *not* available in actions based on breach of contract. An exception to this rule is a situation where an insurer breaches its duty to act in good faith. The duty to act in good faith requires an insurer to deal ethically and fairly with its customers when deciding whether to pay or deny a claim. Many jurisdictions allow plaintiffs to bring bad-faith tort actions against insurers that breach this duty. In deciding whether an insurer acted in bad faith, the courts most often look for evidence of whether the insurer denied claims unreasonably. In determining whether the insurer's actions are unreasonable, most courts examine an insurer's overall conduct and its reasons for denying claims. Because insurers found to have acted in bad faith may be liable to pay punitive damages in addition to compensatory damages, a plaintiff who proves that an insurer has breached its duty of good faith may recover damages that exceed the amount of the policy's basic death benefit and supplemental benefits.

## Equitable Remedies

Common equitable remedies granted to plaintiffs in civil actions involving life insurance contracts include rescission, reformation, interpleader, declaratory judgment, and restitution.

### *Rescission*

The remedy of rescission is of special importance to insurers because it allows a contract to be cancelled and the parties returned to the positions they would have been in had no contract ever been created. When a contract is rescinded, the contract is void. Contracts may be rescinded in various ways. Parties can mutually agree to rescind the contract. If parties have contractual capacity, they have the contractual capacity to agree to rescind the contract and need not apply to the courts to do so.

> **Example:**
>
> While the insured was still alive, an insurer discovered that the insured materially misrepresented his health in the application for life insurance. The insurer and the policyowner may mutually agree to rescind the contract.

A contract that is voidable at the option of one of the parties can be rescinded when that party exercises her right to rescind the contract. When a party has a legal right to avoid—that is, rescind—a contract without incurring legal liability, that party can exercise that right without having to resort to the courts. A party who has the right to avoid a contract can do so by (1) notifying the other party of the decision to rescind the contract and (2) returning to the other party the consideration given for the contract.

> **Example:**
>
> A minor entered a contract for non-necessaries. The minor may exercise her right to avoid the contract at any time during her minority and within a reasonable time after attaining the age of majority.

In some cases, a contract may be rescinded by a court order.

> **Example:**
>
> An insurer discovers during a policy's contestable period that the applicant for insurance materially misrepresented his health in the application for insurance. The policyowner does not agree to rescind the contract. To protect its right to contest the policy, the insurer must ask the court to rescind the contract while the policy remains contestable.

When a contract is rescinded, each party must return to the other party whatever he has received under the contract. Thus, to rescind a life insurance contract, the insurer must return to the policyowner the total amount of premiums paid plus any interest, less any withdrawals on the policy.

## Reformation

As noted in Chapter 2, reformation is an equitable remedy in which a written contract is rewritten to express the original agreement of the contracting parties. Reformation is available when parties reach an agreement and put it in writing, but the written document does not adequately reflect the parties' intent. If the parties cannot mutually agree to correct such a mistake, one party may ask the court to correct the mistake in the written contract.

A plaintiff who seeks reformation of a contract must present the court with clear and convincing evidence as to the terms of the parties' actual agreement. *Clear and convincing evidence* means evidence that shows that the truth of the facts asserted is highly probable and leaves no reasonable doubt as to the truth of those facts. Clear and convincing evidence is a higher degree of proof than a preponderance of the evidence, which is the degree of proof generally required in civil court actions. Preponderance of the evidence means that the decision as to an issue of fact must be supported by the greater weight of evidence.

> **Example:**
>
> One party to a lawsuit asserted a fact and presented evidence to prove the fact. If the trier of fact believes that the evidence shows with a 51 percent likelihood that the fact is true, then the party has proved the fact by a preponderance of the evidence. That evidence, however, is not clear and convincing evidence of the fact. If, however, the trier of fact finds that the evidence shows with an overwhelming likelihood that the fact is true, then the party has proven the fact by clear and convincing evidence.

## Interpleader

Another equitable remedy available to insurers is *interpleader*, which is a court proceeding under which an insurer that cannot determine the proper recipient of policy proceeds pays the proceeds to a court and asks the court to decide the proper recipient. The court, not the insurer, determines who is entitled to the proceeds. After paying the money into the court, the insurer usually is released from any further liability under the insurance contract. The party who seeks the remedy of interpleader must be a disinterested stakeholder. In other words, the party cannot have a personal claim to the money or property in question.

Interpleader is an important remedy for an insurer that is uncertain about who should receive policy proceeds. For example, because of beneficiary changes, assignments, and other policy transactions, insurers are sometimes faced with conflicting claimants to policy proceeds. If the insurer pays policy proceeds to a claimant who is not entitled to the proceeds, the proper claimant can later assert a claim to the proceeds, and the insurer may be obligated to pay the claim again. Interpleader prevents this possibility because after the insurer pays the policy proceeds into court, the conflicting claimants are prevented from pursuing other legal action against the insurer to recover the proceeds.

## Declaratory Judgment

In common law jurisdictions, courts have the power to make determinations as to legal rights when no one has been injured. A declaratory judgment is a judicial statement that declares or denies the parties' legal rights but does not include specific relief or any means to enforce those rights. A declaratory judgment is available at the discretion of the court and typically is not granted if any other appropriate remedy is available. As to life insurance contracts, an insurer might seek this type of remedy to resolve issues involving interpretation of policy provisions or insurance laws. For example, assume that an insurer has a question about the legality of a new insurance law. The insurer might ask a court to issue a declaratory judgment interpreting the law.

## Restitution

Restitution is a remedy under which a party is ordered to return property to its owner or to the person entitled to it. Restitution sometimes is granted as a legal remedy and at other times it is granted as an equitable remedy. For life insurance contracts, restitution is a remedy that is sometimes sought when an insurer overpays policy proceeds or pays proceeds to the wrong claimant. For example, assume that an insurer pays policy proceeds to the wrong claimant. Later, the proper claimant asserts his claim to the proceeds, and the insurer discovers that it paid the wrong claimant. The insurer can then seek restitution from the claimant who was not entitled to the proceeds. In such a situation, a court likely would order the claimant who was not entitled to the proceeds to repay the insurer the amount of policy proceeds paid in error.

## Key Terms

policy contest
representation
incontestability provision
contestable period
collusion
mistake of law
mistake of fact
unilateral mistake
bilateral mistake
common mistake
mutual mistake
clear and convincing evidence
interpleader

## Chapter 14

# Contract Performance

## Objectives

### After studying this chapter, you should be able to

- Explain an insurer's duties to perform annuity contracts according to the terms of structured settlements and various annuitized payout options

- Describe standard claim procedures that insurers follow when processing life insurance claims and identify unfair claim practices

- Explain how insurers determine the proper payee of life insurance policy proceeds in situations involving conflicting claimants, common disasters, and short-term survivorship

- Calculate the amount of policy proceeds payable under a given life insurance policy

- Explain how insurers handle life insurance claim situations that involve policy exclusions, disappearance of the insured, disqualification of the beneficiary, and accidental death benefits

- Describe how insurers can settle claim disputes through compromise settlements, and explain how conflict of laws rules apply in civil actions involving life insurance policies

## Outline

**Performance of the Annuity Contract**
- Structured Settlements

**Performance of the Life Insurance Contract**
- Standard Claim Procedures
- Special Claim Situations
- Claim Litigation

As we discussed in Chapter 6, a contract is performed when each party has carried out his contractual obligations. Insurers want to fulfill their contractual obligations when presented with valid claims, because fair and reliable claim settlement enhances an insurer's reputation and promotes customer confidence. In this chapter, we describe an insurer's duties to perform individual annuity and life insurance contracts. We then identify special claim situations that can cause insurers to extensively investigate a life insurance claim before approving or denying the claim. We end the chapter by discussing litigation of life insurance claims.

## Performance of the Annuity Contract

An annuity contract is performed when the insurer pays out annuity payments in accordance with the terms of the contract. From an insurer's perspective, performance of an annuity contract is generally not a complicated task because contract owners simply select when and how payees will receive their annuity payments. In most cases, the contract owner and the payee are the same person. These factors lead to few instances of fraud in regard to annuity contracts and allow insurers to use standard procedures in administering annuity claims.

One of an insurer's most important responsibilities regarding performance of an annuity contract is ensuring that annuity payments are disbursed according to the payout option chosen by the contract owner. Annuity contracts contain several different payout options, also called *settlement options*, from which a contract owner may select. Contract owners usually consider factors such as how long they want periodic annuity payments to be made and the income tax advantages associated with various payout options.

Many contract owners select annuitized payout options, which tie annuity payments to the life expectancy of a named person, known as an *annuitant*. Figure 14.1 summarizes the most common annuitized payout options.

It sounds like performing an annuity contract is fairly simple.

Well, it's usually very straightforward. The insurer follows the contract owner's instructions as to who receives the benefits. And companies typically have computerized systems that help them keep track of contract values and the timing and amounts of annuity payments.

## Figure 14.1 Annuitized Payout Options

- **Straight life annuity:** Payments continue for the lifetime of the annuitant and cease at the annuitant's death.

- **Joint and survivor life annuity:** Payments are made to two or more annuitants; the payments continue for the lifetime of the last surviving annuitant and cease at the death of the last surviving annuitant.

- **Life annuity with period certain:** Payments continue for the lifetime of the annuitant or for a certain period specified in the contract, whichever is longer. If the annuitant dies before the end of the period certain, the insurer will make payments to a contingent payee for the remainder of the period certain.

- **Life with refund annuity:** Payments continue for the lifetime of the annuitant. If the annuitant dies before the payee receives payments that total at least the purchase price of the annuity contract, the insurer refunds to the payee or a contingent payee named by the contract owner the difference between the purchase price and the amount that has been paid out.

## Structured Settlements

Sometimes annuities are purchased as a result of a *structured settlement*, which is a settlement of a civil dispute or lawsuit in which a party agrees to make periodic payments to a specified payee for a specified period of time. Structured settlements usually result from out-of-court negotiations between a plaintiff and a defendant and their respective attorneys. These settlement agreements are entered into most often by parties involved in personal injury lawsuits. Once the parties agree on the terms, the settlement agreement is incorporated into the trial court's judgment. Only the individual specified in the structured settlement agreement as the payee can be named as a payee on periodic payment checks, and periodic payments cannot be accelerated or increased without the court's agreement. In most cases in the United States, periodic payments received by a payee from a structured settlement are not subject to federal income taxation.

If you're receiving a structured settlement and your needs change, can you change the terms of the payments?

Not usually. Because the terms of the settlement agreement are put into a court order, that order must be followed.

But couldn't you go back to court and ask for a change?

Well, you'd have the right to do that. But going back to court costs money, and courts aren't likely to change the terms of an earlier order.

Each structured settlement agreement is designed to meet the unique needs of the plaintiff. The payee who receives payments under a structured settlement can be the plaintiff or another person. So, a structured settlement can require a defendant to make payments to someone other than the person who was directly harmed by the defendant's actions.

> **Example:**
>
> A plaintiff filed a personal injury lawsuit against a defendant alleging that the defendant's reckless driving caused the plaintiff to be paralyzed. To resolve the lawsuit, the defendant and the plaintiff entered into a structured settlement that required the defendant to make periodic payments to an education fund for the plaintiff's minor children until those children reach the age of 18.

Annuity contracts used to fund structured settlements usually are owned by the defendant or the defendant's property/casualty insurer. When the structured settlement agreement permits, the defendant or the defendant's property/casualty insurer can assign payment obligations to a third-party assignment company, often referred to as a *factoring company*. In such a situation, the assignment company becomes the owner of the annuity. A third-party assignment company typically purchases an annuity contract from an affiliated life insurance company to fund the periodic payments. Assigning payment obligations to a third-party assignment company can be advantageous to all parties because these companies typically have extensive experience in the administration of structured settlements.

Regardless of who owns the annuity contract, structured settlement agreements typically require the contract owner to irrevocably assign the periodic payments from the annuity contract to the payee specified in the structured settlement agreement. Therefore, the annuity contract owner cannot change the identity of the payee who is entitled to receive periodic payments.

Because the payee does not own the annuity contract, he cannot sell the contract to another party. However, the payee may assign the periodic payments he receives from a structured settlement to another party. A payee who wishes to assign the periodic payments from a structured settlement agreement to another party must obtain a court order approving the transaction.

Contract owners who purchase annuities to fund structured settlements do not have the same freedom in choosing payout options as other annuity contract purchasers. The terms of the structured settlement agreement determine the payout options available to these contract owners. The insurer that issues the annuity contract is responsible for administering the payments according to the terms of the structured settlement agreement. Typically, this responsibility involves ensuring that the specified payee receives periodic payments when they are due.

# Performance of the Life Insurance Contract

As explained in Chapter 6, a life insurance contract is a unilateral contract under which the insurer promises to pay the policy proceeds to the named beneficiary following the insured's death. The insurer performs its contractual promise when it pays the policy proceeds following the insured's death.

To perform its contractual obligations, an insurer carefully evaluates each claim to ensure that it pays the proceeds of each policy to the correct person according to the terms of the life insurance contract. In certain situations, an insurer may deny a claim and refuse to pay policy proceeds if the terms of the contract require such an action. In all cases, insurers review all relevant information before approving or denying a claim.

## Standard Claim Procedures

Insurers establish standard claim procedures that all employees follow when processing life insurance claims. These procedures are designed to verify the validity of all claims. Standard claim procedures for most insurers require them to perform the following tasks:

- Determine whether the policy is in force

- Verify the identity of the insured

- Verify that a loss has occurred

- Verify that the loss is covered by the policy

- Verify the identity of the beneficiary

Although insurers take steps to avoid paying invalid claims, an insurer cannot unduly delay payment of a claim. Most jurisdictions require prompt payment of claims. Figure 14.2 lists requirements of various jurisdictions for making claim payments.

Most jurisdictions also prohibit insurers from using unfair practices when settling claims. Laws in most states list practices that are considered to be unfair claim practices when committed in conscious disregard of applicable laws or when committed frequently enough to indicate a general business practice. The following are examples of practices that typically are deemed to be unfair claim practices:

- Intentionally misrepresenting important facts about insurance coverage

- Failing to provide requested claim forms within a stated time—usually 15 days—after receiving a request

■ Failing to respond promptly to communications about unpaid claims

■ Failing to develop proper guidelines for the timely investigation of claims

■ Failing to render a prompt decision about the payment or denial of a claim after an investigation is complete

## Proof of Claim

A person who files a claim for life insurance policy proceeds must furnish the insurer with proof of that claim by providing evidence that the insured person has died. Acceptable evidence of an insured's death varies among jurisdictions. In the United States, most insurers require claimants to submit an official death certificate as proof that the insured has died. Some insurers also accept an Attending Physician's Statement, which is a document reporting the care given by a physician who has treated a person. Insurers in other countries may require claimants to submit more extensive information, or they may accept other forms of documentation as proof of a claim.

## Establishing the Proper Payee

After determining that a claim is valid, the insurer must identify the proper payee of policy proceeds, or the insurer risks being subjected to multiple claims. If the insurer pays policy proceeds to a payee who is not entitled to them, the proper payee can later assert a valid claim to the proceeds, and the insurer will be obligated to pay the claim again. When this situation occurs, the insurer can seek to recover the amount paid in error to the wrong payee from that person. However, it can be difficult and costly for an insurer to pursue such a claim.

---

### Figure 14.2 Time Limitations for Paying Valid Claims

- **Canada:** Provincial laws require insurers to pay life insurance policy proceeds within 30 days of receiving valid proof of a loss.[1]

- **Hong Kong:** Claims must be promptly considered and determined by an insurer once all of the information required by the insurer has been received. If a claim is admitted and the amount payable determined, payment should be made as soon as is practicable.[2]

- **Philippines:** Insurers must pay life insurance policy proceeds within 60 days after receiving proof of the death of the insured.[3]

- **United States:** Laws in most states require insurers to pay life insurance policy proceeds within 30 days of determining that a claim is valid.[4]

---

> **Example:**
>
> After the ABC Insurance Company paid Levi Rosen the $100,000 proceeds of a life insurance policy, ABC received a claim for those proceeds from Ari Rosen. If ABC determines that Ari Rosen is the proper payee, it will be liable to pay him the $100,000. ABC also will have a cause of action against Levi Rosen to recover the $100,000 it mistakenly paid him.

For most claims, the identity of the proper payee is clear, and the insurer is able to pay policy proceeds to a named beneficiary. Some claims, however, require an insurer to conduct an investigation to determine the proper payee of policy proceeds. We describe three situations that require further investigation by the insurer: conflicting claimants, common disasters, and short-term survivorship situations.

## Conflicting Claimants

Sometimes, two or more claimants assert a right to life insurance policy proceeds. For example, both a beneficiary and an assignee might assert a claim to the policy proceeds. Insurers usually settle these types of claims by encouraging the claimants to agree on how the proceeds should be divided. For some claims, however, claimants are unable to agree. As mentioned in Chapter 13, interpleader is a court proceeding under which an insurer that cannot determine the proper recipient of policy proceeds pays the proceeds to a court and asks the court to decide the proper recipient. The court, not the insurer, determines who is entitled to the proceeds. After paying the money into the court, the insurer usually is released from any further liability under the insurance contract.

## Common Disasters

Sometimes an insured and the primary beneficiary die as a result of a common disaster, such as an automobile accident or airplane crash. In such cases, the insurer must determine whether the beneficiary survived the insured. A primary beneficiary is entitled to receive policy proceeds only if she survived the insured. In the United States, when the insurer cannot determine whether the insured or the primary beneficiary died first, most states have a ***simultaneous death act*** that provides a reasonable solution. Simultaneous death acts state the following general rule:

> If the insured and beneficiary die at the same time or under circumstances that make it impossible to determine which of them died first, the insured is deemed to have survived the beneficiary, and policy proceeds are payable as though the insured outlived the beneficiary, unless the policy provides otherwise.

Figure 14.3 provides an example of how simultaneous death acts affect the payment of life insurance policy proceeds in common disaster situations.

## Short-Term Survivorship

Simultaneous death acts govern situations in which an insurer cannot determine if the primary beneficiary outlived the insured. However, sometimes a beneficiary survives the insured for a short period of time, and the right to receive the life

---

## Figure 14.3 Simultaneous Death Acts

Don and Annie Shepherd died in an airplane crash. Evidence did not show who died first. The state in which Mr. and Mrs. Shepherd lived had enacted a simultaneous death act. Mr. Shepherd was the policyowner-insured of a life insurance policy that named Mrs. Shepherd as the primary beneficiary and their daughter, Luanne, as the contingent beneficiary. Mrs. Shepherd was the policyowner-insured of a life insurance policy that named Mr. Shepherd as the primary beneficiary. Mrs. Shepherd's policy did not name a contingent beneficiary and did not include a survivorship clause.

Because we do not know which spouse died first, the state's simultaneous death act is used to determine how policy proceeds are paid.

- **Don Shepherd's policy:** Mr. Shepherd, the insured, is deemed to have survived the primary beneficiary, Mrs. Shepherd. The policy proceeds are payable to Luanne, the contingent beneficiary of the policy.

- **Annie Shepherd's policy:** Mrs. Shepherd, the insured, is deemed to have survived the primary beneficiary, Mr. Shepherd. Mrs. Shepherd's policy did not name a contingent beneficiary, and the proceeds are payable to her estate.

---

insurance policy proceeds vests in the beneficiary at the insured's death. If the beneficiary then dies before receiving the policy proceeds, the insurer must pay the proceeds to the beneficiary's estate. This situation can cause policy proceeds to be paid in a manner contrary to what the policyowner intended.

To prevent such a result, many life insurance policies contain a survivorship clause, which requires the beneficiary to survive the insured by a stated period of time, usually 30 or 60 days, to be entitled to receive the policy proceeds. If the beneficiary does not survive for the stated period of time, the insurer pays the proceeds as if the insured outlived the beneficiary. When a policy includes a survivorship clause, the insurer must delay paying a death claim until the required survivorship period has expired. For example, assume a policy requires the beneficiary to survive the insured by at least 30 days. The insurer must wait until the specified 30-day period has passed before paying the policy proceeds. Figure 14.4 illustrates how a survivorship clause can affect the payment of life insurance policy proceeds.

### *Computing the Amount Payable*

After establishing the validity of a claim and identifying the proper payee of life insurance policy proceeds, an insurer calculates the amount of policy proceeds that are payable. The face amount stated in the policy usually is adjusted to account for various factors. The following amounts, if applicable, typically increase the amount of the death benefit payable:

- Accidental death benefits

- Accumulated policy dividends

- Unpaid policy dividends

■   Paid-up additional insurance benefits

■   Unearned premiums paid in advance

The following amounts, if applicable, reduce the total death benefit amount payable:

■   Unpaid policy loans

■   Accrued policy loan interest

■   Premiums due and unpaid at the time of the insured's death

---

## Figure 14.4 Survivorship Clause

Doug Lauder and his wife, Florence, were injured in an accident. Doug died two days after the accident, and Florence died seven days after the accident. Doug was insured by a life insurance policy that named Florence as the primary beneficiary and Doug's son, Michael, as the contingent beneficiary.

• Assume that Doug's policy did not contain a survivorship clause. Because Florence survived Doug, the policy proceeds are payable to Florence's estate.

• Assume that Doug's policy contained a 30-day survivorship clause. Because Florence did not survive the insured by the required 30 days, the policy proceeds are payable to Michael, the contingent beneficiary.

---

Figure 14.5 shows an example of how an insurer calculates the amount of life insurance policy proceeds payable.

This is a good illustration of how to calculate policy proceeds. I know that in our company, these calculations are usually done by computer programs.

Yes, most insurers have programs that perform these calculations automatically. But it's still good to know how the computer arrives at the final amount!

## Special Claim Situations

Some claims require an insurer to conduct an extensive investigation to determine their validity. When dealing with these special claim situations, insurers sometimes struggle to determine critical factors, such as who should receive policy proceeds. In the following sections, we discuss some of the situations in which insurers closely examine claims before paying proceeds.

## Figure 14.5 Calculation of Total Policy Proceeds

Vera Cohen bought a $250,000 life insurance policy from the Good Will Life Insurance Company. At the time of her death, Ms. Cohen had accumulated policy dividends of $1,220 on deposit with the insurer, as well as paid-up additions in the amount of $550. Two years earlier, Ms. Cohen took out a policy loan of $4,500. At the time of her death, the unpaid loan amount with interest was $2,200.

The total amount of policy proceeds that Good Will would be liable to pay is calculated as follows:

| | |
|---|---|
| $250,000 | Face amount of policy |
| + 1,220 | Accumulated policy dividends |
| + 550 | Paid-up additions |
| – 2,200 | Policy loan and loan interest |
| $249,570 | Total policy proceeds that Good Will is liable to pay |

## Policy Exclusions

Most life insurance policies contain **exclusions**, which are provisions that specify certain situations under which the insurer will not pay the policy's face amount. If the cause of an insured's death was excluded from coverage, then the insurer has no contractual liability to pay the full policy death benefit. Policies typically state that the insurer's liability is limited to the amount of premiums paid for the policy; sometimes a policy provides that the insurer will be liable only for the policy's cash surrender value.

In the past, during periods of war, insurers sometimes included a war exclusion in life insurance policies. A **war exclusion provision** states that an insurer will not pay the full policy proceeds if an insured's death is caused by war-related activities. U.S. insurers, however, rarely add war exclusions to modern-day life insurance policies, and insurers often do not enforce such clauses found in older policies.

Another type of exclusion, the **aviation exclusion provision**, states that an insurer will not pay the policy face amount if the insured's death is caused by certain aviation-related activities. Insurers usually add these exclusions to policies that insure people involved in military or experimental aviation activities and to those employed by airlines as pilots and flight attendants. Aviation exclusions typically do not exclude coverage for passenger travel on regularly scheduled commercial airlines.

The most common policy exclusion is the **suicide exclusion provision**, which states that the insurer will not pay the policy face amount if the insured dies as a result of suicide within a stated period of time after the date that the policy was issued. Laws in most states limit the length of the suicide exclusion period to a specified maximum, usually two years. According to the terms of a typical suicide exclusion provision, if the insured dies as a result of suicide during the suicide exclusion period, the insurer is not liable to pay the policy face amount. Instead, the insurer's liability is limited to a return of any premiums paid for the policy minus any unpaid policy loans. After the expiration of the suicide exclusion period, the death of the insured as a result of suicide is covered by the policy and the insurer must pay the full policy benefit.

The suicide exclusion is intended to guard against *antiselection*, which is the tendency for people who are most likely to have claims to be the people most likely to apply for insurance. The general opinion is that a one- or two-year exclusion period is sufficient to protect the insurer against "planned suicides." In other words, it is unlikely that a person would purchase life insurance with the intention of committing suicide one or two years later.

Most jurisdictions have developed a strong presumption against suicide—that is, the law presumes that a person's death did *not* result from suicide. If the facts of a case can be interpreted in more than one way, a court usually will presume that the insured did not take his own life. When an insurer refuses to pay a policy's face amount based on the suicide exclusion provision and the claimant later sues the insurer, the insurer has the burden of proving that the insured's death was caused by suicide during the policy's suicide exclusion period. An insurer's assertion that the insured committed suicide is an affirmative defense—that is, it is an allegation of facts that constitutes a defense to a plaintiff's claim. Whether the insured committed suicide is a question of fact that depends on all of the circumstances surrounding the death.

Another question of fact that sometimes arises in these cases concerns whether an insured was sane when she committed suicide. According to laws in most states, suicide requires that the person must have intended to kill herself; a person who is insane cannot form the necessary intent to commit suicide. As a result, the insurer is liable to pay policy proceeds if the insured died as a result of self-inflicted injury while insane. To avoid this result, the suicide exclusion provision included in most policies states that the insurer is not liable to pay the policy proceeds if the insured died as a result of suicide or self-inflicted injury, *while sane or insane.*

## Disappearance of the Insured

When an insured disappears, a claimant to life insurance policy proceeds cannot provide the insurer with proof that the insured is dead. If a claimant cannot provide acceptable proof of her claim, the insurer will not pay the claim. When this situation occurs in the United States, a claimant can ask a court to declare the insured dead. A court's willingness to declare a missing person dead often depends on the circumstances surrounding the person's disappearance.

When an insured disappears from an identifiable cause under circumstances that suggest he is likely dead, a court usually declares the insured dead. A court typically makes this determination when the insured disappears as a result of a specific peril that can reasonably account for his death.

> **Example:**
>
> Goran Milo boarded an airplane for a direct flight from Rome to Hong Kong. Mr. Milo was seen boarding the plane by his wife, son, and several airport officials. While in flight to Hong Kong, the plane experienced mechanical failure and crashed. A subsequent investigation revealed no survivors, and Mr. Milo's body was never recovered. In this situation, the plane crash is an identifiable cause of Mr. Milo's disappearance, and circumstances suggest that Mr. Milo is likely dead. Thus, a court is likely to enter an order declaring that Mr. Milo is dead.

When the insured's disappearance cannot be attributed to an identifiable cause, the claimant has the burden of proving that the insured has died. Most states have laws that require a claimant to prove all of the following facts:

- The insured has been missing continuously for a specified period of time—five or seven years in most jurisdictions.

- The insured's absence is unexplained.

- A reasonable search for the insured has taken place.

- No one has had communication with the insured since his disappearance.

 That sounds complicated. Can we talk through an example of such a case?

 Sure. Assume an insured disappeared. The insurer refused to pay the death benefit, and the beneficiary sued the insurer. The insurer's defense is that there isn't convincing evidence that the insured is dead.

 OK. So, first, the plaintiff-beneficiary presents his case.

 Right, the plaintiff has the initial burden of proof. Let's assume that the beneficiary proves the required elements and creates a rebuttable presumption that the insured is dead.

 It's a rebuttable presumption, so the insurer can present facts that show the insured is not dead.

That's right. The insurer can present evidence that the insured is alive and rebut the presumption of death.

So there's evidence from the beneficiary that the insured is dead and there's evidence from the insurer that he is alive.

At that point, whether the insured is dead is a question of fact for the trier of fact to decide.

If a claimant satisfactorily proves the required facts, a court will presume that the insured is dead. In most jurisdictions, a court's presumption of death is a *rebuttable presumption*, which is a presumption that can be disproven but that stands until adequate evidence is presented to the contrary. Therefore, a party wishing to show that the insured is not dead is allowed to present evidence to the court to prove that fact. If a court's presumption of death is rebutted, the insured's status becomes a question of fact.

When a court declares an insured to be dead, a court order serves as proof of death, and policy proceeds become payable. Many times, the court order states the date on which the insured is presumed to have died. When the court order does not specify the date of death for the insured, the insured is presumed to have died on the date of the court order. Note that when an insured disappears, the contract owner or other interested party must keep the policy in force until the court issues an order declaring the insured dead. Therefore, premiums must continue to be paid or the policy must be continued under a nonforfeiture option such as the extended term insurance option. If the policy lapses for nonpayment of premiums before the date of the court order, the insurer is not liable to pay the policy proceeds.

Sometimes an insured who has been declared dead by a court reappears. If an insurer paid a claim and the insured later reappears, the insurer generally is entitled to recover the amount it paid under the claim because the insurer paid the claim as the result of a mistake of fact. The insurer, however, may be prevented from recovering such a mistaken payment if it paid less than the full amount of policy proceeds as part of a compromise settlement with the beneficiary. We describe compromise settlements later in the chapter.

## Disqualification of the Beneficiary

When a beneficiary designation is clear, an insurer pays life insurance proceeds to the proper recipient as promptly as possible. Sometimes, however, a beneficiary is disqualified from receiving policy proceeds because the beneficiary is responsible or alleged to be responsible for the death of the insured. In the United States and in most common law jurisdictions, laws exist to prevent individuals from profiting from a criminal act. When a beneficiary causes the death of the insured, the insurer must determine if the claim should be paid and, if so, to whom.

A beneficiary who is convicted of wrongfully killing an insured in a criminal or civil court typically is disqualified from receiving policy proceeds. Jurisdictions vary as to what type of wrongful killing results in disqualification.

■ In most jurisdictions, any person convicted in a criminal proceeding of murdering the insured is disqualified from receiving life insurance policy proceeds.

■ In some states, a person convicted of murder or a lesser offense, such as manslaughter, also is disqualified from receiving policy proceeds.

■ A person does not have to be convicted of a crime in a criminal court to be disqualified as a beneficiary. If a civil court finds that an individual wrongfully caused the insured's death, that individual is disqualified from receiving policy proceeds.

 This is another reason that it is so important for us underwriters to establish that the beneficiary has an insurable interest in the life of the insured.

 Right, because if you establish insurable interest before the policy is even issued, hopefully we in claims won't have to deal with situations like the ones described here.

 Well, there are no guarantees. But you're right, establishing an insurable interest helps ensure that the life insurance contract was formed for a lawful purpose.

Even though a beneficiary is disqualified, the insurer usually must pay the policy proceeds to a contingent beneficiary or to the policyowner-insured's estate. That general rule, however, does not always apply. If a beneficiary obtained a life insurance contract with the intent of causing the insured's death, the contract is void from its inception. In such a case, the insurer is not liable to pay policy proceeds and is responsible only for returning policy premiums plus any interest, less any outstanding policy loans and unpaid interest on those loans, to the policyowner. In such a case, the insurer bears the burden of proving that the policy was purchased with the intent to cause the insured's death.

## Accidental Death Benefits

An *accidental death benefit* is a supplemental life insurance policy benefit that requires the insurer to pay a specified amount of money in addition to the policy's basic death benefit if an insured dies as a result of an accident. When a life insurance contract contains an accidental death benefit, the insurer must evaluate the cause of the insured's death to determine whether the accidental death benefit is payable. When a claim is made for accidental death benefits, the insurer usually requires the claimant to submit additional information to show proof of the claim. For example, an insurer may require a claimant to provide an autopsy report in addition to a death certificate. The insurer uses these documents to determine whether the insured's death was *accidental* as defined by the terms of the life insurance contract. A typical definition of *accidental death* found in many life insurance contracts reads as follows:

> **Accidental Death.** Death resulting, directly and independently of all other causes, from accidental bodily injury.

When a claimant sues an insurer over the denial of accidental death benefits, the claimant has the burden of proving that the insured's death was caused by an accident. Whether the insured's death was caused by an accident is a question of fact.

Some life insurance policies contain a ***time limitation clause*** that specifies that the insured's death must occur within a certain period of time—usually 90 days—from the date of an accident for accidental death benefits to be payable. The purpose of a time limitation clause is to ensure to a reasonable degree that the accident was the cause of the insured's death.

Most contracts also contain accidental death benefit exclusions, which state that if an insured dies as a result of certain specified causes, the insurer is not required to pay accidental death benefits. As a general rule, the insurer has the burden of proving that the insured died as a result of a cause excluded from coverage.

## Claim Litigation

Insurers try to avoid litigation because it is time consuming and costly. When an insurer is involved in litigation, the insurer's attorneys spend a great deal of time gathering evidence to justify the denial of a claim. Other employees of the insurer spend time gathering pertinent documents and information requested by the legal staff. Often, insurers must hire outside attorneys to assist with claim litigation. Depending on the length and complexity of a trial, attorneys' fees can be a significant expense for an insurer. Because of the many potential drawbacks of litigation, insurers often try to reach a compromise with potential plaintiffs as a way to avoid litigation.

### *Compromise Settlements*

Sometimes insurers and claimants do not agree on the amount of policy proceeds that should be paid for a claim. Accidental death benefits in particular often cause disputes between insurers and claimants regarding the total amount of policy proceeds for which an insurer is liable. Insurers sometimes seek to settle a claim dispute through a ***compromise settlement***, which is an agreement between two or more parties to settle a dispute regarding the terms and/or performance of a contract.

**Example:**

A life insurance contract contained a $200,000 accidental death benefit. The insured died, and the insurer concluded that the beneficiary's claim for the basic death benefit was valid. The insurer, however, could not clearly determine whether the insured's death resulted from an accident or other intervening causes. Rather than completely denying the claim for accidental death benefits, the insurer and beneficiary entered into a compromise settlement under which the insurer paid the beneficiary the basic death benefit and $75,000 in accidental death benefits. The insurer's liability under the contract was discharged when it paid the agreed-upon amount to the beneficiary.

Most insurers are willing to enter into compromise settlements because they want to avoid the possibility of paying a large damage award if the claimant files a successful lawsuit. Damage awards can decrease an insurer's profits and weaken its reputation in the industry. When a claim is paid under a compromise settlement, the insurer cannot demand repayment of the amount it paid in settlement of the claim. For example, assume that an insurer entered into a compromise settlement with a claimant and later discovered facts that indicate it should not have paid the claim. In the absence of fraud, the insurer cannot recover the amount it paid because the courts will not disturb such a compromise settlement entered into by competent parties.

## Litigation

Most litigation between claimants and life insurers begins after an insurer denies a claim for life insurance policy proceeds. A claimant who disagrees with an insurer's decision may file a civil action against the insurer alleging that the insurer breached the life insurance contract by refusing to pay policy proceeds.

### Conflict of Laws

Actions involving life insurance policies often involve the laws of more than one jurisdiction. As we noted in Chapter 2, conflict of laws rules are used to determine which substantive laws apply to the issues in a civil lawsuit when the laws of more than one jurisdiction are involved in the lawsuit.

**Example:**

A civil lawsuit was filed in a court in State A. The lawsuit involved a policy that insured a person who resided in State B at the time of his death. The policy was issued by an insurer domiciled in State C to a policyowner who resided in State A. The court must apply conflict of laws rules to determine which state's substantive laws are to be applied to decide the issues in dispute.

According to the general rules of contract law, the parties may mutually agree as to which jurisdiction's laws will govern their contract. Such a provision is often referred to as a ***choice of laws provision***. If the parties include a choice of laws provision in their contract, then the courts typically will enforce the contract provision and will apply the law of the state that the parties agreed would govern their contract.

When the parties have not included a choice of laws provision in their contract, the general rules of contract law provide that any question concerning the validity of the contract or the interpretation of any provision of the contract is to be determined in accordance with the law of the state in which the contract was made. As a rule, a contract is made in the state where the last act necessary to complete the contract occurs. In the United States, the last acts necessary to complete the formation of a life insurance contract are (1) payment of the initial premium and (2) delivery of the policy to the policyowner. Thus, a life insurance contract typically is considered made in that state in which the policy is delivered or the initial premium is paid, whichever occurs later. That state is most often, but not always, the state in which the policyowner resided when the contract was made. Generally, the law that governs a life insurance contract when it is issued continues to govern the contract throughout its life.

## Damages

As noted in Chapter 2, compensatory damages in an action for breach of contract usually are measured as the *benefit of the bargain*—that is, the amount that would put the plaintiff in the financial position he would have been in had the contract been performed. For a claimant to life insurance policy proceeds, the benefit of the bargain is the amount of policy proceeds.

An insurer has a duty to act in good faith when deciding whether to pay or deny a claim. This duty requires an insurer to deal ethically and fairly with its customers. Many jurisdictions allow plaintiffs to bring bad-faith tort actions against insurers that breach this duty. No single factor determines whether an insurer has acted in bad faith. The most common factor that a court looks for is evidence that the insurer has unreasonably denied claims. In determining whether the insurer's actions are unreasonable, most courts examine an insurer's overall conduct and its reasons for denying claims. Insurers found to have acted in bad faith may be liable for punitive damages, in addition to compensatory damages. Thus, if a plaintiff proves that an insurer has breached its duty of good faith, he may recover damages that exceed the amount of the policy's basic death benefit and supplemental benefits.

# Key Terms

structured settlement
simultaneous death act
exclusion
war exclusion provision
aviation exclusion provision
suicide exclusion provision
accidental death benefit
time limitation clause
compromise settlement
choice of laws provision

# Endnotes

1. Insurance Act of Ontario, R.S.O., ch. I-8, s. 203 (1990) (Can.); C.C.Q., ch. 64, art. 2436 (1991) (Can.).

2. "The Code of Conduct for Insurers," Hong Kong Federation of Insurers, sec. 27 and 30, <http://www.hkfi.org.hk/en_tips_customer_conduct.htm (19> March 2012).

3. Insurance Code of the Philippines, sec. 242, <http://insurancecode.net/section-242.html (19> March 2012).

4. NAIC Unfair Life, Accident and Health Claims Settlement Practices Model Regulation (1990).

## Chapter 15

# Group Products

## Objectives

### After studying this chapter, you should be able to

- Describe how group life insurance contracts are formed and terminated

- Identify the types of groups that are eligible for group life insurance, and describe the rights of group insureds under a group life insurance policy

- Distinguish between contributory and noncontributory group life insurance plans

- Describe the purpose and operation of required provisions included in group life insurance contracts

- Identify various federal laws that regulate group life insurance plans

- Distinguish among types of qualified retirement plans in the United States and describe various requirements that ERISA places on qualified retirement plans

- Describe two common funding instruments for qualified retirement plans

- Identify the duties of plan administrators and plan fiduciaries, and describe how qualified retirement plans are terminated

## Outline

**Group Life Insurance Contracts**
- Formation of the Group Life Insurance Contract
- The Group Master Contract

**Regulation of Group Life Insurance**
- ERISA
- ADEA
- ADA

**Group Retirement Plans**
- Regulation of Retirement Plans
- Retirement Plan Funding Instruments
- Retirement Plan Administration
- Retirement Plan Termination

Group life insurance has been greatly influenced by various regulatory requirements placed on insurance products and on employee benefit plans. We begin this chapter by discussing how group life insurance contracts are created and performed. Then, we discuss regulation of group life insurance. We also describe qualified retirement plans and how these plans are regulated and funded.

## Group Life Insurance Contracts

A group life insurance contract that provides coverage to a number of people, known as the *group insureds*, is called a *group master contract*. The contracting parties to a group life insurance contract are the group policyholder and the insurer. The *group policyholder* is the employer or other party that purchases group life insurance. A group insured has a defined relationship to a group policyholder, such as an employee of an employer, a debtor who has borrowed money from a lender, or a member of a credit union.

A group insured is not a party to the group life insurance contract, but the group insured does have legally enforceable rights under the contract. Laws in most states in the United States do not require that group insureds receive a copy of the group master contract, but they do require that each group insured receive a written description of the group life insurance plan. A group insured must receive a *certificate of insurance*, which is a document that provides a description of the group insured's coverage and outlines the group insured's rights under the group master contract.

For group life insurance, the certificate of insurance and the group master contract are both considered to be integral parts of the contract. Sometimes information in the group master contract conflicts with information in the certificate of insurance. Under the general rules of contract construction, ambiguities in an insurance contract are construed against the party that drafted the contract. Thus, when information in the group master contract conflicts with information in the certificate of insurance, the disparity is considered an ambiguity and will be construed against the insurer and in favor of the group insured. Figure 15.1 summarizes some important terms associated with group life insurance contracts.

### Formation of the Group Life Insurance Contract

A group life insurance contract is an informal contract that must meet the same formation requirements described in earlier chapters for other informal contracts. As in the formation of an individual life insurance contract, the parties to a group

---

## Figure 15.1 Group Life Insurance Terminology

- **Enrollment:** The procedures by which an eligible group member signs up for group insurance coverage.

- **Probationary period:** The period of time—typically, from one to six months—that a new group member must wait until becoming eligible to enroll in a group insurance plan.

- **Eligibility period:** The period of time—usually 31 days—following the probationary period during which a new group member may first enroll for group insurance coverage.

- **Late entrant:** An eligible group member who enrolls for group insurance coverage after the expiration of the eligibility period. Unless he enrolls during an open-enrollment period, a late entrant generally must provide satisfactory evidence of insurability to enroll for group insurance coverage.

- **Open-enrollment period:** A specified period during which group members who did not enroll during their eligibility periods may enroll for group insurance coverage without providing evidence of insurability.

---

life insurance contract must (1) mutually assent to the contract, (2) exchange legally adequate consideration, (3) have contractual capacity, and (4) meet the lawful purpose requirement. With the exception of the lawful purpose requirement, these requirements are met in the same manner in both group and individual life insurance contracts.

Recall from Chapter 10 that the lawful purpose requirement for an individual life insurance contract is met by the presence of an insurable interest. An insurable interest usually is not required in a group life insurance contract because the group policyholder's interest in the contract does not induce wagering contracts as does a policyowner's interest in an individual life insurance contract. The lawful purpose requirement is met in a group life insurance contract when the group policyholder enters into the contract to provide benefits to covered group members.

Another distinction between the formation of individual and group life insurance contracts is that, to enter into a valid group life insurance contract, the policyholder must represent a group that is eligible for group insurance.

## *Eligible Groups*

The goal of group life insurance underwriting is to produce a group of insureds who present similar underwriting risks and whose mortality experience is reasonably predictable. Thus, group insurance underwriters focus on the risk characteristics of the group proposed for insurance rather than on characteristics of individual group members. To guard against antiselection, group underwriters evaluate the purpose for the proposed group's existence to make sure that the group was formed for purposes other than to obtain insurance for group members. In addition, laws in most states prohibit insurers from delivering a group life insurance policy in the state unless the policy insures an eligible group as specified in the applicable law. The following types of groups are eligible for group life insurance in most states:

- **Single-employer groups**, which consist of the employees of a single employer. The group policyholder is either the employer or the trustees of a trust fund created by the employer.

- **Labor union groups**, which consist of members of a labor union. Federal laws prohibit employers from paying funds directly to a labor union for any purpose. Payments therefore must be made to a trust fund established for the purpose of providing benefits to employees. Labor union groups are often referred to as *Taft-Hartley trusts*. These groups also are referred to as *negotiated trusteeships* because they are created by an agreement negotiated between one or more labor unions and the employers of the union members.

- **Multiple-employer groups**, which consist of the employees of more than one employer. The group life insurance contract is issued to a trust established by two or more employers in the same industry, two or more labor unions, or one or more employers and one or more labor unions.

- **Association groups**, which consist of the members of an association of employers or individuals formed for a purpose other than to obtain insurance. The group policyholder is either the association or the trustees of a trust fund established for the benefit of members of one or more associations. Figure 15.2 describes some typical association groups.

- **Debtor-creditor groups**, which consist of individuals who have borrowed money from a specific lender or lenders. The group policyholder may be the creditor or a parent holding company of the creditor. If a policy insures debtors of more than one creditor, the policy may be issued to one or more trustees or to an agent designated by the creditors. Insight 15.1 describes some of the unique features of group life insurance issued to a debtor-creditor group.

- **Credit union groups**, which consist of the members of one or more credit unions. The group policyholder is either the credit union or the trustees of a trust fund created by one or more credit unions.

- **Discretionary groups** that are approved to purchase group insurance by the applicable state insurance department. Discretionary groups do not fall within any of the traditional categories of eligible groups. In deciding whether to approve a discretionary group, state insurance departments consider factors such as whether issuing the policy is in the best interest of the public and whether the premiums are reasonable in relation to the benefits offered under the contract. Most states permit insurance to be issued to discretionary groups, but regulatory requirements vary a great deal from state to state.

## Figure 15.2 Common Types of Association Groups in the United States

**Professional association.** An association of individuals who share a common occupation, such as doctors, attorneys, or engineers.

**Public employee association.** An association of individuals employed by a state, county, or city government or by a state or local school board.

**Common interest association.** An association of individuals who share a common interest or bond, such as participants in a specific sport or alumni of a specific college.

 So other than determining whether a group is an "eligible" group, how can underwriters determine whether a group is an insurable risk?

 Well, as in all underwriting, there are many factors to consider. We look at the group's characteristics, which include its reason for existence, stability, size, geographic location, nature of business, age and sex of members, and any prior coverage and claim experience.

 That's a lot to evaluate, and I bet it's different for each group!

You've got that right. We also examine the type of coverage that the group is requesting and ensure that the group meets our underwriting guidelines for that type of coverage.

That doesn't sound too different from underwriting an individual's risk for insurance.

Well, in both cases, underwriters have the same goal: to accurately assess risk and calculate an appropriate premium to pay for the coverage.

## Insight 15.1 Credit Life Insurance in the United States

Life insurance issued to a debtor-creditor group is referred to as **credit life insurance**. Although credit life insurance has many features of other group life insurance products, it also has some unique features. One such distinction is that credit insurance generally is sold by lenders rather than by traditional insurance producers who market other life insurance coverages. As a first step in setting up a credit insurance arrangement, a lender enters into a contractual agreement with a credit insurer. In many cases, the lending institution and the insurer are affiliated corporations within a holding company system. The contractual agreement between the lender and the insurer specifies the types of credit insurance coverage that will be available to the lender's borrowers. When an individual applies for a loan, the lender offers the borrower the opportunity to purchase credit insurance that will provide money to repay all or part of the debt if the borrower dies or becomes disabled before repaying the loan.

The regulatory requirements imposed on debtor-creditor group life policies differ considerably from the requirements imposed on other group life insurance policies. The following are some examples of the types of regulatory requirements that are unique to credit life insurance:

- State laws place maximum limits on the amount of credit life insurance that may be issued to a debtor. These limitations are designed to ensure that a debtor's coverage is generally equal to the total amount of the insured debt.

- Laws in many states require group insureds to be given at least a 30-day free look period and the right to cancel the coverage at any time.

- State laws require that specified information be disclosed to debtors before they elect to purchase credit insurance. For example, the lender must disclose that it cannot require the debtor to purchase credit insurance as a condition of obtaining approval of the loan.

### Effective Date of the Contract

The date on which a group life insurance contract becomes effective is usually mutually agreed upon by the insurer and the group policyholder. The agreed-on date serves as the effective date even if the group policyholder pays the initial premium on a different date. If the insurer and the group policyholder do not agree on an effective date, the terms of the group master contract may require that payment of the initial premium and delivery of the contract take place before the contract becomes effective.

The effective date of a group insured's coverage is determined by various policy provisions found in the group life insurance contract, such as the actively-at-work provision and probationary period provision. We discuss these provisions later in the chapter.

### Rights of the Group Insured

Generally, each person insured under a group life insurance policy has the same rights to name and change a policy beneficiary that the owner of an individual life insurance policy has, with one limitation: a group insured generally cannot name the group policyholder as the beneficiary. One exception occurs when a policy is issued to a creditor to insure the lives of its debtors. In such cases, the creditor is both the group policyholder and the beneficiary; the benefit payable following a group insured's death is used to reduce or extinguish the group insured's unpaid indebtedness to the creditor.

Most designated beneficiaries of group life insurance policies are revocable beneficiaries. A revocable beneficiary designation allows the group insured to change the beneficiary at will. Recall that a revocable beneficiary generally has no legal interest in the proceeds of a policy nor any involvement with the policy until after the death of the insured. During the group insured's lifetime, a revocable beneficiary cannot prevent a group insured from exercising ownership rights.

## The Group Master Contract

An insurer's responsibility for performing a group life insurance contract is similar to its responsibility for performing an individual life insurance contract. That obligation is to pay a specified death benefit to the named beneficiary when an insured dies. For a group plan, the policyholder usually is responsible for handling some of the plan's administrative aspects. For example, the policyholder typically is responsible for enrolling new group members in the plan and for making all premium payments to the insurer.

### Premiums

For every group life insurance plan, the group policyholder is responsible for remitting premiums to the insurer. Typically, premiums are due prior to the period of coverage, and in most cases, premiums are payable on a monthly basis. Whether group insureds must pay all or part of the cost of these premiums depends on whether their plan is contributory or noncontributory.

A *contributory plan* is a group insurance plan under which the group insureds pay all or part of the cost for their coverage. When a plan is contributory, eligible group members must be given the choice of whether to participate, and they must authorize the payment of their premium contributions. For example, an employee must authorize the deduction of premiums from his salary. As part of their underwriting requirements, insurers commonly require employers to pay at least part of the premiums for group life insurance. Such a requirement, which is imposed by law in many states, helps to reduce the group insureds' premium costs and, thus, tends to increase participation in the plan.

A *noncontributory plan* is a group insurance plan under which the employer or group policyholder pays the entire cost for the coverage. State insurance laws usually require that all eligible group members be covered if a group life insurance plan is noncontributory.

## Plan Enrollment

Group insureds usually are required to complete an *enrollment form* as a prerequisite to group life insurance coverage. The enrollment form serves several purposes, including providing the insurer with identifying information about the group member and allowing the group member to make beneficiary designations. In employer-employee contributory plans, enrollment forms contain the group members' written authorization for the employer to make payroll deductions to pay the employees' share of required premiums.

## Contract Provisions

Most state insurance laws require that specified provisions be included in group life insurance contracts that are delivered or issued for delivery within the state. The following required provisions are similar to those that must be included in individual life insurance policies:

- A *grace period provision* giving the policyholder a grace period of 31 days for the payment of renewal premiums. The insurer can terminate a group life insurance contract for nonpayment of premium at the end of any grace period.

- An *incontestability provision* stating that, after the policy has been in force for two years, the insurer may not contest the validity of the group insurance contract except for nonpayment of premium. Cases of an insurer contesting a group life insurance contract because of material misrepresentation by the group policyholder are rare. The incontestability provision also limits the insurer's ability to contest the validity of a group insured's coverage after that coverage has been in force for two years during the group insured's lifetime.

- An *entire contract provision* stating that a copy of the application shall be attached to the policy when issued, that all statements made by the policyholder or the group insureds shall be deemed representations and not warranties, and that no statement made by a group insured shall be used in any contest unless a copy of the document containing the statement has been provided to the group insured or, if the group insured is deceased or incapacitated, to the insured's beneficiary or personal representative.

■ A *misstatement of age provision* that specifies an equitable adjustment of premiums, benefits, or both premiums and benefits if the age of a group insured is misstated. The provision must clearly state the method the insurer will use to make such an adjustment. Unlike individual life insurance policies, group life insurance policies do not include a misstatement of sex provision because group insurance premiums typically do not vary according to the sex of the insured.

Group life insurance contracts also contain provisions that are not found in individual life insurance policies. The following are provisions that state insurance laws usually require group life insurance policies, but not individual life insurance policies, to include:

■ An ***evidence of insurability provision*** specifying the conditions, if any, under which the insurer reserves the right to require a person eligible for insurance to provide evidence of insurability satisfactory to the insurer as a condition to part or all of her coverage. When a group member is required to provide evidence of insurability, that evidence generally is contained in a questionnaire included in or attached to the group member's enrollment form. If a group insured makes material misrepresentations of fact in providing such evidence of insurability, the insurer has the right to contest the group insured's coverage during the specified contestable period. Note that a material misrepresentation by a group insured does not affect the validity of the group master contract; it affects only the validity of the coverage on the particular group insured.

■ A ***conversion provision*** that gives a group insured the right to obtain an individual life insurance policy if her group life insurance coverage terminates because of specified reasons. An eligible group insured is entitled to obtain individual life insurance coverage without providing evidence of insurability by applying for the individual policy and paying the initial premium within 31 days after the termination of her group life insurance coverage.

Other provisions also are unique to group insurance policies. For example, each group insurance contract describes which members of the covered group are eligible to be covered under the contract. Group insurance contracts that cover an employer-employee group typically define eligible employees as those employees in a specified class or classes. State laws require that these classes be defined by requirements that are related to conditions of employment, such as salary, occupation, or length of employment. Thus, most contracts state that an employee must work full-time in order to be eligible for coverage and that part-time workers are excluded from eligibility.

Most employer-employee group life insurance contracts also specify requirements that new employees must meet to be eligible for coverage. One of the most common provisions affecting new-employee eligibility is the ***actively-at-work provision***, which states that an employee must be actively at work, not ill or on leave, on the day coverage becomes effective. If the employee is not actively at work on the day coverage becomes effective, the employee is not covered by the group life insurance contract until he returns to work.

Another common contract provision that affects new-employee eligibility is the ***probationary period provision***, which is a provision that specifies the length of time—typically from one to six months—that a new employee must wait before becoming eligible to enroll in a group life insurance plan. Under a contributory plan, the probationary period is followed by an *eligibility period*, also known as an *enrollment period*, which is a period of time, usually 31 days, during which a new employee may enroll for group life insurance coverage. Under a noncontributory plan, an employee who has met all other eligibility requirements is automatically covered at the end of the probationary period after completing an enrollment form. Figure 15.3 gives an example of when group members' coverage begins.

## Figure 15.3 Operation of Eligibility Provisions

Dan and Rosario Moedjio recently moved to a new city and will soon begin working at new jobs. They will be eligible for coverage under group life insurance policies provided by their employers. The group policies provide similar coverage, and both policies include a 30-day probationary period. The primary difference is that Dan's coverage is noncontributory, whereas Rosario's coverage is contributory. Dan and Rosario want to determine when their group insurance coverages will become effective.

- Dan's noncontributory coverage will automatically become effective on the first day following the end of the 30-day probationary period.

- Because Rosario's coverage is contributory, her 30-day probationary period will be followed by an eligibility period. At any time during the eligibility period, she may enroll for the coverage and sign a written authorization allowing her employer to deduct her group insurance premium contributions from her salary. Her coverage will become effective as soon as she signs the authorization within the eligibility period.

## *Termination Provisions*

Group life insurance contracts include a provision specifying the conditions under which the insurer or the group policyholder can terminate the contract. Under most group life insurance contracts, a group insured's coverage terminates when the group master contract terminates. Under certain conditions, however, a group insured's coverage can terminate even when the group master contract remains in effect. In the following sections, we discuss conditions under which a group master contract and a group insured's coverage can terminate.

### Termination of the Group Master Contract

According to the terms of most group life insurance contracts, the group policyholder can exercise its right to terminate the contract by giving the insurer written notice of termination at least a specified number of days prior to the termination date. The notice usually must be given at least 31 days prior to termination.

Under specified conditions, an insurer can terminate a group life insurance contract on any premium due date. For example, group insurers often establish minimum participation requirements to guard against antiselection. Insurers usually require that at least 75 percent of eligible group members participate in a contributory group insurance plan. If a group's participation level falls below the required minimum, the insurer has the right to terminate the group life insurance contract. In such situations, the insurer must give the group policyholder written notice of termination, which usually must come 31 days prior to the date of termination.

As stated earlier, an insurer may terminate a group life insurance contract for nonpayment of premium at the end of any grace period. The coverage provided by a group life insurance contract remains in effect during the grace period, unless the policyholder has notified the insurer that it has elected to discontinue coverage in accordance with the terms of the group master contract. If the group policyholder does not pay the renewal premium by the end of the grace period, the group contract terminates. Unlike a grace period provision in an individual life insurance policy, a grace period provision in a group life insurance contract may state that if a policy terminates for nonpayment of premium, the group policyholder must pay the premium for the coverage provided during the grace period.

### Termination of a Group Insured's Coverage

A group insured's coverage can terminate even though the group life insurance contract remains in force. Most group life insurance contracts specify that a group insured's coverage terminates in the following situations:

- The group insured terminates her employment or group membership.

- The group insured ceases to be eligible for coverage. For example, the employee may no longer be part of the defined class of persons covered under the group life insurance plan.

- The group insured does not make a required contribution to the cost of coverage. For example, an employee may instruct his employer to stop payroll deductions of his premium contributions.

As noted earlier, a group insured whose coverage terminates may have the right to obtain individual life insurance.

# Regulation of Group Life Insurance

In the United States, group life insurance is subject to both state and federal regulation. State insurance laws govern insurers and the group life insurance products they sell. We have already described the types of regulatory requirements that the states impose on group life insurance, including requirements concerning the groups that are eligible for group life insurance and the provisions that group life insurance contracts must include. In this section, we describe some of the federal laws that regulate group life insurance plans.

As noted in Chapter 4, U.S. federal employment laws have been enacted to ensure that all employees are treated fairly in the workplace. Employment laws prohibit discrimination regarding hiring, advancement, wages, and other terms and conditions of employment. Employer-sponsored plans that provide employee benefits, such as group life insurance plans, must comply with all applicable federal employment laws.

# ERISA

Most employer-sponsored group life insurance plans in the United States must comply with the *Employee Retirement Income Security Act (ERISA)*, which is a U.S. federal law designed to ensure that employee welfare benefit plans meet certain minimum plan requirements to protect covered employees.[1] For ERISA purposes, a *welfare benefit plan* is a plan that an employer establishes to provide the specified benefits listed in Figure 15.4 to plan participants and their beneficiaries. Any employer-sponsored plan that provides at least one of the listed benefits becomes subject to ERISA's disclosure and reporting requirements.

So even if a plan provides employees with benefits other than retirement benefits—like medical or disability insurance—it is considered to be a welfare benefit plan?

According to ERISA, yes.

And the ERISA regulations apply to all welfare benefit plans?

Yes. If a plan provides at least one of the benefits listed here, that plan is probably subject to ERISA requirements. There are some exceptions, of course.

## Figure 15.4 Employee Benefits that Subject a Welfare Benefit Plan to ERISA

- Medical, surgical, or hospital care benefits
- Sickness, accident, disability, death, or unemployment benefits
- Vacation benefits
- Day care benefits
- Scholarship funds
- Prepaid legal services
- Apprenticeship or training programs
- Certain benefits, which include severance benefits and housing benefits, described in the Labor Management Relations Act[2]

ERISA requires that welfare benefit plans be established and maintained according to a written plan document. Among other things, the document must describe

- The benefits that are provided by the plan

- How the plan will be funded

- The procedure that will be followed to amend the plan

The plan document must name one or more fiduciaries who are responsible for controlling and managing the operation of the benefit plan. Fiduciaries have a duty to act solely for the benefit of group insureds. Plan fiduciaries who fail to perform their duty can be held personally liable for any losses that result from that breach of duty; in some cases, criminal penalties can be imposed on such plan fiduciaries. ERISA places many of the same requirements on fiduciaries of group retirement plans. We discuss these requirements later in this chapter.

ERISA imposes various disclosure and reporting requirements on welfare benefit plans. A ***plan administrator*** is the individual or organization responsible for ensuring that the plan complies with applicable regulatory requirements. A summary plan description must be provided to each group insured and to the federal Department of Labor (DOL). A ***summary plan description*** is an abbreviated version of the plan document that is understandable by the average plan participant and that reasonably informs participants and beneficiaries of their rights and obligations under the plan. If the plan changes significantly, each participant and the DOL must receive a summary of material modifications. ERISA also requires that an annual report be filed with the Internal Revenue Service. ERISA imposes similar requirements on group retirement plans, as we describe later in this chapter.

## ADEA

As noted in Chapter 4, the Age Discrimination in Employment Act (ADEA) is a federal law that protects workers who are age 40 and older from being discriminated against because of their age. The ADEA applies to employers with 20 or more employees. Because the cost of providing group life insurance benefits to older workers is greater than the cost of providing the same benefits to younger workers, older workers are at risk of experiencing discrimination regarding employee benefits. The ADEA seeks to protect older workers from this type of discrimination.

The ADEA permits employers to reduce the level of certain group life insurance benefits so that the cost of providing these benefits to older workers is no greater than the cost of providing them to younger workers. The Act, however, requires that an employer's premium contributions for benefits provided to older workers at least equal the employer's contributions for the benefits provided to younger workers.

## ADA

As stated in Chapter 4, the Americans with Disabilities Act (ADA) is a federal law that protects people with disabilities against all types of discrimination, including employment discrimination. The ADA requires that people with disabilities have equal access to the same group life insurance benefits available to other employees. The ADA allows coverage benefit limitations but prohibits the denial or limitation of benefits based solely on the fact that a person has a disability. For example, the

ADA allows a plan to contain a benefit limit for treatment of mental disorders, but a plan cannot refuse to offer benefits to a person solely because the person has a mental disorder or other disability.

# Group Retirement Plans

Most group retirement plans in the United States are *qualified plans*, which are group retirement plans that receive favorable federal income tax treatment because they meet specified requirements imposed by the federal tax laws and ERISA. Tax laws provide incentives that benefit both the *plan sponsors*—the employers and unions that establish the plans—and the *plan participants*—the employees and union members who are covered under the plan. *Plan beneficiaries* are individuals specified by plan participants to receive retirement benefits provided by the plan if the plan participant dies. Plan beneficiaries may include spouses, dependents, and other individuals specified by plan participants. Figure 15.5 provides a summary of the types of qualified retirement plans in the United States. Each type of plan can be further categorized as either a defined benefit plan or a defined contribution plan.

- A *defined benefit plan* is a type of retirement plan that specifies the amount of the periodic income benefit—based on the employee's salary or wages and/or years of service—that a participant is to receive after retirement. This retirement benefit usually is described in terms of a monthly annuity, and the plan sponsor is obligated to deposit enough assets into the plan to provide the promised benefit.

- A *defined contribution plan* specifies the annual contribution that the plan sponsor will deposit into the plan on behalf of each plan participant. A *contribution* is a payment from any source to fund the plan's benefits. A contribution is usually a percentage of a plan participant's salary or wages. Contributions are allocated to each participant's account and are invested and accumulated on behalf of each plan participant. The amount of the benefit each participant receives is determined by the value of the individual's account at retirement.

## Figure 15.5 Types of Qualified Retirement Plans in the United States

**Pension plan.** A defined benefit retirement plan established by an employer or union to provide workers with a pension in the form of a lifetime periodic income benefit that begins at retirement. Employers make mandatory contributions on behalf of employees, who typically do not make contributions.

**Retirement savings plan.** A defined contribution retirement plan to which a plan sponsor must make contributions on behalf of a plan participant if the participant makes a specified level of contributions to the plan.

**Profit sharing plan.** A defined contribution retirement plan that is funded by contributions from the plan sponsor's profits.

## Regulation of Retirement Plans

Many employers provide retirement plans for their employees. Qualified retirement plans are subject to federal regulation, as are other employee benefit plans. ERISA provides the majority of the federal regulation for retirement plans in the United States, and its requirements apply to all plans with tax-qualified status. ERISA imposes participation, plan documentation, vesting, nondiscrimination, and distribution requirements that all qualified retirement plans must meet.

### *Participation Requirements*

Each retirement plan defines the requirements employees must meet in order to be eligible for participation in the plan. *Participation* refers to the inclusion of an individual in a retirement plan. Qualified retirement plans must contain at least the following minimum participation standards:

- The plan cannot require that an employee complete a period of service beyond one year or be older than 21 to participate in the plan, whichever happens later. In other words, when an employee attains the age of 21 *and* completes one year of employment, she must be eligible to participate in the plan. For example, an employee who is age 19 when she begins employment may be barred from participation until she attains age 21. An employee who is 21 when she begins employment may be required to complete one year of service before being eligible to participate in the retirement plan. Note that a qualified plan is not required to have a minimum age requirement, and a plan may allow an individual to participate in the plan before she reaches the age of 21. If employees are fully vested after two years of service, then the plan may impose a minimum service requirement of two years. (We describe vesting later in this chapter.) In addition, regulatory requirements define how a year of service is measured.

- The plan generally cannot exclude employees who have attained a specified maximum age.

Defined benefit plans also must meet minimum requirements as to the number of plan participants. Minimum participation requirements are met if the plan covers at least a specified number of employees or a specified percentage of all employees.

### *Plan Documentation Requirements*

ERISA requires qualified retirement plans to be established and maintained in accordance with a written plan document that describes the benefits to be provided, how the plan will be funded, and the procedure that will be followed to amend the plan. Plan participants and plan beneficiaries who are receiving plan benefits must be provided with a summary plan description. Figure 15.6 lists some of the information contained in plan documents and summary plan descriptions.

## Figure 15.6 Plan Documents and Summary Plan Descriptions

Plan documents and summary plan descriptions must contain the following information:

- The name and address of the plan administrator

- The names and addresses of all plan trustees, if applicable

- The plan's named fiduciary

- The plan's requirements relating to eligibility for participation and benefits

- A description of the provisions regarding nonforfeitable retirement benefits

- A description of circumstances that may result in disqualification, ineligibility, or denial or loss of benefits

- The source of financing of the plan

- The identity of any organization through which plan benefits are provided

- The date of the end of the plan year and whether the plan's records are kept on a calendar-year, policy-year, or fiscal-year basis

- The procedures to be followed in presenting claims for benefits under the plan

- The remedies available for the redress of claims that are denied in whole or in part

## *Vesting Requirements*

A plan participant is ***vested*** when he has the right to receive partial or full benefits under the plan even if he terminates employment prior to retirement. Qualified retirement plans must provide that each participant is immediately vested in the accrued benefit funded by his own contributions; a participant's right to such benefits is nonforfeitable, which means that this right cannot be taken away. A qualified retirement plan also must include a minimum vesting schedule that specifies when a plan participant has the right to receive benefits funded by employer contributions.

So do you understand how a vesting schedule works?

Doesn't it specify how I, as a plan participant, am vested in a certain percentage of my employer's contributions at certain points in my employment?

Exactly. And that percentage may increase gradually over several years, or may increase to 100 percent all at once at a certain point in your employment.

So it might be that after three years I am 50 percent vested in employer-funded contributions, and after six years I am fully vested in those contributions?

Yes, or your plan's vesting schedule might specify that you have no vested employer-funded benefits until you have been employed for five years, at which point you become fully vested in those contributions.

So each plan's schedule is different?

They can be, but all plans must comply with U.S. federal tax laws that set minimum vesting schedules.

## Nondiscrimination Requirements

Three general requirements are imposed to ensure that qualified retirement plans do not unfairly discriminate in favor of employees who are "highly compensated" as defined by U.S. federal tax laws.

- Contributions *or* benefits may not discriminate in favor of highly compensated employees. Note that this requirement contains the word "or," which means that either contributions or benefits can discriminate, but both contributions and benefits cannot discriminate.

- Plan benefits, rights, and features must be made available to employees in a nondiscriminatory manner.

- The effect of plan amendments and plan terminations must be nondiscriminatory.

U.S. federal tax laws and IRS regulations contain complex rules and tests that are used to evaluate whether a plan complies with each of these requirements.

ERISA imposes additional requirements on *top-heavy plans*, which are plans under which, for a given plan year, the present value of accrued benefits for key employees exceeds a specified percentage of the present value of accrued benefits for all employees. Tax laws in the United States define which individuals are considered key employees, and that definition includes the employer's officers, owners, and highly paid employees. If a qualified plan becomes top heavy, the plan must comply with additional requirements to remain a qualified plan.

## Distribution Requirements

Federal income tax laws in the United States impose several requirements on distributions of qualified plans. *Distributions* are benefits paid to plan participants, usually following retirement. Some plans, primarily defined benefit plans, must provide that distributions will be paid in the form of a qualified joint and survivor life annuity. Thus, surviving spouses of deceased plan participants must be provided with specified survivor benefits. A plan participant may waive this requirement, but only with the consent of the participant's spouse. The plan may provide unmarried plan participants with a life annuity.

Qualified plans must contain specified provisions regarding when payment of plan distributions will begin. In general, distributions must begin by April 1 of the calendar year following the year in which the participant attains age 70½, even if the participant is still employed at that time. Qualified plans also must comply with requirements specifying the periods over which distributions must be paid. Penalties are imposed on plan participants for whom these distribution requirements are not met, and a plan's failure to meet such requirements may result in the plan losing its tax-qualified status.

## Retirement Plan Funding Instruments

ERISA requires that the assets of a retirement plan be held separately from the plan sponsor's general assets. The plan sponsor can separate retirement plan assets from its general assets by allowing the retirement assets to be held by a bank, a life insurance company under various contracts designated for this purpose, or another financial institution. The financial institution in which a group retirement plan's assets are held is called a *funding agency*.

Regardless of whether retirement plan assets are held by a bank, an insurer, or another financial institution, the plan sponsor must choose a funding instrument when establishing the plan. A *funding instrument*, also known as a *funding vehicle*, is an arrangement for investing group retirement plan assets. A plan sponsor usually chooses funding instruments based on how it wants the plan administered and the amount of flexibility available in the plan design. The most common funding instruments for qualified retirement plans are trusts and group insurance contracts.

## Trusts

Trusts are the most common funding instruments for qualified retirement plans. A trust established for a qualified retirement plan is based on the same legal principles as trusts used for other purposes. The grantor of the trust is the plan sponsor. The plan trustee may be a corporation, such as a bank or trust company, or it may be a named individual. The trust beneficiaries are the plan participants.

The terms under which the trust operates are specified in a trust agreement, which addresses the receipt, investment, and disbursement of the retirement plan's assets. Plan trustees may be required to perform any of the following duties:

- Receiving and investing employer contributions

- Providing periodic reports to the plan sponsor

- Paying benefits under the plan

- Maintaining the appropriate administrative records

Plan trustees have a fiduciary responsibility to manage and invest plan assets solely for the benefit of the plan participants. In some plans, investment managers rather than plan trustees are responsible for investing plan assets. In any case, individuals responsible for investing plan assets must act in accordance with plan documents and plan investment policies. Plan assets may be invested in a variety of investment instruments, including deposit accounts, certificates of deposit, stocks, bonds, or mutual funds.

## Group Insurance Contracts

Group insurance contracts used to fund qualified plans can be classified as *allocated contracts* or *unallocated contracts*. Note that this type of classification focuses on how plan contributions are accumulated and how they are used to satisfy individual benefit claims.

Plans funded through *allocated contracts* have individually assigned participant accounts, and employer contributions to the plan are assigned to individual plan participants. Allocated contracts include

- Individual life insurance and annuity contracts

- Group permanent life insurance contracts

- Group deferred annuity contracts

When a plan is funded through an *unallocated contract*, funds are held in one account and are undivided with respect to plan participants; benefits are then paid from that account. Under an unallocated contract, employer contributions to the plan are not assigned to individual plan participants until benefits are actually paid to plan participants. Unallocated contracts include group deposit administration (DA) contracts and immediate participation guarantee (IPG) contracts. Figure 15.7 identifies and describes these two unallocated contracts.

---

## Figure 15.7 Common Unallocated Contracts

- **Group deposit administration (DA) contracts:** A type of contract under which contributions are deposited in an undivided account and are used to purchase single-premium immediate annuities for plan participants when they retire.

- **Immediate participation guarantee (IPG) contracts:** A type of contract under which plan contributions are deposited in an undivided account and the plan sponsor may either (a) withdraw funds from the account to purchase an immediate annuity when a plan participant retires or (b) pay the participant's monthly retirement benefit directly from the account when the participant retires.

---

## Retirement Plan Administration

Retirement plan administration duties can be divided into two categories: administrative duties and fiduciary duties. Typically, administrative duties directly affect plan participants and are performed by plan administrators. Fiduciary duties encompass a broad range of activities and may include both administrative duties and asset management duties. ERISA specifies the conditions under which an individual may be considered a fiduciary of a qualified plan.

### Plan Administrators

A plan sponsor must name a plan administrator, which may be a specified individual or a committee formed for the purpose of handling the plan's administrative needs. The plan administrator may hire other professionals to help ensure that the plan operates according to its terms. Many financial services providers contract with plan sponsors to provide administrative services, such as accounting, actuarial, disbursement, and reporting services. The plan sponsor, however, is ultimately responsible for ensuring that the plan complies with all applicable laws and regulations.

Plan administrators may perform some or all of the following duties:

- Enrolling new employees in the plan

- Communicating plan changes to plan participants

- Maintaining hiring, participation, and termination records of plan participants

- Acting as a resource for plan participants regarding matters dealing with the plan

## *Plan Fiduciaries*

ERISA requires each retirement plan to name one or more plan fiduciaries in its plan document. Typically, the named plan fiduciary is either the plan sponsor or the plan administrator. The purpose of requiring a named fiduciary is to give plan participants the name of at least one individual who is responsible for the administration and operation of the plan. This requirement, however, does not limit fiduciary responsibility to the fiduciary named in the plan document. According to ERISA, other unnamed persons may be considered fiduciaries if they perform any of the following duties:

- Exercising discretionary authority or control over the management of the retirement plan or over assets held under the plan

- Exercising any discretionary authority or responsibility in the administration of the plan

- Rendering investment advice for direct or indirect compensation

Fiduciaries of qualified plans have a duty to act solely in the interest of plan participants and plan beneficiaries. They must act for the exclusive purpose of providing plan benefits and defraying reasonable administrative expenses. According to ERISA, fiduciaries must use the same care, skill, prudence, and diligence that a prudent person who is familiar with such matters would use under the circumstances. Plan fiduciaries who fail to perform their fiduciary duty can be held personally liable for any losses or unreasonable expenses that result from a breach of that duty.

In addition to being held personally liable for any breach caused by his own actions, a plan fiduciary can be held liable for the breach of another fiduciary, who, in this context, is referred to as a *cofiduciary*. When a fiduciary discovers the breach of a cofiduciary, he must take steps to correct the situation, which may include suing the cofiduciary if necessary. A fiduciary will usually be held liable for the breach of a cofiduciary when

- The fiduciary knowingly participates in or knowingly conceals a breach by a cofiduciary

- The fiduciary has knowledge of a breach by a cofiduciary and does not take steps to correct the situation

- The fiduciary fails to comply with ERISA, and this failure enables a cofiduciary to commit a breach

## Retirement Plan Termination

To meet the requirements for a qualified plan, a retirement plan must be established as a permanent plan. The purpose of this requirement is to prevent plan sponsors from establishing plans for only a few years for the sole purpose of obtaining tax benefits. Despite the "permanence" requirement, retirement plans can be, and many times are, terminated. *Plan termination* describes the ending of a group retirement plan when plan benefits cease to accrue. A retirement plan may terminate for various reasons. The plan sponsor may decide to go out of business, or it may decide to replace its current retirement plan with another type of retirement plan. The plan sponsor also may conclude that it can no longer afford to fund the plan. In this situation, the plan sponsor may elect to initiate a *partial plan termination*, which occurs when a plan sponsor terminates a retirement plan for one group of plan participants but continues the plan for another group of plan participants. For example, an employer may continue a retirement plan for employees who have been employed for longer than a stated number of years, but terminate the plan for newer employees.

What happens if a retirement plan terminates without enough funds to pay benefits to the plan participants?

Good question. ERISA created an insurance program for certain qualified plans to ensure payment of vested benefits up to a certain limit, regardless of the financial status of the plan at the time of termination.

Are all retirement plans required to have this insurance?

No. ERISA requires only qualified defined *benefit* plans to have plan termination insurance. That requirement does not apply to qualified defined *contribution* plans, which are much simpler to terminate.

So what happens if those plans terminate with insufficient funds?

Well, other U.S. laws govern the termination of a defined contribution plan; the plan sponsor must follow specified procedures to divide plan assets among the plan participants.

## Key Terms

contributory plan
noncontributory plan
evidence of insurability provision
conversion provision
actively-at-work provision
probationary period provision
eligibility period
Employee Retirement Income Security Act (ERISA)
plan administrator
summary plan description
qualified plan
plan sponsor
plan participant
plan beneficiary
defined benefit plan
defined contribution plan
contribution
participation
vested
top-heavy plan
distributions
funding agency
funding instrument
plan termination
partial plan termination

## Endnotes

1. 29 U.S.C. §§ 1001 et seq. (2011).

2. 29 U.S.C. §§ 141 et seq. (2011).

# *Glossary*

**absolute assignment.** The irrevocable transfer of all of a policyowner's ownership rights in a life insurance policy to another. [12]

**acceptance.** The offeree's unqualified agreement to be bound to the terms of an offer. [6]

**accession.** A method of acquiring property ownership by which a property owner has the right to all that his property produces and all that is added to or united with the property. [8]

**accidental death benefit.** A supplemental life insurance policy benefit that requires the insurer to pay a specified amount of money in addition to the policy's basic death benefit if an insured dies as a result of an accident. [14]

**accord and satisfaction.** A method of discharging a contract in which one party agrees to accept something other than what he was entitled to receive under the original contract. [6]

**acquisition.** A transaction wherein one corporation purchases a controlling interest in another corporation, resulting in a linkage between formerly independent corporations. [3]

**actively-at-work provision.** A group life insurance contract provision which states that an employee must be actively at work, not ill or on leave, on the day coverage becomes effective. [15]

**actual authority.** The authority to act on behalf of a principal that the principal intentionally confers on an agent and that the agent reasonably believes is conferred. [7]

**actual damages.** *See* **compensatory damages**.

**ADA.** *See* **Americans with Disabilities Act**.

**ADEA.** *See* **Age Discrimination in Employment Act**.

**administrative agencies.** The various departments that make up the executive branch of a government. [1]

**administrative code.** A compilation of the administrative regulations of a given jurisdiction. [1]

**administrative law.** The type of law that consists of regulations issued by administrative agencies. [1]

**administrator.** A personal representative who is responsible for settling the estate of a person who died intestate. [8]

**ADR method.** *See* **alternative dispute resolution method**.

**adverse action.** For purposes of the Fair Credit Reporting Act, a denial or revocation of credit or insurance coverage, a change in the terms of an existing credit arrangement or insurance coverage, or a refusal to grant credit or insurance in substantially the amount or on substantially the terms requested. [4]

**affidavit.** A written statement made under oath. [2]

**affiliates.** Companies that are under the common control of a holding company. [5]

**affirmative defense.** An allegation of facts that constitute a defense to the plaintiff's claim in a civil lawsuit. [2]

**Age Discrimination in Employment Act (ADEA).** A U.S. federal law that protects workers who are age 40 and older from being discriminated against because of their age. [4]

**agency.** The legal relationship between a principal and an agent. [7]

**agency agreement.** A written contract between an insurer and an insurance producer that spells out the rights and duties of the contracting parties, including the scope of the producer's authority to act as an agent of the insurer. [10]

**agency at will.** An agency relationship that is to continue for an unspecified amount of time. [7]

**agency by ratification.** An agency relationship created when a principal ratifies an unauthorized act taken by a purported agent. [7]

**agent.** A party who is authorized by another party, the principal, to act on the principal's behalf. [7]

**aleatory contract.** A contract under which one party provides something of value to another party in exchange for a conditional promise. *Contrast with* **commutative contract**. [6]

**alien corporation.** From the point of view of a given state in the United States, a corporation that was incorporated under the laws of another country. [3]

**alien insurer.** From the perspective of a given state, an insurer that incorporates under the laws of a country other than the United States. [5]

**alternative dispute resolution (ADR) method.** A nonjudicial method of resolving civil disputes. [2]

**Americans with Disabilities Act (ADA).** A U.S. federal law that protects people with disabilities against all types of discrimination, including employment discrimination. [4]

**answer.** A written document filed by the defendant in a civil lawsuit to respond to the plaintiff's complaint. [2]

**antitrust laws.** Laws designed to protect commerce against the monopolization of market power and unlawful restraints of trade, such as price discrimination and price fixing. Known as *competition laws* in most countries other than the United States. [3]

**APL benefit.** *See* **automatic premium loan benefit**.

**apparent authority.** Authority that is not expressly conferred on an agent but that the principal either intentionally or negligently allows a third party to believe the agent possesses. [7]

**appellate courts.** Courts that are authorized to review the decisions of lower courts. [1]

**approval premium receipt.** A conditional premium receipt that provides temporary life insurance coverage only when the insurer approves the proposed insured as a standard or better-than-average risk. [10]

**arbitration.** An alternative dispute resolution method in which impartial third parties, known as arbitrators, evaluate the facts in dispute and render a decision that usually is binding on the parties. [2]

**arbitrators.** Impartial third parties who evaluate the facts in a civil dispute and render a decision that is binding on the parties. [2]

**articles of incorporation.** The primary document that generally must be filed to incorporate a business in a given state and that describes some of the essential features of the corporation. [3]

**assault.** An intentional tort that occurs when a person intentionally creates a reasonable fear in the mind of the victim of imminent bodily harm. [2]

**assignee.** The person to whom ownership rights in property are transferred by means of an assignment. [9]

**assignment.** The transfer of ownership rights in property from the property owner, known as the assignor, to another party, known as the assignee. [9]

**assignment provision.** An individual life insurance policy provision that describes the roles of the insurer and the policyowner when the policy is assigned. [12]

**assignor.** The person who transfers ownership rights in property by means of an assignment. [9]

**assumption of the risk.** An affirmative defense that totally bars a plaintiff's claim when the plaintiff understood the nature of the risk presented by the defendant's conduct and voluntarily incurred that risk. [2]

**automatic nonforfeiture benefit.** The life insurance policy nonforfeiture benefit that will become effective automatically when a renewal premium is not paid by the end of the grace period and the policyowner has not elected another nonforfeiture option. [11]

**automatic premium loan (APL) benefit.** A life insurance policy nonforfeiture benefit under which the insurer will automatically pay an overdue premium by making a loan against the policy's cash value if the cash value equals or exceeds the amount of the premium due. [11]

**aviation exclusion provision.** A life insurance policy provision which states that an insurer will deny payment of policy proceeds if the insured's death is caused by certain aviation-related activities. [14]

**bad faith.** Acting with a dishonest motive by knowingly committing a wrong or failing to fulfill a legal duty. [3]

**Bankruptcy Act.** A U.S. federal law that provides a procedure for dealing with insolvent debtors under the supervision of a federal bankruptcy court. [9]

**bankruptcy proceeding.** A procedure for dealing with insolvent debtors under the supervision of a federal bankruptcy court. [9]

**bargaining contract.** A contract created when both parties, as equals, set the terms and conditions of the contract. *Contrast with* **contract of adhesion**. [6]

**battery.** An intentional tort that consists of an intentional harmful or offensive physical contact with another person. [2]

**bearer paper.** A negotiable instrument that is payable "to bearer" and thus can be negotiated by the holder without having to be signed by a specific payee. [9]

**bilateral contract.** A contract under which both parties make legally enforceable promises. *Contrast with* **unilateral contract**. [6]

**bilateral mistake.** A mistake that occurs when both parties are mistaken when they enter into a contract. [13]

**binding premium receipt.** A premium receipt that provides temporary life insurance coverage that becomes effective on the date specified in the receipt. [10]

**blank indorsement.** The indorsement of a negotiable instrument by signature only, with no additional wording; a blank indorsement makes the instrument bearer paper. [9]

**board of directors.** The group of individual directors who manage and direct the affairs of a corporation. [3]

**breach of contract.** The failure of a party to a contract to perform a contractual obligation. [2]

**broker-dealer.** A term often used to refer to individuals and firms that transact securities businesses. *See also* **securities broker** and **securities dealer**. [5]

**burden of proof.** (1) The duty to present evidence at trial to prove a given fact or set of facts. (2) The duty to persuade the trier of fact in a trial that an alleged fact is true. [2]

**business judgment rule.** A rule generally applied by U.S. courts when corporate directors are alleged to have breached a fiduciary duty. According to the rule, directors will not be held personally liable for making business decisions if there is a reasonable basis to believe the directors acted with due care and in good faith. [3]

**bylaws.** A corporate document that contains the basic rules under which the corporation operates. [3]

**case law.** The body of law that consists of the written decisions of a common law jurisdiction's courts. [1]

**cash payment nonforfeiture option.** *See* **cash surrender value nonforfeiture option**.

**cash surrender value nonforfeiture option.** A life insurance policy nonforfeiture option that permits a policyowner to discontinue premiums payments, surrender the policy, and receive the policy's cash surrender value in a lump-sum payment. Also known as *cash payment nonforfeiture option*. [11]

**cause of action.** A set of facts that gives a person the right to judicial relief. [2]

**center of gravity rule.** A conflict of laws rule under which a court applies the law of the jurisdiction that has the greatest interest in the matter. [6]

**certificate of authority.** A document issued by a state insurance department that grants an insurer the right to conduct an insurance business in the state. Also referred to as a *license*. [5]

**CFPB.** *See* **Consumer Financial Protection Bureau**.

**change of ownership provision.** An individual life insurance policy provision that permits a policyowner to transfer all ownership rights by notifying the insurer, in writing, of the change, without having to enter into a separate assignment agreement. When the insurer records the ownership change in its records, the change generally becomes effective as of the date the policyowner signed the written notification. [12]

**choice of laws provision.** A contract provision that allows the parties to a contract to mutually decide which jurisdiction's laws will govern their contract. [14]

**civil code.** In a civil law jurisdiction, a code that contains the general principles of law that apply to relationships between people that arise through birth, adoption, marriage, death, contracts, and personal liability. The civil code usually also regulates property rights. [1]

**civil laws.** Laws that are concerned with private—that is, nongovernmental—rights and remedies. *Contrast with* **criminal laws**. [2]

**civil law system.** A legal system that is based on the Roman legal system in which the laws are codified into comprehensive written codes enacted by the legislature. [1]

**civil litigation.** A judicial process by which private parties go to court to enforce a legal right or to obtain a remedy for a civil wrong. [2]

**Civil Rights Act of 1964.** A very broad U.S. federal antidiscrimination law that prohibits employment discrimination on the basis of race, color, sex, religion, or national origin. [4]

**class designation.** A beneficiary designation that identifies a certain group of people, rather than naming each person individually. [11]

**clear and convincing evidence.** Evidence that shows that the truth of the facts asserted is highly probable and that leaves no reasonable doubt as to the truth of those facts. [13]

**close corporation.** A corporation that has issued stock which is owned by a relatively small group of people—often members of the same family—and which is not available for sale to the general public. Sometimes referred to as a *closely held corporation. Contrast with* **publicly traded corporation**. [3]

**closed contract.** A contract for which only those terms and conditions that are printed in—or attached to—the contract are considered to be part of the contract. *Contrast with* **open contract**. [10]

**closely held corporation.** *See* **close corporation**.

**closing.** The conclusion of a real estate transaction when the parties fulfill all of the terms of their sales contract. [8]

**code.** A comprehensive written statement of rules that embody the general principles of law that apply in a given civil law jurisdiction. [1]

**codicil.** A testamentary document that supplements a will. [8]

**collateral assignment.** The transfer of some of a policyowner's ownership rights in a life insurance policy to provide security for a debt. [12]

**collusion.** An agreement between two or more people to defraud another person of his rights. [13]

**commercial bank.** A depository institution that accepts deposits from people, businesses, and government agencies and uses those deposits to make loans to people, businesses, and government agencies. [5]

**common law.** In its broadest sense, an unwritten body of general principles and rules of law developed and followed by the courts in a common law jurisdiction. [1]

**common law system.** A legal system that is based on the common law of England. [1]

**common mistake.** A bilateral mistake that occurs when both parties to a contract make the same mistake. [13]

**common stock.** An equity security that entitles its owner to share in the issuing corporation's dividends and provides its owner with the right to vote on certain corporate matters. [3]

**community property.** In some states, certain property owned by a married couple in which each spouse has an undivided half interest. *Contrast with* **separate property**. [8]

**commutative contract.** A contract under which the parties specify in advance the values that they will exchange, and the parties generally exchange items or services that they think are of relatively equal value. *Contrast with* **aleatory contract**. [6]

**company limited by guarantee.** In some jurisdictions outside the United States, a company whose owners agree to pay up to a stated amount if the company is liquidated. [3]

**company limited by shares.** In some jurisdictions outside the United States, a company whose owners' liability is limited to the investment they made when they purchased the company's shares. [3]

**comparative negligence.** A system of apportioning losses between plaintiffs and defendants when both parties' negligence contributed to a plaintiff's losses. [2]

**compensatory damages.** Damages intended to compensate an injured party for the amount of the monetary losses that resulted from a defendant's wrongful conduct. Sometimes referred to as *actual damages*. [2]

**competition laws.** *See* **antitrust laws**.

**complaint.** A written document that sets out the cause of action on which a plaintiff in a civil lawsuit bases her claim against the defendant. [2]

**compromise settlement.** An agreement between two or more parties to settle a dispute regarding the terms and/or performance of a contract. [14]

**conciliation.** An alternative dispute resolution method that is used in many countries other than the United States and that is similar to mediation in that the parties are encouraged to come to a mutually acceptable agreement to resolve the dispute. [2]

**conclusive presumption.** A presumption that cannot be refuted. *Contrast with* **rebuttable presumption**. [2]

**condition.** In contract law, an uncertain event, the occurrence or nonoccurrence of which either creates or extinguishes a party's duty to perform a contractual promise. [10]

**conditional premium receipt.** A type of life insurance premium receipt that provides temporary insurance coverage only if specified conditions are met. [10]

**conditional promise.** A promise to perform a stated act *if* a specified, uncertain event occurs.[6]

**condition precedent.** In contract law, a condition that must occur in order to give rise to one party's duty to perform a promise. *Contrast with* **condition subsequent**. [10]

**condition subsequent.** In contract law, a condition that, if it occurs, cancels one party's duty to perform a promise. *Contrast with* **condition precedent**. [10]

**conflict of laws.** The area of the law that determines which substantive laws apply to each issue in a case when the laws of more than one jurisdiction are involved in the action. [2]

**Congress.** In the United States, the legislative branch of the federal government. [1]

**conservator.** *See* **receiver**.

**conservatorship.** *See* **receivership**.

**consideration.** Whatever a promisor asks for and receives in exchange for his contractual promise. [6]

**constitution.** In most countries, a document or group of documents that sets out the fundamental principles that determine the powers and duties of the government and the rights of the people. [1]

**constructive delivery.** Legally adequate delivery of a life insurance policy to a policyowner that occurs when an insurer parts with control of the policy and intends to be bound to its terms. [10]

**consumer.** For most regulatory purposes, a natural person who purchases or tries to purchase goods or services that are to be used primarily for personal, family, or household purposes. [4]

**Consumer Credit Protection Act.** A U.S. federal law that regulates many aspects of how businesses provide credit to consumers. [4]

**consumer credit report.** For purposes of the Fair Credit Reporting Act, any communication of information by a consumer reporting agency that bears on a consumer's creditworthiness, credit standing, credit capacity, character, general reputation, personal characteristics, or mode of living and is used or collected as a factor in establishing a consumer's eligibility for insurance or credit. [4]

**Consumer Financial Protection Bureau (CFPB).** Created by Dodd-Frank, an independent bureau within the Federal Reserve System charged with establishing clear rules of the road for financial services firms to ensure that consumers can see clearly the costs and features of financial services products and services. [5]

**consumer reporting agency.** A business that assembles or evaluates information on consumers and furnishes consumer credit reports to third parties in exchange for a fee. [4]

**contempt of court.** Any act that hinders a court in administering justice or that lessens the authority and dignity of the court and that is punishable by the court. [2]

**contestable period.** The time period within which the insurer has the right to avoid a life insurance policy on the grounds of a material misrepresentation in the application. [13]

**contingent beneficiary.** The party who will receive life insurance policy proceeds after the insured's death if the primary beneficiary dies before the insured. Also known as *secondary beneficiary* or *successor beneficiary*. [11]

**contingent payee.** The person who will receive any policy proceeds payable under a settlement agreement following the death of the payee. Also known as a *successor payee*. [12]

**continuation statement.** A document that amends a financing statement that has been in effect for the maximum allowable time and, thus, continues the effectiveness of the financing statement for a stated number of additional years. [9]

**contract.** A legally enforceable agreement between two or more parties; the agreement consists of a promise or a set of promises. [2]

**contract of adhesion.** A contract that one party prepares and that the other party must accept or reject as a whole, without any bargaining between the parties as to the terms of the contract. *Contrast with* **bargaining contract**. [6]

**contractual capacity.** The legal power to enter into a valid contract. [6]

**contribution.** A payment from any source to fund a group retirement plan's benefits. [15]

**contributory negligence.** An affirmative defense that is available when the plaintiff's own negligence contributed to her loss. [2]

**contributory plan.** A group insurance plan under which the group insureds pay all or part of the cost for their coverage. [15]

**conversion.** An intentional tort that involves the unauthorized exercise of dominion and control over another person's property. [2]

**conversion provision.** A group life insurance contract provision that gives a group insured the right to obtain an individual life insurance policy if her group life insurance coverage terminates because of specified reasons. [15]

**copyright.** A right that is granted by statute to the author or originator of an original literary or artistic work and that gives the copyright holder the exclusive right to publish, produce, or perform the work for a specified time. [8]

**corporate culture.** The values, beliefs, goals, and patterns of behavior that employees of an organization share. [1]

**corporation.** A legal entity that is created by the authority of a governmental unit, such as a state or nation, and that is separate and distinct from the people who own it. [3]

**counterclaim.** A claim by the defendant in a civil lawsuit against the plaintiff; the claim must arise out of the same facts on which the plaintiff's claim is based. [2]

**counteroffer.** A rejection of an offer to contract and the making of a different offer to contract. [6]

**courts of original jurisdiction.** *See* **trial courts**.

**cover.** Under Article 2 of the Uniform Commercial Code, a remedy available to the buyer of goods who may purchase substitute goods from another seller if the original seller fails to deliver the goods as promised, delivers goods that do not conform to the contract terms, or otherwise refuses to perform the contract. The buyer who covers may recover from the original seller damages equal to the difference between the cost of cover and the contract price. [9]

**credit union.** A nonprofit, cooperative financial institution owned and run by its members. [5]

**criminal laws.** Laws that define certain acts as crimes and that provide specific punishments for each crime. *Contrast with* **civil laws**. [2]

**customary law system.** A legal system in which members of a community have accepted local customs as binding on the community's members. [1]

**damages.** Monetary compensation that may be recovered by a plaintiff who has suffered a loss or injury as a result of a defendant's wrongful conduct; the basic legal remedy for most civil wrongs. [2]

**declaratory judgment.** A judicial statement that declares or denies the parties' legal rights but does not include specific relief or any means to enforce those rights. [2]

**deed.** A written instrument that transfers title to real property from one person to another person. [8]

**defamation.** An intentional tort that occurs when a person, without legal right, makes false statements that injure the good name or reputation of another person. [2]

**default judgment.** In a civil lawsuit, a judgment entered against the defendant because the defendant failed to file an answer within the required time or otherwise failed to defend the lawsuit. [2]

**defendant.** The party against whom a civil lawsuit is instituted. [2]

**defined benefit plan.** A type of group retirement plan that specifies the amount of the periodic income benefit—based on the employee's income and/or years of service—that a participant is to receive after retirement. *Contrast with* **defined contribution plan**. [15]

**defined contribution plan.** A type of group retirement plan that specifies the annual contribution that the plan sponsor will deposit into the plan on behalf of each plan participant. *Contrast with* **defined benefit plan**. [15]

**Department of the Treasury.** The U.S. federal administrative agency with primary responsibility for administering federal banking laws. [5]

**deposition.** A discovery method used in civil lawsuits in which attorneys for each party may question parties and other witnesses, who orally testify under oath. [2]

**depository institution.** A financial institution that specializes in accepting deposits and making loans. [5]

**directors.** Individuals who are appointed or elected by a corporation's stockholders to manage and direct the affairs of the corporation. [3]

**disaffirmance.** A minor's exercise of his right to avoid a contract. [6]

**discharge.** An order that is issued by a bankruptcy court when a debtor has complied with all requirements of a bankruptcy proceeding and that relieves the debtor from any further obligation to pay the debts that were included in the proceeding. [9]

**disclosed principal.** A named principal on whose behalf an agent contracts. [7]

**discovery.** A process in which the parties to a civil lawsuit gather information that is relevant to the lawsuit so that they can prepare to present their respective cases at trial. [2]

**dismissal.** A court order or judgment that concludes a civil lawsuit without a trial of the issues involved in the lawsuit. [2]

**dissolution.** The termination of a corporation's legal existence. [3]

**distribution date.** A specified date on which corporate dividends will be paid to the corporation's stockholders of record. Also known as the *payment date*. [3]

**distributions.** Benefits paid to group retirement plan participants, usually following retirement. [15]

**dividend.** A payment of a portion of a corporation's profits to the corporation's owners. [3]

**dividend additions.** Additional amounts of life insurance that a policyowner purchases with policy dividends. Also known as *paid-up additions*. [11]

**doctrine of stare decisis.** A general rule followed by the courts in common law jurisdictions. According to this rule, when a court finds that a specific principle of law applies to a certain set of facts, the court will apply that principle to all future cases in which the facts are substantially the same. [1]

**doctrine of substantial compliance.** An equitable doctrine which provides that when a policyowner has done everything possible to comply with the beneficiary change procedure set forth in the policy, but has failed because of circumstances beyond his control, the change will be considered effective. [11]

**Dodd-Frank.** *See* **Dodd-Frank Wall Street Reform and Consumer Protection Act**.

**Dodd-Frank Wall Street Reform and Consumer Protection Act.** A U.S. federal law that tightened regulation of the U.S. financial services industry following the financial crisis of 2007-2010, in an effort to improve accountability and transparency in the financial system and protect consumers from abusive financial practices. Also known as *Dodd-Frank*. [5]

**domestic corporation.** From the point of view of a given jurisdiction, a corporation that was incorporated within that jurisdiction. [3]

**domestic insurer.** From the perspective of a given state, an insurer that incorporates in the state. [5]

**domicile.** (1) The jurisdiction in which a business incorporates. Also known as *domiciliary state*. (2) The place where a person has his true, fixed, and permanent home. [3, 8]

**domiciliary state.** *See* **domicile**.

**donee.** A party to whom a gift of property is made. [8]

**donor.** A party who transfers property by making a gift of the property. [8]

**draft.** A negotiable instrument that is an order, or an instruction, to pay a sum of money. [9]

**drawee.** The bank on which a draft is written. [9]

**drawer.** *See* **maker**.

**duress.** The forcing of a person to enter a contract against her own free will by acting wrongfully or threateningly to overpower the person's will. [6]

**easement.** The right to make specific uses of another person's property or to prevent another from making specific uses of his own property. [8]

**economics.** The study of how societies allocate their resources. [4]

**EEOC.** *See* **Equal Employment Opportunity Commission**.

**electronic signature.** A signature on an electronic document. [4]

**Electronic Signatures in Global and National Commerce Act (E-SIGN).** A U.S. federal law that ensures that contracts and signatures made in electronic form are the legal equivalent of paper documents and pen-and-ink signatures. [4]

**eligibility period.** Under a contributory group life insurance plan, a period of time, usually 31 days, during which a new employee may enroll for group life insurance coverage. Sometimes referred to as an *enrollment period*. [15]

**employee.** A person in the service of another, the employer, who has the power or right to control and direct how the employee performs the work. *Contrast with* **independent contractor**. [4]

**Employee Retirement Income Security Act (ERISA).** A U.S. federal law designed to ensure that employee welfare benefit plans meet certain minimum plan requirements to protect covered employees. [15]

**endorsement.** A document that is attached to a life insurance policy and that becomes a part of the insurance contract. [11]

**endorsement method.** A method of changing the beneficiary of a life insurance policy under which the policyowner must submit his policy to the insurer along with a beneficiary change request. [11]

**enrollment period.** *See* **eligibility period**.

**entire contract provision.** An individual life insurance policy provision that defines the documents that constitute the contract between the insurer and the policyowner. [10]

**Equal Employment Opportunity Commission (EEOC).** A U.S. federal agency responsible for administering federal antidiscrimination laws. [4]

**Equal Pay Act.** A U.S. federal law that prohibits sex-based wage discrimination between men and women in the same establishment who are performing the same job under similar working conditions. [4]

**equitable remedies.** Remedies that were developed by common law courts of equity and that are based on moral rights and concepts of justice. *Contrast with* **legal remedies**. [2]

**equitable title.** Ownership rights based on considerations of fairness and equity rather than on legal ownership rights. [12]

**ERISA.** *See* **Employee Retirement Income Security Act**.

**E-SIGN.** *See* **Electronic Signatures in Global and National Commerce Act**.

**estate.** All of the property that a decedent owned at her death. [8]

**estate taxes.** In the United States, federal taxes that are imposed on decedents' estates that are valued at more than a specified dollar amount. [12]

**estoppel.** An equitable doctrine by which someone is restrained—or estopped—from acting in a manner that contradicts her previous conduct. [11]

**ethics.** A system of accepted standards of conduct and moral judgment that combines the elements of honesty, integrity, and fair treatment. [1]

**eviction.** A legal process by which a trespasser is removed from real property. [8]

**evidence.** The means by which the disputed facts in a civil lawsuit are proved or disproved. [2]

**evidence of insurability provision.** A group life insurance contract provision that specifies the conditions, if any, under which the insurer reserves the right to require a person eligible for insurance to provide evidence of insurability satisfactory to the insurer as a condition to part or all of her coverage. [15]

**exclusion.** A life insurance policy provision that specifies certain situations under which an insurer will deny payment of policy proceeds. [14]

**executive branch.** The branch of government that consists of a number of agencies or ministries that are responsible for administering, enforcing, or carrying out the jurisdiction's laws. [1]

**executor.** A personal representative who is responsible for settling the estate of a person who died with a valid will. [8]

**exemplary damages.** *See* **punitive damages**.

**express authority.** Actual authority that a principal explicitly confers on an agent. [7]

**extended term insurance nonforfeiture option.** A life insurance policy nonforfeiture option that allows the policyowner to use the policy's net cash value as a net single premium to purchase term insurance for the full face amount provided under the original policy for as long a term as that net cash value can provide. [11]

**Fair Credit Reporting Act (FCRA).** A U.S. federal law that regulates the reporting and use of consumer credit information and seeks to ensure that consumer credit reports contain only accurate, relevant, and recent information. [4]

**Fair Labor Standards Act.** A U.S. federal law that imposes minimum requirements on the wages that employers must pay workers. [4]

**fair use doctrine.** A legal doctrine that permits third parties to use limited portions of a copyrighted work for purposes such as criticism, comment, news reporting, teaching, scholarship, or research. [8]

**Family and Medical Leave Act (FMLA).** A U.S. federal law that provides for unpaid leaves of absence and reinstatement rights in specific circumstances for covered employees. [4]

**FCRA.** *See* **Fair Credit Reporting Act**.

**FDIC.** *See* **Federal Deposit Insurance Corporation**.

**Fed.** *See* **Federal Reserve System**.

**Federal Deposit Insurance Corporation (FDIC).** A U.S. federal agency that guarantees, within stated limits, the funds deposited in member banks. [5]

**Federal Insurance Office (FIO).** Created by Dodd-Frank, a U.S. administrative office within the Treasury Department that monitors the insurance industry, identifying areas with inadequate state regulation, helping to identify systemically risky insurers, and dealing with international insurance issues. [5]

**Federal Reserve System (the Fed).** In the United States, a system consisting of 12 regional banks and the state and national banks that are members of the Fed, whose functions include conducting the nation's monetary policy, supervising and regulating banks, and maintaining the stability of the nation's financial system. [5]

**Federal Sentencing Guidelines.** U.S. federal rules that set out uniform policies for sentencing individuals and organizations that have been convicted of serious federal crimes. [1]

**federal system.** A type of governmental system in which a federal government and a number of lower level governments share governmental powers. For example, the United States is a federation of 50 states, the District of Columbia, and a number of territories. [1]

**Federal Trade Commission (FTC).** The U.S. federal agency that is responsible for enforcing both federal antitrust laws and federal consumer protection laws. [4]

**FHC.** *See* **financial holding company**.

**fiduciary.** An entity or individual who holds a special position of trust or confidence when handling the affairs of another and who must put that other's interests above the fiduciary's own interests. [3]

**financial condition examination.** A formal investigation of an insurer carried out by one or more state insurance departments to identify and monitor any threats to the insurer's solvency. [5]

**financial holding company (FHC).** A holding company that conducts activities that are financial in nature or incidental to financial activities, such as insurance activities, securities activities, banking, and investment and advisory services. [5]

**Financial Industry Regulatory Authority (FINRA).** A nonprofit organization of member firms responsible for regulating all securities firms doing business in the United States. [5]

**Financial Stability Oversight Council (FSOC).** Created by Dodd-Frank, a U.S. independent agency responsible for monitoring the safety and stability of the nation's financial system, identifying systemic risks to the system, and coordinating regulatory responses to any threats to the system. [5]

**financing statement.** A document that is filed with a specified state or local government official to record the existence of a security interest in identified property of a debtor. [9]

**FINRA.** *See* **Financial Industry Regulatory Authority**.

**FINRA Rules.** Requirements for how broker-dealers and registered persons must conduct business; all registered members of the Financial Industry Regulatory Authority must comply with the rules. [5]

**FIO.** *See* **Federal Insurance Office**.

**fixture.** Personal property that has been attached to real property and, thus, has become part of the real property. [8]

**FMLA.** *See* **Family and Medical Leave Act**.

**foreclosure.** A process by which a mortgagee may put mortgaged property up for sale to raise funds to pay off the mortgagor's unpaid debt when the mortgagor has failed to repay a mortgage loan according to its terms. [8]

**foreign corporation.** From the point of view of a given state in the United States, a corporation that was incorporated under the laws of another state. In most other countries, a corporation that was incorporated under the laws of another country. [3]

**foreign insurer.** From the perspective of a given state, an insurer that incorporates under the laws of another state. [5]

**formal contract.** A contract that is enforceable because the parties met certain formalities concerning the form of the agreement. [6]

**fraud.** An act by which someone intentionally deceives another party and induces that other party to part with something of value or give up a legal right. [3]

**fraudulent misrepresentation.** An intentional tort that occurs when a person knowingly or willfully makes a false statement with the intent that another person will rely on the statement and will be harmed as a result of that reliance. [2]

**free and open market.** A market in which prices are established by the forces of supply and demand with little or no intervention from the government or other powerful economic entities, such as monopolies. [4]

**freedom of contract.** In the United States and many jurisdictions, a contract law principle which states that parties have the right to contract with whomever they choose and on whatever lawful terms they choose. [6]

**free look provision.** An individual life insurance policy provision that gives the policyowner a specified period—usually 10 days—following delivery of the policy within which to cancel the policy and receive a refund of all premiums paid. [10]

**FSOC.** *See* **Financial Stability Oversight Council**.

**FTC.** *See* **Federal Trade Commission**.

**functional regulation.** The principle that a single regulatory body should oversee similar financial activities, regardless of which type of financial institution engages in the activity. [5]

**funding agency.** The financial institution in which a group retirement plan's assets are held. [15]

**funding instrument.** An arrangement for investing group retirement plan assets. Also known as *funding vehicle*. [15]

**funding vehicle.** *See* **funding instrument**.

**garnishment.** A legal process by which a creditor can obtain a debtor's property that is in the possession of a third party. [4]

**general partner.** A partner who has unlimited personal liability for partnership debts. [3]

**general partnership.** A partnership in which all of the partners have unlimited personal liability for partnership debts. [3]

**gift.** The voluntary transfer of property ownership from one person to another without the exchange of consideration. [8]

**grace period provision.** A life insurance policy provision that allows the policy-owner to pay a renewal premium within a stated time following a premium due date. [11]

**grantee.** A person to whom title to real property is transferred by means of a deed. [8]

**grantor.** A person who transfers title to real property to another person by means of a deed. *See also* **settlor**. [8]

**gratuitous promise.** In contract law, a promise that is not supported by consideration. [6]

**gross negligence.** A knowing failure to perform a legal duty in reckless disregard for the consequences of that failure. [3]

**guardian.** An individual or group of individuals who is authorized by a court to take care of a person, known as a ward, and manage the ward's property and affairs. [6]

**holder.** The person who has possession of a negotiable instrument that is payable to the person or "to bearer" and who is entitled to negotiate the instrument. [9]

**holder in due course.** The holder of a negotiable instrument who paid value for the instrument, obtained it in good faith, and obtained it without knowledge of defenses or claims against its payment. [9]

**holding company.** A company that owns and controls another company or companies. [5]

**holding company system.** A corporate ownership structure in which one company, known as a holding company, owns and controls another company (or companies), known as a subsidiary. [5]

**holographic will.** A will that is handwritten and signed by the testator. [8]

**immovable property.** *See* **real property**.

**implied authority.** Actual authority that a principal intends an agent to have and that arises incidentally from an express grant of authority. [7]

**incontestability provision.** A life insurance policy provision that denies the insurer the right to avoid the contract on the grounds of a material misrepresentation in the application after the contract has been in force for a specified period of time. [13]

**indemnification.** Compensation or reimbursement of another's loss. [7]

**independent contractor.** A person who contracts to do a specific task according to her own methods and who generally is not subject to the employer's control except as to the end product or final result of the work. *Contrast with* **employee**. [4]

**individual retirement account.** An individual retirement arrangement that takes the form of a trust or custodial account set up in the United States for the exclusive benefit of a taxpayer and his beneficiaries; the trustee must be a bank, brokerage firm, mutual fund company, or similar financial institution. [11]

**individual retirement annuity.** An individual retirement arrangement that takes the form of an individual annuity issued by an insurance company. [11]

**individual retirement arrangement (IRA).** A retirement savings plan that allows individuals with taxable compensation to deposit a stated amount of that income into a savings arrangement that meets requirements specified in the federal tax laws and, thus, receives favorable federal tax treatment. [11]

**inducing a breach of contract.** An intentional tort that occurs when a person who is not a party to a contract persuades a contracting party to breach a contractual obligation. [2]

**informal contract.** A contract that is enforceable because the parties met requirements concerning the substance of the agreement rather than requirements concerning the form of the agreement. [6]

**infringement.** Any violation of the exclusive rights belonging to the owner of intellectual property. [8]

**injunction.** A court order that prohibits a party from committing a specific act. [2]

**inside directors.** Corporation directors who are otherwise employed by the corporation or are major stockholders of the corporation. [3]

**insurability premium receipt.** A conditional premium receipt that provides temporary life insurance coverage on condition that the insurer finds the proposed insured to be insurable as a standard or better-than-average risk. [10]

**insurable interest.** An interest that exists when a person is likely to suffer a genuine loss or detriment should the event insured against by an insurance policy occur. [6]

**insurance producer.** A person who is licensed to market and sell insurance products. [5]

**insurance trust.** An irrevocable trust for which the trust property consists of insurance policies on the life of the settlor or the proceeds of such policies. [12]

**intangible property.** Property that consists of one or more intangible legal rights that have value because, if necessary, the rights can be enforced by the courts. *Contrast with* **tangible property**. [8]

**intellectual property.** Intangible personal property that is a product of the human intellect and in which the creator has ownership rights. [8]

**intentional tort.** A private wrong committed by a person who intended to do something that the law declares a wrong. [2]

**inter vivos transfer.** A transfer of property ownership that is made by a property owner during his life. *Contrast with* **testamentary transfer**. [8]

**inter vivos trust.** A trust that takes effect during the settlor's lifetime. Also known as a *living trust*. [12]

**interpleader.** A court proceeding under which an insurer that cannot determine the proper recipient of policy proceeds pays the proceeds to a court and asks the court to decide the proper recipient. [13]

**interrogatories.** A discovery method used in civil lawsuits in which one party prepares written questions that the other party must answer in writing within a specified time. [2]

**intestate.** Not having a valid will at one's death. [8]

**investment company.** A company that issues securities and engages primarily in investing and trading securities. [5]

**involuntary petition.** A bankruptcy petition that is filed by one or more creditors of an insolvent debtor. [9]

**IRA.** *See* **individual retirement arrangement**.

**irrevocable beneficiary.** A life insurance policy beneficiary whose rights to policy proceeds are vested when the beneficiary designation is made. [11]

**Islamic legal system.** A legal system in which the law is set out in the Koran (or Qur'an) and is unchanging. [1]

**issue of fact.** An issue in which the parties to a civil lawsuit disagree as to the facts involved in the lawsuit. [2]

**issue of law.** An issue in which the parties to a civil lawsuit disagree on how the law should be applied to a given set of facts. [2]

**joint and several liability.** Liability in which each defendant is independently liable for the entire amount of damages awarded to a plaintiff regardless of a defendant's share of responsibility for the losses. [7]

**joint venture.** An arrangement between two otherwise independent businesses that agree to undertake a specific project together for a specified time period. [3]

**judge.** A judicial officer who presides over a trial court. [1]

**judgment.** An official decision of a court that resolves a dispute and determines the rights and obligations of the parties to the action. [2]

**judgment creditor.** A creditor who has sued a debtor who failed to repay a debt and has obtained a judgment against the debtor. [12]

**judicial branch.** The branch of government that consists of a system of courts that are responsible for applying and interpreting the jurisdiction's laws. [1]

**jurisdiction.** (1) The authority of a court to hear specific cases. (2) A geographic area of legal authority. [1]

**laches.** An equitable principle that bars a plaintiff from equitable relief if he unreasonably delayed in pursuing a claim against a defendant and the defendant was harmed in some way as a result of the undue delay. [2]

**landlord.** A real property owner who conveys the right to possess the property for a period of time to a tenant. Also known as the *lessor*. [8]

**late payment offer.** An insurer's conditional offer to waive its right to require timely payment of a premium. [11]

**law of agency.** The body of law that defines the rights, duties, and liabilities that arise among the parties when an agent represents a principal in dealings with third parties. [7]

**lease.** A contract under which the owner of real property conveys to another party the exclusive right to possess the property for a period of time. [8]

**legal remedies.** Limited and specific common law remedies that primarily involve the payment of money damages to injured parties. *Contrast with* **equitable remedies**. [2]

**legislative branch.** The branch of government that consists of one or more legislative bodies that are responsible for enacting laws to govern the applicable jurisdiction. [1]

**lessee.** *See* **tenant**.

**lessor.** *See* **landlord**.

**license.** *See* **certificate of authority**.

**lien.** A generic term used to describe a claim against property resulting from a debt or other obligation. [8]

**liquidated damages.** Damages for breach of contract that are agreed upon by the parties to the contract and are included as a term of the contract. [9]

**liquidation.** A process in which a corporation that is being dissolved pays its debts or makes arrangements to pay those debts. If any assets remain after the debts are paid, then those assets are distributed on a pro rata basis to the corporation's stockholders in the order of their priorities. [3]

**liquidation proceeding.** A type of bankruptcy proceeding in which a bankrupt debtor's assets are liquidated and the proceeds are used to pay the debtor's creditors. *Contrast with* **rehabilitation proceeding**. [9]

**living trust.** *See* **inter vivos trust**.

**maker.** The person who writes a draft. Also known as the *drawer*. [9]

**market.** In economics, an environment in which buyers and sellers of a product or service meet. [4]

**market conduct examination.** A formal investigation of an insurer's nonfinancial operations conducted by one or more state insurance departments to determine whether the insurer's market conduct operations comply with applicable laws and regulations. [5]

**market conduct laws.** State insurance laws designed to make sure that insurance companies conduct their businesses fairly and ethically. [5]

**market economy.** An economy that relies primarily on the market forces known as supply and demand to allocate resources. [4]

**material misrepresentation.** A misrepresentation by one contracting party that induces the other party to enter into a contract that it would not have entered had it known the truth. [6]

**McCarran-Ferguson Act.** A U.S. federal law that gives the states primary authority to regulate insurance as long as Congress finds state regulation to be adequate. [5]

**mediation.** An alternative dispute resolution method in which an impartial third party, known as a mediator, facilitates negotiations between the parties in an effort to create a mutually agreeable resolution of the dispute. [2]

**mediator.** An impartial third party who facilitates negotiations between disputing parties in the process of mediation. [2]

**merger.** A transaction in which one corporation is absorbed into another corporation by combining its assets and liabilities with those of the surviving corporation; the merged corporation is liquidated and ceases to exist. [3]

**minor.** A person who is younger than a stated age, often 18, and thus does not have full contractual capacity. [6]

**misrepresentation.** An untrue statement of fact. [6]

**mistake of fact.** A mistake that occurs when one or both parties is mistaken as to the existence of something or as to the identity of something or someone. [13]

**mistake of law.** A mistake that occurs when, with full knowledge of the facts, one or both parties make a mistake as to the legal effect of those facts. [13]

**mitigate.** To minimize the amount of damages that result from a defendant's wrong. [2]

**mixed legal system.** A legal system that contains elements of more than one basic type of legal system. [1]

**model act.** *See* **model law**.

**model law.** A sample law that has been created and adopted by a national or international organization of regulators, lawmakers, lawyers, and/or academics and that the sponsoring organization encourages legislatures to enact. Sometimes referred to as a *model act*. [3]

**Model Privacy Act.** *See* **NAIC Insurance Information and Privacy Protection Model Act**.

**monopoly.** A market scenario in which one firm, or a group of firms acting together, controls the production and distribution of a product. [4]

**mortgage.** An agreement under which a borrower transfers its interest in real property to another party as security for a loan or other obligation. [8]

**mortgagee.** A creditor to whom an interest in real property is transferred as security for a mortgage loan. [8]

**mortgagor.** A borrower who transfers an interest in real property to a creditor in exchange for a mortgage loan. [8]

**movable property.** *See* **personal property**.

**multinational corporation.** A corporation that operates in more than one country and makes major operational decisions within a global context. [3]

**mutual mistake.** A bilateral mistake that occurs when both parties to a contract make a mistake, but they make different mistakes. [13]

**NAIC.** *See* **National Association of Insurance Commissioners**.

**NAIC Insurance Information and Privacy Protection Model Act (Model Privacy Act).** An NAIC model law that establishes standards for the collection, use, and disclosure of information gathered in connection with insurance transactions. [5]

**National Association of Insurance Commissioners (NAIC).** A nonprofit association of the insurance commissioners of all U.S. states and territories; one of its primary functions is to promote uniformity of state regulation by developing model insurance laws and regulations. [3]

**necessaries.** Goods and services that a minor or other incapacitated person actually requires to sustain her well-being. [6]

**negligence.** A private wrong committed by a person who failed to exercise the legally required degree of care in (1) doing something that is otherwise legally permissible or (2) omitting to do something that is otherwise legally required. [2]

**negotiability.** A feature of a negotiable instrument which means that possession of the instrument can be transferred—or negotiated—from person to person and the instrument generally is accepted as a substitute for cash. [9]

**negotiable instrument.** A written document that represents an unconditional promise or order to pay a specified amount of money upon the demand of the owner of the instrument. [9]

**net cash surrender value.** The amount of a life insurance policy's cash value that the policyowner will receive upon surrendering the policy. The net cash surrender value is calculated by adjusting the cash surrender value for amounts such as dividend additions, advance premium payments, policy loans, and policy withdrawals. [11]

**net policy proceeds.** The amount of life insurance policy proceeds that remain after any overdue premiums and any outstanding policy loans and interest have been deducted. [12]

**nominal damages.** Damages that may be awarded to a plaintiff who was wronged but did not suffer a loss as a result of the wrong, cannot prove the amount of the loss with reasonable certainty, or the loss was trivial. [2]

**noncontributory plan.** A group insurance plan under which the employer or the group policyholder pays the entire cost for the coverage. [15]

**nonpublic personal information.** According to U.S. federal laws, personally identifiable information about a consumer that is *not* publicly available. [5]

**note.** A negotiable instrument that is a promise to pay a sum of money. [9]

**OCC.** *See* **Office of the Comptroller of the Currency**.

**Occupational Safety and Health Act (OSHA).** A U.S. federal law that sets a wide range of safety and health standards for workplaces. [4]

**offer.** A proposal that, if accepted by another according to its terms, constitutes a binding contract. [6]

**offeree.** The party to whom an offer to contract is made. [6]

**offeror.** The party who makes an offer to contract. [6]

**Office of the Comptroller of the Currency (OCC).** A bureau of the U.S. Department of the Treasury directly responsible for regulating national banks and most state banks. [5]

**officers.** The individuals, such as the president and treasurer, who are responsible for carrying out important management functions for the day-to-day operation of a corporation. [3]

**open contract.** A contract that identifies the documents that constitute the contract between the parties, but the enumerated documents are not all attached to the contract. *Contrast with* **closed contract**. [10]

**order paper.** A negotiable instrument that is payable to the order of a specific payee and, thus, can be negotiated only by the named payee. [9]

**OSHA.** *See* **Occupational Safety and Health Act**.

**outside directors.** Corporation directors who are not otherwise employed by or have no direct interest in the corporation. [3]

**paid-up additions.** *See* **dividend additions**.

**parliamentary democracy.** A country in which the legislative branch of government, usually known as the Parliament, has ultimate authority for making all laws. [1]

**parol evidence.** Evidence that is extrinsic to—that is, outside of—a written agreement. [6]

**parol evidence rule.** A procedural rule that states that parol evidence is *not* admissible to add to, vary, or contradict the terms of a written contract. [6]

**partial plan termination.** A type of group retirement plan termination that occurs when the plan sponsor terminates the plan for one group of plan participants but continues the plan for another group of plan participants. [15]

**partial surrender provision.** *See* **policy withdrawal provision**.

**partially disclosed principal.** A principal on whose behalf an agent contracts by disclosing the existence of the principal but without identifying the principal. [7]

**participation.** The inclusion of an individual in a group retirement plan. [15]

**partners.** Two or more individuals who enter into an agreement to own and operate a business for profit.

**partnership.** An association between two or more individuals who enter into an agreement to own and operate a business for profit. [3]

**party.** The plaintiff or defendant in a civil lawsuit. [2]

**past consideration.** In contract law, a promise made in exchange for actions or events that have already taken place and, therefore, not considered adequate consideration for a contract. [6]

**patent.** A governmental grant of property rights to the inventor or creator of an original process, machine, manufactured article, or chemical compound. [8]

**payee.** (1) The person to whom a draft is made payable. (2) The person who, if still living at the insured's death, will receive life insurance policy proceeds under a settlement agreement. [9, 12]

**payment date.** *See* **distribution date**.

**payout options provision.** An annuity contract provision that identifies each of the payout options from which the contract owner may select. Also known as a *settlement options provision*. [11]

**per capita beneficiary designation.** A class designation in which the class members all stand in the same relationship to the policyowner and the class members who survive the insured share the policy proceeds equally. [11]

**per stirpes beneficiary designation.** A class designation in which the descendants of a deceased class member take the decedent's share of the policy proceeds by representation. [11]

**perjury.** A crime that is committed when an individual knowingly makes false statements under oath. [2]

**person.** In the context of civil litigation, a natural person or an entity, such as a corporation, that the law recognizes as having legal rights and duties. [2]

**personal property.** Any property other than real property. In some jurisdictions, referred to as *movable property*. *Contrast with* **real property**. [8]

**personal representative.** The person appointed by a probate court to settle a decedent's estate. [8]

**plaintiff.** The party who institutes a civil lawsuit in the courts. [2]

**plan administrator.** Under the Employee Retirement Income Security Act, the individual or organization responsible for ensuring that an employee welfare benefit plan complies with applicable regulatory requirements. [15]

**plan beneficiary.** An individual specified by a group retirement plan participant to receive retirement benefits provided by the plan if the plan participant dies. [15]

**plan participant.** An employee or union member who is covered under a group retirement plan. [15]

**plan sponsor.** An employer or union that establishes a group retirement plan. [15]

**plan termination.** The ending of a group retirement plan when plan benefits cease to accrue. [15]

**pleadings.** The formal, written statements that set out the claims and defenses of each of the parties to a lawsuit. [2]

**police power.** Governmental power to enact laws to promote the public's health, safety, and welfare. [8]

**policy contest.** A court action to determine the validity of a life insurance contract. [13]

**policy loan provision.** A life insurance policy provision that gives the policyowner the right to take out a loan for an amount that does not exceed the policy's net cash value less one year's interest on the loan. [11]

**policy withdrawal provision.** A provision included in some life insurance policies, such as universal life policies, that permits the policyowner to make withdrawals from the policy's cash value. Also known as a *partial surrender provision*. [11]

**precedent.** In common law jurisdictions, a court's decision that generally must be followed by that court and the lower courts in the same jurisdiction in cases that involve substantially the same facts. [1]

**preexisting duty.** In contract law, a duty that a party has a legal obligation to perform and, therefore, not considered adequate consideration for a contract.

**preferred stock.** An equity security that entitles its owner to certain preferences— or first rights—that common stockholders do not have. [3]

**preponderance of the evidence.** The degree of proof generally required in a civil action, in which the decision as to an issue of fact must be supported by the greater weight of the evidence. [2]

**presumption.** A rule of law under which a fact is assumed to be true because another fact or set of facts was proven. [2]

**price fixing.** A prohibited practice that occurs when competing businesses act together to affect the price of a product or service. [4]

**prima facie case.** In the trial of a civil lawsuit, evidence that is sufficient to prove the elements of a party's case and that entitles the party to judicial relief unless the opposing party presents evidence to the contrary. [2]

**primary beneficiary.** The party who, if still living, will receive life insurance policy proceeds after the insured's death. [11]

**principal.** (1) In the securities industry, an officer and/or manager who is involved in the day-to-day operation and supervision of a securities business, has qualified as a registered representative, and has passed additional examinations administered by the Financial Industry Regulatory Authority. (2) A party who authorizes another party, the agent, to act on the principal's behalf. [5, 7]

**private law.** Those areas of the law that primarily involve disputes between non-governmental parties. *Contrast with* **public law**. [2]

**private property.** Property that is owned by anyone other than a government entity. *Contrast with* **public property**. [8]

**probate court.** A local court that is responsible for supervising the administration of decedents' estates. [8]

**probate estate.** Any property owned by a decedent that does not pass at his death automatically by operation of law. [8]

**probate process.** A process established by each state to handle the distribution of decedents' estates. [8]

**probationary period provision.** A group life insurance contract provision that specifies the length of time—typically from one to six months—that a new employee must wait before becoming eligible to enroll in a group life insurance plan. [15]

**procedural laws.** Laws that define the methods that exist to enforce substantive laws. *Contrast with* **substantive laws**. [1]

**property.** In legal terminology, anything tangible or intangible that is capable of being owned by someone. [8]

**prospectus.** A communication, usually written, that offers a security for sale and that must contain detailed information about the issuer of the security and the security itself. [5]

**proxy.** A written authorization given by one person, such as a stockholder, to another person who is thereby enabled to act on behalf of the first person. [3]

**prudential regulation.** A term used to describe solvency regulation in many countries other than the United States. [5]

**public law.** Those areas of the law that affect the public interest and that govern relationships between the government and nongovernmental parties. *Contrast with* **private law**. [2]

**public property.** Property that is owned by a government entity. *Contrast with* **private property**. [8]

**publicly traded corporation.** A corporation whose stock is available for sale to the general public. *Contrast with* **close corporation**. [3]

**punitive damages.** Damages awarded in addition to compensatory damages when a defendant's conduct was malicious or willful. Also referred to as *exemplary damages*. [2]

**pure competition.** A market scenario in which there are many producers and consumers of a product and prices are established by market forces with no interference from outside economic forces. [4]

**qualified plan.** A group retirement plan that receives favorable federal income tax treatment in the United States because it meets specified requirements imposed by the federal tax laws and the Employee Retirement Income Security Act. [15]

**quitclaim deed.** A deed that conveys whatever ownership rights the grantor had in the transferred real property when the deed was executed. [8]

**quorum.** A specified percentage of an entire body, such as a corporation's board of directors, who must be present in order to take actions that are legally binding. [3]

**ratification.** The adoption by a principal of an act that was taken by an agent on the principal's behalf but without the principal's authorization. [7]

**real estate.** *See* **real property.**

**real property.** Land and whatever is growing on or affixed to the land. Also known as *real estate*. In some jurisdictions, referred to as *immovable property*. *Contrast with* **personal property**. [8]

**rebating.** A sales practice, prohibited in most states, in which an insurance producer offers a prospect an inducement to purchase a policy from the producer and the inducement is not offered to all applicants in similar situations and is not stated in the policy itself. [10]

**rebuttable presumption.** A presumption that can be disproven but that stands until adequate evidence is presented to the contrary. *Contrast with* **conclusive presumption**. [2]

**receiver.** In a receivership, the person responsible for formulating a plan to distribute the assets of the impaired insurer and for making sure the insurer's obligations to customers are met to the extent possible. Also known as a *conservator*. [5]

**receivership.** A process in which the state insurance commissioner, acting for a state court, takes control of and administers an impaired insurer's assets and liabilities. Also known as a *conservatorship*. [5]

**record date.** A specified date on which parties who are listed on a corporation's records as owning the corporation's stock are identified as being entitled to receive a dividend as declared by the corporation's board of directors. [3]

**recording method.** A method of changing the beneficiary of a life insurance policy under which the policyowner must provide the insurer with a written and signed notification of the beneficiary change. [11]

**recording statute.** A state law that establishes an administrative system for recording all transactions that affect real property in the state and, thus, creates a way for conflicting claims to real property to be resolved. [8]

**redemption.** The sale by a mutual fund shareholder of the shareholder's shares back to the mutual fund. [11]

**reduced paid-up insurance nonforfeiture option.** A life insurance policy nonforfeiture option that allows the policyowner to use the policy's net cash value as a net single premium to purchase paid-up life insurance of the same plan as the original policy. [11]

**reformation.** An equitable remedy in which a written contract is rewritten to express the original agreement of the contracting parties. [2]

**registered representative.** A person who is associated with a member of the Financial Industry Regulatory Authority (FINRA), engages in the securities business on behalf of the member by soliciting the sale of securities or training securities salespeople, and has passed a special examination administered by FINRA. [5]

**regulations.** Rules or orders that are issued by administrative agencies and that have the same force and effect as statutes. [1]

**rehabilitation proceeding.** A type of bankruptcy proceeding in which a bankrupt debtor works out a plan for paying its creditors over a period of time. *Contrast with* **liquidation proceeding**. [9]

**reinstatement.** The process by which an insurer puts back into force a life insurance policy that has either (1) been terminated for nonpayment of premium or (2) been continued under the extended term or reduced paid-up insurance nonforfeiture option. [11]

**reinstatement provision.** An individual life insurance policy provision that describes the conditions the policyowner must meet to reinstate the policy. [11]

**reorganization proceeding.** A type of rehabilitation proceeding provided by Chapter 11 of the federal Bankruptcy Act under which a debtor can work out a plan for paying its creditors. [9]

**representation.** A statement made by a contracting party that will invalidate the contract if the statement is not substantially true and the statement induced the other party to enter into the contract. [13]

**request to produce documents and things.** A discovery method used in civil lawsuits in which one party requests the other party to produce documents and items related to the lawsuit. [2]

**rescission.** An equitable remedy in which a contract is cancelled and the parties are returned to the positions they would have been in had no contract ever been created. [2]

**res judicata.** A judicial doctrine under which the judgment in a civil lawsuit becomes final and binding on the parties. [2]

**restitution.** A civil remedy in which a party is ordered to return property to its owner or to the person entitled to it. [2]

**restrictive covenant.** An agreement entered into by the owner of real property that places restrictions on how the owner may use her property. [8]

**restrictive indorsement.** The indorsement of a negotiable instrument by signature with instructions as to how the instrument can be used. [9]

**revocable beneficiary.** A life insurance beneficiary whose designation as beneficiary can be changed by the policyowner during the insured's lifetime. [11]

**right of survivorship.** A property right belonging to joint tenants; when one joint tenant dies, her share automatically passes to the surviving joint tenant or tenants. [8]

**rules of evidence.** Procedural rules that govern the admissibility of evidence at trials and determine whether the evidence presented is sufficient to prove the issues involved in an action. [2]

**S&L association.** *See* **thrift institution.**

**sale of goods.** The transfer of ownership of tangible personal property in exchange for some other property, money, or services. [9]

**savings and loan (S&L) association.** *See* **thrift institution**.

**savings bank.** *See* **thrift institution**.

**secondary beneficiary.** *See* **contingent beneficiary**.

**secured party.** A creditor who has obtained a security interest in a debtor's property. [9]

**secured transaction.** A credit transaction in which a creditor extends credit and receives a security interest in the debtor's property as a way to guarantee that the creditor will be protected if the debtor defaults on the loan. [9]

**securities broker.** An individual, corporation, or other legal entity engaged in the business of buying and selling securities for the accounts of others. [5]

**securities dealer.** An individual, corporation, or other legal entity that is engaged in the business of buying and selling securities for its own account. [5]

**security agreement.** A contractual agreement in which a debtor gives a creditor a security interest in specific property of the debtor. [9]

**security interest.** A claim against a debtor's property that gives a creditor the right to possession of the property if the debtor defaults on the underlying loan. [8]

**separate property.** In community property states, property that belongs entirely to one spouse. *Contrast with* **community property**. [8]

**service mark.** A word, phrase, symbol, design, or combination thereof that identifies and distinguishes the source of one party's services from those of other parties. [8]

**service of process.** The act of delivering—or serving—a complaint to a defendant in a civil lawsuit. [2]

**settlement agreement.** A contractual agreement between a life insurance policyowner and an insurer governing the rights and obligations of the parties after the death of the insured. [12]

**settlement options provision.** An individual life insurance policy provision that grants the policyowner or beneficiary several choices as to how the insurer will pay the policy proceeds. *See also* **payout options provision**. [12]

**settlor.** The person who creates a trust and transfers ownership of property to the trustee. Also known as *grantor*. [12]

**shareholders.** *See* **stockholders.**

**SIFI.** *See* **systemically important financial institution.**

**simultaneous death act.** A state statute which provides that if an insured and beneficiary die at the same time or under circumstances that make it impossible to determine which of them died first, the insured is deemed to have survived the beneficiary, and policy proceeds are payable as though the insured outlived the beneficiary, unless the policy provides otherwise. [14]

**sole proprietorship.** A business that is owned and operated by one individual. [3]

**solvency laws.** State insurance laws designed to ensure that insurance companies are financially able to meet their debts and to pay policy benefits when they come due. [5]

**special indorsement.** The indorsement of a negotiable instrument by a signature along with words indicating to whom the instrument should be paid. [9]

**specific performance.** An equitable remedy that requires a party who has breached a contract to carry out the contract according to its terms. [2]

**spendthrift clause.** A provision that may be included in a life insurance policy or settlement agreement to protect the policy proceeds from being seized by the beneficiary's creditors. Also known as *spendthrift trust clause*. [12]

**spendthrift trust.** A trust that is designed to keep trust property out of the hands of creditors of the trust beneficiary, by prohibiting the beneficiary from assigning or otherwise transferring her interest in the trust. [12]

**spendthrift trust clause.** *See* **spendthrift clause**.

**state code.** The compilation of the laws that have been enacted by a U.S. state. [1]

**state insurance code.** The portion of a state code that is devoted to regulating the insurance industry within the applicable state. [1]

**state insurance department.** A state administrative agency that is responsible for enforcing the state insurance code and ensuring that insurers conducting business within the state comply with all state insurance laws. [1]

**state legislature.** In the United States, the legislative branch of a state government. [1]

**statute.** A law that is enacted by the legislative branch of government and that declares, commands, or prohibits something. [1]

**Statute of Frauds.** A law that declares certain types of contracts to be unenforceable unless they are evidenced by a written document signed by the party to be charged with performing the contract. [6]

**statutory law.** The body of law consisting of the statutes enacted by the legislative branch of government. [1]

**stockholders.** The owners of a corporation's stock. Also known as *shareholders*. [3]

**strict liability.** Liability imposed by tort law in very restricted situations without regard for whether the defendant was at fault. [2]

**structured settlement.** A settlement of a civil dispute or lawsuit in which a party agrees to make periodic payments to a specified payee for a specified period of time. [14]

**subsidiary.** A company that is owned and controlled by another company. [5]

**substantive laws.** Laws that create, define, and regulate legal rights and duties and that courts apply to specific cases. *Contrast with* **procedural laws**. [1]

**successor beneficiary.** *See* **contingent beneficiary**.

**successor payee.** *See* **contingent payee**.

**suicide exclusion provision.** A life insurance policy provision which states that an insurer will not pay policy proceeds if the insured dies as a result of suicide within a stated period of time—usually two years—after the date that the policy was issued. [14]

**summary plan description.** Under the Employee Retirement Income Security Act, an abbreviated version of a group retirement plan document that is understandable by the average plan participant and that reasonably informs participants and beneficiaries of their rights and obligations under the plan. [15]

**supplementary contract.** A settlement agreement between an insurer and a life insurance policy beneficiary. [12]

**survivorship clause.** A clause that is included in some life insurance policies and that requires the beneficiary to survive the insured for a stated number of days to be entitled to the policy proceeds. Also known as a *time clause*. [11]

**systemically important financial institution (SIFI).** As identified by the Financial Stability Oversight Council, a financial institution whose failure could potentially pose a risk to the U.S. financial system and which is therefore subject to more stringent regulatory standards than other firms. [5]

**systemic risk.** A risk, such as the failure of a very large and interconnected financial institution, that affects the entire financial system. [5]

**tangible property.** An object or thing that can be physically possessed and that has value as an object. *Contrast with* **intangible property**. [8]

**tenant.** A person or business to whom a real property owner conveys the right to possess the property for a period of time. Also known as the *lessee*. [8]

**termination statement.** A document that is filed with a specified state or local government official to record that a debtor has repaid a secured creditor, who thus no longer has a security interest in the debtor's property. [9]

**testamentary capacity.** The legal capacity to make a will. [8]

**testamentary transfer.** A transfer of property ownership that occurs after a property owner's death. *Contrast with* **inter vivos transfer**. [8]

**testamentary trust.** A trust that takes effect at the settlor's death. [12]

**testate.** Having a valid will at one's death. [8]

**testator.** A person who makes a will. [8]

**thrift institution.** A depository institution that receives the majority of its deposits from consumers and makes the majority of its loans as residential mortgage loans. Sometimes known as a *savings and loan (S&L) association* or *savings bank.* [5]

**time clause.** *See* **survivorship clause.**

**time limitation clause.** A life insurance policy provision which specifies that the insured's death must occur within a certain period of time—usually 90 days—from the date of an accident for accidental death benefits to be payable. [14]

**title.** A claim to ownership of property that is superior to anyone else's ownership claim. [8]

**top-heavy plan.** A group retirement plan under which, for a given plan year, the present value of accrued benefits for key employees exceeds a specified percentage of the present value of accrued benefits for all employees. [15]

**tort.** A private wrong—other than a breach of contract—for which the law provides a remedy to the wronged party. [2]

**trademark.** A word, phrase, symbol, design, or combination thereof that identifies and distinguishes the source of one party's goods from those of other parties. [8]

**transferee.** A party who obtains ownership of property by purchasing it. [8]

**transferor.** A party who sells property to another. [8]

**treaty.** A legally binding agreement entered into by two or more nations, which agree to abide by the terms of the treaty. [1]

**trespass to land.** An intentional tort that consists of the unauthorized physical invasion of another person's land. [2]

**trial.** A formal proceeding at which the parties to a civil lawsuit appear in court along with their respective attorneys and present their cases to the court. [2]

**trial courts.** Courts that first hear disputes and apply the law to controversies brought before them. Sometimes referred to as *courts of original jurisdiction.* [1]

**trier of fact.** The party that is responsible for deciding issues of fact in a civil trial. In a jury trial, the jury is the trier of fact; in a nonjury trial, the judge is the trier of fact. [2]

**trust.** An arrangement in which one person holds title to property for the benefit of another. [12]

**trust agreement.** A written document that spells out the terms of a trust, including instructions as to how the trustee is to handle the trust property. [12]

**trust beneficiary.** In a trust, the person for whose benefit the trustee holds title to property. [12]

**trustee.** In a trust, the person who holds title to property for the benefit of another. [12]

**UCC.** *See* **Uniform Commercial Code.**

**UETA.** *See* **Uniform Electronic Transactions Act**.

**undisclosed principal.** A principal on whose behalf an agent contracts without mentioning the existence of the principal. [7]

**undue influence.** The misuse of a position of power or trust to overcome the free will of another person. [6]

**Unfair Trade Practices Act.** An insurance law enacted by most states that defines certain practices as unfair and prohibits those practices in the business of insurance if they are committed flagrantly in conscious disregard of the Act or so frequently as to indicate a general business practice. [10]

**Uniform Commercial Code (UCC).** A U.S. model law that has been adopted in some form in all states to govern commercial transactions. [9]

**Uniform Electronic Transactions Act (UETA).** A model law adopted by the National Conference of Commissioners on Uniform State Laws and enacted by almost all U.S. states to provide for the effectiveness of electronic signatures. [4]

**unilateral contract.** A contract under which only one of the contracting parties makes a legally enforceable promise. *Contrast with* **bilateral contract**. [6]

**unilateral mistake.** A mistake made by only one of the parties to a contract. [13]

**unsecured transaction.** A credit transaction in which a creditor extends credit and receives only the debtor's promise to pay the debt. [9]

**U.S. Code.** The compilation of the laws that have been enacted by the U.S. Congress. [1]

**valid contract.** A contract that is enforceable by law. [6]

**vested.** In regard to a group retirement plan, a plan participant's right to receive partial or full benefits under the plan even if he terminates employment prior to retirement. [15]

**vested right.** A right that cannot be altered or changed without the consent of the person who owns the right. [11]

**vicarious liability.** Indirect liability, such as an employer's liability for the torts of an employee committed during the course of the employee's employment. [7]

**voidable contract.** A contract under which a party has the right to avoid her obligations under the contract without incurring legal liability. [6]

**void contract.** An agreement that was never enforceable by law. [6]

**voluntary petition.** A bankruptcy petition that is filed by a debtor. [9]

**wagering contract.** An illegal contract in which either party may gain or lose depending on the outcome of an uncertain event, such as a lottery or a soccer game. [6]

**waiver.** The voluntary giving up of a known right. [6]

**ward.** A person for whom a court has appointed a guardian. [6]

**war exclusion provision.** A rarely used life insurance policy provision which states that an insurer will deny payment of the full policy proceeds if an insured's death is caused by war-related activities. [14]

**warranty.** A promise or guarantee recognized by law that a statement of fact is true. [7]

**warranty deed.** A deed that conveys clear title to real property and contains warranties that the grantor has clear title to the property. [8]

**warranty of authority.** A guarantee recognized by law that an agent is acting on behalf of a principal who has contractual capacity and that the agent has authority to act for the principal. [7]

**will.** A legal document that directs how a person's property is to be distributed at his death. [8]

**work for hire.** Under U.S. federal copyright laws, a work prepared (1) by an employee within the course of his employment or (2) as the result of an agreement of the parties that it is a work for hire. [8]

# Index

Numbers in *italics* indicate figures

———

# A

absolute assignment, 12.2, 12.5

acceptance, of offer, 6.8, 6.12–6.14

 in formation of insurance contracts, 10.3–10.5

 in formation of annuity contracts, 10.18

 in sales contracts, 9.4–9.5

 international requirements for, 6.20

acceptance by conduct, *6.14*

accession, 8.4

accidental death, 14.15

accidental death benefit, 14.14–14.15

accord and satisfaction, 6.22

accounting, for the principal's money, 7.6

acquisitions, 3.13

 regulatory review of, 4.5, 4.6

act, performance of as consideration, 6.15

actively-at-work provision, 15.7, 15.9

actual authority, 7.3, 7.6, 7.9–7.10, 7.16, 10.21

actual damages. *See* damages

ADA. *See* Americans with Disabilities Act

ADEA. *See* Age Discrimination in Employment Act

administrative agencies, 1.7–1.8

administrative code, 1.7

administrative law, 1.7

administrative regulations, 1.3, 1.8

administrator, 8.18

ADR. *See* alternative dispute resolution methods

adverse action, 4.9–4.10

adverse underwriting decision, 5.20

advertising, 10.22

affidavit, 2.5

affiliates, 5.4–5.5

affirmative defense, 2.4

 assumption of risk as, 2.14–2.15

 contributory negligence as, 2.14

 duty to mitigate damages as, 2.17–2.18

 insured's suicide as, 14.11

affirmative easement, 8.8

Age Discrimination in Employment Act (ADEA), 4.17, 15.13

agency, 7.2

 law of, 7.2

 terminating the relationship, 7.14–7.17

agency agreement, 7.3, 10.20

agency contract, 10.20

agency relationship, 7.2–7.4, 7.14–7.17, 10.20–10.21

agency by ratification, 7.10

agency at will, 7.15–7.16

agents, 7.2. *See also agency listings*

 contract liability of, 7.13

 duties of, to the principal, 7.5–7.6

 knowledge of, 13.11–13.12

 liabilities of, to third parties, 7.12–7.14

 remedies of, for principal's breach of contract, 7.8

 tort liability of, 7.14

 warranty of authority, 7.13

aleatory contracts, 6.6, 6.7, 6.19, *10.3*, 11.11

alien corporation, 3.5

alien insurer, 5.7–5.8

allocated contracts, 15.19

alternative dispute resolution (ADR) methods, 2.21–2.22

American Bar Association, 3.5

American Law Institute, 9.2

Americans with Disabilities Act (ADA), 4.17, 15.13–15.14

Annual Statement, 5.8

annuitant, 14.2

annuities. *See also* variable annuity

 as commutative contracts, 6.5, 6.6

 as contracts of adhesion, 6.7

 formation of contract, 10.18–10.19

 as intangible personal property, 11.20

 ownership of, 11.20–11.21

 performance of the contract for, 14.2–14.5

 required provisions in contracts for, 10.19

 sales of, 10.20

annuitized payout options, 14.2, *14.3*

annuity considerations, 10.19

annuity trust, *12.12*

answer, 2.4

anticompetitive tactics, 4.4

antidiscrimination laws, 7.15, 10.5. *See also* discrimination

anti-money laundering acts, *3.16*

antiselection, 14.11, 15.3, 15.10–15.11

antitrust

 international regulation of, 4.7

 regulation of, 5.10

 specific prohibitions against, 4.4

 U.S. laws against, 3.13, 4.4–4.7

 U.S. regulation of, 4.2

APL. *See* automatic premium loan benefit

apparent authority, 7.9–7.10, 7.16, 10.21

appellate courts, 1.8, 1.12, 2.9

applicable law, 2.9

# P

pacts, 1.8
paid-up additions, 11.15–11.16
pain and suffering, 2.17
Parliament, 1.4, 1.5
parliamentary democracy, 1.4, 1.5
parol evidence, 6.25–6.26
parol evidence rule, 6.25–6.26
partially disclosed principal, 7.8, 7.13
partial (retirement) plan termination, 15.22
partial surrender provision, 11.18
participating policies, *10.12*
participating preferred stock, *3.12*
participation, in retirement plan, 15.15
parties, to civil action, 2.3
partners, 3.3
partnership, 3.3
past consideration, *6.16*
patent, 8.20–8.22
Patent Cooperation Treaty (PCT), 8.21
payee
    of annuity benefit payments, 11.20, 14.2,
        14.3, 14.4, 14.5
    of life insurance policy proceeds,
        12.14–12.15, 14.6–14.8
    of negotiable instrument, 9.6, 9.8, *9.9,*
        *9.10*, 9.16
payment date, 3.11
payout options, for annuities, 14.2
payout options provision, 11.20
PC. *See* professional corporation
PCT. *See* Patent Cooperation Treaty
pension plan, *15.14*
per capita beneficiary designation, 11.4–11.6
perfecting a security interest, 9.17–9.20
performance, 7.14, 7.15
periodic tenancy, 8.14
perjury, 2.5
permanent life insurance policies, *10.12*
person, 2.3
personal check, for premium payments, 11.12
personal injury, 2.17
personal property, 8.2, *8.3*
    assignment of, 12.2
    right of the parties to, 9.20–9.21
    security interests in, 9.17–9.20
per se violations, 4.4, 4.5
personal representative, 8.18
per stirpes beneficiary designation, 11.5–11.6
Philippines
    copyright laws in, *8.19*
    time limit in, for paying valid claims, *14.6*
plaintiff, 2.3, 2.7
plan administrator, 15.13, 15.20
plan beneficiary, 15.14
plan documents, 15.15, *15.16*
plan enrollment, for group life insurance, 15.8

plan fiduciaries, 15.21
planned suicide, 14.11
plan participant, 15.14
plan sponsor, 15.14
plan termination, 15.22–15.23
pleadings, 2.3–2.5
police power, 8.7–8.8
policy contest, 13.2–13.3
    barriers to, on grounds of material
        misrepresentation, 13.7–13.14
    grounds for, 13.3–13.6, 13.14–13.17
    remedies, 13.17–13.20
policy delivery, 10.11
policy dividends, applied to premium
    payments, 11.13
policy exclusions, 13.3, 14.10–14.11
policy forms, 5.8
policy issue, 10.13
policy loan provision, 11.17, 11.18
policyowner's estate, designated as beneficiary,
    11.9, 11.10
policy withdrawal provision, 11.18
political treaties, 1.8
precedent, 1.9–1.10
preexisting duty, *6.16*
preferred stock, 3.11, *3.12*
premium notices, 11.13–11.14
premium payments, 11.10–11.15
premium receipt, 10.13–10.18, 10.20
premiums
    assignment and, 12.3–12.4
    for group life insurance, 15.7–15.8
    payment methods for, 11.12–11.13
    person paying, 11.13
    refund of, 10.4, 10.5, 10.6, 10.11, 10.19,
        11.11, 13.2, 13.6, 13.15
preponderance of the evidence, 2.8
presumption, 2.8, 14.12, 14.13
price discrimination, 3.13, *4.6*
price fixing, 3.13, 4.5
prima facie case, 2.7
primary beneficiary, 11.2–11.3, 11.7, 14.7
prime minister, 1.5
principal, 5.17, 7.2. *See also* agency listings
    contract liability of, 7.8–7.10
    duties of, to the agent, 7.6–7.8
    duty of, to notify third parties, 7.16–7.17
    liabilities of, to third parties, 7.8–7.12, *7.14*
    remedies of, for agent's breach of con-
        tract, 7.6
    tort liability of, 7.10–7.12
privacy, 4.12–4.13, 4.14
    international regulation of, 5.23
    U.S. federal regulation of, 5.21–5.23
    U.S. state regulation of, 5.20–5.21
privacy notices, *5.22*
private disputes, 2.10
private law, 2.2